First World War
and Army of Occupation
War Diary
France, Belgium and Germany

48 DIVISION
Headquarters, Branches and Services
Royal Army Medical Corps
Assistant Director Medical Services
29 March 1915 - 31 October 1917

WO95/2748/1

The Naval & Military Press Ltd
www.nmarchive.com
Published in association with The National Archives

Published by

The Naval & Military Press Ltd

Unit 10 Ridgewood Industrial Park,

Uckfield, East Sussex,

TN22 5QE England

Tel: +44 (0) 1825 749494

www.naval-military-press.com

www.nmarchive.com

This diary has been reprinted in facsimile from the original. Any imperfections are inevitably reproduced and the quality may fall short of modern type and cartographic standards.

© Crown Copyright
Images reproduced by permission of The National Archives, London, England, 2015.

Contents

Document type	Place/Title	Date From	Date To
Heading	WO95/2748 48 Div Apr 15-Oct'17 ADMS		
Heading	48th Division Bef A.D.M.S. Apr 1915-Oct 1917 To Italy		
Heading	121/5099 March 29th To April 30th-1915 ADMS South Midland Div 48th Div Vol I		
Heading	War Diary Of I.R.I. Raywood From March 29.1915 To April 30th 1915		
War Diary	Chelmsford	29/03/1915	29/03/1915
War Diary	Boulougne	30/03/1915	30/03/1915
War Diary	Oxelaeire	31/03/1915	06/04/1915
War Diary	Merris	07/04/1915	11/04/1915
War Diary	Crois De Bac	12/04/1915	14/04/1915
War Diary	Merris	15/04/1915	15/04/1915
War Diary	Nieppe	16/04/1915	30/04/1915
Miscellaneous	A.D.M.S. 48th Div Apr 1915		
Heading	A.D.M.S. 48th Div May 1915		
Miscellaneous	ADMS. 48th (S.M.) Division Vol II May 1915		
War Diary	Nieppe	01/05/1915	31/05/1915
Heading	48th Division ADMS. 48th Division Vol III June 1915		
War Diary	Nieppe	01/06/1915	27/06/1915
War Diary	Busnes	27/06/1915	30/06/1915
Heading	48th Division ADMS 48th Division Vol IV July 1915		
Heading	War Diary Of ADMS 48th Division From 1st July 1915 To 31st July 1915 (Volume IV)		
War Diary	Lillers	01/06/1915	17/06/1915
War Diary	Terramesnil	18/07/1915	18/07/1915
War Diary	Lillers	18/07/1915	18/07/1915
War Diary	Terramesnil	19/07/1915	20/07/1915
War Diary	Authie	21/07/1915	31/07/1915
Heading	48th Division A.D.M.S. 48th Division Vol V From 1-31.8.15		
Heading	War Diary Of ADMS 48th (H) Division From 1st To 31st August 1915		
War Diary	Authie	01/08/1915	03/08/1915
War Diary	Bus	04/08/1915	31/08/1915
Heading	A.D.M.S. 48th Division Vol VI Sept 15		
Heading	War Diary Of ADMS 48th (H) Division From 1st September To 30th September To 30th September 1915		
War Diary	Bus	01/09/1915	30/09/1915
Miscellaneous	ADMS 48th Div Oct 1915		
Heading	A.D.M.S. 48th Division Vol VII Oct 15		
Heading	War Diary Of ADMS 48th Division From 1st To 31st Oct 1915		
War Diary	Bus	01/10/1915	31/10/1915
Map	Map		
Heading	ADMS 48th Divn Nov 1915 Vol VIII		
Heading	War Diary Of ADMS 48th Division From Nov 1st 1915 To Nov 30 1915		
War Diary	Bus	01/11/1915	30/11/1915
Heading	ADMS 48th Division Dec 1915		

Heading	War Diary Of ADMS 48th Division From Dec 1st To 31st 1915 Vol IX		
War Diary	Bus	01/12/1915	31/12/1915
Heading	F/54/2 A.D.M.S. 48th Div Jan Vol X Jan 1916		
Heading	War Diary Of ADMS 48th Division From 1-1-16 To 31-1-16		
War Diary	Bus	01/01/1916	31/01/1916
Miscellaneous	A.D.M.S 48th (Self Div)		
Heading	War Diary Of ADMS 48th Division From 1st Feb 1916 To 29th Feby 1916 Vol XI		
War Diary	Bus	01/02/1916	29/02/1916
Map	48th Division Area		
Miscellaneous	A.D.M.S. 48th (S.M) Div March 1916		
Heading	War Diary Of A.D.M.S 48th Division From 1.3.16 To 31.3.16 Vol XII		
War Diary	Bus	01/03/1916	26/03/1916
War Diary	Couin	27/03/1916	29/03/1916
Map	4th Divn		
War Diary	Couin	30/03/1916	31/03/1916
Heading	War Diary Of A.D.M.S. 48th Division For April 1916		
Heading	War Diary Of A.D.M.S 48th Division From 1-4-16 To 30-4-16 Vol XII		
War Diary	Couin	01/04/1916	30/04/1916
Heading	A.D.M.S 48th Division May 1916		
Heading	War Diary Of A.D.M.S. 48th Division From 1.5.16 To 31.5.16 Vol 14		
War Diary	Couin	01/05/1916	31/05/1916
Heading	A.D.M.S. 48th Division June 1916		
Heading	War Diary Of ADMS 48th Division From 1-6-16 To 30-6-16 Vol 15		
War Diary	Couin	01/06/1916	30/06/1916
Operation(al) Order(s)	48th Division R.A.M.C. Operation Order No. 1	18/06/1916	18/06/1916
Operation(al) Order(s)	R.A.M.C. Operation Order No. 2 By Colonel C.A. Young A.M.S. C.M.G. A.D.M.S. 20th June 1916	20/06/1916	20/06/1916
Operation(al) Order(s)	48th Division R.A.M.C. Operation Order No. 3	23/06/1916	23/06/1916
Operation(al) Order(s)	48th Division R.A.M.C. Operation Order No. 4	30/06/1916	30/06/1916
Miscellaneous	48th Division Scheme Of Medical Arrangements In The Event Of Heavy Fighting		
Heading	War Diary Of ADMS 48th Division From 1st July To 31st July 1916 Vol 16		
War Diary	Couin	01/07/1916	01/07/1916
War Diary	Mailly-Maillet	02/07/1916	03/07/1916
War Diary	Couin	03/07/1916	16/07/1916
War Diary	Bouzincourt	17/07/1916	28/07/1916
War Diary	Le Plouy	29/07/1916	31/07/1916
Operation(al) Order(s)	R.A.M.C. Operation Order No. 5 By Colonel C.A. Young A.M.S. C.M.G. A.D.M.S. 48th Division	02/07/1916	02/07/1916
Operation(al) Order(s)	48th Division R.A.M.C. Operation Order No. 6	17/07/1916	17/07/1916
Heading	War Diary Of ADMS 48th Division From 1.8.16 To 31.8.16 Vol 17		
War Diary	Le Plouy	01/08/1916	09/08/1916
War Diary	Beauval	09/08/1916	13/08/1916
War Diary	Bouzincourt	13/08/1916	31/08/1916
Miscellaneous	48th Division Scheme Of Medical Arrangements During Active Operations	15/08/1916	15/08/1916

Heading	War Diary Of A.D.M.S. 48th Division From 1-9-16 To 30-9-16 Vol 18		
War Diary	Bertrancourt	01/09/1916	03/09/1916
War Diary	Beauval	04/09/1916	18/09/1916
War Diary	Bernaville	19/09/1916	30/09/1916
War Diary	Henu	30/09/1916	30/09/1916
Miscellaneous	Attached RAMC 48th Division Operation Order No. 7		
Miscellaneous	48th Division Royal Army Medical Corps, Order 7		
Heading	War Diary Of ADMS 48th Division From 1-10-16 To 31-10-16 Vol 19		
War Diary	Henu	01/10/1916	21/10/1916
War Diary	Doullens	21/10/1916	22/10/1916
War Diary	Baizieux	23/10/1916	31/10/1916
War Diary	Millencourt	31/10/1916	31/10/1916
Heading	War Diary Of ADMS 48th Division From 1-11-16 To 30-11-16 Vol 20		
War Diary	Millencourt	01/11/1916	02/11/1916
War Diary	Lozenge Wood	03/11/1916	30/11/1916
Heading	War Diary Of ADMS 48th Division From 1-12-16 To 31-12-16 Vol 21		
War Diary	Lozenge Wood	01/12/1916	15/12/1916
War Diary	Albert	16/12/1916	31/12/1916
Heading	War Diary Of ADMS 48th Division From 1st Jany 1917 To 31st Jany 1917 Vol 22		
War Diary	Baizieux	01/01/1917	08/01/1917
War Diary	Hallencourt	09/01/1917	27/01/1917
War Diary	Mericourt-Sur-Somme	28/01/1917	28/01/1917
War Diary	Mericourt	29/01/1917	31/01/1917
Heading	War Diary Of ADMS 48th Division From 1-2-17 To 28-2-17 Vol 23		
War Diary	Mericourt-Sur-Somme	01/02/1917	02/02/1917
War Diary	Cappy	03/02/1917	28/02/1917
Miscellaneous	48th Division Scheme Of Medical Arrangements In The Event Of Heavy Fighting	03/03/1917	03/03/1917
Heading	War Diary Of A.D.M.S. 48th Division From 1.3.17 To 31.3.17 Vol XXIV		
War Diary	Cappy	01/03/1917	26/03/1917
War Diary	Quinconce	27/03/1917	31/03/1917
Heading	War Diary Of A.D.M.S. 48th Division From 1-4-17 To 30-4-17 Vol XXV		
War Diary	Tincourt	01/04/1917	22/04/1917
War Diary	K11a79.	23/04/1917	24/04/1917
War Diary	Tincourt	18/04/1917	20/04/1917
War Diary	K11a7.9.	25/04/1917	30/04/1917
Miscellaneous	48th Division Medical Arrangements For Evacuation Of Sick & Wounded From Present Line	03/04/1917	03/04/1917
Heading	A.D.M.S. 48th Divisions		
Heading	War Diary Of A.D.M.S. 48th Divn From 1.5.17 To 31.5.17 Vol 26		
War Diary	K11a79	01/05/1917	01/05/1917
War Diary	Flamicourt	03/05/1917	14/05/1917
War Diary	N.11.C	15/05/1917	24/05/1917
War Diary	I34.a.2.5	25/05/1917	31/05/1917
Heading	War Diary Of A.D.M.S 48th Division From 1-6-17 To 30-6-17 Vol 27		
War Diary	I34a.2.5	01/06/1917	30/06/1917

Miscellaneous	Relief Of 48th Division By 3rd Division	29/06/1917	29/06/1917
Heading	War Diary Of ADMS 48th Division From 1-7-17 To 31-7-17 Vol 28		
Miscellaneous	Summary Of Medical War Diaries Of 48th Div. 18th Corps. 5th Army	22/07/1917	22/07/1917
War Diary	I 34a.4.2	01/07/1917	04/07/1917
War Diary	Adinferwood	05/07/1917	22/07/1917
War Diary	Border Camp Camp 'D' A30.b	22/01/1917	22/01/1917
War Diary	'D' Camp	23/07/1917	31/07/1917
Miscellaneous	48th Div. 18th Corps. 5th Army A.D.M.S. Colonel C.A. Young C.M.G. Col. R. Pickard To A.D.M.S From 24th July	00/07/1917	00/07/1917
Miscellaneous	48th Division R.A.M.C. Orders By Colonel C.A. Young	19/07/1917	19/07/1917
Miscellaneous	R.A.M.C. Orders By Lieut-Colonel T.A. Green R.A.M.C. (T)	02/07/1917	02/07/1917
Miscellaneous	O.C. 1/2nd S.M. Field Ambulance	02/07/1917	02/07/1917
Miscellaneous	Two Bearer Sub did us Leave Beaumetz 14 Hus advance Party report 1 1/2 Hus beforehand. To be rationed for the 18th.	16/07/1917	16/07/1917
Miscellaneous	C Form Messages And Signals		
Miscellaneous	A Form Messages And Signals		
Miscellaneous	48th Division R.A.M.C. Order By Colonel C.A. Young	16/07/1917	16/07/1917
Miscellaneous	48th Division R.A.M.C. Order By Colonel C.A. Young	20/07/1917	20/07/1917
Operation(al) Order(s)	R.A.M.C. 48th Division Operation Order No. 1	30/07/1917	30/07/1917
Miscellaneous	Instructions To Medical Officers During Operations		
Miscellaneous	48th Division, R.A.M.C. Circular Memorandum No. 2	31/07/1917	31/07/1917
Heading	War Diary Of A.D.M.S. 48th Division From 1-8-17 To 31-8-17		
War Diary	D Camp A.30.b	01/08/1917	01/08/1917
War Diary	Map Sheet 28 1/40000 Belgium	02/08/1917	02/08/1917
War Diary	D Camp	03/08/1917	07/08/1917
War Diary	C Camp	08/08/1917	28/08/1917
War Diary	Wormhoudt	29/08/1917	31/08/1917
Miscellaneous	Summary Of Medical War Diaries Of 48th Div. 18th Corps 5th Army		
Miscellaneous	Military Situation		
Miscellaneous	B.E.F. 48th Div. 18th Corps. 5th Army	00/08/1917	00/08/1917
Miscellaneous	Military Situation.		
Miscellaneous	B.E.F. 48th Div. 18th Corps. 5th Army A.D.M.S. Col. R. Pickard	00/09/1917	00/09/1917
Miscellaneous	Chart Shewing Sick		
Operation(al) Order(s)	Operation Order No. 6 D.D.M.S XVIII Corps	03/08/1917	03/08/1917
Operation(al) Order(s)	R.A.M.C. 48th Division Operation Order No. 2	04/08/1917	04/08/1917
Operation(al) Order(s)	R.A.M.C. 48th Division Operation Order No. 3	11/08/1917	11/08/1917
Miscellaneous	Alterations R.A.M.C. 48th Division Operation Order No. 3	11/08/1917	11/08/1917
Miscellaneous	To Accompany 48th Division R.A.M.C. Operation Order No. 3	11/08/1917	11/08/1917
Miscellaneous	48th Division R.A.M.C. Circular Memorandum No.3	09/08/1917	09/08/1917
Operation(al) Order(s)	R.A.M.C. 48th Division Operation Order No. 4	27/08/1917	27/08/1917
Operation(al) Order(s)	Operation Order No. 10 D.D.M.S XVIII Corps	25/08/1917	25/08/1917
Miscellaneous	Distribution		
Miscellaneous	Chart Shewing Wounded Adms By Unit 1		
Heading	War Diary Of A.D.M.S. 48th Division Period September 1st-30th 1917 Vol 30		

Miscellaneous	Summary Of Medical War Diaries Of 48th Div 18th Corps 5th Army	01/07/1917	01/07/1917
Miscellaneous	Moves F.A. 1/2nd S.M.F.A. To Licques	16/09/1917	16/09/1917
War Diary	Wormhoudt	01/09/1917	17/09/1917
War Diary	Zoutkerque	18/09/1917	27/09/1917
War Diary	Brake Camp Sheet A.30.d.15	28/08/1917	30/09/1917
Operation(al) Order(s)	48th Division R.A.M.C. Operation Order No. 5	14/09/1917	14/09/1917
Miscellaneous	48th Division R.A.M.C. Order	18/09/1917	18/09/1917
Miscellaneous	With reference to D.M.S. Instructions under his No 11/76 d/d 13-7-17. this Office No M.18/58 d/d 14-7-17. all sick West of Berques-Noorpeene Railway to St Omer except self-inflicted wounds. App 3		
Miscellaneous	Administrative Instructions Issued With XVIII Corps Order No. 76	25/09/1917	25/09/1917
Miscellaneous	Distribution		
Miscellaneous	48th Division R.A.M.C. Order	25/09/1917	25/09/1917
Miscellaneous	Orders For Move Of 1/2nd And 1/3rd S.M. Field Ambulances	25/09/1917	25/09/1917
Miscellaneous	48th Division Total Admission By Units For Month Of September 1917		
Miscellaneous	Chart Shewing Sick ADMS And Wastage-By Units		
Heading	War Diary Of ADMS 48th Division From 1.10.17 To 31.10.17 Vol 31		
War Diary	Brake Camp (Sheet 28 A.30.d.15)	02/10/1917	04/10/1917
War Diary	Brake Camp	04/10/1916	10/10/1916
War Diary	X Camp (Sheet 28 A. 16.C. 37)	11/10/1917	12/10/1917
War Diary	Pernes (Lens 1/10000 E. 1)	13/10/1917	14/10/1917
War Diary	Villers Chatel (lens 1/100000 H.2)	17/10/1917	17/10/1917
War Diary	Chateau D'Acq	18/10/1917	18/10/1917
War Diary	Sheet 36b W.30.B. 2.5	19/10/1917	31/10/1917
Miscellaneous	48th Division R.A.M.C. Operation Order No. 7	03/10/1917	03/10/1917
Operation(al) Order(s)	48th Division R.A.M.C. Operation Order No. 8	04/10/1917	04/10/1917
Operation(al) Order(s)	48th Division R.A.M.C. Operation Order No. 9	07/10/1917	07/10/1917
Operation(al) Order(s)	Administrative Instructions In Connection With 48th Div. Order No. 223	08/10/1917	08/10/1917
Miscellaneous	Administrative Instructions In Connection With 48th Div. Order No. 223	08/10/1917	08/10/1917
Operation(al) Order(s)	48th Divn R.A.M.C. Operation Order No. 10	09/10/1917	09/10/1917
Miscellaneous	Casualties Deal With At Advanced Dressing		
Operation(al) Order(s)	48th Division R.A.M.C. Order No. 122	11/10/1917	11/10/1917
Operation(al) Order(s)	R.A.M.C. 48th Division Operation Order No. 11	14/10/1917	14/10/1917
Miscellaneous	48th Division Medical Arrangements	14/10/1917	14/10/1917
Miscellaneous	48th Division Medical Arrangements No. 194	18/10/1917	18/10/1917
Miscellaneous	Evacuation from The Line Held By The 48th Division	25/10/1917	25/10/1917
Miscellaneous	Chart Shewing Sick Admission & Wastage By Units		

WO95/2748 ①
48 Div
Apr '15 - Oct '17
ADMS

48TH DIVISION

BEF

A. D. M. S.
APR 1915 — ~~D~~

Oct 1917

TO ITALY

12/5099

12/5099
March 29th to
April 30th 1915

Been over and copies 23/4/17

A.D.M.S. South Midland Div" 48th Div.
Vol I

Apr '15
|
Dec '18

Confidential

War Diary

of

J.R.R. Raywood

Colonel,
Assistant Director Medical Services,
1/1st South Midland Division.

April 3rd. 1915.

From March 29. 1915 to April 3rd. 1915.

Army Form C. 2118.

J.F. Roywood
Colonel,
Assistant Director Medical Services,

WAR DIARY
or
INTELLIGENCE SUMMARY.
(Erase heading not required.)

Hour, Date, Place	Summary of Events and Information	Remarks and references to Appendices
7pm 29/3/15 CHELMSFORD	Left for FOLKESTONE & embarked for BOULOGNE arriving at 1.30pm with HQrs S.M.D.	Good passage, fine weather.
1pm 30/3/15 BOULOGNE	Proceeded by train to OTELAERE with HQrs S.M.D.	
31/3/15 OTELAERE	D.A.D.M.S. rem'd sick to St. C.C.G. HAZEBROUK.	F Ambulance S.M.D. at HAVRE.
1 4/15 OTELAERE	Reported to D.M.S. 2nd Army. Visited 1st F.A. who had moved up to OUDEZEELE. 2nd F.A. at HARDIFOOT. 3rd F.A. ST JAW CAPELLE.	
2 4/15 OTELAERE	Motor Convoy Workshop with Ambulances arrived to complete establishment of F. Ambulances. Stations further W. OUTERSTEEN with Sanitary section who are very busy.	This wo no account of teatram detailed to it & in horses who move daily. Very wet.
1 am 3 4/15	Sanitary section arrived permille temperules complete. Visited Sanitary Sections of 5 into.	
4pm 4/15	With Ambulance. 2 cars departed to F.A. one Cars Cerebro-Spinal fever reported.	2 mulliers received Goulbourn YELLOWING to Independence Cover
5 4/15	Interviewed D.M.S. 2nd Army re general readiness etc. Visited Unit at OUDEZEELE. expressing no reference to SORE FEET.	
6 4/15	Moved to Jn. HQrs S.M.D. to MERRIS	
7 4/15 MERRIS	D.M.S. 2nd Army visited JHQrs. D.A.D.M.S. left for temporary attachment to Div. IV NIEPPE. Visited 3rd F.A. at LE FIETRE.	Cours of Instructions arrange 4 2nd Army
8 4/15 MERRIS.	Visited Workshop Ballieol at BALLEOL. D.A.D.M.S with Comm. G.O.C. inspected Motor Workshop of S.M.D. D.D.M.S. 3rd Corps. Came.	

Forms/C. 2118/10

Army Form C. 2118.

WAR DIARY
or
INTELLIGENCE SUMMARY.
(Erase heading not required.)

Instructions regarding War Diaries and Intelligence Summaries are contained in F. S. Regs., Part II. and the Staff Manual respectively. Title pages will be prepared in manuscript.

Hour, Date, Place	Summary of Events and Information	Remarks and references to Appendices
9.4/15 MERRIS	Visited 1st & 2nd F.A. at KIEPPE.	
10 4/15	Special report on Motor Cars received.	
11 4/15	Tent drawn A.S.C. VI. with workshop evacuated to CCS.	—wanted—
	Visited Hdqrs Warwickshire Duty Brigade re Sanitation Orders. Visited 2 F.A. Offrs re accommodation. D.A.D.M.S. returned from ct.b. a Journee to DIV VI	
12 4/15 to 14 4/15 CROIS de BAC	Attached to DIV VI. Visited & examined Convalescent Depot BAC ST MAUR. WASHING & BATHING FACTORY, ERQUINGHEM. 16th, 17th, 18th & 19th F. Ambulances attached DIV VI. Recruit which is under S/Arc details. Visited A.D.M.S. DIV VI returned HQrs S.M.D. MERRIS. 7pm.	Obj'ns arranged hybrid Corps.
15 4/15 MERRIS	Signed Dmg. 2nd Army re Sanitation Reports & offic'l work visited Ambulances & schedules to F.As with workshop attached 2nd F.A.	
10am 16 4/15 NIEPPE	Arrived NIEPPE with HQrs S.M.D. Visited 1st, 2nd & 3rd F.A.s Consultation respect'g re disposition of F.As	
17 4/15 NIEPPE	3rd F.A. billets in Billeter & Promyplane at ROMARIN, & PLOEGSTREET to take up SWD's wounded 1st F.A. billeted in ROMARIN. The orders. 2nd F.A. remains at BALLEUL	To take up WD's to take up 2nd F.A. near NIEPPE
18 4/15 NIEPPE	While SWD occupy line & heads from NOUVE GHEM to MESSINES DA to S.E. n bank R. WARANNE Visited FA SMD & remaining sick and fors.	
19 4/15 NIEPPE	Visited 1st & 2nd F.A. with B.D. and 3rd Cyclist F.A. saw re evacuation of sick to BAILLEUL.	Heavy Art'y attacked on A.C.W. Don & interp. to BAILLEUL.

WAR DIARY
or
INTELLIGENCE SUMMARY.
(Erase heading not required.)

Army Form 2118.

Hour, Date, Place	Summary of Events and Information	Remarks and references to Appendices
20/4/15 NIEPPE	1st & 2nd F.A. H.Qrs S.MIDLAND Infantry Brigade — 1st & 2nd Fd. W. Baths re Working.	
21/4/15 "	Arrangements when Sanitary Section defects in NIEPPE. 1st & 2nd Wondrous Battalion 1st F.A. 2nd F.A. St Quin. Drone & Annexe. Col LE FLETRE. Supply wh CAESTRE. Lieut Shardlaw R.A.M.C. arrived posted to 2nd F.A. vice Cuthbertson offered fire (to Rufwd.)	
22/4/15 "	St Omer. Wrote Adm. Infantry Brigade — Inspected various billets. St.Qn. Gr. Wondrous Baths.	
23/4/15 —	Formed Brigade Sanitary Committee, & attended work of In-To-[?]ghynes Committee. Visited 1st, 2nd & 3rd F. Ambulance. Various billets. RONINARIN	Precautions & treatment wanted in Divl. Orders re Asphyxiating Gas
24/4/15 —	LE FLETRE & CAESTRE	
25/4/15 —	Conference with A.D.M.S. & 31st Divn. re Asphyxiating Gases. Conference with D.D.M.S. 3rd Lines A.H.Q. D.M.S. L.of C. D.M.S. 2nd VI. Visited Divisional Chirurgical Depot. Spent an Section 1st F.A. between 3rd Cavalry Clearing Station	
26/4/15 —	Al BAILLEUL. Regimental stretcher entrapped with OXYGEN cylinders. Meeting Sanitary Committee. Wrote office Infantry Brigade. Visited 2nd F.A. billets situation	
27/4/15 —	Visited billets of R.F.A. Batteries & Divisional Trains. Station. Special reports on use of Oxygen. Sent offered Army Cylinders.	
28/4/15	Took on Baths at PONT de NIEPPE from A.D.W. took an heads 1st A.D.W. under Bedlam 1st F.A. to PONT DE NIEPPE 2nd A.D.W. Sup intended for Leaving Station in BIZET PLUG GIBEET Rd.	All sect offered injury & delinc cayt & F2 fact Lavaughs.

A.D. OF M.S.
Date 1/5/15
SOUTH MIDLAND DIVISION

WAR DIARY
or
INTELLIGENCE SUMMARY.
(Erase heading not required.)

Army Form C. 2118.

Instructions regarding War Diaries and Intelligence Summaries are contained in F.S. Regs., Part II. and the Staff Manual respectively. Title pages will be prepared in manuscript.

Hour, Date, Place	Summary of Events and Information	Remarks and references to Appendices
28/4/15 NIEPPE	Conference with G.O.C SWD 40I Infantry Brigade - all troops now effn. Sgt. Ryde - Visited Sgt F.A. BAILEY.	
29/4/15 "	Visited bath. Present station 1st F.A. Railhead ADVANCED wedding Depot BAILLEUL. Sent out C.W.L members to Officers Quarters. Visited Billets in great St Andrienne. Sanitary admin Depot on Sandulau of NIEPPE to DuMS. were engaged with Billets St Glos. & Petits PONT de NIEPPE with Sergeant of Course S.N. Vermalroft Russian Hussars attached to Staff. Received special instruction for making emergency supples of Respirators to A.S.W.B. north of Gophendres from	
30/4/15 "	Remarks. Sanitation. Billets moderate. Troops mainly in barns & farm buildings, duty & heavily overcrowded by troops - with unglazed windows serving one stable friends. In hands of fields - Small amount of billety already in use - Very good. Anterdeeds ample. Water Supply. Indiff. Cameraterrally shallow wells - Water getting low in general use a week of conclusion here - In water, or been dried up - except in this is a few & best full. Burel frienda carnot now with more Climate	

WAR DIARY or INTELLIGENCE SUMMARY

Army Form 2118

A.D. of M.S. Date 15/5/15 South Midland Division

Hour, Date, Place	Summary of Events and Information	Remarks and references to Appendices
	Disease. General clean. good. Epidemic deemes Merle - 7 cases } Pneumonia 2 cases - Diphtheria 1 case - Cerebro Spinal Fever 2 cases.	
	Sick in Cafes: S.W. 182. Wounded, 106. Venereal cases 12. (2 contracted weekly). No enteric fever. Con ad. = Divisional Rest Station. Establishment totalled by 2nd F.A. BALLEUL is a great deal of fever and unlafe. It is hoped I am allowed to Barbeuil & other. Very few with Bathin at PONT NIEPPE are taken in hospital arrangements are unknown made & more to have where Division are Being reduced. Divn Staples. BALLEUL will 2 F.A. is trembling under its present accommodation. Field Ambulances had been attached to the Division for sanitation & are working to ROTHEN. MUMPS & SEPTIC THROATS. well. very satisfactory Others - Very good all round.	

R.R. Allwood Colonel,
Assistant Director Medical Services,
1/1st South Midland Division.

A.D.M.S. 48th Div. Apr. 1915

Appx. A - has been detached & filed under "Ypres"

Sept 1915
Summoned - not cited 23-7-17

a D M f H? = 5/-

121/5556

A.D.M.S. 48th (S.M.) Division

Vol II

May. 1915

WAR DIARY or INTELLIGENCE SUMMARY

Army Form C. 2118.

Hour, Date, Place	Summary of Events and Information	Remarks and references to Appendices
1 5/15 NIEPPE	Visited Hosp. Pte. LA CRÈCHE. re takes for Reparation. Visited 3rd F.A. ROMARIN, & 1st F.A. ROMARIN. Inspected billets Glorieux. Visited Baths PONT NIEPPE. Arranged for walking Reparations. Cloudy. Parade Ptes and Baths, PONT NIEPPE. Visited 1st F.A.	No Gas Cases in 3 W Dws. since June.
9 5/15	Visited 1st and Batty cleared for repairs. Visited Hosp. at 9 ½ hr. Conferred with D.D.M.S. 3rd Corps. re Gassing Cases. Visited Gt. C.C. BALLEUL & eventually procured supply of morphine by Cav. Corps. Ease supply of Sod Bicarb. reserve of Rosehead. Served Bottles of Hp. dus & special inhalers to Usobtp &	Weather Showers in n/k and v.n/k. Previous Australian Divnup to G.O. ? Chemin
3 5/15	Visited Baths PONT NIEPPE. Visited 1st F.A. also 2nd Div. 1st F.A. removed to ROMARIN & Rd NIEPPE (rue St Sophie) Grunill. D.D.M.S. 3rd Corps BAILLEUL. Visited Divisional RAV Station. BAILLEUL & 2nd F.A. Visited Pt. of 1st F.A. (Hp's) Batt. re Reparation. Issued 5000 men Reparation & Supply of Sod Bicarb. to 1st Gas Brigade.	Very lty weather.
4th – 9 am 11 am	Attended Conference e Gov't & Hps staff 9 am Attended Meeting. S.W Infantry Rykes & PLOEGSTEERT. Ind Lecture. S.W. Private attended. Visited Baths. 3rd F.A Hpes removed to ROMARIN via h/k Representation from Inf. Gos for Collective Wh. Wounded touche	Formed Rykes Sanitary Committee been Lutr organise distributed

Army Form C. 2118.

WAR DIARY
or
INTELLIGENCE SUMMARY.
(Erase heading not required.)

Hour, Date, Place	Summary of Events and Information	Remarks and references to Appendices
5/5 NIEPPE	Visited Baths. Visited 1st F.A. Visited 9th F.A. Visited 8th C.C. BAILLEUL. (re 9 Cas.) Visited Advanced Medical Stores. re supplies. Road Back to Capt Thompson and arrived to take on duties of ADMS and Authd. Store Report. d 250 bottles disinfectant Royan...	No Amb N.S. to evacuate. Shortage realised. Urgent.
6	Visited 1st F.A. Visited Baths. re Report on Cromwell DDMS. 31 Capt W 2nd F.A. & Div. Rail Station Visited 3.1 F.A. attended CO JHQrs re Green Standing or. to Capt Thompson. A.m.L. Orders Amb. leave granted to orderly of BAH Eot. Every man of Div. can will be ready with Report — NO CASE OF OPHTHALMIA GO in this Division to date	No Amp. N.S. to evacuate
		New from Rs. Pmil. day of Mule. Sage Reports enclosed. Intact. Monday, all wered Ambulance. this Report.
		G.R.P. Callwood
		Assistant Director Medical Services 41st South Midland Division
NIEPPE May 7 = 7 a.m.	Situation unchanged. Weather fine but cloudy.	
9 a.m.	Col. H.N. THOMPSON arrives & takes over office of ADMS 3 Division	
10.30 a.m.	The SODed water baths & discusses new pattern respirator, 2.7 One 6" grease & 1" March, 1 pressed, with cotton waste, with SM III Cap in arrangement of Baths for making these respirators	
12 p.m.	Major-General H. Keith J.O.C. S.M. Division places on record that	

Forms/C. 2118/10.

WAR DIARY or INTELLIGENCE SUMMARY

Army Form C. 2118.

Hour, Date, Place	Summary of Events and Information	Remarks and references to Appendices
NIEPPE May 7 — 12.10 pm	Suffering from Conjunctivitis. Col. Sir Wilmot Herringham Consulting Physician came and put Roth in consultation. Recommends a fortnight's change, completed.	
2.0 pm	Message received from O.Bn. (2 Wks) "One more draft of 9 R Harris Apt Col H. R. Foster now in Servells Asylum Col Cheshire inoculates." Yes all the conjunctival wounds follows as inoculated.	Appendix 1.
3.30 pm	Message sent to O.C. 4 & 5 Foster inquiring if R Harrison inoculated.	Appendix 2.
	Engagement to commanding 5th Bn Warwicks meeting Capt. F.J. CLAYTON to attend this Offr, Gen. Hughes Divisional Road.	
6 pm	Message from Capt. CLARKE M.O. 9th R. Gloster — Sent "Harrison received one dose of antityphoid vaccine 500,500 million) this brought on a sharp attack from D. ambulances. Was afterwards informed by the R.C.O. in billet that he has been melancholic retains a doubt as was has Harrison this I shall not have inoculated him as I have no doubt in my mind that the inoculation was a shan even.	Appendix 3
	Message to D.M.S. 2nd Army — Forwarded officers sickness list. P.J. Garatt S.R. Royal Warwicks sworn N.D. Hure Captain AJC	

Army Form C. 2118.

WAR DIARY
or
INTELLIGENCE SUMMARY.
(Erase heading not required.)

Instructions regarding War Diaries and Intelligence Summaries are contained in F.S. Regs., Part II. and the Staff Manual respectively. Title pages will be prepared in manuscript.

Hour, Date, Place		Summary of Events and Information	Remarks and references to Appendices
NIEPPE 7th May	6 p.m.	Reynolds, Lt. F.W. Bowyer and Lieut. R. Green of Bucks B.C. Dm. to Bucks C.J. O.R. sick seven wounded, twenty from Staff Division sick list	
"	6 p.m.	Message to 3rd Corps Divisions to establish bombers from 12 noon 6th to 12 noon 7th. Officers sick nil Bowers from 8 p.m. Drne J. Worcesters Captains Reynolds, L.F.C Bowyer (21st East Green B of Bucks B". O.R. sick thirty-one, twenty-two, twenty-two Evacuated Officers last twenty-four hours and right arm 7.0. S.E Warwicks List seven wounded, twenty officers sick to other Divisions admitted fifteen evacuated two sick	Appendix 5
NIEPPE 8th May	8 a.m.	Situation unchanged. Weather showery	
	10.30 a.m.	O.D.M.T with Col REILLY A.A. & Q.M.G. 5th Divn consulted with Brigades as to which is practicable with the use of the latest respirators to holds against twenty-four (24) trenches. Question of one able fully with the officers on the spot.	
	3 p.m.	Instruction issued & viewed regarding use of latest	

Army Form C. 2118.

WAR DIARY
or
INTELLIGENCE SUMMARY.
(Erase heading not required.)

Instructions regarding War Diaries and Intelligence Summaries are contained in F.S. Regs., Part II. and the Staff Manual respectively. Title pages will be prepared in manuscript.

Hour, Date, Place		Summary of Events and Information	Remarks and references to Appendices
NIEPPE May 8		respirators & a proportion issued. Also a telephone.	
"	5 pm	Message to 3rd Sth & 8th Army "Evacuate" officers at one, rest of Range Rivic at 8 & wounds OR & left twelve wounded	Appendix 6.
		twelve Other Ranks from	
		Message to 9th Div & 3rd Corps "Arrivers to 2nd Wimbledon 3 Officers and OR each party"	Appendix 7.
		from 12 noon 7th to 12 noon 8th. 8 Officers and OR each party	
		four wounded fourteen evacuated. Officers such had	
		Lieut Payer Rivic & att 8th wounds. Sgt twelve wounded	
		twelve Sick Sie Jonn. The Division admitted two sick	
		evacuated four wounded.	
NIEPPE May 9	8 am	Situation in charge. Weather bright & sunny.	
	10 am	O Day issued and Instructions regarding the next few	
		months. Enroll nos. & no. + ability to procure & collect	
		flowers all country by stream.	
	5 pm	Received from the 2nd Division the Nightly Report of wounded, sitter	
		on sie. & a telegram re making an adjusted to follow	
		Total wounded &	
		Sick Carbon & OR	
		Officers —	
		Wounded	

Army Form C. 2118.

WAR DIARY
or
INTELLIGENCE SUMMARY.
(Erase heading not required.)

Instructions regarding War Diaries and Intelligence Summaries are contained in F.S. Regs., Part II. and the Staff Manual respectively. Title pages will be prepared in manuscript.

Hour, Date, Place	Summary of Events and Information	Remarks and references to Appendices
NEDAH May 9th 7 pm	In the trenches & ends to be in readiness with full kit. new trenches made for Battalion = 350. Transport 1 to 2 Officers and 15 Other Ranks OR cut. 6 & Do Officers one OR to upper Scout & 2nd Munichs OR cut. 6 & Do Officers one OR to 7 do thirteen S.B. do Officers and 2 Signallers & 2 Machine Gun one OR to fight on S.B. do Officers to 4 Coy. Stores 25 Gunners one OR to Gunners Rec. Stn. Do Batch.d. Seven Bn. ch. Bn. do Officers one OR to Bomb Offrs L.R.P.S. 24.7.8 Bomb. (1) Do to 5. No one LRP S & Officers one OR ten one Lt. W. Prest. Armstrong Hee & two Dr's to Horse from Immoral Cyclists one Cpl & P.P.N.Q. one Staff Officer all OR are Brigadiers & P.t.s nine... transport to Field Ambulance — two orderlies Officers march (4) Captains F.T. CLAYTON J.B. Somerich & A. HAGUE 2 Ensigns Munich to Captain SEYMOUR Lieut O DINEN 5 to Munichs OR each transported a seventeen then... war no District lines	Appendix 8 ... October 9

WAR DIARY or INTELLIGENCE SUMMARY

Army Form C. 2118.

Place	Hour, Date	Summary of Events and Information	Remarks and references to Appendices
NIEPPE	May 9th 7 p.m.	Message to III Corps. Admissions to Field Ambulances from noon 8th to noon 9th. Sick Officers one. Sent to Sir William's Hospital, Boulogne: Captain F. T. Clayton 5th Warwicks. Capt. R. Hayes 5th Lincolns. D.R. for Etaples - Wounded Officers: Lt. (a/Capt.) J.O. SEYMOUR & Lt. O. OWENS 5th Warwicks. Sick other ranks twenty four. Wounded officers fr Capt. Lt. (a/Capt.) Clayton Hayes Seymour & Lieut. O. Owens 5th Warwicks. O.R. seventeen. Ambulance from Divisional Rest Station attached. Admissions sick and wounded one and One officer admitted Lieut. C.A. MIDGLEY North Lancs. in service.	Appendix 10
NIEPPE	May 10th 8 a.m.	Situation unchanged. Weather brightening.	
	10 a.m.	O./C. 2nd Div Hd Qrs Headquarters left Nieppe July 6th with officers to Neuve Chapelle ordering all that they ... should be evacuated to Bruay.	

WAR DIARY or INTELLIGENCE SUMMARY.

(Erase heading not required.)

Army Form C. 2118.

Hour, Date, Place	Summary of Events and Information	Remarks and references to Appendices
NIEPPE May 10th 10 a.m.	No aid posts for regimental medical officers as the present situation of aid posts is not considered suitable to a terrain in case of heavy fighting. Visited aid posts of 2nd Ox & Bucks, 1/4 Berkshire & Rifle Bde. Conferred with medical officers of the C.O.s Battalion medical officers. Visited advanced dressing station (3.) R.A.M.C Ambulance. For reinforcements of billets of 2nd Fd. Coy R.E. & Headquarters 5th Bgd. 1.8.2.F.	
2 p.m.	Proceeded to HÔTEL BOULOGNE — Brigr. transferring found health not improving and a great fortnight. Can you accommodate him in Chateau Roben General Hospital? He confirmed tomorrow few arranged. Enft. applied sick.	Appendix 11
4.30 p.m.	Telegram to Adm. 2nd Army. — Evacuated officers sick 8 sick. Nine wounded forty-five other Divisions sick one wounded one	Appendix 12.

WAR DIARY
or
INTELLIGENCE SUMMARY.
(Erase heading not required.)

Army Form C. 2118.

Hour, Date, Place		Summary of Events and Information	Remarks and references to Appendices
NIEPPE May 10th	4.30 pm	Message to III Corps. Officers sent from 2nd Field Ambulance to 12 noon	Appendix 13
"	9 to 12 noon	10 L. Officers and O.R. sick twenty seven. Wounded fifty two, Gassed nine, wounded forty five. Other Divisions admitted at 2nd wounded two Gassed one, sickness wound one.	
"	9 pm	Message received from D.D.M.S. Boulogne - All Officers commanded urgently required. Received Bed and Permission sent to REPORT on Couch to send from now.	Appendix 14
"	9.30 pm	Message arrived ADMS. REPORT - Propose sending large Camp head as after fortnight on Road great requires us. Nos. Capacity if you can accommodate in Bill forces summer. D/Officers. (no total number of the new mess/mass issued = 3200	Appendix 15
NIEPPE May 11-	8 am	Situation unchanged weather bright + sunny	
"	9 am	O. Pont attended Conference of My Staff at Headquarters	
"	11.30 am	Visited Headquarters Posts + proceed to My B.E. met Lieut Col. Young 2nd Field Ambulance went reference to	

Army Form C. 2118.

WAR DIARY
or
INTELLIGENCE SUMMARY.
(Erase heading not required.)

Instructions regarding War Diaries and Intelligence Summaries are contained in F.S. Regs., Part II. and the Staff Manual respectively. Title pages will be prepared in manuscript.

Hour, Date, Place		Summary of Events and Information	Remarks and references to Appendices
NIEPPE July 11	11.30 am	Collection of wounded & provision of dry-nts for wounded awaiting evacuation	
"	10.30 am	Message received from M.O. TREPORT - Can accommodate any further wounded. 3 General Hospital	Appendix 16
"	10.45 pm	Message read - DDMS BOULOGNE - Major Genl Pratt left for forward areas this morning. Forward documents and report to you by post	Appendix 17
"	3.30 pm	O Dist visited the trenches with C.R.E with reference to provision of dug outs for regimental aid posts	
"	4 pm	Message sent HqRs. II (2nd) Army - Evacuations offices and OR sick twenty two - wounded nil	Appendix 18
"		Message sent III Corps - Admissions to Field Ambulances from 12 noon 10-11 to 12 noon 11-11 - Officers and OR sick forty two - wounded six - Evacuated sick twenty two wounded nil - Remaine the	Appendix 19
"	7 pm	Total wounds admitted and evacuated A.T.O. + month ships 30.0.0	
NIEPPE July 12th	8 am	Situation unchanged. Weather changeable.	
	11.30 am	O Dist II Corps interviewed O Dist with reference to the	

WAR DIARY
or
INTELLIGENCE SUMMARY.

Army Form C. 2118.

Hour, Date, Place	Summary of Events and Information	Remarks and references to Appendices
NIEPPE May 12 11.30 a.m.	New pattern face pad. O'Brien's B.M. ordered to the Divisional R.A. Who notes that pads are being made. And then to 3 rd F.M. Field Ambulance at POPERIN	
2.30 pm	Conference at ADMS Office with O.Cs Field Ambulances and Regimental Medical Officers. DADMS visited Trenches with Sanitary Officer Capt DALE with reference to wearing of face pads seeing they were up to date as per instructions. Also enquiring into sanitary matters (DMS 2nd Army inspected Sanny. Evacuated Officers and men) Wire composed Lieut MacEnery Inspected F.O.S. & Indn Captain D. Root full BWC Heath CO of DC division wounded. Two Captains Road Dm Buck and 29 class Lieut JAS Cannon knocked O.R. and fifteen wounded, fourteen sick one other sick and air	Appendix 20
7 p.m.	Message to ADMS Corps — advance to Field Ambulance 12 noon 11th to 12 mdn 12 officers sick one hyp and Kelt C.B. (O.C. division wounded) This Capt S Rose : Lieut J.O.S. Cannon : & (N.W.B. ruch; 89 OR sick/influenza wounded fifteen Evacuated Officers as above OR sick fifteen wounded fourteen & one other Division admitted OR sick like & wounded his Total number remaining in hospital 7300.	

WAR DIARY or INTELLIGENCE SUMMARY.

Army Form C. 2118.

(Erase heading not required.)

Instructions regarding War Diaries and Intelligence Summaries are contained in F.S. Regs., Part II. and the Staff Manual respectively. Title pages will be prepared in manuscript.

Hour, Date, Place		Summary of Events and Information	Remarks and references to Appendices
NIEPPE	May 13th		
	8 a.m.	Situation unchanged. Weather rainy.	
	9 a.m.	A Dud mortar hurled at 12th (S.R.) Bryds (late Moucade's) Evacuated (App 15.2.) to destroy himself as the offensive. Officers pads already issued, & for present emergency appoint	
		Message to 21st & 23rd Army - Evacuated officers & one Regt. Appendix to ADWCT as to 7 & 8th Wounded. Evacuated 22nd lieut OR exclusive wounds two litter Brios.	Appendix 22
	4 p.m.	Cooper Keeg. Sent? Knew OR exclusive wounds two litter Brios. Returns one —	
		Message to III (1 p.m.- Ambrems & Dieth ambulances from 12 noon to 12 noon 13. 3 officers sick two Regt. Admitted, the	Appendix 23
		(amot. sd) 3 : 14 wounded Staff Knight Offrs & five two wounded) one field (other five wounded) OR sick forty men wounded) fourteen evacuated offrs, one Regt & two OR. Die "A" Corps - OR sick men wounds, two OR wounded one evacuated) men wounds.	
		Total number of men pads issued 9500.	
MERRIS	May 14.		
	8 a.m.	Situation unchanged. Weather rainy (cool)	
	10.30 a.m.	A Dud visits 2nd RW Lib Ambulance & Dud 2 Army.	

WAR DIARY or INTELLIGENCE SUMMARY

Army Form C. 2118.

Hour, Date, Place	Summary of Events and Information	Remarks and references to Appendices
NIEPPE May 14th 4pm	George sent 2nd and 3rd army evacuated Officers and hit wounded, two Lieut Bedgood & 8 other ranks killed & 4 P. evacns 5th Berwicks of which seven wounded, seven other ranks wounded one. Present III Corps — Divisions to Field Ambulances from 12 noon 13th to 10 noon 14th. Officers sick two Capt H.B. Green & Lt Warwick, Lieut N Bower 2nd Cyclist Corps wounded, two Lieut Birdyer & 8 Worcester Lieut Menlove wounded. O.R. 5th Warwicks O Rates twenty (20 missing) nine (9 evacuated) Officers two other ranks OR each seven remaining seven Other Div. sum admissions three two available remaining) Total weaken (special list issued) 11,450	Appendix 24 Appendix 25
NIEPPE May 15th 8 am	Situation unchanged. Weather sunny but cold	
8:30 am	DADMS visited field ambs with Capt Dale with reference to the recovery of kit pads with reference to sanitary matters	
11 am	A.D.S. issued explanation of rays form in paper application	
2 pm	ADMS inspected 2nd Lts Field Ambulance at BAILLEUL Chateau	

Army Form C. 2118.

WAR DIARY
or
INTELLIGENCE SUMMARY.
(Erase heading not required.)

Instructions regarding War Diaries and Intelligence
Summaries are contained in F. S. Regs., Part II.
and the Staff Manual respectively. Title pages
will be prepared in manuscript.

Hour, Date, Place		Summary of Events and Information	Remarks and references to Appendices
NIEPPE	May 15 2pm	inspected new billets	
	4pm	Heard to find 2nd Army - evacuated sick Officers one Lieut Riddell C.E. 5th Warwicks. O.R. ten. Wounded Officers one Lieut. Sibeo 6th Warwicks O.R. five. Other Ranks sick. Present to HQ 46 - Officers one & Field Ambulances from 12 noon 16.6.15 noon 15. Sick officers one Lieut Riddell C.E. 5th R. Warwicks. O.R. twenty (20). Wounded Officers one Lieut Jobeo 6. Warwicks. O.R. five. Evacuated Off inclusive 1st Army to 10 Yesterday OR five. Other Ranks sick sixty one incl. ten. wounded. Sick & other Ranks evacuation ambulance since all. Total number in hospitals now 12700	Appendix 26 Appendix 27
NIEPPE May 16/15	8am	Situation unchanged. Weather enemy reserve	
	10am	A.D.M.S. visited Baths with reference to filling vacancy of O.C. to do. Went to 1st 2nd Field Ambulances regarding the preparation of return for same.	
	3pm	A.Army Hosp Conference with OCs 1st & 3rd Field Ambulances regarding returns of Advanced Dressing Stations & the collection of wounded.	
	4pm	D. find inspected Riddell #5 Warwickshire Post Bridge	

WAR DIARY or INTELLIGENCE SUMMARY

Army Form C. 2118.

Place	Hour, Date	Summary of Events and Information	Remarks and references to Appendices
NIEPPE	May 16 / 4 pm	Message to H.Q. 2nd Army - Evacuated Officers two one Capt. Davies E.Y. 5th Warwicks OR Evacuated sick two wounded one	Appendix 28
"	"	Message to III Corps - Admissions at Field Ambulances from 12 noon 15th to 12 noon 16th Officers sick three Capt. Davies E.Y. 5th Warwicks heat Apo ASD Lieut. Pullman A of 7th Worcester OR shrapnel wounds Officers sick 2 Sgt. Evacuated Officers one Capt. Davies shell wounded OR 4 sick. Evacuated sick admissions forward evacuated ten wounded four sick one wounded one	Appendix 29
"	"	Message to H.Q. I Base - Sick wounds from 12 noon 15th to 12 noon 16th. Officers five OR eighteen 6th S. Staffs one OR sight 7th S. Staffs OR twenty-two 8th S. Staffs sixteen 4th Lincolns ten OR seven 5th S. Staffs OR nine 6th S. Staffs eleven 7th Worcester OR seven 8th S. Staffs OR one 8th Sherwood Foresters OR one Officers two OR fourteen Bucks R. 2nd Field Amb. Battalion right 3rd R.F.A. five R.E. one 3rd Ambulance four Divl Engineers four Train one two OR three 4 & 8 one 3rd Ambulance one Divl R.Sigs. one Divl Cyclists one R.F. Vice Ammunition Column one 2nd R.F.A. transferred to Baths and two Head Quarters Drawn Officers one OR ult. Total Officers thirteen OR one hundred and fifty one Total number respirators issued 14,200. Situation unchanged. Weather cloudy rainy.	Appendix 30
NIEPPE	May 17 / 8 am	Message to H.Q. 2nd Army - Evacuated Officers nil OR	Appendix 31

Army Form C. 2118.

WAR DIARY
or
INTELLIGENCE SUMMARY.
(Erase heading not required.)

Instructions regarding War Diaries and Intelligence Summaries are contained in F.S. Regs., Part II. and the Staff Manual respectively. Title pages will be prepared in manuscript.

Place	Hour, Date	Summary of Events and Information	Remarks and references to Appendices
NIEPPE	May 17. 4pm	Sick twelve wounded thirteen Other Divisions sick two. Message to III Corps — A.D.M.S. not. Field Ambulances from 12 m.n. on 18 8 to 12 m.n. on 19 8 Officers nil OR sick thirty wounded nineteen Evacuated sick twelve wounded nineteen Other Divisions admissions sick OR six Evacuated two Officers nil OR sick five wounded. Weather dry raining.	Appendix 32.
NIEPPE	May 18. 8 am	O. and with D.A.D.M.S. visited Aid posts of 16 Gloucesters	
	10 am	16 Gloucesters with reference to home nursing of Scabies.	
	3 pm	O. and visited 1st Field Ambulance	
	4 pm	On Ops. O.6.b wounds interviewed O. and regarding the Evacuation from this Battalion at night. Details rather working out the details. Message to III Corps — Admissions to Field Ambulances from 12 m.n. on 18 to 12 m.n. on 19 Bn. Sick Officers one Capt Austin RAMC 1 18 July two wounds OR three Evacuated OR sick eleven Other four Evacuated hand. Nil for a prisoners 1645 P. Situation unchanged. Weather this raining	Appendix 33 Appendix 34
NIEPPE	May 19. 9 am		

(73089) W4141-163. 400,000. 9/14. H.&J.,Ltd. Forms/C. 2118/10.

Army Form C. 2118.

WAR DIARY
or
INTELLIGENCE SUMMARY.
(Erase heading not required.)

Hour, Date, Place	Summary of Events and Information	Remarks and references to Appendices
MEPPE May 19.	A.D.M.S. visited trenches of 145th & 143rd Brigades with further reference to wearing catching, & keeping greatcoats.	
2.30 pm	Conference AD.M.S. with OC's Field Ambulances. Regimental & Medical Officers.	Appendix 35
	Many cases from Gloster BAILLEUL - Pte Hunt No 1900 8th Gloucesters is suffering from Pemphigus see Academy Acton Dethemouth reference Otitis	Appendix 36
4 pm	Message to 8 W.Y 2nd Army - wounded Officer cases chin. Lieut Goulford A. wounded and 2nd Lieut Kay J.W. struck. Message to 8 W.Y 2nd Army - wounded one Officer & two others missing the division nil. Twelve wounded two others missing the division nil. Message to 8 W.Y III Corps - Wnd cases two Capt Tilley, C.J. & Lieut Goulford A. 5th Warwicks & Lieutenant & 2nd Lieut Kay J.W. 8th Gloucester; 2nd Army 1 sick officer 12 noon 19; Sick officers two Capt Tilley C.J & Lieut Goulford A 5th Warwicks & Lieutenant & 2nd Lieut Kay J.W 8th Glos V.R. wounded Officers two instead Kay & Lieut Caulfield YR. Sick twelve wounded two. Other divisions admissions two. Sick created nil.	Appendix 37
NIEPPE May 20. 8 am	Situation unchanged. Weather warm & sunny	

WAR DIARY
or
INTELLIGENCE SUMMARY.
(Erase heading not required.)

Army Form C. 2118.

Instructions regarding War Diaries and Intelligence Summaries are contained in F.S. Regs., Part II and the Staff Manual respectively. Title pages will be prepared in manuscript.

Hour, Date, Place	Summary of Events and Information	Remarks and references to Appendices
MIEPPE May 20th 9am	O. in C visited trenches of 143rd & 146th Brigades with reference to gas, out of gas posts, warning posts & sentries.	
2.30 pm	A.D.M.S. interviewed O. in C. D.D.M.S. gave information as to farms on its army with chemicals the farm to be Keg Q. 2. D.D. leaving to arrive from Infirm.	
1 pm	9 camp to stand to Army - Reconnd. of Raid & improv. Dams. Other Divisions Officers to instruct Ridgley & M. Klein's	Appendix 38
	Faith R. Battery 8 R. Pied 9 came to III Corps. Ambulances Field Ambulances from 12mm L to 12 noon 20 & 2 store Antoigne Wounded Officers in it me tingle D.B.S. 2 & Evacuation. Arrd MA 48 6 Dr. 65 11 Eleven So central Officers and OR wick in wounds since. Other Serans Admitted sick. Officers 2 OR - Kind Tingley M. Placeton 1 C Batty 319 and Evacuated Officers one A. Tinteley 12 mins. Total Number of prisoners taken 1.16,650.	Appendix 39
NEPPE May 21st 9 am	Situation unchanged. Weather warm & sunny. O.in C. inspected progress of work in connection with the	

WAR DIARY or INTELLIGENCE SUMMARY.

Army Form C. 2118.

Hour, Date, Place	Summary of Events and Information	Remarks and references to Appendices
NIEPPE May 21st 10 a.m.	Making of dug-outs for ourposts of the 144 H.B.S. Also visited Headquarters 144 & 143rd with reference to sanitation. The obtaining water for drinking purposes.	
4 p.m.	Waded up to 2nd Army Vaccinated Officers one Capt. Lucken. O.R. Branch O.R. sixteen Wounded O.R. eight Other Divisions. O.R. Own. Waded up to D.D.M.S. III Corps. Admissions to Field Ambulances from B men 20 to 12 normal. Officers nil. O.R. sick fatigue. Wounded eight. Evacuated Officers sick one Captain Lucken 1st Warwicks. O.R. sick sixteen Wounded eight Other Divisions admissions sick O.R. four evacuations. All units except A.E.E. equipped with face pads mouth plugs Situation unchanged. Weather warm & Sunny.	Appendix 40 Appendix 41
NIEPPE May 22nd 8 a.m.	A.D.M.S. visited TOUQUERT BERTHE with reference to drinking water drawn from a well in the 144 K.B.S. Trench Engineers & specimen of water sent to D.W.D. Armentières 45th Division.	
2 p.m.	Visited Maison Crème de Ponchin PONT DE NIEPPE with a view to ensuring billets of Women & rats to men of the Division. Inspected the billets of men & littered them.	

(73989) W4141—463. 400,000. 9/14. H.&J.Ltd. Forms/C. 2118/10.

Army Form C. 2118.

WAR DIARY
or
INTELLIGENCE SUMMARY.
(Erase heading not required.)

Instructions regarding War Diaries and Intelligence Summaries are contained in F.S. Regs., Part II. and the Staff Manual respectively. Title pages will be prepared in manuscript.

Place	Hour, Date	Summary of Events and Information	Remarks and references to Appendices
NIEPPE	May 22nd, 4 pm	Message to DAA & QMG 2nd Army - Evacuations Officers wounded one Capt Haywood by J.6? Proton OR twelve sick OR thirteen other Division nil.	Appendix 42
		Message to III Corps - R Division no 1 Field Ambulance from 12 noon 22nd to 12 noon 23rd Sick OR fifteen wounded Officers nil Captain Haywood WJR 6th Proton OR eighteen Wounded Officer wounded A.D.R at thirteen (evacuated) twelve of the Division a Divisions a & even OR sick Evacuated nil	Appendix 43
	11.12 am	Message from 3rd Field Ambulance — 16.00 g. Week 0 sufferers from scarlet fever — removed to Bailleul. Precautions taken. Situation unchanged.	Appendix 44
NIEPPE	May 23rd, 5 am	Weather bright sunny. O.R.M.S. inspected 1st (Fld) Field Ambulance at Ecole d'Alpha PONT DE NIEPPE with its transport wagons.	
	2 pm	Message received from the C.C.L. 2600 Pte Ockley 76 Muster to officers from Celebs Found meningitis.	Appendix 42 e.
	After	Embarked map also transport sent to OR & while Returning Railway bullion saw Ambulance to take a Battalion wounded directly — this evening. Calais Entry machine gun would commit be taken away from rendez for four days.	Appendix 45.

WAR DIARY or INTELLIGENCE SUMMARY

Army Form C. 2118.

Place	Date	Hour	Summary of Events and Information	Remarks and references to Appendices
MEPPE	23.5.15	4 pm	Message to G.O.C. 2nd Army - Evacuated Officers two sick one about Pavillon S.K. 6 1/2 Plus two DR eighteen Wounded officers nil DR twenty - Other Divisions nil	Appendix 46
			Message to D.M.S. Corps - Admissions to Field Ambulances from 8 noon past 57 mn 22nd to this officers one about Pavillon S.K. 6 1/2 Plus two OR fifteen OR sixty one wounded OR sixteen. Evacuated officers none of such eighteen sum OR twenty other Division admitted sick own four, wounded nil.	Appendix 47
		6 pm	Message to D.M.S. Base - Richards to from 15th to Nov 22nd 5th Warwicks officers one OR six 6 Warwicks OR fifteen 5th Warwicks officers one OR twelve 8 Warwicks officers two OR twenty 4th Plus two OR seven 6.C. Plus two officers no main 7 Wor--ters Officers nil RE twelve 5 Worcesters OR twelve 4th Plus two OR sixteen Worc--ter O. R. eleven 4 F.R. Banks OR seven 1st DM 8 F. (R.30) DR two 2nd Batt--n one 3rd Batt--- one Girl Dragoons 7 S R form No 1 Field Ambulances to 3rd Batt--n from King Edward Horse two Battn Cyclist Corps form R.F.A. 114 Heavy 8.15 RE one 7 Fat officers one ORs two from Section officers one O RS two from Divine strongly mine	Appendix
MEPPE	24.5.15	8 am	Situation unchanged. Weather warm sunny.	
		11 am	About inspected 3rd & 1st FA Field Ambulances, Transport lines, hospital	
		4 pm	Message to G.O.C. 2nd Army Evacuated O.R. sixteen Wounded never the sick Appendix 48 Message to DMS Corps - Admissions to Field Ambulances from Noon 23 to noon 24 Sick Officers one Cpl six O.R.s & Warwick O.R. fifty seven Brown DS OR	Appendix 48

1577 Wt. W10791/1773 500,000 1/15 D. D. & L. A.D.S.S./Forms/C. 2118.

WAR DIARY
or
INTELLIGENCE SUMMARY.
(Erase heading not required.)

Army Form C. 2118.

Place	Date	Hour	Summary of Events and Information	Remarks and references to Appendices
NIEPPE	24.5.15	4 pm	eight Evacuated sick 1 PR 3 BRO wounded 7 3 sever Other Division's O.R. sick in	Appendix 50
NIEPPE	25.5.15	9 am	Situation unchanged. Weather bright sunny.	
		11 am	Every man in division furnished with respirator night cap.	
			Letter from Capt Walpole Lieut Smith 2nd Bn. A.M.C. reporting from Base from	
			Base. 1/7. Transfer to C.C. O.O. of	
			Inspected billets to rooms men of 6. B. R. Warwick.	
		2 pm	Proceeded to Strazeele. Army Group sent (3) Wounded Officers to Capt Loukes 2nd	Appendix 57
			R.W. Kent. 2 Cpl R.Q 3 gr R. Inniskillings. 10 H to 15 2 attached to Rhin R 30 R 3 Bn 1 D.R.	
			thirteen other division's it own	
		4 pm	George to Sit (Capt - Division's field Ambulances from 10 am 24 to 12 noon	Appendix 52
			25 th Sick 8 R. Hostly from. Wounded Officers Capt Chamberlain 1st W. Riding	
			Capt Louke E. 3rd R.M. R.J. 2 Loams (Lieut Ambrose H.Q. 104. A.B. R.Q. attached)	
			3. R.M. B. 9, R.J.G. 2 of E.M. evacuated Officers to ... two Died ... 1 of ...	
			Sick O.R. thirteen of the Division administrative two wounded sick in	
NIEPPE	26.5.15	8 am	Situation unchanged. Weather warm sunny.	
		11 am	About visited Headquarters H.D. of 8.15 with reference to the wearing of the	
			Puff's vacuum apparatus. This is considered cumbrous thus only the	
			woad by myself. It is entirely unsuitable to treatment	
			letter to 8 A.B.A. Warwick with reference to men leaving their respirators Pipe	

WAR DIARY
or
INTELLIGENCE SUMMARY.

Army Form C. 2118.

Place	Date	Hour	Summary of Events and Information	Remarks and references to Appendices
NIEPPE	26/5/15	2 p.m.	Message sent to D.D.M.S of Corps & collect sample of water from wells concerned in Kendles of 1914 2 & 3rd Offensive Stance Shuffle.	Appendix 53
		2.30 p.m.	Conference with O.C. Field Ambulances & various Regimental Medical Officers.	Appendix 54
		4.30 p.m.	Message to D.M.S. 2nd Army — Evacuated O.R. ten wounded since 9 a.m. to Divisional Rail	
			Message to III Corps — Admissions to Field Ambulances 9 p.m./9 a.m. 25th to 12 noon 26th. O.R. sick forty, O.R. wounded eleven. Evacuated March ten wounded, six other	Appendix 55
			Divisional admissions sick O.R. two.	
			Situation unchanged. Weather cold. Dull windy.	
NIEPPE	27/5/15	9 a.m.	A.D.M.S inspected 2nd (R.M) 2nd Ambulance with the Nurse of this Ambulance. A.D.M.S visited Isolation Hospital BAILLEUL. Visited proposed site for expanding Divisional Rest Station	
		2 p.m.	Explosion at bomb factory at 9 a.m. (?) DOUCE R 2 9 9th Division at NIEPPE Station. 2 killed, 14 wounded, also Evacuees wounded arrived.	
		2.30 p.m.	Much damage done. Shelters —	
			Col. C.O. Yeomanry Unit arrived to take over duties of O.M.S of 28th Division.	
		6 p.m.	Message to D.M.S 2nd Army — Evacuating sick O.R. twelve wounded officers one.	Appendix 53
			Captain Chamberlain 7th Worcesters O.R. seven. Nil Divisional	
			Message to III Corps — Admissions to Field Ambulances from 12 noon 26th to 12 noon 27th.	Appendix 54
			Sick officers one. Capt. Clarke 1/6 Gordons O.R. seventy three wounded eleven. So under	
			Sick O.R. twelve wounded officers one Captain Chamberlain 7/4 Worcester O.R.	
			Seven. Nil Divisional.	

Army Form C. 2118.

WAR DIARY
or
INTELLIGENCE SUMMARY.
(Erase heading not required.)

Instructions regarding War Diaries and Intelligence Summaries are contained in F. S. Regs., Part II. and the Staff Manual respectively. Title pages will be prepared in manuscript.

Place	Date	Hour	Summary of Events and Information	Remarks and references to Appendices
NIEPPE	27.5.15	6.30 p.3	Message from Isolation Hospital BAILLEUL – 492 Cpl Beatty T.V. R.D.A. 45th Dig Batt attached Divisional Ammunition Park admitted to-day as unsuspected (typhus) – men al investigation carried on	App. 55
NIEPPE	28.5.15	8 a.m.	Situation unchanged – Weather cold & dull	
		9.30 a.m.	Col C.A. Young took over duties ADMS 4th Division from Col S.N. Thompson who proceeds to Outyr a Sury III Corps. ADMS with Col Young visited new baths at PONT-DE-NIEPPE also the Officers Baths where men of 6 Division are temporarily billeted. Visited Headquarters of 11th & B.92.	
		2 p.m.	Visited 2 Bd III Corps at BAILLEUL Then Headquarters 143rd Brigade. Visited 2 & 3rd Field Ambrys – Evacuated Officers one Lieut Hargreaves J.B. 6th Warwicks App 52 B.R. twenty & from 2nd Field Station other Division Officers from 2 end Rands B.R. twenty & from 3rd Field Station other Division Officers B.R. ten	
		5 p.m.	Bagley V.C., Chy Al. 2nd Gl J.R. Hogan Egontefoni Col B.R. ten. Message to Sary III Corps – Omissions – 3rd Field Ambulance from 12 noon 27th to 12 noon 28th. Sick Officers one Second Lieut Hargreave J.B. 6th Warwicks B.R. Continue wounded B.R. eleven. Evacuated Officers & Ir twenty and from 4th Division Field Station other Division Officers Wounded Officers one	

Army Form C. 2118.

WAR DIARY
or
INTELLIGENCE SUMMARY.
(Erase heading not required.)

Instructions regarding War Diaries and Intelligence Summaries are contained in F. S. Regs., Part II. and the Staff Manual respectively. Title pages will be prepared in manuscript.

Place	Date	Hour	Summary of Events and Information	Remarks and references to Appendices
NIEPPE	28/5/15	5 pm	2nd Lieuts Bageley VA. Clay OA. Ross JR. Lieutenant Cheetham Capt Smith M.B. from hospital. Cpl all J.G. Field C R.3. OR Warwick OR from 3ra created officers 2nd Lieutenants Royeley, Clay, Ross & high J. a type. OR. 100.	app 57
	29/5/15	8am	Situation unchanged. Weather cooler one.	
		2 pm	O Duty inspected 2nd Field Ambulance. BALLOU also the Isolation hospital	app 58
		2 pm	Message received from D.S. 1 FAR — 438 Jones 4D R War R Entries ...	
		11.30pm	Message to 4rd 2nd Army. Evacuated 38 IR fourteen	app 59
			Message to III Corps — Admissions + Field ambulances from 12 noon 28th to noon 29th	app 60
			Officers sick one. Lieut Hot H.P.6.B. Montre VA fat Wound. TR nine. Evacuated IR fourteen. Other Ranks admissions Roads one Evacuated IR fourteen.	
		7.30pm	Message from Sanitation Hospital — 1870 Pt. Team Jur 1/2 Km. 2 Auto-impresa system	app 61
			Situation unchanged. Weather cold, windy, but sunny.	
NIEPPE	30/5/15	8am	Message from ADY 14th Motor Dt. Boulton D Coy 2nd Platoon suffering from diphtheria	app 62
		11.30am	Message from ADMS 4th Div 2nd Field Ambulance visited HQ Quarters 143rd Brigade. huts in	
		10 am	O Duty inspected 3rd 2nd Field Ambulances and ascertained arrangements supply to the men in the trenches of this Battalion.	
			PLOEGSTEERT WOOD of 4 & 6 on Ducks Roads	
		4 pm	Message to Divisional Army — Evacuations officers sick one Lieut Jaffe A.H. IR	app 63

1577 Wt.W10791/1773 500,000 1/15 D. D. & L. A.D.S.S./Forms/C. 2118.

WAR DIARY or INTELLIGENCE SUMMARY

Army Form C. 2118.

Place	Date	Hour	Summary of Events and Information	Remarks and references to Appendices
NIEPPE	30/5/15	4 pm	Message to III Corps Division re Field Ambulances from 11 am 29th to 5.75 a.m 30th Sick Officers seven, Rank & File forty, R.N.D. Warwicks O.R. twenty six, Wounded Officers one and Lieut Young 2/8th Cheshires O.R. nine. Evacuated Officer one Lieut Jagger. Died Lieut Young O.R. two. Mrs Giovarno kid	App X 64
		6 pm	Message to D.A.G. Base – reports III Corps – Weekly sick wastage from 21 am 22nd to 6 am 29th at Divisional rends 6 & Do. Officers one 27.D. twelve 7 & Do. fourteen 8 & Do. seventeen 4 Cavalry Division one R.D. twelve 1/8th cavalry Officers one R.D. five 8 & Do. five 5 & Do. Division 1/8 North British Division Batts. 8 4/8. 4 & tanks three 1st R & R D. to 3 & Do. Officers two O.R. one 4 & Do. one 4th Division fifteen A/C Three Ammunition Column three Cyclist Corps 3rd Field Ambulance three R & B Officers five	App X 65
			Other ranks one hundred & forty five	
		6.30 pm	Message from Isolation Hospital – 23.04 Pte Bolton 16 Gordons wil Syphilis to Brother	App X 66
NIEPPE	31/5/15	9 am	Situation unchanged. Weather warmer & sunny	
		11 am	Alfred visited trenches of 14th & Brigade ringholds returns considerably. Also visited aid posts of H.L. of R. in cavalry trees. Dynamited & S.C. Scots R.H.	
		2 pm	R.C.H. Asquith O.P. waters men Batts. Away in afternoon	
		4 pm	Message Genl. 2nd army – Evacuated O.R. Sick five Warwickshire Chs. Officer one Lieut five Warwickshire Officers sick two. Remaining Officer sick one O.R. thirty three Wounded thirteen	App X 67
			Message to III Corps – A. Division & Field Ambulances from 12 am 30th & 12 am 31st	App X 68

WAR DIARY
or
INTELLIGENCE SUMMARY.

Army Form C. 2118.

Place	Date	Hour	Summary of Events and Information	Remarks and references to Appendices
DIEPPE	31/5/15	4 pm	Sick OR Thirty eight Wounded seven Evacuated sick OR five Wounded brother other Division Divisions Officers sick one Sent Y/hospital Cpl Brown RE Rheumatism OR nine Evacuated OR Rheumatism	

Murray Colonel AMS
ADMS 48th Divn.

On His Majesty's Service.

12/5930-

48th Division

121/5930

ADMS. 48th Division (2nd...)

Vol III

June 1915.
Issues raised – 2nd Oct d 25/11/17.

amd.

S/

WAR DIARY or INTELLIGENCE SUMMARY

Army Form C. 2118.

Place	Date	Hour	Summary of Events and Information	Remarks and references to Appendices
NIEPPE	1-6-15	8 a.m.	Situation unchanged from that of May 3rd. Weather chilly but sunny	
		10 a.m.	ADMS visited ECOLE PROFESSIONALE, ARMENTIERES with reference to taking over the chemical apparatus from 1st Field Ambulance for the examination guards	
		12 p.m.	for Avenue de Cysoing on arriving. ADMS inspected 1st Field Ambulance — PONT DE NIEPPE	
		2 p.m.	ADMS visited 2nd Field Ambulance — BAILLEUL	
		4 p.m.	Proceeded to DMS 2nd Army — Evacuated sick officers one 7th Warwicks Captain (ADM) 9R OR sight Wounded Officers one 6th Warwicks 2nd Lieutenant Rec. R.C. OR nine. Remaining OR sick twenty to Wounded nineteen. The Wounded evacuated. OR sick two Wounded three	Appendix 1.
			Proceeded to III Corps Admission to Field Ambulances from Regiment to mount of Officers sick one 7th Warwicks (Captain Mitchell) OR 9R OR sightly since above OR Officers one 6th Warwicks 2nd Lieut Lowe IC OR twenty Wounded Officers none OR sight Wounded OR nine. Dead two Other Divisions Admissions OR sick none Wounded none. Evacuated OR sick two Wounded three	Appendix 2.
NIEPPE	2-6-15	8 a.m.	Situation unchanged and the night rainy	
		11 a.m.	ADMS inspected Regimental Aid posts of 5th Warwicks 1st R. Berks also 3rd Field Amb.	
		2.30 p.m.	Conference with DD of Field Ambulances & Regimental M.O.'s. The following points were discussed regarding Sanitary Guards & the disinfect establishments generally instructors	

WAR DIARY
or
INTELLIGENCE SUMMARY.
(Erase heading not required.)

Army Form C. 2118.

Place	Date	Hour	Summary of Events and Information	Remarks and references to Appendices
NIEPPE	2/6/15	2.30 p.m.	Men in first field proceed. Ambulance to Divine for same. Instructions to Junior Officers on Anti Louse effects. The Sanitary arrangements in trenches billets. The prevention of food contamination is same. The method of carrying responsibilities. Ambulance, an of ambulances can of scrap to receive from D.D.M.S.(?) - 1810 FEARN. Relief 1/2 3rd W. Munt. relieve.	Appdx 3 Appdx 4
		4 p.m.	Message to D.D. 2nd Army - Wanted sick Officers signed CRE(?) 3rd line. ELLIS. E.H.F. 2nd Details in Am von Fd Ain Wounded Officers the Arch B/ 2/Lieut infant HAMPDEN M.M. A 4th Supt. 8 D.R. mine Remaining ex? Operations (Wounded) OR Kitchen Message to III Corps — Admission to Field Ambulance from 2 arm (at 6/2 noon 3rd) sick Officers ten 2/Lieuts. TRANNELL H Infantry arm. 3rd Fd sick C.RE./Lieut ELLIS 547 1/Lieut Ins Ams(?) OR 1/Thirty one Wounded Officers are Arch B(?) 2/Lieut Infant HAMPDEN M.M. all rifle (?) OR sixteen Evacuated Officers eight Evacuated names(?) 3 sick air wounds in mine Gas Poisoned other Remains O. Divisions explain sick & evacuated	Appdx 5
NIEPPE	3/6/15	8 a.m.	Situation unchanged. Weather warm sunny. O. Divil visited the extension of the Divisional Rest Station in tents. BAILLEUL.	Appdx 6
		2 p.m.	Evacuation Divl sick & distrib worms 2nd from	
		4 p.m.	Message to Aml 2nd Army III Corps - Admission Field Ambulances from 18 noon 2nd to 6 noon 2nd Evacuation to Amb III Corps. 3rd Lieut O.R. forty nine (Wounds) Devon 3/Lieutn ten Evacuated OR such sickline wounds from other Divisions admission Sick Officers one six/h Division train A.S.C. Lieut Wilson R.W. Lancaster knee OR J. Jenn	Appdx 7

1577 Wt. W 10791/1773 500,000 1/15 D. D. & L. A.D.S.S./Forms/C. 2118.

WAR DIARY
or
INTELLIGENCE SUMMARY.

(Erase heading not required.)

Army Form C. 2118.

Place	Date	Hour	Summary of Events and Information	Remarks and references to Appendices
MEPPE	4.6.15	8am	Situation unchanged. Weather dull & damp.	
		12am	A. D.M.S. attend Conference at Headquarters 48th Division.	
		2.30 pm	S Divn III (Intradia) together with A.D.M.S. visited 14th & 15th Field Ammunition Cyclist Coy.	
		4 pm	Nrs.my to Div 2nd Army. Wounded officers and one 5th Warwicks Lieutenant Kemp.	App. 8
			S.D. sprains ankle. O.R. nine wound. O.R. five. O the Divisn O.R. sick one. Remaining	
			O.R. sick twenty four from Bivouacs & elsewhere.	
			Message to III Corps. Division to III Corps Divn sick to 10 & O.R. sick to 17 N.C.O.s &	App. 9
			Lieut officers tr. 6 Warwicks Lieut KEMP S.D. sprained ankle, 7th Warwicks Lieutenant	
			CARR-GRIGGS Bn. M.O. O.R. thirty eight wounded. Off. sick evacuated one. Prisoners of war O.R.	
			sick nine wounded five & three to the Division. 9 Divns one O.R. with ser wounds.	
			Ditto one	
		6 pm	D.A.D.M.S. with Lt. Col. HOWKINS O'Phs Field Ambulance looks over debris both waste	
			which he reports attach Myers sono ND room 10 x 10 x 14' filled with large quantity of Chlorine	
			Bromine for 40 minutes without any ill effects and Nurse states the could stay lugn.	
NIEPPE	5.6.15	8am	Situation unchanged. Weather warm & sunny.	
		10 am	A Digt. much Sickness fr. two cases of sick several. Sent 80 Dysn. triggered	
			Message to Div 2nd Army - Evacuated sick wounded O.R. five	
		4 pm	Remaining officers sick one O.R. twenty four. Wounded D.B. Lee	App. 10
			& escape Nrs III Corps. ADivisions Field Ambulances from wounds & O.R. nine	App. 11
			5th Lieut. officers one 4. R. Berks Lieut AVIS SJN Sprainankle 7 th Warwicks Lieut	
			4 A 16 H. D.H. Branchito 8 th Warwicks 2 Lieut PIKE J.C.R. Ingham. C.E. Goode 2 Lieut.	

WAR DIARY
or
INTELLIGENCE SUMMARY.

(Erase heading not required.)

Army Form C. 2118.

Instructions regarding War Diaries and Intelligence Summaries are contained in F.S. Regs., Part II. and the Staff Manual respectively. Title pages will be prepared in manuscript.

Place	Date	Hour	Summary of Events and Information	Remarks and references to Appendices
NIEPPE	5.6.15	4 p.m.	NOTT N.P. and N.P.D. O.R. thirty eight wounded S.O.A. fire. S.A. awaited O.R. wounded three Other airmen admitted O.R. from acct.	
		8.15 p.m.	Group from SAP gHQ & 2nd BEATTY RFC S and Air Ammnt Park attacked 3.29	App 12
			Cpl A.L.C. ENTERIC.	
MEPPE	6.6.15	8 a.m.	Situation unchanged — weather warm & sunny	
		10.30 a.m.	A Duty visits 11th E.R. Hy (Carrier Group) with reference to medical examining arrangements generally & a case of respirators	
		12.45	Message from 48 F. Ammunition Park stating Cpl BEATTY has been inoculated twice before leaving England	App 13
		3.30 p.m.	O Auld & ADMS attended lecture by M BARLEY f III Corps in wood neighbouring	
		4.30 p.m.	message to O.R. Bone & III Offrs — Lieut MacKay from wounds gun shot arm St b Devonshire Officers two O.R. right w. S. Lincolns S.R. right f. S.S. one O.R. from 6 R.E. Officers one S.A. right 7 h. S.O. Offrs. two O.R. right w. Inniskilling three Burks 10 W. African ADVRS Officers admitted other ranks 2nd Br. R.F.A. two 7. Pal Ff. two air other Ranks Column one King Edward Horse one nine to five	App 14
			message to Dind 2nd Army. Evacuated Officers Lieut AULD F.Amb. & E.K. Berks	App 15
			Inniskilling S.R. sick trip Wounded Sick Walker Divisions S.R. sick	
		9 p.m.	message to 1TR n/ps — Admissions to Field Ambulances from 12 noon 5.6. 12 noon 6.6. Lich S.R. twenty seven wounded S.R. eight Evacuated Lieut AULD 2nd Lt. & Panul Auld/lt 8 R Berks S.R. sick two other ranks Flve Airmen admissions O.R sick twenty Evacuates one S.H.	App 16

WAR DIARY or INTELLIGENCE SUMMARY

Army Form C. 2118.

Place	Date	Hour	Summary of Events and Information	Remarks and references to Appendices
NIEPPE	7.6.15	8 a.m.	Situation unchanged. Weather warm windy.	App 17
		4 p.m.	Bearer to 9th & 2nd Army - Evacuated sick Officers & men/prisoners/Field No 7 & N.O. 6 I. Stokes H.Q. D.R. 3 bro to 3 D.R. one. Bearer to III Corps Advanced Field Ambulance from 12 noon to 6 p.m. 10 men. 15 Sick, OR Thirty-one Wounded, OR Three Evacuated Field Officers / Cardl NO 77 H.Q. 6 I. Posten H.Q. OR Three Wounded. 27 O.R. sick. O.R. Divisions admitted Eleven.	App 18.
NIEPPE	8.6.15	8 am	Situation unchanged. Weather warm sunny.	
		11 am	A Dull visited PLOEGSTEERT area road with a view to situation of Wagon Rendezvous for Field Ambulances to collect wounded	App 19
		4 pm	Bearer to 9th & 2nd Army. Evacuated Wounded Officer one 8 Warwicks Lieut Cattan(?) I am fifty Right shoulder. took took sick Officer Other Divisions (Admitted)	
			Sick Thirty one Wounded/Men. Leave(?) to III? Corps Advance from 12 noon 7 a.m. to 10 a.m & 9 o'clock OR fifty nine. Wounded Officers one 8 Warwick Lieut Cattan. Jos Officer R. Wilts OR took Evacuated Officer as above OR six eleven wounded Men. Other Divisions Admitted OR sick for Evacuated to etc.	App 20
NIEPPE	9.6.15	8 am	Situation unchanged. Weather too damp.	
		11 am	Bearer from Isolation (In patio) Batteries - 3370 Pte Bird SR/8 R Warwicks inspected. Evacno.	App 21
		2 pm	Conference with O.C. Field Ambulances & Regimental Medical Officers - the following points	

WAR DIARY
or
INTELLIGENCE SUMMARY.
(Erase heading not required.)

Army Form C. 2118.

Place	Date	Hour	Summary of Events and Information	Remarks and references to Appendices
NIEPPE	9.6.15	2 p.m.	were discussed. Scheme of divisional area medical aid in time of active operations. The latest memorandum from 2nd Army regarding Respirators & the helmets. The replenishing of medical & surgical equipment of divisional units. The keeping roads & grooming sick. The daily inoculation of all labor gangs. Antityphoid inoculation. The sanitation of the trenches.	Appendix 22
		4 p.m.	Message to DDMS 2nd Army – Evacuated O.R. sick eight wounded five remaining sick Officers one O.R. twenty six Wounded Officers one O.R. thirteen	App 23.
			Message to III Corps – Admissions to Field Ambulances from 12 noon 8th to 12 noon 9th twenty 9 Red Officers one 8th Worcesters Capt BURLINGHAM R.H. Bold 8th Worcesters since Wounded Officers one 8th Worcester Lieut DAVIES C.C. filled left arm O.R. ten – Evacuated O.R. sick eight wounded five Other divisions a divisions O.R. sick nine	
			A DMS attended DDMS's inspection by G.O.C. of 1st Field Ambulance. Sanitation an along ad. Weather rainy & clear. Flight Thunderstorms.	
NIEPPE	10.6.15	8 a.m.	Message from 8th Warwicks 33/0 Pte BIRD inoculated once	App 23
		2 p.m.	A sent DADMS Noisdu BAILEUL for a demonstration as to the use & effect of Chlorine gas when using respirators & smoke helmets. Chlorine at first is funny head – So if all effects experienced when using either offers antidote.	
		2.30 p.m.	Message to DMS 2nd Army – Evacuated officers at two 6th Gloster Lieut Co ANDERSON B.G. Gsw. 8th Worcesters Captain CLARKE S.A. Gsw right Wound S.2 m.	
		4.30 p.m.		App 24

WAR DIARY
or
INTELLIGENCE SUMMARY

Army Form C. 2118.

Place	Date	Hour	Summary of Events and Information	Remarks and references to Appendices
DIEPPE	10.6.15	4.30 pm	8th Worcesters Lieut DAVIES C.C. and few left arm OR sick six Wounded three Remaining Officers from OR sick twenty eight Wounded eleven. Released to the Corps – Admissions to Field Ambulances from 18 evening to 12 noon	App 25.
			10th Officers sick four Lieut Col ANDERSON B.J. & Capt J.H. Worcesters Lieut GORE 2/S. Suffolk attach Lieut SYNE C.W. Syenna 2/6 Worcesters Captain CLARKE 2.G. Indigestion OR twenty six Wounded Officers 4 Clarkes Lieut PHIPPEN G. and few left arm OR four – Evacuated Officers three Lieut Col ANDERSON Cap tain CLARKE and S.G. Worcesters Lieut DAVIES C.C. and few left arm OR sick six Wounded three The Division	
			Admissions sick OR nine. Situation unchanged. Weather damp & close.	
DIEPPE	11.6.15	8 am	Army visited Rue de Nord Arras Entries with reference to Hyserine loops holding bay numbers. Also referred to A.D.M.S. 27th Division in whose area two is situated. United Advance Status LA CRECHE Europe also official pattern respirators for officers.	
		11 am		
		12.30 p.m.	France. Message to DM.S and Army – Evacuated sick Officers two 4 Evacuated sick O.R.E. six E.S. 7th Warwicks Lieut PIKE J.C.n. OR Twelve Wounded Officers one 4 Clarkes Lieut PHIPPEN H.C. and few left arm OR seven Remaining Officers three OR thirty nine Released to III Corps – Admissions to Field Ambulances from 12 am 10th to 12 noon 11th the Rest OR Thirty four Wounded Officers two 4 Clarkes Lieut Castle H. and f.i.n scalp slight Lieut GAUNTLET R.C.W.R. and G.4th 4.13 arms injury OR seven. Evacuated sick Officers two	App/p 26

WAR DIARY or INTELLIGENCE SUMMARY

Army Form C. 2118.

Place	Date	Hour	Summary of Events and Information	Remarks and references to Appendices
NIEPPE	11.6.15	4.30pm	7th Worcesters 2/Lieut GORE E.S, 7th Warwick Lieut PIKE J.C.R. OR twelve wounded. Officers one H.Glosters Lieut PHIPPEN H.S. and 2/Lieut BORE OR seven died ORALL Divisions OR sick form	App 37
NIEPPE	12.6.15	8 am	Situation unchanged. Weather warm sunny.	
		2 pm	DDMS II Corps interviewed O.Sick Message to 2nd & 3rd Army - Evacuated sick Officers one L Class Bucks L/ Lieut GRIFFEN - fifford. 2/6 Worcesters 2/Lieut GWILLIAM A.S. Wounded nipally OR seven wounded officers one L Gloster Lieut MERRICK H and 4 Glo L/Jaw OR seven L the Division OR sick one. Remaining sick Officers one OR nineteen Wounded Officers resits OR eleven	App 38
			Message 6 DAy III Corps - Admissions Field Ambulances from 12 noon 11.6.15 to noon 12.6.15 Officers three L Corps three L Div. 3 Rnch Lieut GRIFFEN I.E half of 7th 5th centuring L Lieut GWILLIAM sick R Q M Sgt attached 6 E.A. anicks Lieut 8yms ga hid from horse OR twenty one wounded. Officers 1 L Gloster Lieut MERRICK 14 am f/b L/jaw OR seven. Evacuated sick Officers in last 24 hours OR seven. Wounded Officers one L Gloster and OR seventh. Lit transit	App 39
NIEPPE	13.6.15	8 am	Situation unchanged. Weather warm sunny	
		11 am	Message from Salvation Hospital BAILLEUL 974 Spr KING W.H. 1st Field Cay R.E. suspected Influenza	App 40
		4 pm	Message to No 1 2nd Army - Evacuated sick OR eight wounded two remaining sick officers one OR twenty. Wounded Off one OR fourteen. Other Division so evacted OR sick one	App 41
			Message to III Corps - Admissions Field Ambulances from 12 noon 12 to 12 noon 13	

WAR DIARY or INTELLIGENCE SUMMARY

Army Form C. 2118.

Place	Date	Hour	Summary of Events and Information	Remarks and references to Appendices
NIEPPE	13.6.15	4 p.m.	Sick Officers one Lieut DRAKE C.S. Jas. Chipadis 4th Gloster OR thirty Wounded OR four OR two OR sick eight Wounded two Other Divisions admissions sick OR two Wounded OR one.	App 42
		6 p.m.	In escape to D.A.T. Race. Sick wastage from 12 noon 6th to 12 noon 12th Lieut 5th Warwicks OR six OR R.O. one J.J. R.O. Officers one OR. J.J. R.O. Officers one OR Nine 4th Gloster Officers two OR twelve 5th Gloster OR seven 7th Worcester Officers two OR nine 8th D. Officers two OR seven 4th Oxon Bucks Officers one OR ten 4th R.Berks Officers one OR four 3rd WR R.F.O. OR one 1st Field Ambulance one 2nd Do. two 3rd Do. two 1st Wels Coy R.E. two Signals Do. one Cyclist Co. one A.S.C. Supply Column two King Edwards Horse one 2nd Mountain Battery R.G.A. att three 2nd Brigade Reg. Detachment att one H.Q. Officers twelve OR.	App 43
			Visibility & weather unchanged. Weather changeable.	
NIEPPE	14.6.15	9 a.m.	A.D.M.S. present at inspection by the G.O.C. 28th Div: (the 3rd) Fd Ambulance.	
		11.45 a.m.	A.D.M.S. interviewed C.R.E. with reference to laying pillar for water supply to men in the trenches - also as to providing receptacles to same.	
		3 p.m.	De. letter written to O.B.O.X XIIth Division asking that the sick wounded of 35th Inf Brigade should be sent to 10 (5th) Fd Ambulance Pont de Nieppe for evacuation by escape to D.M.S. 2nd Army - Do casualties OR thirteen wounded OR six Remaining sick Officers three OR eighteen Wounded Officers two OR six.	App 44

1577 Wt. W10791/1773 500,000 1/15 D. D. & L.   A.D.S.S./Forms/C 2118.

WAR DIARY or INTELLIGENCE SUMMARY

Army Form C. 2118.

Place	Date	Hour	Summary of Events and Information	Remarks and references to Appendices
NIEPPE	14/6/15	4 pm	Message to III Corps - Admissions to Field Ambulances from 12 noon 13th to noon 14th. Sick Officers nil. Sth Worcesters Captain CLARKE Sa Indigestion. 2nd Worcesters Lieut HARRIS T.C.? and M.Y.D. acc. O.R. twenty nine Wounds O.R. eight. Evacuated Officers nil (first name) O.R. sick fifteen Wounds six. Other divisions 2 divisions OR sick four.	App 45
NIEPPE	15/6/15	9 am	Situation unchanged. Weather warm sunny.	
		3 pm	DADMS inspected BRASSERIE BOULET NEUVE EGLISE to ascertain if any mineral water could be obtained as there is scarcity in this area. Found only been made—no mineral water.	App 46
		4 pm	En route to 2nd Army. Evacuated OR sick two Wounds OR three. Divisions OR nine wounds one. Remaining sick Officers one three OR fifteen Wounds Officers two OR nine	
			Message to III Corps - Admissions from Ambulances from 12 noon 14 to noon 15th. Sick OR forty five Wounds Officers one 8th Wor cesters Lieut Colts "A" 4th Glo Rt. shell slight OR five. 2nd Worcesters OR two wounds three. Other Divisions OR sick eight Wounds one. Evacuated OR wounded one.	App 47
NIEPPE	16/6/15	9 am	Situation unchanged. Weather warm sunny. Officers left for Cargo leave in England.	
		11 am	Dr Paul visited "Stinking Farm" M.26.7a.57 Ref Map Sheet 36 (south) with reference to vacation as the well is being occupied a couple of the watch was taken, to test with Howarth apparatus & found 1.9° quality.	App 48
		11 am	Message from Jerusalem hospital. 9740 Spr KING 1st Field Co Ry E.S? proves bacteriologically water provisionally to Inflicere.	
		4 pm	Message to III LOD 2nd Army - Evacuated OR sick nine Wounds five. Remaining sick Officers	App 49

WAR DIARY
or
INTELLIGENCE SUMMARY.
(Erase heading not required.)

Army Form C. 2118.

Instructions regarding War Diaries and Intelligence Summaries are contained in F. S. Regs., Part II. and the Staff Manual respectively. Title pages will be prepared in manuscript.

Place	Date	Hour	Summary of Events and Information	Remarks and references to Appendices
MIEPPE	16.6.15	4 pm	Three O.R. twenty four wounded officers and two O.R. sick	App 50
			Message to III Corps admin in Field Ambulance from 12 noon 15th 9 am 16th Officers wounded five (Capt. HALL P.H. invalids O.R. fifty five wounded) one Lieut CURTIER W.L. S.R. evacuated five O.R. sick R. high O.R. five (2 cases) S.R. sick nine wounded nine — Other divisions admissions and officers one one 7th Suffolks Lieut CHITTY - THOMAS Gen.? Diphtheria. O.R. eleven towards two	
MIEPPE	17.6.15	8 am	Situation unchanged. Weather very rainy	App 51
		4 pm	Message to Div and Army - Evacuated officers sick two 5th R Warwicks Lieut Col STEWART C.A. tachycardia Manager wounded - two	
			Bay Loren 7th Worcester Lieut DRAKE D.B. tachycardia O.R. three other Divisions officers nil	
			8th Worcesters Lieut CARTER H. and Officer Reflected J.M. Diphtheria O.R. wounds three remaining sick officers	
			7th Suffolks Lieut CHITTY-THOMAS J.M. Diphtheria O.R. wounds one O.R. twelve	
		"	Message to III Corps - Admissions to Field Ambulances from 12 noon 16th to noon 17th Jct.	App 52
			Officers one 5th R Warwicks Lieut Col STEWART C.A. (Tachycardia) seven O.R. fatigues wounded	
			O.R. nine . Evacuated officers nil two Lieut Col STEWART and 7th Worcester Lieut DRAKE D.B.	
			Tachycardia. Wounds five and Diphtheria Lieut CARTER H. and Reflect J.M. - - three O.R. wounded	
			seven wounds three Other Divisions Admissions March two wounded three wounded officers	
			nil one Lieut CHITTY-THOMAS 7th Suffolks Diphtheria - wounded O.R. three	
NICPPE	18.6.15	12 am	Message from 8th M.L. 9741 KING 1/Field Ay RE Bulline	App 53
		8 am	Situation unchanged. Weather cold but fine	

WAR DIARY
or
INTELLIGENCE SUMMARY.
(Erase heading not required.)

Army Form C. 2118.

Place	Date	Hour	Summary of Events and Information	Remarks and references to Appendices
NIEPPE	18/6/15	2.30 p.m.	Staff Officers conference at Headquarters. Staff, in the absence of C.O. present.	App/54
		4.30 p.m.	Message to III Corps - Ambulances to Field Ambulances from R.A.M.C. 17th Div wounded Sick Officers nine. Capt GREENHALL C. 2. Remainder in 6th Londons. Lieut JACKMAN W.A. pneumonia. Other ranks to Casualty Clearing Station H. Colonel Ramahita's Field Dressing Station. One O.R. Ninety three wounded. B Rifles. Evacuated Sick Officers one. Lieut GREGG C Benedict Pneumonia. 2 L.R. Warwicks. Other ranks. Evacuated Sick one. O.R. Wounded B.R. Nine. Other ranks. evacuated sick one. O.R. Wounded two. Remainder O.R. wounded one.	
			Message to 2nd Div 2nd Army. Evacuated Sick Officers one. Lieut GREGG C Benedict Pneumonia. 2 L.R. Warwicks. O.R. six wounded O.R. the Remaining sick Officers & Ranks one. Wounded Officers nil. O.R. seven. Other Divisions evacuated O.R. wounded five.	App/55
			Situation unchanged. Weather cold, but sunny.	
NIEPPE	19/6/15	8 a.m.	Message to III Corps ambulances. Evacuated sick Officers one. Lieut ADSHEAD R.N. 2nd Bn. R.F.A. Measles. O.R. in England O.R. 2) Officers one. M/Lieut CARTER E.D. 4 R Berks Rifle left Eye. Other ranks & Other Divisions O.R. wounded two Remaining sick Officers one O.R thirty three wounded.	App/56
		5 p.m.	Message to III Corps. A Divisions Field Ambulances from R.A.M.C. 18/6/15 12 noon 19th Sick Officers intwo. Lieut ADSHEAD R.N. 2nd Bn. R.F.A. Measles. Lieut KNIGHT-ADKIN J.H. 4 R. Londons fracture intwo. O.R. Thirty one evacuated. Officers one. M/Lieut CARTER E.D. 4 R. Berks Rifle left Eye. O.R. fifty six. evacuated Officers sixfirst Remaining O.R. sixty two Wounded two. Other Divisions evacuated Officers one. Wounded nil. O.R. five. Remaining O.R wounded two.	App/57

Wt. W.10791/1773 500,000 1/15 D. D. & L. A.D.S.S./Forms/C. 2118.

WAR DIARY
or
INTELLIGENCE SUMMARY.

Army Form C. 2118.

Place	Date	Hour	Summary of Events and Information	Remarks and references to Appendices
NIEPPE	20/6/15	8 a.m.	Stratton in charge. Weather warm sunny.	App 58
		4 pm	Messages to S.A.C. Base - Lieut unstop from 12 noon 3 to 4 am 19 just 3rd Warwicks Officers one OR three 6 to OR six 7th D. Officers ten OR three 8th S. OR five 10 S. Florestin right 6 Cheshire nine 2 Worcestin Officer one Brig General 2 S.S. Officer two OR two 3rd Worcs Offrs 9 Wars Bucks seven Bucks Bn nine O.R. Rihn Ten Regt nine O.R. nine 2 Wars Bucks OR 12 OR 12 to one Ammunition Park one 1st Aus Field Ambulance three 3 S. one King Edward's Horse three A.S.C. Supply Column two 2nd Mountain Bty nine total Officers seven OR seventy eight.	
			Messages to DSS, 2nd Army Son evacuated Officers one Capt GREGG O.M.7th Warwicks Gunshot wound OR five Evacuated OR from the Division OR wounded 27 sick two Remaining 3rd Officers M twenty seven Wounded OR nine.	App 59
			Messages to III Corps - A Division Field Ambulance from 12 noon 19 to noon 20th Sick Officers one - Capt GREGG O.M.7 Warwicks Gunshot wounds 27 twenty five wounds many we evaluated Officer one above OR sick five seven mild form Other Division Officers First Officers one Lieut MYERS H.2 9 th Essex S.P. Division OR seventeen wounded OR two five minutes OR sick ten wounded 27 OR one	App 60
NIEPPE	21/6/15	8 a.m.	Stratton in charge. Weather warm sunny.	
		3 pm	A Draft XII Servant called with ofference to rendering medical assistance to working party of XII Division working in this area.	
		11 pm	Message to Sub DoM Army Wounded Officers one Capt GREENTREE C.C. 6th Florida Gunshot wound OR right Wounded OR five The Division OR wounded 9 D OR ten Officer one OR in catafalk Wounded OR Remaining sick	App 61

Army Form C. 2118.

WAR DIARY or INTELLIGENCE SUMMARY.
(Erase heading not required.)

Place	Date	Hour	Summary of Events and Information	Remarks and references to Appendices
NIEPPE	21.6.15	4 p.m.	Greetings to III Corps. Admissions 8 Field Ambulance from 12 noon 20.6 to 12 noon 21st. Sick Officers one Lieut BURCHER F.D.W. & 80 o.r. cases. Diphtheria O.R. Wounded in Wounds O.R. evacuated Officers one Capt. GREENHALL C.S.6 O.R. Photos Pneumonia O.R. right. Wounds O.R. five other Divisions admissions sick O.R. seven wounds one other Division wounds one.	App. 62
NIEPPE	22.6.15	8 a.m.	Situation unchanged. Weather very rainy. O.Sul. returned off leave.	
		2.30 p.m.	I find III Corps called here O.Sul. with officers to witness to withstanding approaches to the Victory of water at ECOLE PROFESSIONELLE ARMENTIERES.	App. 63
		5 p.m.	Greetings to 3 rd Army. Evacuated O.R. sick seven Wounded five other Divisions sick one. Remainder Lieut officers ten O.R. thirty one Wounded Officers no O.R. eleven.	
			Greetings to III Corps. Admissions & Field Ambulance from 12 noon 21st 12 noon 22nd. Field Officers two Lieut BEAVAN L.A.W. & H Photos Lieut EARNSHAW Wounds I.C.I. nighttime O.R. forty Wounded Officers one & Lieut WILLIAMS A.S.C. Warwicks of the Scalp & left arm. O.R. seven evacuated O.R. sick & eight Wounded five other Division. Admissions O.R. sick fourteen wounded one left.	App. 64
NIEPPE	23.6.15	9 a.m.	Situation unchanged. Weather close warm. Some rain.	
		9 a.m.	O.Sul. interviewed D.D.M.S. with reference to 2nd Field Ambulance & closing of Divisional Rest Station at BAILLEUL. The D.D.M.S. 2nd Army was present at the same time.	
		12.15 p.m.	O.Sul. instructed 3 Div Ambulance with reference ther.	
		2.30 p.m.	Conference with O.Cos Field Ambulances & Regimental M.O.s Officers Pure of the Division.	

WAR DIARY or INTELLIGENCE SUMMARY

Army Form C. 2118.

Place	Date	Hour	Summary of Events and Information	Remarks and references to Appendices
MEPPE	23/6/15	7.30 pm	Met of the Field Ambulances discussed. Also viewed measures of Chlorination should not instructions being taken to ensure enforcement. Arrangements made to transport to the nearest R.E. water station to increase supply of fresh water. Passage to WID? Sanny - No casualties of officers - Lieut EARNSHAW ?Ro. ? Worick T.C.T. Rifle knee. 2/Lieut GREG. A.N. D.A. head cha Inf? Morse. Lieut HAND 2nd Mountain R.B.? R.F.A. ?symrites R. shoulder D.A. mine. Wounded officers same. 2/Lieut WILLIAMS O.& Warwicks ?to scalp shell am. D.A. seven other Divisions sick D.A. one wounded D.A. two. Remaining sick officers on bed losing ?eight. Wounded D.A. Thirteen.	App 65
			Message to III Corps - admissions Field Ambulances from noon 22nd to 12 noon 23rd Sick Officers five 2/Lieut GREG A.N. ? T.R.R Warwicks Inf? Male Lieut HAND 2 Mountain ?shoulder D.A. twenty seven wounded D.A. nine ?ra cases sick officers three Lieut EARNSHAW H.M. ? R.R. ? wounded T.C.T. Rifle knee 2/Lieut GREG ? Lieut HAND named above nine wounded officers one 2/Lieut WILLIAMS O.& Warwicks ?th Scalp? eff. am. D.A. seven Other Divisions admissions D.A. eight these wounds fire D.A. ... D.A. ...	App 66
		6 pm	2/Lieut XII Division called with reference to ambulance of his Division taken on the way.	
MEPPE	24/6/15	8 am	18th Division in car eaten by them. Situation unchanged. Weather close many Air. Officers 2.30 am of 18 Field Ambulance XII Division took over charge running of the Divisional Baths at Pont DE MEPPE	
		4 pm	O Dw? XII Division called with reference to no cooler packs wounded from the area which he takes one from the AS ? Doveren	
		7 pm	Message to Devs? 2nd Army - Evacuated sick officers four 2/Lieut SIMS.C.M.?.B.	App 67

WAR DIARY
or
INTELLIGENCE SUMMARY.

Army Form C. 2118.

Place	Date	Hour	Summary of Events and Information	Remarks and references to Appendices
MIERIS	24.6.15	4pm	Worcesters Eugene Lieut BURCHER FAH, 2 Worcesters Suffolks Lieut BEAVAN LDW. & Suffolks Boils Lieut JACKMAN WA. 6 Suffolks Queens Colitis OR eighteen Wounded Officers one Lieut KNIGHT-ADKIN JR 8th St Gastro 50 Contusion abdomen OR nine Lieut one. Officers OR sick three Wounded five Remaining OR sick ten Wounded five.	
			Progress to III Corps Advising Field Ambulances from 10 noon 23rd June 24th of Revel. Seventy two Wounded from Evacuated Officers four Sprain LSame C.n 2nd Worcesters Eugene Lieut BURCHER FAH, 2nd Worcesters Suffolks Lieut BEAVAN LDW, 11th Suffolks Boils Lieut JACKMAN WA, 6th Suffolks Queens Colitis OR eighty seven Wounded Officers on Lieut KNIGHT-ADKIN 2nd 8th Suffolks 50 Contusion abdomen OR nine hies no other Divisional Admissions OR sickness Evacuated OR sick three Wounded five.	App 68
	"	8pm	3rd Field Ambulance XII Divisional took on billeting area vacated by 1st Res Ambulance Solid Arrangements for new Divisional area.	
			Lieut A.BOWIES ADC. to Major Genl Donaghow S.o C.H 28th Division Evacuated on account 2 Invincible Rd. Inguinal Hernia to hypocrate the C.n.D + Hernia.	
MIERIS	25.6.15	9am.	143 H.B42 proceeds en route for new area with IV Corps 1st Army to VIEUX BERQUIN	
		11am	0 Divl Hr's 3rd Field Ambulance with reference to above Handing over 18th Field Ambulance XII Division	
		4pm	Proceed to First 2nd Army Evacuated sick Officers one Lieut BOWLES J.B. Noagasala Division Hyscole 1 OR oundy ten Wounded OR twenty three Other Divisions M.ichen Wounded two Remaining OR sick ten Wounded one.	App 69
	"		Message to III Corps Admissions Field Ambulances from 12 noon 24th to 12 noon 25th with.	

Army Form C. 2118.

WAR DIARY
or
INTELLIGENCE SUMMARY.
(Erase heading not required.)

Instructions regarding War Diaries and Intelligence Summaries are contained in F. S. Regs., Part II. and the Staff Manual respectively. Title pages will be prepared in manuscript.

Place	Date	Hour	Summary of Events and Information	Remarks and references to Appendices
NIEPPE	25/6/15	4 p.m.	Officers viz. Lieut BOWES I.A. Headquarters, Divison Cyclists and 2 Lieut PLAYSTOWE A & B Worcesters. Slight shrapnel wound Scalp (caused Officers and 2/Lieut PLAYSTOWE A & B Worcesters. Slight shrapnel wound Scalp (Duty. 8/R twenty two casualties. All officers were first named 7/R twenty two wounded. 8/R twenty three wounded. 7th Division admitting field 8/R two wounded, three wounded CR with one wounded two.	App/70
		8 p.m.	1st Fld Ambulance takes over station (3 w/Rn) 2 Fld Ambulance which proceeds with 14/3rd 8/R to newara. 14/3rd 8/R proceeds to ambulance at [illegible] BAILLEUL	
NIEPPE	26/6/15	8 a.m.	Situation as above. Weather close & damp.	
		8.30 am	O. Duty visits 3rd Fld Ambulance – 3 July @ C/pcal PRUGER with reference to chevrons provisional Rail Station & the overflow ambulance train seen.	
		1 p.m.	Answer from H. OFF 1st Army North R.3 Carps POPPIED I.P.C R3 letter LEEF SAYS Rec'd	App/71
			VIEUX BERQUIN Diphtheria – social meantime taken.	
		3 p.m.	journey to Houpleand Army – Sir Alex Ophir met our Reinforcing OR sent two thousand	App/72
			Arrived 7pm & Jo Division PI to ambulance from 8 noon 25th Div noon 26th OR	App/73
		8 p.m.	1st & Brigade proceeds in motor bus over VIA BOULOGNE & 2nd Field Ambulance attached to this Bg	
NIEPPE	27/6/15	5.30 am	Headquarters, Brigade 28th Division proceeds en route to BUERNES.	
		8.30 am	A pril office closes at NIEPPE	
BUSNES	1/6/15	6 am	Headquarters office opens at BUSNES. 28th Division bivouacs & bivcs on offit Piepo 1st Army	
		11 am	A Duty office opens at BUSNES	
			1st Div FtdG Ambulance proceeds to GONNEHEM night 29/26	

WAR DIARY
INTELLIGENCE SUMMARY

Army Form C. 2118.

Place	Date	Hour	Summary of Events and Information	Remarks and references to Appendices
BUSNES	27/6/15	4 pm	Proceed to W Caper. Divisions to Field Ambulances from 8 noon 26 to 8 noon 27.	App 75
			OR sick evacuated. Brackets [?].	
			Proceed to A of Base + M. Type. Sick unaltered from 8 noon 19 to noon 26: 5 all Ranks. OR Sick 8.90. admd. 7 do. Officers. Nees 8.90 Sick. Nee 8. do. Officers. Wounded at Station Officers. Nee OR Sk 6.90 Officers. Nee OR sick [?] J.H. Worcester Officers. Nee TR Wounded S.S. 2/d	App 76
			OR (wounded noon to 8 am. Busnes to Verchin Breeks. BM Lecture [?] WR Resha[?]on S [?] Officers. 2nd 3B2 RJ A two 3rd to do. fine to do. to 3rd Ambulance. BS+AS a attached Officers. See M.O.on. Kin[?]adgeorter Officers one do. One + 1st Field Cog RS Off. one Vaud[?] one Signal [?] Kin[?] Towards Officers. two one 1st Field Ambulance one + 20 three 2nd 9.5 two Q.C. to form Q.O.C. Division the Mal Off. are twelve + R one hundred ninety three.	
			This RMD is due to evacuation of the Divisional Red [?] in a recent Quene Prisoner to [?]	
		4.15 pm	Sources from Isolation Hospital SAILLEVL 17.37. Spr PROFIELO 1st Field CARS worture + Stykes.	App 77
			1st Field Ambulance arrived SONNEBIER with 145 U.B. 87s	
			2nd Field Ambulance arrived at HAM-EN-ARDS with 143 -- 139s	
			3rd Field Ambulance arrived at VIEUX BERQUIN with 144 -- 137s. all evacuated. Business.	
			The change (on + lorce night 26/27 B. 6. 15.	
			Situation of Divisional Area Question unaltered.	
BUSNES	28/6/15	9 am	A Day twelve reported to DD [?] Corps + Army. Then proceed to J and Field Ambulance at VIEUX BERQUIN.	

Army Form C. 2118.

WAR DIARY
or
INTELLIGENCE SUMMARY.
(Erase heading not required.)

Place	Date	Hour	Summary of Events and Information	Remarks and references to Appendices
BUSNES	28/6/15	2 p.m.	O.O. (D) visited 3rd Field Ambulance at HAM-EN-ARTOIS. Then to 1st Field Ambulance which had proceeded to ALLOUAGNE with 145th F.A. (night 27/28th). The formation of a Divisional Rest Station was under consideration for some time past.	
BUSNES	29/6/15	9 a.m.	Headquarters at BUSNES. Weather rainy & cold.	
			1st Field Ambulance arrived at ALLOUAGNE	
			3rd Field Ambulance arrived at AUCHEL	
			2nd Field Ambulance proceeding to-night BURBURE	
			Headquarter Officers & P.M.O.(?) A.D.M.S. A.A. & Q. occupied themselves opening a Divisional Rest Station.	
		12 p.m.		
		2.30 p.m.	A.D.M.S. interviewed O.C. 1st Field Ambulance with reference to opening Divisional Rest Station at ALLOUAGNE & gave directions for the scheme to be taken up for this purpose of accuracy.	App 78.
		4 p.m.	Message to Hd of Amy. Remained O.R. sick seventeen. Evacuated nineteen. Remaining thirty one	
BUSNES	30/6/15	9 a.m.	Situation as yesterday. Weather cold & showery.	
		2 p.m.	Message to D.M.S. 1st Army. Remained March thirty one. Wounded Officers one. Evacuated Officers one Men seventeen.	App 79.
			O.R. sick 18 O.R. 29 A.R. Admit fourteen. Remaining O.R. sick thirty.	
			A.D.M.S. visited 2nd Field Ambulance situated at RAIMBERT near BURBURE; the 3rd Field Ambulance at AUCHEL; 1st Field Ambulance. The last named with further reference to opening a Divisional Rest Station	

Mull Colonel
A.D.M.S.
48th Divn

121/6242.

131/6242.

48th Division.

A.D.M.S. 48th Division

Vol IV

Summarised but not copied.

Dec. 1927.

AMD

July 1915.

S1

Army Form C. 2118.

WAR DIARY
or
INTELLIGENCE SUMMARY.
(Erase heading not required.)

Confidential

War Diary
of
48th Division

— from 1st July 1915 — to — 31st July 1915 —

(Volume IV)

Army Form C. 2118.

WAR DIARY
or
INTELLIGENCE SUMMARY.
(Erase heading not required.)

Place	Date	Hour	Summary of Events and Information	Remarks and references to Appendices
LILLERS	1.7.15	9 a.m.	Message from 2nd Div Cyclists. Outbreak of measles reported at HORIONVILLE travel near LILLERS on unbeaten Gloucesters to be killed. Recce to investigate report.	App 1
"	"	9 a.m.	Situation of billeted groups of PHUDNEL – ADMS offices moved to LILLERS.	
"	"	10.30 a.m.	ADMS interviewed OC 2nd Field Ambulance. Then proceeded MARLES-MINES with reference to Divisional Baths. Then to 1st Field Ambulance to inspect Divisional Rest Station.	
"	"	12.30 p.m.	Message to AD of Army. Remained DR sick thirty five males. Officers sick Capt. PARKES H.H. Captain BOWATER. Captain FYSHE & CR R Warwicks. Remainder DR right sick thirteen Rest Station OR sick nineteen. Remaining DR sick thirty.	App 2
"	"	6 p.m.	ADMS attended GS conference at Headquarters.	
LILLERS	2.7.15	8 a.m.	Situation as above. Weather warm sunny.	
"	"	10 a.m.	ADMS inspected billets at HORIONVILLE & interviewed MO of 4th & 6th Gloucesters billets there with reference to the outbreak of measles at that place & precaution necessary regarding the troops. No cases have occurred amongst the troops.	
"	"	12.30 p.m.	Message to AD of Army. Remained 879 sick thirty. Evacuated sick extern. Remaining DR twenty two Rest Station Remaining Divisional Rest Station officers sick one.	App 3
"	"	6 p.m.	Rec'd ALSTON R.L 2/1st Field Cy R.L Serffes Lcpl DR sick thirty two. ADMS attended GS conference at Headquarters.	
LILLERS	3.7.15	9 a.m.	Situation unchanged. Weather warm sunny.	
"	"	11 a.m.	ADMS interviewed OC 1st Field Ambulance.	
"	"	2 p.m.	Orders off to AD of Army. Remained 879 sick twenty two for cavalry out & ten Divisional	App 4

Army Form C. 2118.

WAR DIARY
or
INTELLIGENCE SUMMARY.
(Erase heading not required.)

Instructions regarding War Diaries and Intelligence Summaries are contained in F. S. Regs., Part II and the Staff Manual respectively. Title pages will be prepared in manuscript.

Place	Date	Hour	Summary of Events and Information	Remarks and references to Appendices
LILLERS	2/7/15	10 pm	Ditto twenty four.	
		2.30 pm	ADMS inspected all Field Ambulances.	
LILLERS	4/7/15	8 am	Situation unchanged. Weather fine & sunny.	
		11 am	ADMS interviewed O/C 1st Field Ambulance with reference to the wearing of on the helmets.	App 5
		12.30 pm	Message to D.A.[?] Bde — Sick wastage from 9 am 20th inst to 9 am 3rd inst 5 Warwicks OR fourteen, 6 & 9th Worcester OR twelve 7 & 8th Worcester OR fifteen, 4 & 5 Gloucester 5th Do three, 6th Do one, 7 & 8 Worcester OR fifteen, 8th Do four, 1 & 2 Berks 7th Do five, 2/4 Ox & Bucks Bth four, 4th Berks three, 1st Fd Coy RE four 2/Fd Co RE's five & 2nd Co to one, 2nd Field Ambulance three 3rd Do three 2nd Bde RFA four 3rd to Officers one 87? me, Cyclist Coy 8A, one Ammunition Col. one A.O.C attached one 82 nil, Officers four O.R seventy nine. Speaking to D.D.M.S. 1st Army remained 98 sick twenty four, Evacuated five remaining fifty seven.	App. 6
		3.30 pm	Medical Board difficients B.C.103 LOWNDES 2nd 159 x 299 & Lieut Moore 1 1 & 9 Berkshire Rgt. for a Commission in Regular Army.	
LILLERS	5/7/15	8 am	Situation unchanged. Weather bright & sunny. Captain Beckton RAMC DADMS departed on eight days leave to England.	
		11 am	ADMS visited all Field Ambulances.	
		12.30 pm	Message to Bde. 1st Army "Remained OR sick forty seven, Evacuated fifth seven, remaining ditto eighty six.	App 7

Army Form C. 2118.

WAR DIARY
or
INTELLIGENCE SUMMARY.
(Erase heading not required.)

Instructions regarding War Diaries and Intelligence Summaries are contained in F. S. Regs., Part II. and the Staff Manual respectively. Title pages will be prepared in manuscript.

Place	Date	Hour	Summary of Events and Information	Remarks and references to Appendices
LILLERS	6/7/15	3 pm	D.D.M.S. 1st Army visited & gave instructions re daily messages. Replied to D.D.M.S. 1st Corps' wire asking for names of medical officers of British Battns. S.M. o Brsh. 2.1.	
LILLERS	6/7/15	8 am	Situation unchanged. Weather hot & sunny.	
		11 am	Visited A.D.M.S. 47th Division at Noeux les Mines in anticipation of possible move of this Division to that area & made supervision of functions of Field Ambulances & Divisional stations.	
		1 pm	Wire from No 8 Casualty Clearing Station asking for discharge of Pte Carron all admitted there on 22nd inst with self inflicted wound. Wired O.C. 4th Div. Amb. L.9 to send them enquiry.	
			Received orders re Divisional Reserve. Conf held on 7th 8th 9th & 5th & sent them on to O.C. 1st Gen. Ta.	
		4 pm	Sent transport to husband Clearing Station for 2 men of this Division returning to Duty.	
			Directed Sanitary Officer to enquire into alleged case of diphtheria at Hurionville amongst civilian population, have such had been reported to local authorities.	
LILLERS	7.7.15	10 am	Attended lecture given by Genl. Ketankile on care of smoke helmets, and afterwards conducted Dept. for Anti Oxlem	
			re same. Attended a Divisional review under the direction of the G.O.C.	
		4 pm	Received wire from Ordnance, 48th Division, asking number of 1st & C.S.L carried by each Field Ambulance. Wired to each O.C. for necessary information.	
			Telegram received from 4th C.C.S that No 2534 Pte G Wright 8th Worcesters had been admitted with cerebro-spinal meningitis.	
			Usual daily returns went to D.M.S. & returns to A.D.M.S. & A.& S. – Officers sick – OR 28 admitted, 16 discharged 13 remained, 10 H. remaining all sick – sick percentage .15	

1577 Wt. W10791/1773 500,000 1/15 D. D. & L.   A.D.S.S./Forms/C. 2118.

WAR DIARY
or
INTELLIGENCE SUMMARY.
(Erase heading not required.)

Army Form C. 2118.

Instructions regarding War Diaries and Intelligence Summaries are contained in F. S. Regs., Part II. and the Staff Manual respectively. Title pages will be prepared in manuscript.

Place	Date	Hour	Summary of Events and Information	Remarks and references to Appendices
LILLERS	8.7.15	10 am	Wired Ordnance, 1st 6th Divn. re history of Divisional Field Ambulance. Sent Sanitary Officer to enquire who case of cerebro-spinal meningitis reported last night — None of the contacts shew any symptom of the disease; all have been installed in accordance with DMS' circular. Usual daily returns wire to DDMS & returns to DDMS & A.A.G — Captain Leonard E. Slater admitted & evacuated with rupture of the muscles of the thigh — O.R. 42 admitted, 18 discharged, 18 evacuated, 110 remaining	
"	9.7.15		Wire from 8th C.C.S. saying that no documents re Pte Cornwall (see entry of 6.7.15) had been received — Wired him that action had been meanwhile, on receipt of his telegram & also wired to re H.H. Div. & Bucks that the C.C.S. had not received any documents	
		3 pm	Visited all Field Ambulances & found all correct. Gave verbal instructions to each that all eye cases were to be evacuated to nearest C.C.S. for special transfer to No 4 Stationary Hospital. Usual daily routine wire to DDMS & returns to DDMS & A.A.G. — Officers nil — O.R. 9 admitted, 19 discharged, 7 evacuated, 93 remaining ; all sick — Sick percentage ·05	
		6 pm	DMS visited office & enquired re history in provision of Field Ambulances —	

1577 Wt.W10791/1773 500,000 1/15 D. D. & L.   A.D.S.S./Forms/C. 2118.

WAR DIARY
or
INTELLIGENCE SUMMARY.
(Erase heading not required.)

Army Form C. 2118.

Place	Date	Hour	Summary of Events and Information	Remarks and references to Appendices
LILLERS	10/7/15		Situation unchanged. Weather storm & heavy. Usual routine. Subject to shell, and one 2 Grp[?] aug. Officer kld. & 2 aux[?] whilst 2 S. Discharged 14, 2 awaits, 12 remaining 92. Batteries up to 9/9 strength. Battery reported that there were considerable enemy efforts with lowering and him inactive at present. Headquarters proposed new Divisional Headquarters with D.A.D.O.N. Sick in & exchange - no exchange actually seen. Usual daily routine when return to duty. D.O.M.S. off admitted.	
"	11/7/15		Remaining (& Lieut C DAVIES 8 b Lowealers) O.M. 80 admitted. 9 discharged, 9500 cases 91 remaining. Divisional Sanitary Officer in regiment can locate suffering from future fever in house where some men of the 4th R Berks are billeted - billets to cool[?] all necessary precautions taken.	
LILLERS	12/7/15	9 a.m.	Weather unchanged. 2 case of Dys. (Army. admitted Officers show some wounded) in 28 and twenty eight wounded, one 2 awaits (one wounded) are seven wounded, sick wounded and new rendered in 89 sick one hundred & two, wounded	app. 13.
		4:30 p.m.	Preceding increases nil in Sick 75, no 17. A bomb accidentally exploded whilst being handed, for instruction purposes by the	

WAR DIARY
or
INTELLIGENCE SUMMARY.
(Erase heading not required.)

Army Form C. 2118.

Instructions regarding War Diaries and Intelligence Summaries are contained in F. S. Regs., Part II. and the Staff Manual respectively. Title pages will be prepared in manuscript.

Place	Date	Hour	Summary of Events and Information	Remarks and references to Appendices
LILLERS	12/7/15	4.34 p.m.	145th Inf'y Bde. — Two Officers & twenty two men wounded, one man killed.	
LILLERS	13/7/15	9 a.m.	Billeting Division Orders & Instructions. K. 145th Bde (New orders) 2nd ocean and NEUX-LES-MINES — the 143rd Bde. to HOUCHIN, the 144th Bde to HES DIGNEUL	
		11 a.m.	A. Adj. visited HES DIGNEUL to arrange site for Dressing Station & instructing them to send tent sub-division of Field Ambulance from the Brigades around this area.	
		3 p.m.	Journey to Dep't rel. Army. Admitted Officers from wounds this day sick officers twenty, twenty two and thirteen (15) occurred in wounded in the intervening remained twenty one remaining Officers wounded five wounded Send orders received to sick - one hundred eleven wounded - nil. Previous figures - nil - Sick personnel 50 Lieut. Pepper C.2 Flesnes (I.C.) arrived for duty up to No 6 Gd. Ambulance 8th Division.	Ap/7/14
LILLERS	14/7/15	9 a.m.	Situation as above. Weather windy but summer.	
		9.30 a.m.	O. Adj. visited 2 Field Ambulances with reference to being Divisional Rest Station. The Ambulance is to be moved from ALLOUAGNE.	
			D.A. Adj. with D.A.Q.M.G. arranged for billet of 143rd Bde about 2 LIERES and of the latter place for the 2 Field Ambulance & transport.	
		10.27 p.m.	Message to D.A. Adj. 1st Army. Admitted Officers sick wounded nil. OR sick seventy two wounded nil as one group nil-sick - one group nil as ever occurred on leave army of the later Officers send Six wounded nil OR sick seventy two wounded nil OR one hundred Ap/7/15	

WAR DIARY or INTELLIGENCE SUMMARY

Army Form C. 2118.

Place	Date	Hour	Summary of Events and Information	Remarks and references to Appendices
LILLERS	15/7/15	8 am	Situation unchanged. Weather warm & sunny. Rained very hard during night.	
		12.15 pm	O.D.M.S. interviewed R.O. of 2nd Division by chief C in C who stated that one platoon of this Coy was infected with lice.	
		12.30 pm	M.O. in charge received from hospital a bacteriologist MEERS - from a Civilian MORTEN THOURELL	App 16.
	16/7/15		at ZAPUSNOY Culture injections for inoculation	App 17.
			Reinforcements Staff & Army Admitted Officers wounded and evacuated sick and sick (officers) wounded) Soldiers wounded & sick mostly wounded nil Remaining Officers and sick wounded nil in hospital, wounded Sick 97 : 09	
			The above number sick 99 evacuated an account of Wounded Sick being closed by army 1st Field Ambulance to AMES	
			A 2nd night to White (11th Division) Cycled Coy 13 of our Lieutenants the remainder of the Division in buses. They proceeded to prepare an extension for field ambulance at AMES.	
LILLERS	16/7/15	8 am	Situation unchanged. Weather windy & raining.	
		12.30 pm	Moved up to find 1st Corps - Admitted Officers sick nil nil OR sick twenty. App. 18	
			Wounded nil an evacuated Officers sick nil none OR sick four wounded Remaining Officers sick wounded nil OR sick twenty (wounded) nil mostly	
			Diseases all lied percentage - nil	
			Lieut Baker C.W. Rawe Gr Dix & Brereton reported sick remained sick	
		5.30 pm	D.M.S. 1st Army called. Saw O D.M.S. with reference to same	
LILLERS	17/6/15	8 am	Situation Divisional Headquarters as above 145 L B.G.S. moved to AMES. 146 L.B. AT.S. 16	

WAR DIARY
or
INTELLIGENCE SUMMARY.

Army Form C. 2118.

Place	Date	Hour	Summary of Events and Information	Remarks and references to Appendices
LILLERS	17/6/15	9am	BURBURE 3 & 14 Sdn N.Z.F.A. RUCHEL.	
		12.15pm	In camp. 2 O/Rs at Army - admitted Officer sick are wounded nil OR sick of. (11 wounded) nil am evacuated Officers wounded nil 82 sick right wounded nil 2 by ambulance nil am evacuated nil OR sick sixty wounded nil. Remaining Officers — injured sick sick percentage .49%	App/19
		2.30pm	O Dud visited 1st Field Ambulance with reference to forming of a dressing station in new area as an advanced dressing station.	
		6pm	Instructions issued to Field Ambulances as to move towards at DOULLENS and Vic (Abbeville)	
TERRAMESNIL	18/7/15	10am	The 2 gyn Arc moved to TERRAMESNIL by Map AMIENS sheet 12. O Duf Officer in charge of Ambulance also Dressing Station opened up division in new form part of VII Corps 4th Army.	
		2.30pm	O Dud III Corps interviewed O Duf with reference to 2nd & Cavalry Clearing Station being formed at BEAUVAL. Officer sick & wounded evacuated there.	
* LILLERS	18/7/15	*8am	Message to O Duf 1st Army - admitted Officer sick and wounded nil OR sick wounded 1 (wounded) nil am evacuated Officers sick wounded nil of such & 4 wounded OR sick 4 wounded nil. Remaining Officers sick & wounded nil of sick & wounded evacuated Poorburg & received Proforma.	App/20
		5.35pm	Message to 2nd Army Field Ambulance & new Dressing Officer for Corps to HQg. (minus)	App/21
			by Motor Lorries very urgent.	
TERRAMESNIL	19/7/15	7am	O Duf visited ROUVRENCOURT of Map AMIENS sheet 12 French Field Ambulance at the Chateau with reference to taking over wounded (French) in event of the move.	
		9.44am	Message from 7th Corps that Sanitation of MAP 13 ex on right identity at O Duvision Sanitation (...)	App/22

WAR DIARY or INTELLIGENCE SUMMARY

Army Form C. 2118.

(Erase heading not required.)

Place	Date	Hour	Summary of Events and Information	Remarks and references to Appendices
TERRAMESNIL	19/7/15	10.35am	Message from 2 And. 7th Corps that 9 serious cases at LOUVENCOURT to be taken over	App 23
		12.30pm	Message from A.D.M.S. to 5th Division at BARTON that case of diphtheria (not case of diphtheria now) there where 5th Division billeted & ambulance (he are) proceed there. Enquiries made & precaution taken	
		2 pm	2 And visited BEUVAL to enquire to 4 Casualty Clearing Station ready to receive cases. 2 officers & 160 other ranks	
		6 pm	Two officers & 10 other ranks sent to take over at LOUVENCOURT Chateau & Sanitary Section arrived at TERRAMESNIL	
TERRAMESNIL	20/7/15	9am	Situation as before. D.M.S. II Army called on A.And.	
		10.30am	A And visited BARTON (Ref Map AMIENS sheet 13), with reference of encampment for 1st Field Ambulance & forming Divisional Rest Station	
		12.30pm	A And visited Field Ambulance at LOUVENCOURT with reference to the evacuation of German & French wounded	
			Two motor ambulances attached here temporarily & rack Brigade ready were too in purpose of picking up wounded on the move.	
		4 pm	Headquarters moved to AUTHIE. Dressing Station at TERRAMESNIL closed - all sick sent to And Field Ambulance at LOUVENCOURT.	
		5 pm	A And visited Section of 1st Field Ambulance at BARLY giving instructions to	
AUTHIE	21/7/15	9am	Position of Field Ambulances: Headquarters Brigade Train, 1st & 2 & organs 1st And Field Ambulance LOUVENCOURT	App 26
		11am	Situation as before. Weather Enemy unknown	

WAR DIARY or INTELLIGENCE SUMMARY

Army Form C. 2118.

Place	Date	Hour	Summary of Events and Information	Remarks and references to Appendices
AUTHIE	21/7/15	9.30am	O.C. W[?] visited ST LEGER-LES-AUTHIE, COIGNEUX, BAILLY, COURCELLES at the two latter places interviewed the French Officers in charge of the Advanced Dressing Stations with a view to taking them over. Also visited the Field Ambulances with reference to forming Rest Stations.	
"		12.15pm	A.D.M.S. visited 2nd Field Ambulance & gave instructions as to viewing the ready 1st Division.	
"		5pm	A.D.M.S. visited Advanced Dressing Station at COISNEUX & gave instructions as to taking over Advanced Dressing Station at BAILLY & forming another at COURCELLES & sending a party to take over Advanced Dressing Station at HEBUTERNE also from the French Division.	
"		5.7pm	Message received from A.D.M.S. 2nd Corps to take in each of the Division temporary:	App 25
			Orders to 2nd & 3rd W. army — Ivan instructed as remaining &c received right half wounded	App 26
"		7pm	Message to 3rd & 1st W. Corps A.D.M.S. Divisions to Field Ambulances from 6 noon to 6 noon	App 27
			21st Officers and 9th W each seventy six Wounded No acute milk cases midnight there.	
			Situation of Headquarters as above — 1/5th W. Bde. took over Rifle Relay Trenches from patients of HEBUTERNE. The line extending about 2 miles were Namery.	
HUPY	22/7/15	9am		
		9a.m	A.D.M.S. visited BAILLY with O.C. 3rd Field Ambulance also O.C. HEBUTERN & gave instructions the Advanced Dressing Station. Then proceeded to inspect some fifth between the left & right of the Trenches — Instructions given that 3rd Field Ambulance are to take charge of wounded than Allied Villages in parties 2nd Field Ambulance Save instructions as others.	
		12.15pm	A.D.M.S. visited 1st Div. Field Ambulance with reference to the D Wounded Rest.	

1577 Wt. W10791/1773 500,000 1/15 D. D. & I. A.D.S.S./Forms/C. 2118.

Army Form C. 2118.

WAR DIARY
or
INTELLIGENCE SUMMARY.
(Erase heading not required.)

Instructions regarding War Diaries and Intelligence Summaries are contained in F. S. Regs., Part II. and the Staff Manual respectively. Title pages will be prepared in manuscript.

Place	Date	Hour	Summary of Events and Information	Remarks and references to Appendices
AUTHIE	22/7/15	5 pm	Message to D.D.M.S. III Army & D.A.A.G. 7 Corps. Situation as above. Eleven sick other ranks.	App. 28
AUTHIE	23/7/15	9 a.m.	Situation of [headquarters] as above – 143 w. Duty 13 Dr. took on hundred (N sick) from the French night 22/23 D. Weather raining	
		9 am	A D.M.S. visited refns as to the collection of sick. Annex BARTON AUTHIE-VAUCHELLES by [1st Rly. Field] Ambulance. Recce LOUVENCOURT, COURCELLES, BUS, & army hy. 3rd Field Ambulance. And an. 23 ST CÆSIER COIGNEUX & BAYENCOURT by 3rd Field Ambulance.	
		5 pm	A D.M.S. visited 3rd Field Ambulance, 2nd Field Ambulance, 1st & 3rd Ambulance, 2 H the First Armoured Giving Memorandum of Collection of sick & Lieut named regarding Divisional Rest Station	App 29
		7 pm	Message to D.D.M.S. II Army & D.D.M.S. 7 Corps. Situation & sick form.	
AUTHIE	24/7/15	8 am	Situation unchanged. Weather windy & cloudy	
		9.30 am	A D.M.S. called with O.Offr. visited Ancony Station at Sailly & advanced Dressing Station at HEBUTERNE. Also the bivouac of 5th Battalion, H.E. 2nd April. Back at Sailly	
		3 pm	A D.M.S. visited 2nd Field Ambulance & rode to new building of Divisional Rest Station	
		7 pm	Message to D.D.M.S. III Army & D.D.M.S. 7 Corps. Sick and wounded office Officers and one Capt H&W F.W. Ira & Lieut. Situation & six	App 30
		7 1/2 pm	Wounded nil and sick from ranks Division the above.	
AUTHIE	25/7/15	8 am	Situation unchanged. Weather still damp	
		11 am	A D.M.S. visited 2nd Field Ambulance.	
		3 pm	A D.M.S. in company with D.C. 3rd Field Ambulance visited VAUCHELLE & fixed upon site for accommodation of that Unit in the Chateau's ground. The provision for pumping arrangements with the C.R.E. for battery brand D.A.D.Y. thereof.	
			[illegible] with this C.C.C. for name	

WAR DIARY or INTELLIGENCE SUMMARY

Army Form C. 2118.

Place	Date	Hour	Summary of Events and Information	Remarks and references to Appendices
AUTHIE	25/7/15	5 pm	Message to 2nd & 7th Army & 2nd & 7th Corps. Evacuated Officers and wounded other Ranks and nine wounded men of the Divisional Troops and one Sgt THOMSON R.E., 96th Batty R.F.A. Machine gun bullet wound nil. Off. sick and twenty-two wounded nil. B. Stanton exchanged, ten taken and nine wounded.	App 31
AUTHIE	26/7/15	8 am	A Dvy with O.C. 3rd Field Ambulance visited Dressing Station at 8 may & the Batty arranging for further bathing accommodation. Then proceeded to 2nd Field Ambulance and to not Field Ambulance.	
"	"	5 pm	Message to 2nd & 7th Army & 2nd & 7th Corps. Evacuated Officers sick and wounded nil. Off. and nine wounded and one other Divisional Officer and nil wounded O.R. each County. Sick nine wounded nil.	App 32
"	"	9 pm	Three wounded nil. Instructions sent to O.C. 3rd Field Ambulance to move to ST LEGER via Henin on 29/7/15. Then Down to VAUCHELLE after on 9 may on 29/7/15.	
AUTHIE	27/7/15	9 am	Situation unchanged. Weather very rainy.	
"	"	11 am	A. Dvl. visited 1st (Mr.) Field Ambulance.	
"	"	2.30 pm	A. Dvl. visited DOUIENS with A. D. a. e. Officer with a view to making contained for concentration plan to be now with Hound Spragen.	
"	"	5 pm	Message to 2nd & 7th Army. 2nd & 7th Corps. Evacuated officers nil. O.R. sick eight wounded eighteen. The Divisional Officers enclose hugh HANKESLEY J.M. 135 R.F.A. Casualties wounded nil.	App 33
AUTHIE	28/7/15	9 am	Situation unchanged. Weather fine but windy.	
"	"	11.30 am	8 Mil. 7 K. Corps. Cables from A. Dvl.	
"	"	9 pm	A. Dvl. visited 3rd Field Ambulance at VAUCHELLE which had just moved in	

WAR DIARY or INTELLIGENCE SUMMARY

Army Form C. 2118.

(Erase heading not required.)

Place	Date	Hour	Summary of Events and Information	Remarks and references to Appendices
AUTHIE	28/7/15	2.30pm	Conference with Brigade Major re Orderlies of 144 & 143 Bdes	
		5pm	Message to OC 3 Army & DDMS 3rd Army (Major Tweedie) re Officers sick and Bed (Capt Clarkson) & two officers seventeen men sick and Cap of Robinson & two men dangerously ill, through TROOPERS LONDON (Capt of Robinson & 2 W/Os & 2 Sgts)	App/34
			2nd N Midl Field Ambulance - 24 sick. App/Ordnance	App/35
AUTHIE	29/7/15	9am	Situation unchanged. Weather warm & dry.	
		9.30am	ADMS visited 1st W Midl Field Ambulance. Discussed Statn then proceeded to MARICOURT re the D Duty & OC re regarding transport of Sick Ambulance their precept to	
			to ADM III Army with reference to loan of wagon	
		11.15am	ADMS proceeded to inspect baths at SAILLY, proceeding to APP VESTA & Inspect	
			for Divisional Baths	App/36
		5pm	Message to DADM & Army & DDMS III C.p. - two wounded Officers and Rank (one wounded) nil Sick	
			Situation unchanged. Weather warm but rainy	
AUTHIE	30/7/15	9am	ADMS visited 1 & 2/3rd (WM) Field Ambulances also 1st Ambulance Establishment	
		9.30am	Message to DADM III Army & DDMS III C.p. - two wounded officers and M'ride Sufstin Wounded	App/37
		5pm	from the Divisional officers nil OR sick & expense ill	
		9pm	Message from 2nd Field Ambulance - Captain O.C Robinson & 2 W/Os & Sgts Recovery	App/38
AUTHIE	31/7/15	9am	Situation unchanged. weather warmer & sunny	

VOUCHERS

Army Form C. 2118.

WAR DIARY
or
INTELLIGENCE SUMMARY.
(Erase heading not required.)

Instructions regarding War Diaries and Intelligence Summaries are contained in F.S. Regs., Part II. and the Staff Manual respectively. Title pages will be prepared in manuscript.

Hour, Date, Place	Summary of Events and Information	Remarks and references to Appendices
HOTHIE 31/7/15	A Drill issued instructions for Reorganization for adoption for imitation & kellyfina. Breakfast with II Army & Draft 2 Opera received. Officers and Died one (Capt. C.G. Rawlinson 7th Worcestershire) & one sick remembers another sent on to other Divisions. Officers sick OR sick 2 men wounded sick.	Appx 39.

Army Colonel
admis 48th Division

48th Division

12/6598
—

A.D.M.S. 48th Division

Vol V

from 1 – 31. 8. 15

Summarised & not copied.
Dec. 1917.

August 1915

5

Confidential

War Diary
of
A.D.M.S. 48th (Sth) Division
from 1st to 31st August 1915

Army Form C. 2118.

WAR DIARY
or
INTELLIGENCE SUMMARY.
(Erase heading not required.)

Instructions regarding War Diaries and Intelligence Summaries are contained in F. S. Regs., Part II. and the Staff Manual respectively. Title pages will be prepared in manuscript.

Place	Date	Hour	Summary of Events and Information	Remarks and references to Appendices
RUTHIE	1.8.15	8 a.m.	Situation unchanged from that of last July. Weather warm & sunny.	
		9.30 a.m.	A bird visited ARQUEVES with O.C. 1st Field Ambulance to inspect field sites, ammunition/ 1st Field Ambulance. Then proceeded to 3rd Field Ambulance, HQ & Co'y camps, chose site for divisional dressing station at SAILLY then returning to O.C. 1st Field dressing station at SAILLY then returning O.C.	App I
		12.30 pm		
		5 pm	Arranged for 2nd & 3rd Army's Sanit. W. Reps. See awaited officer hit. O Reid for wound. till O/C of Division tel.	
RUTHIE	2.8.15	8 a.m.	Situation unchanged. Weather. Camp raining. O.C. 1st Field Ambulance interviews. O Reid with reference to situation of Advanced Dressing Station	App 2
		11 a.m.	of Co'ys camp	
		5 pm	A Brit attended conference with G.O.C.	
		5.30 pm	In company of Maj 3rd Army & Maj. 3rd Corps. Proceeded to C.C.S. & vised Capt. WINBUSHIER 7.F.R. Branch Regt. Quite talkative but not free from wound but other Divisional officers recovered. Of Major J.K. PRICE RLC Hydro Coy. & Lt Duncan of the Apply D.T. list	
RUTHIE	3.8.15	8 a.m.	Situation unchanged. Weather. Cold & rainy.	
		11 am	O'Reid & R. Capt. called round Offd and Divl. cdn. C. camps from nearby 2nd Field Ambulance.	
		2.30	Divisional Headquarters moved to SUS-LES-MARETS (Refrng Union Shots)	
		5 pm	In company of Revd D. army & 3rd Corps. Proceeded to E.C. of officers and M rich High	App 3
BUS	4.8.15	8.30 am	D/Mul. Division HQ arrived here morning nil	
		11 am	Situation as above. Weather very rainy.	
		5 p.m.	A Brit inspected area of Hd. Qty Dr. Co. for accommodation for Permanent Base.	App 4

WAR DIARY
or
INTELLIGENCE SUMMARY.
(Erase heading not required.)

Army Form C. 2118.

Instructions regarding War Diaries and Intelligence Summaries are contained in F. S. Regs., Part II. and the Staff Manual respectively. Title pages will be prepared in manuscript.

Place	Date	Hour	Summary of Events and Information	Remarks and references to Appendices
BUS.	4.8.15		1 O.R. Mine wounded — Other Divisions nil	
BUS	5.8.15	9.30 am	Situation unchanged. Weather warmer & sunny	
"	"	10 am	A.D.M.S. visited Dressing Station of 3rd A.M.L. & O.C.'s of 2nd and 3rd Field Ambulances	
"	"	2.30 pm	A.D.M.S. proceeded to Doucieux to see chose washing tubs & equipment & bath.	
"	"	5 pm	Gave orders to 2nd & 3rd Army & Mnts. & Cyclists. Evacuated to C.C.S. 1 officer wounded & 28 sick & other wounded — other Divisions sick & wounded nil	Appx 5.
"	"	6.30 pm	Gave orders to 1st Field Ambulance to proceed tomorrow to BREUVES. Sick to Armond	Appx 6.
BU 6	6.8.15	8.30 am	Rec Stat'n to be transferred to 3rd Field Ambulance. Situation unchanged. Weather damp & rainy	
"	"	6 pm	1st Field Ambulance arrived at new station BREUVES	
"	"	5.30 pm	Proceeded to 2nd & 3rd Army & 2nd & 3rd Cyps. Evacuated to C.C.S. 8 officers and 172 sick & other wounded	Appx 7.
BUS	7.8.15	6 pm 8.30 am	Visited Dressing Stn 2nd A.M.L. one officer wounded. Situation unchanged. Weather damp & rainy	
"	"	11 am	Sgt Mr J. Coyne Q.M.A.A.C. killed a gun	
"	"		A.D.M.S. visits 1st Field Ambulance.	
"	"	5 pm	Gave orders to 1 Mnt.A., & Cyps & 2nd 3rd Army. Evacuated to C.C.S. 1 officer wounded & 83 sick	Appx 8.
"	"		Other wounded nil	
BUS	8.8.15	9.30 am	Weather warmer & sunny. Situation unchanged	
"	"	9.30 am	A.D.M.S. visited 2nd & 3rd & 1/2 Field Ambulances	
"	"	4 pm	Gave orders to 1 Mnt.A., Mnts., & Stats & Cyps. Evacuated to C.C.S. 1 Officer sick, one R & 1st H.C. Western Officer sick, one R & 1 H.C. Western right arm. Nil.	Appx 9.

WAR DIARY
or
INTELLIGENCE SUMMARY.

Army Form C. 2118.

Place	Date	Hour	Summary of Events and Information	Remarks and references to Appendices
BUS	9/8/15	9.30 am	Situation unchanged. Weather warm & sunny	
		10.15 am	O/Visit 3rd Army CCS's and ADMS	
		11 am	ADMS attended Board 145th Infy Bde. Examined men for permanent base abroad	
		11.30 am	O/Visit visited advanced Dressing Station at Hebuterne, also giving instructions & advice from the him div	
		12.30 pm	Notification received that Dodd, a Sgt or civilian at Courcelles, who was suffering from severe fever had been removed to Civil Hospital Doullens on 8th inst. No known contact, no one also at GRANDRUE farm where he had been working where the family brought their butter there	App 10
		5.30 pm	Messages to Adv 3rd Army, 7 Divs & Corps: Evacuated to C.C.S. Officers sick Capt Bartram ASC Division train, Stanhal Jamieson, Capt Hewitt JP Durh Amm Colum. Other Rank Drive CC&J.Sergeant A/S Immens and Pvt King A/S/T Stanton Davidson Capt Rose O/K H/S Oastbacker & J. Hatton. OR ranks Hickinson and Missand OR sick wounded men evacuated	
10/8/15	8.30 am	Situation unchanged. Weather improving. Thunderstorm	
BUS			O/Visit inspected all Field Ambulances	
		2.15 pm	O/Visit inspected 6.O.T Officer, one Aust:	App 11
		5 pm	Messages to A in C III Army & 7th Corps. Evacuated to C.C.S officers one Aust: Colonel WK PFDKE SW Worcesters Wounded in Bus OR sick (after wounds) nil	
BUS	11/8/15	8.30 am	Situation unchanged. Weather warm & sunny	
		11 am	O/Visit visited all Field Ambulances in & inspected patients	
		6.30 pm	Messages to A in C III Army & D.M.D & 7 Corps. Evacuated to CCS Officers sick one Lieut H.E. Bartlett RAMC A/FA 46th Glosters. Lena, two rank. OR sick twenty six non wounded officers nil OR sick and other Divisions OR sick from area examined	App 12

1577 Wt.W10791/1773 500,000 1/15 D. D. & L. A.D.S.S./Forms/C. 2118.

Army Form C. 2118.

WAR DIARY
or
INTELLIGENCE SUMMARY.
(Erase heading not required.)

Instructions regarding War Diaries and Intelligence Summaries are contained in F. S. Regs., Part II. and the Staff Manual respectively. Title pages will be prepared in manuscript.

Place	Date	Hour	Summary of Events and Information	Remarks and references to Appendices
BUS	12/8/15	8.30 am	Situation unchanged. Weather warm & sunny	
"		4 pm	D. D. of D. Corps called & saw D. D. M. S.	
"		6.30 pm	Messages to D. of D., 3rd Army & D. D. M. S. Corps, evacuated B. C. O. & 1 sick officer & 1st Maid	Appx 13
			seven wounded from a [?]. The Divisions first intervened at 8 am.	
BUS	13/8/15	8.30 am	Situation unchanged. Weather warm & sunny	
"		9.30 am	O. D. M. S. visited & & evacuated 11 & 6 B. of Shelter & [?] to & interviewed the Div. Officer on	
			instructions & then to form a divining station for sick	
"		2.30 pm	A. D. M. S. visited & inspected the orderly arrangements of the French Ambulance at Gron	
"		5.15 pm	Messages to 2nd & 3rd Army & D of D 9 Corps - no cases B C O & 1 sick officer on	
			Capt W Lewis 1/1st Shelton dental Corps. off and twenty seven wounded sick.	
BUS	14/8/15	8.30 am	Situation unchanged. Weather warm & sunny.	
"		2.30 pm	Letter from the Commander Column stating that Cu Fields & Ambe. Syringe by numbers	
			asked urgently forward.	
"		9 pm	A. D. M. S. & A. Dist. Infanteer stroppeds stretcher place also H. Arther or stretcher samples from	Appx 14
			which was then taken to 9 & 9 by yeme & according for examination	
"		9 pm	Messages to Div. 2nd Army & D. D. M. S. Corps. Evacuated & C. C. S 1 off. escorted sick & R.	Appx 15
			& sick nineteen & wounded of men. & the Divisions on act on.	
BUS	15/8/15	8.30 am	Situation unchanged. Weather cold & rainy	
"		10 am	O. D. M. S. visited 3 & Field Ambulance. Then attended a conference at Staff & also my	
"		10.30 am	Messages from Div. & Hygiene Laboratory methylferrine &c to sample between R. Arther	

1577 Wt.W10791/1773 500,000 1/15 D. D. & L. A.D.S.S./Forms/C. 2118.

WAR DIARY
or
INTELLIGENCE SUMMARY.

Army Form C. 2118.

Place	Date	Hour	Summary of Events and Information	Remarks and references to Appendices
BUS	15/8/15		Acting Bde: so far no prisoners met with found	app/16
"		4:30 p.m.	Message to Bde 3rd Army & Bde 7th Corps - Evacuated to C.C.L. Officer sick Capt. O.H. BUTCHER 7/8 Worcestr. To 8th Canadian Gen: Hosp. Capt. R.C. CLARKE R.A.M.C. attached 4th Gloster.	app 17
BUS	16/8/15	5:30 a.m.	Intents: OR sick nineteen (Eleven 2nd Div. Officers and WR three. Situation unchanged. Weather cool & dull	
"		9:30 a.m.	Bde L't visited all Field Ambulances. Also held conference with ship their new Field Ambulance in the trenches primary to	
"		2:30 p.m.	Message to Bde 3rd Army & Bde 7th Corps - Evacuated no C.C.L Officer and an Capt. O A Willcock WR Bde. O.C.Ks March Medrem Seven Dr. Officer list OR three	app 18
BUS	17/8/15	5:30 a.m.	Situation unchanged. Weather cool & dull.	
"		11:30 a.m.	Bde called upon O.M.S. also interviewed Lt. Langton & Sullivan R.A.M.C. at this office.	
"		1 p.m.	Message to Bde 3rd Army & Bde 7th Corps - Evacuated to C.C.L Officers and two hosp. Lieut E.F.G. BRENAN 4/8 Div. Cyclist Coy. Dental Caries.	app 19
"			O.R. sick twenty me nac. (eleven) Officers hit WR six. Situation unchanged. Weather cool & dull	
BUS	18/7/15	5:30 a.m.		
"		12:30 p.m.	O. Bde L't visited & form and dressing station at COIN CAMP. Then proceeded to the Dressing Room He B 2 Warwicks at COURCELLE, 7 & Wor'stres at BOIRY OU BOIS, 5 & 4 Warwicks at BRYENCOURT, 8 & Warwicks at LEGER	
"		4:30 p.m.	Message to Bde(3d) Army & Bde 7th Corps - Evacuated to C.C.L. Officers sick n Retul an officer for temporary duty with 5/11 Field	app 20
			sick eight OR seven den out	

WAR DIARY
or
INTELLIGENCE SUMMARY.

(Erase heading not required.)

Army Form C. 2118.

Instructions regarding War Diaries and Intelligence Summaries are contained in F. S. Regs., Part II. and the Staff Manual respectively. Title pages will be prepared in manuscript.

Place	Date	Hour	Summary of Events and Information	Remarks and references to Appendices
RUA	18/7/15		Ambulance at BERTRANCOURT. An Officer from 2nd & 7 Amble Outside	
BUS	19/7/15	8.30 am	Situation unchanged. Weather cold, dull.	
		10.30 am	⅔ Bud? R Capitulated. Then with O Bay visited Advanced Dressing Station at COURCELLES	
			HEBUTERNE & Dressing Station at BAILLY.	
		4.30 pm	Messages to find 3rd Army & D Bay & R Corps – Evacuated to C.C.S. Officers and Wounded men	App 21
			Lieut G HAWKINS 1/5 Londons, flds Hughes & Chester a.a. O.R sick fifteen wounded two	
			Privates sent to R.D. & Wimbleton – Pte 8261 Pte G GRAHAM 5th London Contagtil notes	App 22
BUS	20/7/15	8.30 am	Situation unchanged. Weather warm, dull	
		1.30 pm	O Bay visited all Field Ambulances.	
			Orders issued to O C 2nd Field Ambulance to inspect Latrines in their respective areas	
			with regard to Sanitation & measures adopted generally in every fort & hypo the Most	App 23
		4.30 pm	Messages to find 3rd Army & D Bay & R Corps – Evacuated to C.C.S. Officers and Wounded	
			nil a.a. O.R and eleven wounded two	
		7 pm	To a Bay 3rd Army called now Officer	
BuS	21/7/15	8.30 am	Situation unchanged. Weather warmer but dull	
		10 am	A Bay visited 8 no Field Ambulance	
		4.30 pm	Messages to find 3rd Army & MMed? & Corps – Evacuated to C.C.S. Officers and wounded	App 24
			nil a.a. O.R sick and wounded none from	
BUS	22/8/15	8.30 am	Situation unchanged. Weather cts & sunny	
		4 pm	O Bay accompanied by the Distinguished Commanding. Capt S.S. AUSTIN & No 1000 20 J. Visited	

WAR DIARY or INTELLIGENCE SUMMARY

Army Form C. 2118.

Place	Date	Hour	Summary of Events and Information	Remarks and references to Appendices
B.U.F	22.8.15		COURCELLES, BAILLY, HEBUTERNE, RAYENCOURT, COIGNEUX, LOUVENCOURT, ARQUEVES & VAUCHELLES	Appx 25
	22.8.15	11.30pm	Two cadets to C.C.S. Officers – one Lieut R.C. NORWOOD of Bucks 3/R. Second, where one wounded hit on CH and severe wound. One little received from A.D.G. stating that Lieut GAUNTLETT RAMC, T.M.O.P. & Flander had been evacuated to England.	
B.U.F	23.8.15	8.30am	Situation unchanged. Weather warm & sunny.	Appx 26
	"	4.30pm	2 cases to 2nd/1st S Army, 1 D.W. 1/1 Oxon. We asked 1 C.O.Y. Officer visited 2 T.R. sick officers wounded etc.	
	"	6pm	Two members of the British Red Cross Society called saw A.D.M.S. with reference to making of equipment – The 2nd Field Ambulance for Officer was satis.	
B.U.F	24.8.15	8.30am	Situation unchanged. Weather warm & sunny.	
		12.30pm	A.D.M.S. visited 2 and 43rd Field Ambulances	
	"	4.30pm	Horse go to 2nd/3rd S Army, 1 Dbly/1 Cap. Doc - visited & C.C. Officers visited 2 T.R. sick & one wounded one.	Appx 27
			Received from D.A.& Q.M.G. Re stating that Major PHILPOTT RAMC had attended off the strength. Ambulance had been evacuated to England.	
B.U.F	25.8.15	8.30am	Situation unchanged, weather warm & sunny.	
	"	9.30am	One case to A.D.M.S. Brown, stating his taking over duties of Camp operation officer at his station (evacuation sigs & Divisions) A.D.M.S. visited all the Field Ambulances.	Appx 28
		11.30am	A message received from A.D.M.S. IV Division stating he will inform us when he will	

WAR DIARY
or
INTELLIGENCE SUMMARY.

Army Form C. 2118.

Place	Date	Hour	Summary of Events and Information	Remarks and references to Appendices
BUS	25/8/15		Take over Dressing Station	App 29
		12.30 pm	Messages from O. field Amb on those clothing Dressing Station at Potijze with the Picken as 11 pm	App 30
			From [illegible] by No 11 Field Ambulance	
			Messrs [?] to O.C. 1st Field Ambulance. Med S.o 11 Field Ambulance taken on Dressing Station	App 31
		4.30 pm	Message to Maj S. D. Army S. D. and S. R. Corps — Evacuates to C.C.S. Officers and en. R. Warwicks, Appendicitis aen wounded aen D.R. sickness (numbers) aen	App 32
BU 4	26/5/15	8.30 am	Lieutenant in charge Walker enemy	
			A.D.M.S. visited 3rd Field Ambulance	
		10.4 pm		
		4.30 pm	Messages S.D. and S. D. and S. R. Corps — evacuated C.C.S. sick Officers en R. Warwickshire [illegible] E.F. 1010 Sick R	App 33
			Lieut. Rept. Starbuck on D.R. sick thirteen wounded eight	
			Memo from S.Q.M. Hospital S275 Ph. by Lt. M.S. Foster Officers from Ypres to O.D.C.Sanity	
			S[illegible] informed	
BUS	27/8/15	8.30 am	Situation unchanged. Weather warm rainy	
		12.30 pm	A field visited Corbie, S. Engineering assistance, about Sailly, Dressing Station at BAYENCOURT.	App 34
		1.30 pm	Messages to S.D. and S. Army S.D. and S.R. Corps - Evacuated to C.C.S. Officers and [illegible] sick [illegible]	
			numbers from	
BUS	28/8/15	8.30 am	Situation unchanged. Weather warm rainy	
		4.30 pm	A.D.M.S. attended meeting by Maj S. Army at the 3rd 31st Field Ambulance the Patients there	
			Was agreed himself as keen followed with A.A. Shute	
			Messages S. and S. Army S. D. and S. R. Corps - Evacuated C.C.S. Officers sick See Capt. H. Davies, 48	App 35
		4.30 pm	R. Warwicks Pneumonia news Lieut. O.H. [illegible] H/R Bonnard, [illegible] aen D. Rick S. [illegible] sick	

Army Form C. 2118.

WAR DIARY
or
INTELLIGENCE SUMMARY.
(Erase heading not required.)

Instructions regarding War Diaries and Intelligence Summaries are contained in F. S. Regs., Part II. and the Staff Manual respectively. Title pages will be prepared in manuscript.

Place	Date	Hour	Summary of Events and Information	Remarks and references to Appendices
BUC	29/8/15	8.30am	Situation unchanged. Weather colder, wet.	
"		11.30am	O.C.cdg with S.S. of O visited A.S. LEGER with officers to Divisional Baths & Barges to the Docks. There & the news & exam made clothing, staff fatigue.	
"		4.30pm	Arranged with 3rd Army & 8 Bnd. F. C.a. Pn. 300 crates to C.C.S. Officers and one Capt. L. Kenwood & 3 W.C. enters hospital cases in O.R. sick seventeen. Evening: 2 nil. Wentworth moved to H. of Bger P. and wastage during the week. Situation unchanged. Weather fair but showery.	app 36
DUC	30-8-15	8.30am	O.R & infects sent to 5, 6, 7, 14, 18, Warwicks for command Baths.	
"		11.30am	9/Worcs to H/Sul. 3/Sely & 8/Dly/L. 16 Cpls. Evacuated to C.C.L Officers out two, Capt of Button 17. I.R. Warwicks hospital Cases. The Rev H.A. MEEK Wesleyan chaplain app 13 F. M. Dil. Ambulance On Leave. There are O.R. sick twelve attended one in the Divisions sick O.R one	app 37
"		6pm	A Draft wanted 3rd Glos Field Ambulance Situation unchanged. Weather colder & dull.	
BUS	31/8/15	8.30am	Arrangement to 2nd 3rd Army & 2nd/6th & 16th - Evacuated L.C.C.S Officers nil O.R. sick eleven wounded nil san & the Division O.R. sick one	app 38

Colonel,
Assistant Director Medical Services,
48th (South Midland) Division.

48th b. Alpini

A.D.M.S. 48th Division

9th VI

Sept. 15

Summarised & not copied.
Dec. 1917.

121/6918

Sept '15

S

Confidential

War Diary
of
A.D.M.S. 8th (Rlw.) Division
from 1st September to 30th September 1915.

Army Form C. 2118

WAR DIARY
or
INTELLIGENCE SUMMARY.
(Erase heading not required.)

Instructions regarding War Diaries and Intelligence Summaries are contained in F. S. Regs., Part II and the Staff Manual respectively. Title pages will be prepared in manuscript.

Place	Date	Hour	Summary of Events and Information	Remarks and references to Appendices
B.W.F	1.9.15	8.30 a.m.	Situation unchanged from 31st July. Weather wet + cold.	
"	"	10 a.m.	A.D.M.S. inspected men of 1/5th R. Warwicks for permanent base.	
"	"	11 a.m.	A.D.M.S. visited 3rd (Bn) Field Ambulance.	
"	"	4 p.m.	Increase to Strength 3rd Army, 2 Subs., 7 O.R.s.- Evacuated to C.C.S. Officers nil, for Major D. TAYLOR 1/5th R Warwicks Haemorrhoids on Rest G.440 N. REAY 1/7 hallux wounded 18 Warwicks (back eighteen) wounded one	App I
B.W.B	2.9.15	8.30 a.m.	Situation unchanged. Weather cold + wet	
"	"	9 a.m.	A.D.M.S. attend conference G.O.C.	
"	"	"	A.D.M.S. visited 70 N.QUELLIERS (HQ. & 1 sec. Ambulance) (Lief' 25 Amiens St (2) with O.C. 1st (Bn) Field Ambulance to select position (adv. dressing station, as troops of the Div.).	
"	"	"	taking over part of line from 63 & 64 french Divns.	
"	"	4.30 p.m.	Increase to Strength 3rd Army, 2 Subs., 4 O.R.s. Evacuated to C.C.S. Officers nil OR. sick twelve wounded nil.	App 2
"	"	"	Sanitary Officer visited THIEVRES with reference to care of Typhus fever amongst Civilians, patient removed to Hospital at DOULLENS. No men fit at frontline.	
B.W.B	3.9.15	8.30 a.m.	Situation. Part of line recently 56. B. French Division of 1/6 N.QUELLIERS taken over by 143rd Infy Bde. - Weather cold + wet.	
"	"	10 p.m.	A.D.M.S. with H.Q. & 1/1, & 1/2 1st F.A. (12 noon) D.DMS Journey now visited 2 French Dressing Stations	

WAR DIARY
or
INTELLIGENCE SUMMARY.

(Erase heading not required.)

Army Form C. 2118

Instructions regarding War Diaries and Intelligence Summaries are contained in F. S. Regs., Part II. and the Staff Manual respectively. Title pages will be prepared in manuscript.

Place	Date	Hour	Summary of Events and Information	Remarks and references to Appendices
BUS	3/9/15	12.15pm	FOR QUEVILLERS. Instructions issued to D/s to leave all walking sick in billets. Rolls place noted.	Appx 3
"	"	4.30pm	Pieces of Lieut 3rd Army & D.A.D.S. of infra. Evacuated to C.C.S. officers in two Ricart A.W. NEWMAN 11/3rd Glou B73 R.F.A. H B-17 Dental cases. Cpl 87 Jones 117 R.Shanoels Eve on each of ten wounded O.R. from the Division R. sick one O.R. wounded one.	
"	"	8pm	Lieut J.H. Mackay R.A.M.C. (T.C.) reported for duty from 2nd Home Hosp 1/6 Gloucester. Situation unchanged. Weather warm & sunny.	
BUS	4/9/15	8.30am	Re evacuated to 3rd & 2nd Corps & D.A.H. & Cpt. Brand 10/2 C.C.S officers one Lieut 1/8 KING 1/5 Gloucester Duntol Caine on each fourteen wounded Done other sickness wounded one	Appx 4
BUS	5/9/15	8.30am	Situation unchanged. Weather warm & sunny.	
"	"	12.30pm	A.D.M.S. attend conference at D.H.Q. 3rd Army.	
"	"	1.30pm	Re evacuated to 3rd Br Army & D.A.D.S. & D.A.H. 7/3 Corps. Eve vacated to C.C.S. officers nil O.R. sick seven wounded nil	Appx (5)
BUS	6/9/15	8.30am	Move to D.R. of 3rd Echelon forwarded each wantage Situation unchanged. Weather warm & sunny.	
"	"	4.15pm	O.R.W. wrote to all patients in Divisional Rest Station. Visits to Field Ambulance.	Appx 6
"	"	4.30pm	Re evacuated to 3rd & 2nd Army & D.A.D.S. & H. of infra. Evacuated to C.C.S officers nil O.R. sick fourteen wounded three	
BUS	7/9/15	8.30am	Situation unchanged. Weather warm & sunny.	
"	"	11.15pm	O. Died visited 2 and 3 3rd Field Ambulances	

WAR DIARY
or
INTELLIGENCE SUMMARY.

(Erase heading not required.)

Army Form C. 2118

Instructions regarding War Diaries and Intelligence Summaries are contained in F. S. Regs., Part II. and the Staff Manual respectively. Title pages will be prepared in manuscript.

Place	Date	Hour	Summary of Events and Information	Remarks and references to Appendices
B.U.S.	7.9.15	4.15pm	Proceeded to 2nd and 3rd Army & 29th and 7th Corps – Evacuated to C.C.S. Officers sick two & head G.R.P. WILLSON 5th R Sussex Bronchial Catarrh and Capt E.N.R. HADDEN 1/4 Oxfords sendo L.S. Brutal Carie one O.R. sick Rheumatic Wounds 2nd OR two	app 7.
B.U.S.	8.9.15	8.30am	Sent S. MOORE Yorks R. reported on duty as a N.C.O. to Officer in Duties in the 3rd Wells Field Amb [?] Situation unchanged. Weather warm & sunny	
		12.15pm	O.B.W. visited St. LEGER, then to THIEVRES enquired as to sanitation of that place.	app 8.
		4.30pm	Proceeded to 2nd and 3rd Army & 29th and 7th Corps – Evacuated to C.C.S. Officers sick two OR sick twenty two one Officer Wounded OR one [?]	
B.U.S.	9.9.15	8.30am	Situation unchanged. Weather warm & sunny	
			Wrote report of Corporal & William Donavan to be of 6th Dragoons to 8 Stat Hospital	
			Sent M. Army returns for DHI & Hygienic return approved. They are as annexed	
			Sent the proposal of Lieutenant S. Moore for Musketry Instructor.	
		4.30pm	Proceeded to 2nd and 3rd Army & 29th and 7th Corps – Evacuated to C.C.S. Officers sick two OR sick twenty five wounded OR one	app 9
			Situation unchanged. Weather warm & sunny	
B.U.S.	10.9.15	8.30am	O.B.W. visited the Field Ambulance with reference to 10 cases of Jaundice admitted [?]	
		12.30pm	one officer to have. These proved not to be so.	
		4.30pm	Proceeded to 2nd and 3rd Army & 29th and 7th Corps – Evacuated to C.C.S. Officers sick one OR sick sixteen SUTTON 7 R Warwicks Double Carie on OR sick thirty wounded OR one	app 10

1577 Wt. W10791/1773 500,000 1/15 D. D. & L. A.D.S.S./Forms/C. 2118.

WAR DIARY or INTELLIGENCE SUMMARY

Army Form C. 2118

Place	Date	Hour	Summary of Events and Information	Remarks and references to Appendices
BUZ	11.9.15	8.30am	Situation unchanged. Weather warm & sunny	
"		9am	Issue from Office Director 2nd Army stating No 1876 Pte Bell A 5th R.Irish Rifles admitted with Cerebro-spinal fever. can'd only be exchanged for anti-microbial sole	
"		12.30pm	Message to O/C Div. 2nd Army & DADMS 3rd Div. Details as to Ambulance that will send to (Centre-spinal meningitis suspects	App 11
"		3pm	Message to O/C Field Ambulances where he can send & examine contacts	App 12
"		4pm	Message to D.D.M.S 7 Corps & DMS 3rd Army. Re evacuation to C.C.S B officer with late Capt R.A.M.C ROTTER R & D Bark. Do cerebro-spinal to Major D.W. POWELL R.F.C. DMS evacuated to civil internment was on No 1876 Pte. Poole A 5th R.I. Rifles & message in writing to Hospital in England to Cerebro-spinal meningitis	App 13
"		6.15pm	Message from Bgd D Bactr Laboratory stating he has examined contacts of afternoon & found	App 14
BUZ	12.9.15	8.30am	Situation unchanged. Weather warm & sunny	
"			O. D.M.S proceeded on 8 days leave to England.	
"		12.45pm	DADMS visited Dressing Stations at BAILY, Q.Donners Dressing Station & HEBUTERNE and for Queviours Class to bring of Signers Daygrams & appointments	
"		2.30pm	ADMS attended conference of S.O.C & Divisional Staff re Dressing Stations.	
"		4.30pm	Message to DMS 3rd Army & DMS 3rd Div. Re Capt J.Cobs. Swaine R.A.M.C. Officer sick R.I.H.A sick & ordinary time also the Divisions that he Somme one	App 15
BUZ	13.9.15	8.30am	Situation unchanged. Weather warm & sunny	
"		11.30am	Message to DMS 3rd Army & DMS 14 Corps. Re evacuation to C.C.S 8 officer sick Captain A.H. ROTCHER	App 16

Army Form C. 2118

WAR DIARY
or
INTELLIGENCE SUMMARY.
(Erase heading not required.)

Instructions regarding War Diaries and Intelligence Summaries are contained in F. S. Regs., Part II. and the Staff Manual respectively. Title pages will be prepared in manuscript.

Place	Date	Hour	Summary of Events and Information	Remarks and references to Appendices
B.U.Z	13.9.15		1/7 Worcester Imaamia OR sick nineteen	
B.W.Z	14.9.15	8.30am	Situation unchanged. Weather warm but cloudy	
"	"	11am	JADrew visits R.O.Yo & Scooters with officers to number of sick occurring in that unit	App 17
"	"	4.30pm	Messages to D.M.S. 2nd Army & D.D.M.S 3rd Corps. Evacuated to Ccp officers and sick of twenty from OR wounded three	
B.U.Z	15.9.15	8.30am	Situation unchanged. Weather cloudy	
"	"	12.7pm	Message from 4 Cavalry Station – Blood chilling gave/15 A Clifton positive Widal Group –	App 18
"	"	4.30pm	M.D.Yo & O.C. Sanitary Section accordingly informed. Messages to DMS 2nd Army, D9Md 3 & Ccrps – Evacuated to C.C.S officers seven and sick one 2/R.W.&B. DIXON 1/6 R.Warwick Dunkel Casino OR sick eleven wounded D.N. three on other Divisions OR wounded ten	App 19
B.O.Z	16.9.15	8.30am	Capt. Cawdry DADMS 48th Division sent to 2nd Field Ambulance reffering from phlebitis R.Leg. Situation unchanged. Weather cloudy & close	
		11.30pm	Message to DMS 2nd Army, DMS 3 Corps. Evacuated to C.C.S. officers weck one Capt E. TAYLOR 1/4 Glos Regt, Gastritis DR sick thirteen wounded four our other Divisions OR sick even	App 20
B.O.Z	17.9.15	8.30am	Situation unchanged. Weather warm & sunny	
"		4.30pm	Message to DMS 3 Army, DMS 3 Corps – 16 Corps – Evacuated to C.C.S officers sick from Lieut LADKIN 1/5 R.Warwick Pyrexia Capt E.G. FORTESCUE 1/6 Worr Bucks chronic catarrh Lieut A.H. RHODES 2/M. & B. 1095. RGA Machine Fever Lieut A.B. DUNN 1/6 R Warwick Dent Carine OR sick eighteen DR wounded three on other Divisions OR sick two DR wounded one	App 21
B.U.Z	18.9.15	8.30am	Situation unchanged. Weather warm & raining	

WAR DIARY
or
INTELLIGENCE SUMMARY

(Erase heading not required.)

Army Form C. 2118

Place	Date	Hour	Summary of Events and Information	Remarks and references to Appendices
B'u'p	18/9/15	4.30 pm	Evacuated to 87th F.A. 3 Army & 2nd Batt'n 7th Cop'n. Evacuated to CCS 1 officer sick one officer wounded. Capt. I.R. Parr CALDICOTT 1/7 R. Warwicks sprained ankle, OR sick 4, one OR wounded. One prisoner OR wounded two.	App 22
B'u'p	19/9/15	9.30 am	Situation unchanged. Weather warm sunny.	
		4 pm	Evacuated to 87th F.A. 3 Army & 2nd Batt'n 7th Cop'n. Evacuated to CCS 1 officer sick one OR. Capt. A. PROFFEIT 8th K.R.R. shrapnel wound head, OR sick twenty four wounded one. Prisoners of war sick one OR wounded two.	App 23
B'u'p	20/9/15	8.30 am	Situation unchanged. Weather warm sunny. O. Batt'n James Evans Inspection as regards to 1/7th Warwicks & visit Officer's resuscit'n in ACC 2 men to sent to M.O. CCS Colo'll Duff invited Colin Bailey to courseilles.	
		9 am		
		5 pm	Evacuated to 87th F.A. 3 Army & 2nd Batt'n 7th Cop'n. Evacuated to CCS 1 officer sick one OR sick eighteen wounded two other Pioneers in sick line. Lieut W. MUNDY COX R.A.M.C. (T.F) reported for duty to 87th F.A. 3 Army (8th Corp.) Field Ambulance	App 24
B'u'p	21/9/15	8.30 am	Situation unchanged. Weather warm sunny.	
		1 pm	O. Batt'n visited FONQUEVILLERS & noted P.C. OCRI (?) Field Amb and reference to evacuation of wounded. Itinerary P.o. Becom, 8 show, R. 00, 15 al (?) 18 Warwicks, inspecting their aid posts. He then visited AUTHIE & M.D.f.o.4 & spoke to Bayonet. To the numerous except blanks all made in the company. Cars namely 8/8 at another probably half a mm. Colo'll Duff Cecovaugh 5 days.	
		4.15 pm	Evacuated to 87th F.A. 3 Army & 2nd Batt'n 7th Cop'n. Evacuated to CCS 8 officer sick one OR wounded	

WAR DIARY or INTELLIGENCE SUMMARY

Army Form C. 2118

Place	Date	Hour	Summary of Events and Information	Remarks and references to Appendices
B.U.B	21.9.15		JONES 1/6 Warwick Dental Caries. O/R sick eighteen wounded nil	app 25
		7 p.m.	A.D.M.S. visited 2nd & 3rd Field Ambulances with reference to evacuation of wounded	
B.U.B	22.9.15	8.30 a.m.	Lieut J. ALLISON detailed to 1st Field Ambulance for duty. Situation unchanged. Weather warm & sunny	
		10 a.m.	A.D.M.S saw O.C. 1st Can Field Ambulance & O.C. 3 F.d Ambulance	
		11.30 a.m.	A.D.M.S examined men at Berkofs transport lines & Reducing Grange	
		4.30 p.m.	Message to Railhead Coy. 1 D.A.C. & C. Co. Sanctuary - sent order to C.O. 2 F.d. Ambulance	app 26
			to send 1/2 Field Ambulance to sector for field parties for evacuation of wounded. Sick	
			Persons O/R sick 20 wounded one.	
		6.30 p.m.	D.D.M.S. 1/6 Corps called. A.D.M.S.	
			Lieut J. ALLISON R.A.M.C. T.C. proceeded to 1/2 Florries for duty relieving Lt MACKAY who had	
B.U.B	23.9.15	9 a.m.	also to Ypres Miss Office on 23.9.15 at 9 a.m. Situation unchanged weather close	
		10 a.m.	Lieut MACKAY RAMC T.C. proceeded to form 6th Division Board held at RUTHIE - Capt. DOYLE - Resident to give into residence Division 1/6 Florries	app 27
		1.30 p.m.	Message to 2nd 3rd Army & D. Adj 1/6 Corps - Evacuated C.C.S Officer sick one Captive's Cross	
			4/4 Slorden Pyrexia - 10 other 3 men Capt. H.U. MC. F Mus 16" Siege B'y 1/5 4 St B.F.A Shellshock O/Rank	
			Total O/R wounded three Other Division O/R sick three wounded none	
B.U.B	24.9.15	8.30 a.m.	Situation unchanged. Weather rainy & close.	
		11 a.m.	O.D.M.S saw O.C. 1 & 3 F.d. 2/3rd Field Ambulances	
		11.30 a.m.	A.D.M.S Inspected mess of 2nd & 3rd Field Ambulances & lines for transport & Base	

WAR DIARY
or
INTELLIGENCE SUMMARY.
(Erase heading not required.)

Army Form C. 2118.

Instructions regarding War Diaries and Intelligence Summaries are contained in F. S. Regs., Part II. and the Staff Manual respectively. Title pages will be prepared in manuscript.

Place	Date	Hour	Summary of Events and Information	Remarks and references to Appendices
BUS	24.9.15	4.30pm	Nieneport Shut 3rd Army & 9 Ind. 7 W. Corps - Evacuated to C.C.S. 8 Officers sick nil OR sick 4 O R wounded 12	A/App 28
BUS	25.9.15	8.30am	Situation unchanged. Weather dull & rainy	
		12.30am	A.D.M.S. visited all Field Ambulances	
		4.30pm	Nieneport 3rd, 3rd Army & D. Ind. 7 W Corps - Evacuated to C.C.S. 8 Officers sick nil OR sick eleven	A/App 9
			OR wounded four	
		5.30pm	A.D.M.S. called on A.D.M.S. with reference to evacuation of wounded & the collecting of information regarding casualties	
BUS	26.9.15	8.30am	Situation unchanged. Weather dull & raining	
		11.30am	A.D.M.S. visited Dressing Stations S.A.24 & Advanced Dressing Station HESDIGNEUL	
		9.30pm	Nieneport 3rd 3rd Army & D Ind 7 W Corps - Evacuated to C.C.S. 8 Officers sick two Kent C.W. 12 RFA 4/6 R Warwicks and Lieut A.G. F.15H 41 Abt. R.F.A. R.F.A. Horses OR sick twenty one OR wounded two. 5th Division 89 sick two	A/App 30
		7pm	A.D.M.S. attended A.D.M.S. 7 W Corps returning wounded forwarded from 6 am to 6 pm (This message he sent every day for 12 hours ending 6am & 6pm.)	
BUS	27.9.15	8.30am	Situation unchanged. Weather rainy	
		4.30pm	Nieneport 3rd Shut 3rd Army & D Ind 7 W Corps - Evacuated to C.C.S. 8 Officers sick one Lieut & Greener 1/R Warwicks	A/App 31
			H.Q. Div Rcl 3 Cay A.S.C. Fire field Amb. One wounded Lieut P.A. Turner 1 RCB 4th Division OR sick twenty OR wounded three nil 47th Division OR	
			sick nil OR wounded one	
BUS	28.9.15	8.30am	Situation unchanged. Weather rainy & cold.	

Army Form C. 2118.

WAR DIARY
or
INTELLIGENCE SUMMARY.

(Erase heading not required.)

Instructions regarding War Diaries and Intelligence Summaries are contained in F. S. Regs., Part II. and the Staff Manual respectively. Title pages will be prepared in manuscript.

Hour, Date, Place		Summary of Events and Information	Remarks and references to Appendices
R.W.B.	12.30 a.m. 28.9.15	A.D.M.S. visited all Field Ambulances.	
"	4.30 p.m.	Evacuees to 3rd Fd Amb'y. D.S.M.d-7-(Cpr.) Evacuated to C.C.S. Officers sick two. Lieut J.M FOWLER 1/6 Gloucesters Pyrexia. Lieut CM AH ROBERTS A.S.C. ad ½ Field Bearer Headquarters. OR sick twenty. OR wounded three.	App 33
B.W.B.	29.9.15 8.30 a.m.	Situation unchanged. Weather rainy, cool.	
"	10 a.m.	Medical Board on Capt BYWATER 1/6 Warwicks.	
"	4.30 p.m.	Evacuees to 3rd Fd Amb'y. D.S.M.d.7. (Cpr.) Evacuated to C.C.S. Officers sick Nil. OR sick twenty nine. wounded one.	App 34.
B.W.B.	30.9.15 8.30 a.m.	Situation unchanged. Weather cold & sunny. A.D.M.S. visited 2nd Fd Ambulance. Went into the matter of moving its situation, but no suitable place being found, it was decided that it remain where it is now at the Gabrez.	
"	4.30 p.m.	The A.D.M.S. Evacuees to 3rd Fd Amb'y & D.S.M.d-7. (Cpr.) Evacuated to C.C.S. Officers sick one. 2/Lieut JH HERRING R.F.C. Stge Ambulance OR sick twenty three.	App 35

[signature]
Colonel,
Assistant Director Medical Services,
South Midland Division.

121/7384

A.D.M.S. 48th Division
Vol VII
Oct 15

Oct 1915

Confidential

War Diary
A.D.M.S. 8th Division
from 1st to 31st Oct 1915

Army Form C. 2118.

WAR DIARY
or
INTELLIGENCE SUMMARY.
(Erase heading not required.)

Instructions regarding War Diaries and Intelligence Summaries are contained in F.S. Regs., Part II. and the Staff Manual respectively. Title pages will be prepared in manuscript.

Hour, Date, Place		Summary of Events and Information	Remarks and references to Appendices
BUS 1/10/15	9.30 am	Situation unchanged from 30 & Sept. Weather cold & rainy	
" "	11.30 am	ADMS 4th Corps called & saw ADMS	
" "	4.30 pm	Messages to Med. 3rd Army & D. Dir. of Supplies - sou. anxted to C.C.S. Officers	app. endor. 1
BUS 2/10/15	9.30 am	Put BR sick & wounded BR wounded Situation unchanged. Weather cold & rainy	
" "	10 am	Capt D Buchanan RAMC (T.F.) reported for duty, posted to 2n K(W) Field Ambulance	
" "	2.30 pm	Messages to Med. 3rd Army, DDMS 3 & 4 Corps. Evacuated to C.C.S. Officers sick. Lieut A.S. DUMAS 17th Division. Sick&Cases BR sick	app. 2
BUS 3/10/15	9.30 am	After Situation unchanged. Weather cold & rainy	
" "	1 pm	ADMS attended conference DMS 3rd Army	
" "	4.30 pm	Messages to Med. 3rd Army & DDMS 4th Corps. Evacuated to C.C.S. Officers sick but BR sick twenty four BR wounded one other	app. 3
" "	"	BR wounded one. Message from No2 C.C.S. 2371 Pt Egerton 7 Carpenter intern.	
BUS 4/10/15	9.30 am	Situation unchanged. Weather cold & rainy	app. 4
" "	2.30 pm	Message to Med. 3rd Army, DDMS 4 Corps. Evacuated to C.C.S. Officers sick nil	app. 5
" "	5.7 pm	BR sick twenty seven BR wounded from Message from No 4 C.C.S. 1157 Pte Marshall R.5 Remses & 357 P/S Perrins 2nd	

Army Form C. 2118.

WAR DIARY
or
INTELLIGENCE SUMMARY.
(Erase heading not required.)

Instructions regarding War Diaries and Intelligence Summaries are contained in F.S. Regs., Part II. and the Staff Manual respectively. Title pages will be prepared in manuscript.

Hour, Date, Place		Summary of Events and Information	Remarks and references to Appendices
BWB	4/10/15	a.d. 1292 Pte LAMBERT & 5th R Warwicks - all suspected Enteric	app 6
BWB	5/10/15	9.30 am	Situation much as per previous day - weather still wet	
"	"	10.30 am	O/but visits all Field Ambulance & Bakes at Couin	
"	"		Reception HCCS Pot. Pte Egerton fires of arm - blood culture	app 7
"	"	4.30 pm	Message to Studs Army, D.Stat & M.C.PO - evacuated to C of 8 Officers sick nil. O.R. sick 68 et al O.R. wounded nil. Officers Division BA et al nil	app 8
"	"		2 nd (Lon) Field Ambulance relieved 3 rd (Lon) Field Ambulance. Took over Advanced Dressing Station at HEBUTERNE - Dressing Station & Baths at BAILLY	
"	"		O.C. Sanitary Section reports two cases (Typhus) at Couin us among civilians. The AD.MS. & B. evacuated RAMC asked to inquire into above calling & take precautions taken	
BWB	6/10/15	8.30 am	Situation much as per - Weather variable	
"	"	10.15 am	O/but visits Dressing Station at BAILLY	
"	"		Message from D.Stat saying 300 men of R Inniskillings sickened during	app 9
"	"		VAUGHELLES. No 3 Field Amb. ord. to take medical charge. Instructions sent to O.C. 3 (Lon) Field Ambulance accordingly.	app 10
"	"	4.30 pm	Messages to Studs Army, D.Stat, A.P. etc. - evacuated to C of 8 Officers sick nil. O.R. sick 68 O.R. wounded nil. Officers wounded nil	app 11
"	"	6.15 pm	D.D.M. writes to 5th R Warwick with reference to numbers of sick being sent to Field Ambulance as suspected Typhus.	app 12

Army Form C. 2118.

WAR DIARY
or
INTELLIGENCE SUMMARY.
(Erase heading not required.)

Instructions regarding War Diaries and Intelligence Summaries are contained in F.S. Regs., Part II. and the Staff Manual respectively. Title pages will be prepared in manuscript.

Hour, Date, Place		Summary of Events and Information	Remarks and references to Appendices
BUS	6.10.15	The O i/c 8 Bacteriological Lab. visited Coigneux took civilian Stools for cultures & interia. Arrangements made to move Field Laboratory to DOULLENS.	
BUS	7.10.15 8.30 am	Situation unchanged. Weather dull	
"	" 11 am	Message from A.C.C.S. — PERRINS & LAMBERT negative blood cultures	App 12.
"	" 5 pm	O i/c visited Advanced Dressing Station at FONQUEVILLERS & Dressing Station at BOIS RETZ [?]	App 13
"	"	Arranged to take 3 Army & Suff & Cambs Evacuates to CCS Officers sick two 2/Lieut HOTROP "; Sm Field CoR 2. Orderly Jaundice Lieut Ph. WRIGHT Bucks 6/15 Auretropia OR a k trinity two OR wounds fifteen Other Services sick OR one	
BUS	8.10.15 8.30 am	Situation unchanged. Weather dull	
"	" 11.45 am	Message from ACCS. 10719 Pte A WATSON 1st Bedfords 2/7 H. R.	App 14
"	"	Sick intake July 8/15 — accepted interior.	
"	" 11.30 pm	Message from Divns. Diarted 7 h Copno — Evacuated to CCS. Officers three. Officers sick NIL Rank & File fifteen OR wounds two three O.C. Sanitary Section marks Coigneux with reference turnculating civilian inhabitants against interic.	App 15
"	" 2 pm	Message from 34 Field Amb. — Civilian at Coigneux — BAILLY 38 I DOWN 14 [?] Blood cultures fromitive Bacillus Typhosum	App 16
"	" 4 pm	Message from Highlands CCS. B/3 A Ansell 6 ath [Camo.] R&S Scarlet fever	App 17

(73989) W4141—463. 400,000. 9/14. H.&J.Ltd. Forms/C. 2118/10.

Army Form C. 2118.

WAR DIARY
or
INTELLIGENCE SUMMARY.
(Erase heading not required.)

Instructions regarding War Diaries and Intelligence Summaries are contained in F.S. Regs., Part II. and the Staff Manual respectively. Title pages will be prepared in manuscript.

Hour, Date, Place		Summary of Events and Information	Remarks and references to Appendices
BUQ 9.10.15	8.30 am	Situation unchanged. Weather mostly cold & dull	
"	12.30 p.m.	A Draft wanted all Field Ambulances.	
"	4 p.m.	Draft fund for 2/L Warwicks (who there had had to use infantry pigeons) Instruction to pigeons Itrioques) with reference to interrupting the enemy's line	
"	4.30 p.m.	Messages to Shrewsbury & DAMS Upper Wanted & CO of Warwicks OR sick leaving OR wounded from site.	app. 18
		Divisional OR sick one.	
RUF 10.9.15	8.30 am	Situation unchanged - weather warm a sunny	
"	10.30 am	2 Lieut 7th Cape. called was Ayr?	
"	4.30 p.m.	Lieut Capt Bond 3rd Army 3 S. Staffs & Capt - Lieuts 4/CC8	app 19
		Officers died two Cape Barnard 5th R. Lancs Doubloons Capt S	
		Revisited 1/6 R Warwicks - In conference of Cap. A/100 & A/7.103 Major	
		fifteen OR wounded & three	
		Sanitary Officer visited Courmus with reference to present amt of	
		Enteric was accompany accept Ciserow + 4 officers mere	
		inoculated against Enteric. Besides 6 Upper being taken	
		at BAILLY, PUTHIE & THIEVRES.	
BUF 11.10.15	8.30 am	Situation unchanged. Weather mild & sunny	
"	4.30 p.m.	Rx created to 0.08 Officers and 1/8 OR sick Thirteen OR wounded 1 two	app. 20

WAR DIARY
or
INTELLIGENCE SUMMARY.

(Erase heading not required.)

Army Form C. 2118.

Instructions regarding War Diaries and Intelligence Summaries are contained in F.S. Regs., Part II. and the Staff Manual respectively. Title pages will be prepared in manuscript.

Hour, Date, Place		Summary of Events and Information	Remarks and references to Appendices
B.U.B. 12.10.15	8.30 a.m.	Situation unchanged. Weather cold.	
"	12.30 p.m.	O.C MD visited all Field Ambulances	
"	4.30 p.m.	Messages to D.M.S. Army, D.D.M.S. I.K. Corps. - Evacuated to CCS & Fieldwick all OR sick and wounded Div. Division OR sick &c one	App. 21
B.U.B. 13.10.15	8.30 a.m.	Situation unchanged Walker Drill	
"	12.30 p.m.	O.C MD visited Field Baths at Bailey & Cour	
"	3.1 p.m.	No developed probable laboratory in a D.M.L. with reference to suspected Typhoid carriers in St. Warwicks. Investigations being carried out.	
"	4.30 p.m.	Messages to D.M.S. Army, D.D.M.S. and I.K. Corps - Evacuated to C.C.S. & Fieldwick all OR sick & Officers for wounded. Division OR wounded one	App. 22
B.U.B. 14.10.15	8.30 a.m.	Situation unchanged. Weather mild.	
		Instructions issued to O.C 60 Battalion regarding the precautions against "Frostbite" "Trenchfoot" &c.	
"	11.30 p.m.	Messages to D.M.D. & D.Army & D.D.M.D. I.K. Corps. Evacuated to A.C.S. Fieldwick all OR sick & OR sent headquarters sick, wounded. Division OR sick one.	App. 23

Army Form C. 2118.

WAR DIARY
or
INTELLIGENCE SUMMARY.
(Erase heading not required.)

Instructions regarding War Diaries and Intelligence Summaries are contained in F.S. Regs., Part II. and the Staff Manual respectively. Title pages will be prepared in manuscript.

Hour, Date, Place		Summary of Events and Information	Remarks and references to Appendices
RUS 15.10.15	8.30am	Situation unchanged. Weather dull	App p 24
"	11.30 am	Message to Brit. 2nd Army District & H.Q. — Evacuated to C.C.S. Officers 2/Lt Hore 2/Lieut A.D. ANDERSON 1/5 Gloucester Details carried Lieut H.P. SNOWDEN 1/5 Glosters. Wounded in action Major H.J. ROSLING 1/5 RM Field Ambulance. Pyrexia OR and twenty-five OR wounded) one OR sick no TP sick no me	
RUS 16.10.15	8.30am	Situation unchanged. Weather dull.	
"	12.4 pm	O.P.H.L. similar. Brewing Station at Sully where dug-out for snipers for individuals being made. & observed Brewing 9 stretcher multitudinous. Evacuated to C.C.S. Officers sick and all OR sick seventeen Others Enemies OR sick less	App p 25
"	4.30 pm	Message from Brig.Gen. W.C.C.95 2693 Pte LOWE F 1/4 R.Berks	App p 26
		German Mancurn	
RUS 17.10.15	8.30 am	Situation unchanged. Weather dull	
"	12.30 pm	R.A. of attack in Advance Army Hd.Qrs. I.I. Army	
"	4.30 pm	In respect Births & Army, B. Bnd. L.Cpls. H.H.G. BENNETT 1/8 Worcester & officers disabled from Capt R.N. WAUGH 45 R. Sussex & private Pte L.C. ARFAXLEY 1/5 R.Sussex. Details OR sick Ten OR wounded one Pte Burnes OR sick one	App p 27
		Usual average. Sick no sufferer. No sick at B, H, G, Bases.	

Army Form C. 2118.

WAR DIARY
or
INTELLIGENCE SUMMARY.
(Erase heading not required.)

Instructions regarding War Diaries and Intelligence Summaries are contained in F.S. Regs., Part II. and the Staff Manual respectively. Title pages will be prepared in manuscript.

Hour, Date, Place		Summary of Events and Information	Remarks and references to Appendices
RUS	18/10/15 8.30 am	Situation unchanged. Weather seasonable (cool).	
	12.45 p.m.	O.R.U.L. visited all the Field Ambulances	
	3.30 p.m.	Welcome Draft of 2/Lieut B.H.B Allan and (him) D.2 N.C.O. from communication to the Regular Army	
	4.30 p.m.	Evacuated to hospital 3 Army O.R. sick 24 (four - evacuated to C.C.S) Officers sick nil. O.R. sick twenty seven, O.R. wounded eleven (five serious O.R. sick (four wounded) three	App 28
		Situation unchanged. Weather seasonable (cool)	
RUS	19.10.15 8.30 am		
	5 p.m.	O.R.U.L. inspected billets (i n.c.o & Pvt communication & farm at ATHIENVE transferred to Pud.3rd Army, 1 Pvt Pud.2 Corps - evacuated to C.C.S Officers sick nil. O.R. sick fourteen, O.R. wounded three	App 29
RUS	20.10.15 8.30 am	Situation unchanged. Weather cool but sunny. O.R.U.L. inspected all billets at AUTHIE	
	12.45 p.m.		
	4.30 p.m.	Evacuated to hosp. 3rd Army, 1 Officer, 1 Officer & Corps - evacuated to C.C.S Officers sick nil. O.R. sick twenty two, O.R. wounded one. Other Services O.R. sick	App 30
RUS	21-10-15 8.30 am	Situation unchanged. Weather dull.	
	4.30 p.m.	Evacuated to C.C.S Officers sick two Lieut J Griffiths 1/1 R Welsh Fusiliers Attd 3/4 R & Lieut Percivitta Reto of Lieut. U.J. Field 1/1R Percivitta Total Service O.R. sick sixteen Other Services O.R. sick one wounded one	App 31

(73989) W4141—463. 400,000. 9/14. H.&J.Ltd. Forms/C. 2118/10.

WAR DIARY
or
INTELLIGENCE SUMMARY.
(Erase heading not required.)

Army Form C. 2118.

Instructions regarding War Diaries and Intelligence Summaries are contained in F.S. Regs., Part II. and the Staff Manual respectively. Title pages will be prepared in manuscript.

Place	Hour, Date	Summary of Events and Information	Remarks and references to Appendices
RWB	22.10.15 8.30am	Situation unchanged. Weather mild & sunny.	
"	12.30pm	O/C Med. inspected billets of Bucks & 6th Conn. Also the Bn.l Baths at same place.	
"	4.30pm	Reverent. Hutchisbury & D. Ord. J.H. Opps. – evacuated to C.C.S. Officers sick two Lieut P.H.W. HICKS 1/7 R.Warwicks. Dental Caries Rem.t WNO Bell KEH B. Sqdn. Dental Caries OR sick twenty two OR wounded three Other Ranks OR sick three OR wounded one.	App 32
RWB	23.10.15 8.30am	Situation unchanged. Weather mild & raining.	
"	10.46pm	O/C Med. visited all Field Ambulances	
"	2pm	Civilian in Spicey reported to have returned to Ranal.	
"		(notified Hotel de Ville) AMIENS	
"	4.30pm	Messages to 1/Ber. (3rd) Army 1 D Ord. 7 HCps. – wounded 1 OO.F. Officers sick one e/Lieut R.W. HASSELL 1/2.9.15 B.M.D. Bronchitis OR sick thirty five OR wounded one Ober Grosserino Machine	App 33
"		Weekly messages to D.D.M.S. 4. Opps. – sick wounded	
BOS	24.10.15	D.A.D.M.S. departed on 8 days leave to England Situation unchanged. Weather cold & foggy. There are a large number of scabies cases in Bnsn. 51 cases having been admitted during the past week. I must circular to all medical Officers re health inspections	

WAR DIARY
or
INTELLIGENCE SUMMARY.

(Erase heading not required.)

Army Form C. 2118

Place	Date	Hour	Summary of Events and Information	Remarks and references to Appendices
BUS	24/10/15	—	Usual messages to A.D.M.S. 7th Corps & D.M.S. 3rd Army — Captain Muller 1/6 R Warwicks evacuated to C.C.S. suffering from "Dental Caries". Other ranks, sick 10, other division other ranks, sick one, wounded one.	
"	25/10/15		Usual messages to D.A. & 3rd Division. 6 Officers 172 other ranks, an increase of 33 other ranks over previous week. Of these evacuated, over 50% are dental & eye cases, the majority of which return to the Division. Weather very wet and cold — Situation unchanged. Divisional Sanitary Officer inspected Latrines & afterwards went to Doullens to buy branch for the storage of drinking water for the civilian population at Souastre and Thievres.	
"	26/10/15		Medical Board on Captain Bramall 5/R Sussex Reg. Evacuated to CCS other ranks, 24 sick, 1 wounded died. Sent wires to ADMS & DMS. Weather fine but cold — Situation unchanged — Visited all three Field Ambulances. Received Hospital instruction on care of Sanitary Section — Messages to ADMS & DMS, Evacuated to CCS other ranks, sick 17, wounded 1.	
"	27/10/15		Weather wet & cold. Situation unchanged. Usual messages to ADMS & DMS, evacuated to C.C.S. other ranks sick 17, wounded 1. other Divisions other ranks sick 5	
"	28/10/15		Weather wet & cold. Situation unchanged — Medical Board on Captain Haigh & Whitehill 1/8 R Warwick Regt. Found both suffering from "Nervous debility". Messages to ADMS & DMS evacuated to CCS Lieut P.T. Cosfield R.M.A. "C" Battery Dental Caries other ranks sick 22, wounded 2, other Divisions other ranks sick 11, wounded 1.	
"	29/10/15		Weather fine but cold — Visited 3/Sn Field Ambulances & arranged for transfer of marquees & operation tents. Messages to ADMS & DMS Evacuated to CCS other ranks sick 9.	

WAR DIARY
or
INTELLIGENCE SUMMARY

Army Form C. 2118

Place	Date	Hour	Summary of Events and Information	Remarks and references to Appendices
Bus	30/10/15		Weather showing cold - Situation unchanged. Letters received from DMS through ADMS meeting. Staff Sergt Davis - SM of No 3 Gen Field Ambulance to report to ADMS 11th Division for duty. Period to OC 31st Gen Field Ambulance for necessary action. ADMS visited at Office. Then up to ADMS & DMS, wounded other ranks sick 19; other divisions other ranks, sick 1, wounded 1. There are still a large number of drawn men for scabies, 50 during the past week.	
Bus	31/10/15		Weather wet, stormy & cold. Situation unchanged. Evacuations to ADMS & DMS - Evacuated to CCS Capt. Tilley 1/4 Gloster "D.A.H." & Captains Haigh & Whitehill 1/8 R Warwick Regt "Neuros debility" - 2nd Lt E.J. Chadwick 1/7 Royal Warwicks "Fracture of superior maxilla" other ranks sick 15, wounded 2. Other Divisions, other ranks, sick 2. Went to Bde 6, 3rd Echelon "sick wastage" 5 Officers, 12 other ranks, a decrease of 1 Officer & 25 men compared with last week.	

Lynn Colonel
A.D.M.S. 48 Divn

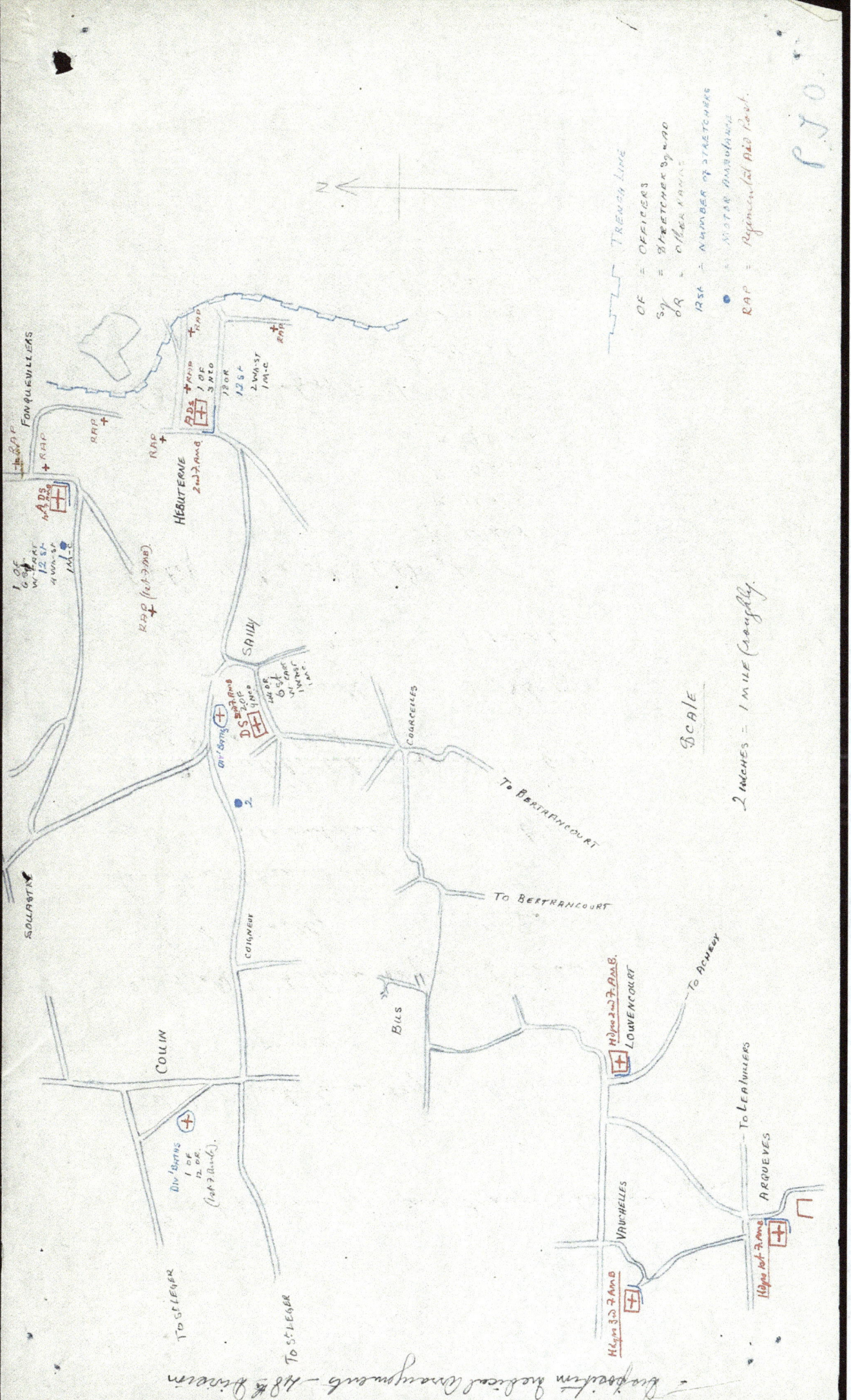

12/637

A.D.M.S. 48th Division.

No 2 copy

Vol VIII

Nov 1915

CONFIDENTIAL

War Diary
of
A.D.M.S. 18th Division
from Nov 1st 1915 to Nov 30 1915

WAR DIARY
or
INTELLIGENCE SUMMARY

Army Form C. 2118

(Erase heading not required.)

Place	Date	Hour	Summary of Events and Information	Remarks and references to Appendices
BUS	1-11-15	9.30 a.m.	Situation unchanged from that in 31st Oct 1915. Weather nice & still.	
		4.30 p.m.	Message to 3rd Army & 6th Bgd. Evacuated to C.C.S. Officers sick Lieut D.R. Washington O.R. sgnrs. (The Division O.R. at 3rd three 3R squaring(?)) one	App 1
BUS	2-11-15	8.30 a.m.	Situation unchanged - weather raining	
		1 p.m.	O.B.S.L. visited all Field Ambulances	
		4.30 p.m.	Message to 2nd 3rd Army & D.M.S. 4 Corps. Evacuated to C.C.S. Officers sick Capt J.L. TOMLINSON 1/7 Worcesters Dental caries. Lieut H.J. PULLMAN R.A.M.C. 13th Wiltshires Bronchitis. fifteen other Division Officers sick and one 2/Lieut J.H. McLEANE 10 R Inniskilling Fusiliers Appendicitis at each two.	App 2
			Lieut A.F. GRAVELLE R.Que (?) (TC) reports for duty & posted to 96 Floaters vice Capt R.N. CLARKE R.Que (TF) ordered hospital for duty with 19 C.C.S.	
BUS	3-11-15	8.30 a.m.	Situation unchanged - weather colder	
		12.30 p.m.	O.Bn.J. visited all Field Ambulances.	
		4.30 p.m.	Message to 3rd & 2nd Army - Evacuated to C.C.S. Officers sick one Capt H.R. MASON 1/4 R. Warwicks. Intolerable (?) O.R. sick twenty one of the Division O.R. sick too.	App 3
BUS	4/11/15	8.30 a.m.	Situation unchanged - weather seemy hot(?) cold	
		1 p.m.	O.B.S.L. inspected men of 5th R Warwicks for "D.S." at 7 O.N. 40 soldiers. Then visited Drawing Station at BAIZY.	
		4.30 p.m.	Message to 3rd & 2nd Army - Evacuated to C.C.S. Officers sick one Lieut N.H. GUETT 1/7 R Warwicks Dental Caries. O.R. sick eighty. (The Division O.R. sick too.	App 4

WAR DIARY
or
INTELLIGENCE SUMMARY.
(Erase heading not required.)

Army Form C. 2118.

Place	Date	Hour	Summary of Events and Information	Remarks and references to Appendices
BUZ	5/11/15	8.30 am	Situation unchanged. Weather raining hard	
"		4.30 am	Reconnaissance to 8th R.Ir F. & 2nd R.W.F. – Evacuated 6 O.O.B. Officers and 14 O.R. sick and 12 O.R. wounded. About the Division sick OR 184/am.	App 5
			9th O. & 6th Warwicks reported cases of measles of small pox (Warwicks in fourth 4 in Warwicks). One seen by D.A.D.M.S.; a case reported the proud of preventing taken to the G.O.C. his opp. mostly been taken.	
BUZ	6/11/15	8.30 am	Situation unchanged. Weather sunny but cold	
"		4.30 pm	ADMS attended lecture on the uses and constraints for the rescue helmets at Dig Casualty Clearing Station DOULLENS.	App 6
			Reconnaissance to 8th R.Ir F. & 2 R.Inf. – Evacuated to C.C.S. Officers sick nil & wounded nil. R.C. Lowe 1/6 R. Warwicks S&W. Sligt. OR sick thirty seven IR wounded two. The Division OR sick two.	
			Instructions issued regarding general sanitary measure to be taken during the coming winter to all Units. Brigades & Headquarters	
R U Z	7/11/15	8.30 am	Situation unchanged – weather fine	
"		4.30 pm	Reconnaissance to 8th R Ir F & 2 R.Inf. – Evacuated to C.C.S. Officers sick nil Capt. N. MURRAY 17 R. Warwicks wounded (accidental). OR sick twenty nine IR wounded one.	App 7
			Message to D.A.G. Rouen re light wreckage – Sick Officers, 149 men – an increase of 1 Officer 25 men compared with last week.	
BUZ	8/11/15	8.30 am	Situation unchanged. Weather fine	
		4.30 pm	O.M.G. visited A.R.I HEBUTERNE. VDS of SAILLY	

WAR DIARY
or
INTELLIGENCE SUMMARY.
(Erase heading not required.)

Army Form C. 2118

Place	Date	Hour	Summary of Events and Information	Remarks and references to Appendices
But	8/11/15	12.15pm	D.M.D.S. Confce called now O.B.M.	
"	"	2.30pm	Messages to D.M.D. + D.D.M.S.- Evacuated to C.C.S. Officer sick Major J.O. Summerhayes R.A.M.C. A.D.M.S. Office Bucks. R.Regt. Dental cases Revd H.J Deacon 1/4 Oxf J Bucks L.I. Southam Yeo Wounded on Captain G.E Tomkinson 1/1 Worcesters Shrapnel wound leg O.R. and twenty one O.R. wounded two other Brown O.R. sick one O.R. own own.	app 8. app 7
But	9/11/15	8.30 am	Situation unchanged. Weather warmer.	
"	"	4.30pm	Messages to D.M.D. + D.D.M.S. Evacuated to C.C.S. Officer sick one Lieut C.K Reed 1/4 Glouctrs Battalion O.R. sick twenty three O.R. wounded two other Division O.R. sick one	app 9
"	"		Civilian named LE FEVRE of Thievres suffering from Typhoid removed to AMIENS	
But	10/11/15	8.30am	Situation unchanged. Weather warmer.	
"	"	4.30pm	Messages to D.M.D. + D.M.D. + D.D.M.S.- Capt T.H Capr Two crates to C.C.S. Officer sick two Lieut E.F Chamberlain A.S.C for 3 Coy Train S.+ plce absence of Lieut F.H. Gullett 1/7.R Warwicks henorrhiditis O.R. sick twenty three O.R. wounded one.	app 10
But	11/11/15	8.30am	Situation unchanged. Weather rainy.	
"	"	4.30pm	R.D.M.S. attended Confce G.O.C. Messages to D.M.D + D.M.S. Evacuated to C.C.S. 8 Officers sick Lil 87 sick nineteen wounded two other Division O.R. sick two.	app 11
But	12/11/15	8.30am	Situation unchanged. Weather stormy	
"	"	11 am	A.D.M.S. attended D.D.M.S. + D.D.M.S. - Board Examination on one Sanitation R. Brook	
"	"	4.30pm	Messages to D.M.D + D.M.D. + D.D.M.S. Evacuated to C.C.S. Officer sick Rev C.G.B Groom Bradfe 1/7 Worcester O. Crile Shepmater Capt 2/Lt F.H Grisewood 1/4 Oxf + Bucks L.I. Kent O.R. sick O.R. Regt sick three. Oths Divn O.R. sick two	app 12

WAR DIARY
or
INTELLIGENCE SUMMARY.

(Erase heading not required.)

Army Form C. 2118

Instructions regarding War Diaries and Intelligence Summaries are contained in F. S. Regs., Part II. and the Staff Manual respectively. Title pages will be prepared in manuscript.

Place	Date	Hour	Summary of Events and Information	Remarks and references to Appendices
B.u.p	13.11.15	8.30am	Situation unchanged. Even thing stormy.	
		2.30-4pm	O/Rd. + all Med'l Officers attend J. Lecture on ambulances/Helmets delivered by Captn Hartley, Chemical Advisor to Army.	App 13.
		4.30pm	Arrived to Hd. Qrs. 8.Ind. Div. evacuated b C.C.S. Officers sick 1 OR sick and two OR wounded.	
B.u.p	14.11.15	8.30am	One OR Driver on sick list. Situation unchanged. Weather rainy.	
		12.30pm	O/Rd. visited all Field Ambulances.	
		4.30pm	Evacuated to 8.Ind.S.Hosp. - two evacuated to C.C.S. Officers sick, nil. OR sick fifteen, OR wounded - nil. The Division G.R. sick rate	App 14.
	15.11.15	8.30am	is very low. The beginning of the sick per Officers + Men & Officers + Men compared to last week. + Fallen all through. Improvement due to issue of (cold weather clothing) and falling asleep in night.	
			O/Rd. informed G.S.O.2. that he had come to his knowledge that certain units had not tube helmets to practise with any tube helmets to practise with.	
		4.30pm	Proceed to Hd. Qrs. 1.D. Vl.Vd. so evacuated to C.C.S. Officers sick one Capt H.W.H THORNE 1/4 R.Berks Inf. Hussars. OR sick thirty, OR wounded three. Other Divisions sick rate	App 15
B.u.p	16.11.15	8.30am	Situation unchanged. Weather cold + heavy fall of snow during night.	
		4.pm	O/Rd. visited 2nd Field Ambulance with reference to trench feet.	
		4.30pm	Proceed to Hd. Qrs. 1.D. Vl.Vd. Evacuated to C.C.S. Officers sick nil. OR sick twenty nine, OR wounded nil. Other Division Return me.	App 16
B.u.p	17.11.15	8.30am	Situation unchanged. Weather misty, snowy.	
		4.30pm	Evacuated Officers & men. Evacuated to C.C.S. Officers sick two, Majr R.H.H CREAR 1/8 Worcester Worcestershire - Capt B.W DUNCAN 5th R Sussex Duke Cairo. OR sick twenty one, OR wounded. OR wounded two. Further Officers evac. with afflicts. The prevalence of trench feet	App 17

1577   Wt.W10791/1773   500,000   1/15   D. D. & L.   A.D.S.S./Forms/C. 2118.

WAR DIARY
or
INTELLIGENCE SUMMARY.

(Erase heading not required.)

Army Form C. 2118

Place	Date	Hour	Summary of Events and Information	Remarks and references to Appendices
B.u.p	18/11/15	8.20 am	Situation unchanged. Weather milder, thawing.	
"	"	12.30 pm	O. Dud. visited all Field Ambulances	
"	"		A.D.M.S. Army called in re O.Ps.Md. Reference the delivery of Lectures by Capt Salt &c. Officer of the 1/4 Highland Instruction at Frévencourt.	
"	"	4.30 pm	Messages to A.md. of 8 Ind. Evacuated to C.C.S Officers nil O.R. sick thirty-three – sick nil OR sick ten wounded one	App 18.
B.u.p	19/11/15	8.30 am	Situation unchanged. Weather misty & damp	
"	"		Messages A.md. to 8 Ind. Div. Evacuated to C.C.S Officers and nil O.R. sick twenty two Other Divisions Officers nil. One of 6 Field Ambulance G 1/3 R. Irish Rifle Ambulance. O R sick three wounded one	App 19
B.u.D.	20/11/15	8.30 am	Situation unchanged. Weather cold	
"	"	1 pm	O.Dud. accompanied S.O.C. on an inspection of billet 17th Division, covering also an inspection of the 1st (Fd.), 2nd (Fd) Field Ambulances. Also visited dressing station at Forquevillers	
"	"	4.30 pm	Evacuated to C.C.S Officers sick nil OR sick under the Arms OR sick four	App 20
B.u.p	21/11/15	8.30 am	Situation unchanged. Weather relatively fine	
"	"	4.30 pm	Messages to A.md. & 8 Ind. Evacuated to C.C.S Officers sick nil OR sick eight wounded one Officers Divisions 7A sick eight	App 21
B.u.p	22/11/15	8.30 am	Weight yesterday message to ADS 205. Scene of Archangel – Officers three OR 152. Ambulance off OR compartnered with Situation unchanged. Weather bright fine	
"	"	12.30 pm	About visited 1st, 3rd (RM) Field Ambulances	
"	"	4.30 pm	Messages to A.md. & 8 Ind. Evacuated to C.C.S Officers sick one Capt. Powell R.S Dental	

WAR DIARY
or
INTELLIGENCE SUMMARY

Army Form C. 21

Place	Date	Hour	Summary of Events and Information	Remarks and references to Appendices
B.U.D	22/11/15		Casualties 1/h O.M. Bach R. Infy - wounded, hd D.R. sick twentyfour wounded sick three Division DR sick three. Lieut. Col. C Hoskins Commanding 8th Field Ambulance placed on sick list suffering from maltitis.	App. 22
B.U.D	23/11/15	8:30 am	Situation unchanged. Weather foggy - warm.	
		4:30 pm	Discharged to duty, 9 Ord. - Evacuated to C.C.S. Officers hd & other ranks sick twelve wounded nil. Other Divisions DR sick five.	App. 23
B.U.D	24/11/15	8:30 am	Situation unchanged. Weather milder.	
		11:30 pm	Average to duty & Ord. Evacuated to C.C.S. wounded one Major Knox T.M. 1/5 R Warwicks wounded. Other Ranks wounded eighteen wounded from Other Divisions DR sick two wounded two.	App. 24
B.U.D	25/11/15	8:30 am	Situation unchanged. Weather cold, sunny. (A.D.M.S. visits all 3 Field Ambulances)	
		11:30 am	Evacuated to C.C.S. Officers sick one 2/Lieut Bagshaw R.F.C. 1/5 R Warwicks Anothifian wounded hd D.R. sick seventeen wounded two Other Divisions Officers sick one Capt. BURROUGHS TS 13 R Irish Rifles. Rheumatism DR sick two.	App. 25
B.U.D	26/11/15	8:30 am	Situation unchanged. Weather cold but fine.	
		4 pm	A.D.M.S. called - saw O.D.M.S.	
		11:30 pm	Evacuated to C.C.S. Officers - Lieut BRYCE T.T. evacuated to C.C.S. Officers wounded two 2/Lieut BROGDEN M.C. 1/6 Cheshires wounded, 1/6 Gloster's wounded elsewhere. Other ranks sick seventeen. Other Divisions DR sick two wounded one Pres. Officer one.	App. 26

WAR DIARY or INTELLIGENCE SUMMARY

Army Form C. 2118

Place	Date	Hour	Summary of Events and Information	Remarks and references to Appendices
B.H.Q.	26/11/15		Capt IRVINE R.T. 1/6 Stratton wound about — (The above number appears necessary to bring to notify a.g and out & kept the former [illegible] day not) Information received & admitted to [illegible] Field Ambulance.	
B.H.Q.	27/11/15	8.30am	Situation unchanged. Weather cold but fine.	App 27
"	"	11.30pm	Message to O. & 1/D.H.Q — Evacuated to C.C.S. R.O. wounded nil O.R. wounded thirty one wounded two, Other Divisions O.R. sick one wounded nil. Stratton unchanged. Weather cold but fine.	
B.H.Q.	28/11/15	9.30am	One Case Anthrax occurred in H.R. Drake at A.O.T.11/15 — No 2596 Pte Walker. Investigation [illegible] A.C.C.B. stating [illegible] [illegible] pork & [illegible] fresh fish further.	App 28.
"	"	4.30pm	Message to A.H.L & L.D.M.S. — Evacuated to C.C.S. R.O. wounded nil, O.R. wounded 40. Other Divisions Head Col. D. [illegible] R.O. wounded [illegible] for [illegible] A.R.120 admitted R.M. [illegible] [illegible] fifty one O.R. compound fractured week. [illegible] unchanged. Weather cold but fine — Raining.	App 29.
B.H.Q.	29/11/15	9.30am	[illegible] sent 1 Off & 1 D Stat. — Evacuated twenty two wounded R.O's sick to two Other Divisions O.R. sick two wounded one a few prisoner farm.	
"	"	1.30pm	[illegible] to A.H.L & L.D.M.S — Evacuated to C.C.S. R.O. wounded O.R. sick twenty nine wounded 1	App 30
B.H.Q.	30/11/15	8.30am	Stratton unchanged. Weather mild. 3 Officers, 6 R.C.Rs & 97 Field Ambulance 30th Division joined 3 W(Sh) Field Ambulance for instructional purposes under [illegible] D. Stat.	
"	"	9.30pm	Message to A.H.L & L.D.M.S — Officers nil R.O. sick twenty three O.R. wounded nil Other Divisions O.R. sick one.	App 31
			The hrs of the Divisional area &c is identical in all particulars with that out with the Army Field & months.	

[signature]
COLONEL,
A.D.M.S. 43th (S.M.) DIVISION.

A.D.M.S
4th Division

Dec 1915

Dec 1915

CONFIDENTIAL F/54/1

With Henry

Asked 48th Division
from Dec 1st to 31st 1915.

Vol IX

WAR DIARY
or
INTELLIGENCE SUMMARY.

(Erase heading not required.)

Army Form C. 2118.

Instructions regarding War Diaries and Intelligence Summaries are contained in F. S. Regs., Part II. and the Staff Manual respectively. Title pages will be prepared in manuscript.

Place	Date	Hour	Summary of Events and Information	Remarks and references to Appendices
BHQ	1.12.15	8.30am	Situation unchanged from that of the month ending 30th Novr 1915.	
"	"	12.30pm	ADMS visited all three Field Ambulances	
"	"	4.30pm	Messages to DDS & DDMS – Evacuated to C.C.S. 8 Officers sick no Nest GAYTHORNE-HARDY 6 1/4 R. Berks Reserve OR sick twenty nine OR wounded. The Division OR sick three. Situation unchanged. Weather mild, raining.	App 1.
BHQ	2.2.15	8.30am	Message to Adml + DDMS - We evacuated to C.C.S. 8 Officers sick two Capt A.I.M. WRIGHT 1/4 Med Fd Coy R.S. T.F. by train 2nd Lieut PERKINS - DYSON 2nd Bn. 8 & R.F.C. Dental cases - Erysipelas OR sick twenty OR wounded one. The Division OR sick three. Situation unchanged. Weather raining.	App 2.
BHQ	3.12.16	8.30am	Message to Adml + DDMS - We evacuated to C.C.S. 8 Officers sick OR sick twenty OR wounded nil. Other Division OR sick three.	App 3.
"	"	4.30pm	Situation unchanged. Weather mild, raining.	
BHQ	4.12.15	8.30am	Message to Adml. D.D.M.S. - Evacuated to C.C.S. 8 Officers sick nil OR sick sixteen OR Wounded OR nil three. Situation unchanged. Weather could but not raining.	App 4.
BHQ	5.12.15	8.30am	ADMS visited 1/7 H.L.I. Wheelers at COURCELLES with reference to setting up permanent quarters for	
"	"	4.30pm	Message to Adml + D.D.M.S. - Evacuated to C.C.S. 8 Officers sick two Capt H.R. HOSKINS 1/7R. Warwick Scaled caries OR sick twenty 8R. wounded one. Other Division OR sick two.	App 5.
"	"	10pm	Message from High'd C.C.S. 29.21 D.W. LAWRENCE W. 1/7R Warwick suffering from Cerebro-Spinal Meningitis. Reference above sent Instructions read the DDI Warwick to regard as infected by available for another bayonet (Section 9). Reserve to be kept under Medical Supervision for a period of about fourteen days from M.149.	n.4./b.

1577 Wt. W10791/1773 500,000 1/15 D. D. & L. A.D.S.S./Forms/C. 2118.

Army Form C. 2118.

WAR DIARY
or
INTELLIGENCE SUMMARY.
(Erase heading not required.)

Instructions regarding War Diaries and Intelligence Summaries are contained in F. S. Regs., Part II and the Staff Manual respectively. Title pages will be prepared in manuscript.

Place	Date	Hour	Summary of Events and Information	Remarks and references to Appendices
Bulz	6.12.15	8.30 am	Situation unchanged. Weather mild, sunny	
		3.45 pm	ADMS visited all three Field Ambulances. He went for review amongst the Officers men of 4/6th Warwicks by the Divl Med Mobile Laboratory. Lieut MacClure. La proved negative	App 7
		4.30 pm	Weary got to C.C.S. Officers sick one Lieut DE RIDDELL 1/5 R Warwick. Debility ORsick Morlyport	
Bulz	9.12.15	8.30 am	Situation unchanged - Weather mild, sunny	
		1.30 pm	Weary got to Hd 1 S Myd - D.O evacuated to C.C.S. Officers sick one Lieut H.B. KING 1/5 Gloucester Dental Caries OR sick twenty two ORs Evacuated to Field Amb [illegible]	App 8
Bulz	8.12.15	8.30 am	Situation unchanged. Weather mild	
		3 pm	ADMS visited 2nd (EY) Field Ambulance with reference Levny transport for R. Hqrs - 5th number fully Ill Officers sick R. Infs - one ready for 3 weeks leave	
		4.30 pm	Weary got to Hqrs DADMS to a centre to C.C.S. M[illegible] one 2/Lieut UTTWHATT 1/5 R Warwick Sprd OR sick nine ORs Evacuated to ambulance	App 9
Bulz	9.12.15	8.30 am	Situation unchanged. Weather mild, rainy	
		11.30 pm	Weary got to Hq Hqrmd - Evacuated to C.C.S. M[illegible] one 2/Lieut C.V NEAVE Bucks BM Dental Caries OR sick nineteen [illegible] ambulance one Gen Duncan Misseigeur[?] on Lieut F.E BEHRINS 16th Warwickstars Shrapnel wound by OR sick three wounds fine	App 10
Bulz	10.12.15	8.30 am	Situation unchanged. Sick a/Musling rainy	
		12.45 pm	ADMS visited Clearing Station FONQUEVILLERS; 1/5 R Warwicks BAYENCOURT, Evacuating latem Sailly.	
		3.15 pm	Weary from Offr 6 R Inf Lab Laboratory for with reference to the Camp Cirubo Spinal Menyephorus from the	App 11

WAR DIARY
or
INTELLIGENCE SUMMARY.
(Erase heading not required.)

Army Form C. 2118.

Place	Date	Hour	Summary of Events and Information	Remarks and references to Appendices
BUF	10/2/15		17 R Cannots sent to Highland C.C.S on 8 wick) — Result of examination J.C.S to sent to son	
			2010 Adams and 2451 Gillingham sent as sent (wounds) to neighbour	App 12
		2.25 pm	Message from Buff & later of all positive cases in C.S.M & P and 1st Highland C.C.S	
		4.30 pm	Message to Buff & 3rd DMS (vacated) to C.C.S Officers & NC 1 R sick Twenty OR wounded	App 13
		8.30 am	Situation unchanged. Weather fine, raining	
"	11/2/15	4.30 pm	Message to Buff Board. Vacinated C.C.S Officers nil and OR sick twenty. OR wounded	App 14
			OR sick one	
BUF	12/2/15	9.30 am	Situation unchanged. Weather colder —	
		4.30 pm	Message to Buff 1 & Buff. Vacinated to Officers B O.C.S Officers sent nil sick twenty three OR	App 15
			wounded one. Other Division OR wounded	
			Message sent meeting N O of Base Officers from TP.160. Arrivions of 11 other ranks employed with	
BUF	13/2/15	2.30 am	Situation unchanged. Weather cold	
			Message to Buff's Field Vaccination C.C.S Officers nil Lieut W.H. HAYLOR 1/6	App 16
			Gordon Highland Lieut F. PROTER 1/6 Gordon Dental Corps. Capt H.C.R SEXTON 1/6 Gordon sent to	
			cover Buff and W.K. McCLINTOCK 1/6 R Buffs 692 S. O.R. sick twenty one and OR wounds	
			nil sick two	
			OR nil wounded all Field Ambulances	
			Message from Highland C.C.S - no D1 Pt. Lavin admitter with Carbo geunicheough	
			The usual routine messages & directions sent by Officer Buff concerned	
BUF	14/2/15	8.30 am	Situation unchanged. Weather cold but fine.	
		4.30 pm	Message to Buff & Buff. Vacinated & C.C.S Officers nil and OR sick fourteen OR wounded two	App 17

WAR DIARY
or
INTELLIGENCE SUMMARY.

(Erase heading not required.)

Army Form C. 2118.

Instructions regarding War Diaries and Intelligence Summaries are contained in F. S. Regs., Part II. and the Staff Manual respectively. Title pages will be prepared in manuscript.

Place	Date	Hour	Summary of Events and Information	Remarks and references to Appendices
B.U.P.	15/12/15	8.30 a.m.	Situation unchanged. Weather cold, wet.	
"	"	12 noon	A.D.M.S. visited Advanced Dressing Station, R&B UTERNE, Dressing Station at A&BUTERNE.	
			RAVENCOURT:	
"	"	1.30 p.m.	Lieut. BATCHAM M.M.S. 96 OR. arrived from 30th Division. He attached to 2nd (the) Field Ambulance for instruction.	
"	"	1.30 p.m.	Arrangements made to A.D.M.S. Evacuated to C.C.S. Officers sick one, Lieut. F.W. BANTOR R.F.A. No. 3 Coy. 13th Train Somersham Officers wounded one, Lieut. A.B.D. VM & G Steward R.S. High Vr Royal Warwicks O.R. sick nine.	App 18
R.M.B	16/12/15	8.30 a.m.	Situation unchanged. Weather changeable.	
"	"	1/p.m.	A.D.M.S. visited all three Field Ambulances.	
"	"	4.30 p.m.	Arrangements to A.D.M.S. D.D.M.S. Officers sick his O.R. sick eleven, O.R. wounded one. Other Divisions O.R. sick one.	App 19
B.U.P	17/12/15	8.30 a.m.	Situation unchanged. Weather rainy.	
"	"	4.30 p.m.	Arrangements to Adjut. & D.D.M.L. Evacuated to C.C.S. Officers sick three Lieut. R.J.B. & 2nd Y.&R. Berks. Dental Carries Cap G.B. ELLIOT 16 Scottish Dental Carrie Lieut. A.T.E. HARBARD Connaught Rangers attd. No. 86 French Mortar Bty. Sciatica O.R. sick eighteen O.R. wounded two	App 20
B.U.P	18/12/15	8.30 a.m.	Situation unchanged. Weather milder, changeable.	
"	"	4.30 p.m.	Arrangements to Adjut. & D.D.M.L. Evacuated to C.C.S. Officers sick one Major R.L. ROWSEE 1/6 Offers & Doctors Dental Carries O.R. sick fifteen.	App 21
B.U.P	19/12/15	8.30 a.m.	Situation unchanged. Weather sunny & cold.	
"	"	1 p.m.	A.D.M.S. attends Conference Chief 3rd Army	

Army Form C. 2118.

WAR DIARY
or
INTELLIGENCE SUMMARY.

(Erase heading not required.)

Place	Date	Hour	Summary of Events and Information	Remarks and references to Appendices
13 M.B	19.12.15	4.30 pm	Message to Brig. D. Maj. - Evacuated to C.C.S. Mericourt two Capt. I.R. CALDICOTT 1/7 R. Warwick. Much fever. Major O.B.W. DOKE 1/7 Worcesters. Dental Caries 1/7 Wrecester Rented. Caries of ariel/tubes OR wounded two other Divisional OR sick one. Weekly message to a & Base - next average officers 11 OR 101. Average of officers but because of 59 OR compare that week.	App 22
B.M.B.	20.12.15	8.30 am	Situation unchanged. Weather cold. Off it's have been made during last two months to obtain fluid for Divisional Laundry, three barges to obtain in the Divisional area for washing purposes, of preceding men wanting their clothes, but this has been negatived, no washing being done by the men, thro' oldness themselves.	
		4.30 pm	Evacuated sick message to ADJ + D Maj - Evacuated to C.C.S. officers sick nil OR sick eighteen one Divisional OR sick two	App 23
B.M.B	21.12.15	8.30 am	Situation unchanged. Weather cold & raining. Two more men/contact 1/4 Oxf.'s & Bucks. & Infy. notified by Bge. & should out an Carriers C.B.M. Thoroo mated.	
		4.30 pm	A.D.M.S (visited) #3 Dy B.F. A.Bye. LA HAIE FARM + 85 Burenhs at BAYENCOURT.	
B M B	22.12.15	8.30 am	Message to ADJ + D Maj - Evacuated to C.C.S. Officers sick nil OR sick twelve & other Divisional OR sick two OR wounded one.	App 24
		4.30 pm	Situation unchanged. Weather raining.	
			Message to ADJ + D Maj. Evacuated mil OR sick fifteen - no Divisional OR sick three.	App 25
B M B	23.12.15	8.30 am	Situation unchanged. Weather raining.	

WAR DIARY
or
INTELLIGENCE SUMMARY.
(Erase heading not required.)

Army Form C. 2118.

Instructions regarding War Diaries and Intelligence Summaries are contained in F. S. Regs., Part II. and the Staff Manual respectively. Title pages will be prepared in manuscript.

Place	Date	Hour	Summary of Events and Information	Remarks and references to Appendices
B.u.B.	23/12/15	1 pm	O i/c M/ visited all Field Ambulances.	
"	"	1.30 pm	Messages to D.M.L. & D.Dy.S. Evacuated to C.C.S. Officers sick one Lieut P.E. ROBINSON 15R Warwicks various kinds TR sick thirteen TR wounded three on the Division TR sick two	App 26
B.u.B.	24/12/15	8.30 am	Situation unchanged. Weather rainy	
"	"	9.30 pm	Messages to D.M.L. & D.Dy.S. Evacuated to C.C.S. Officers sick nil TR sick five OR wounded three on the Division TR sick four	App 27
B.u.B.	25/12/15	8.30 am	Situation unchanged. Weather rainy changeable.	
"	"	9.30 pm	Messages to D.M.L. & D.Dy.S. Evac. on diem to C.C.S. Officers sick at one - Capt W. Lewis V/Staffs Insomnia TR sick six on the Division TR sick two	App 28
B.u.B.	26/12/15	8.30 am	Situation unchanged. Weather mild, sunny	
"	"	4.30 pm	Messages to D.M.L. & D.Dy.S. Evacuated to C.C.S. Brigade sick nil TR sick four OR wounded eight on the Division OR sick two. Weather mild, sick nicely. Wicklow po 86 Case. Officers 2 OR 75. above App 26 OR wounded subrack. Situation unchanged. Weather changeable	App 29
"	27/12/15	8.30 am		
"	"	10 am	O i/c M/ held Medical Board at BAYENCOURT to examine every battalion of 143rd Infy Bgd for selecting to Permanent Base & no case may be under above VII Corps.	
"	"	4.30 pm	Messages to D.M.L. & D.Dy.S. Evacuated to C.C.S. Officers sick one Lieut KING H.J. 1/5 Glosters Battalion (above) TR sick seventeen OR wounded two on the Division TR sick two	App 30
B.u.B.	28/12/15	9.30 am	Situation unchanged. Weather mild.	
"	"	10 am	O i/c M/ examined men of 144 Infy B.D. & apply for Permanent Base.	
"	"	1 pm	O i/c M/ visited baths at COCUN	
"	"	4.30 pm	Messages to D.M.L. & D.Dy.S. Evacuated to C.C.S. Officers sick nil TR sick nine OR wounded.	App 31

1577 Wt.W10791/1773 500,000 1/15 D. D. & L. A.D.S.S./Forms/C. 2118.

WAR DIARY
or
INTELLIGENCE SUMMARY.
(Erase heading not required.)

Army Form C. 2118.

Instructions regarding War Diaries and Intelligence Summaries are contained in F. S. Regs., Part II. and the Staff Manual respectively. Title pages will be prepared in manuscript.

Place	Date	Hour	Summary of Events and Information	Remarks and references to Appendices
B.u.B	28/12/15	pre a.m	Other Formations TR sick Lieut G. AITCHIM R.F.C. 88 2/7 Fr. alun Dub.	
B.u.B	29.12.15	8.30 am	Situation unchanged. Weather changeable.	
"	"	11.30 am	G Genl I.D.M. official found ament 145 Infy Bgde known for permanent Base	
"	"	5 p.m	A Diet visited No 165 Stratm Count + attn [illegible] Ambulance	
"	"	11.30 p.m	Evacuees to Divl D.R.M. was in a [later] to C.C.S. Officers sick nil OR sick nine	App 32
B.u.B	30.12.15	8.30 am	Situation unchanged. Weather mild.	
"	"	11 a.m	A Divl examined men of other corps of the Division for permanent Base	
"	"	11.30 p.m	Evacuees to Divl D.R.M. was in a [later] to C.C.S. Officers sick an Capt G.E. ELLIOTT 1/6 Staffs	App 33
"	"		O.R. sick twenty TR wounded three	
"	31.12.15	8.30 am	Situation unchanged. Weather mild, raining.	
"	"	11.30 p.m	Evacuees to C.C.S. Officers sick nil OR sick ten OR wounded five	App 34
"	"		Divisional Area same as in November 1915, with 27th Division on our left + 2. Div. on our right.	

[signature] Colonel,
A.D.M.S. 48th (S.M.) DIVISION.

A.D.M.S. 48th Div.

Jan / Vol XI

F/54/2.

Jan. 1916.

CONFIDENTIAL

WAR DIARY
OF
ADMS 48th DIVISION
FROM 1-1-16 to 31-1-16.

Army Form C. 2118.

WAR DIARY
or
INTELLIGENCE SUMMARY.
(Erase heading not required.)

Instructions regarding War Diaries and Intelligence Summaries are contained in F. S. Regs., Part II. and the Staff Manual respectively. Title pages will be prepared in manuscript.

Place	Date	Hour	Summary of Events and Information	Remarks and references to Appendices
BUZ	1.1.16	8.30am	Situation unchanged. Learn that on 31.12.15, owing to army	
		4.30pm	messages to 3rd & 5th Dist. Evacuated to C.C.S. Officers sick Nil. OR sick Ten wounded four	App 1.
BUZ	2.1.16	8.30am	Situation unchanged. Weather changeable	
		12 noon	A.D.M.S. attended conference 3rd & 2nd Army	
		4.30pm	Messages to 3rd & 5th Dist - Evacuated to C.C.S. Officers sick nil OR sick Thirteen OR wounded five Other admissions OR sick one	App 2
		5.25pm	Message from Highland C.C.S. - 2468 Pte John 5735 5/17 Worcesters confirmed Czecho-Speud Meningitis - The R.M.O. informed. The O/c. 8 Mobile Laboratory wired to make a examine the contacts - Message to 3rd/2nd Army, 2nd Div. 5th Div. also informing them.	App 3
			Weekly average to S.A.G. Base of Sick knowledge officers 2.87.96 a nicrew of 21.OR. Corps and Staff locat	
BUZ	3.1.16	8.30am	Situation unchanged. Weather stormy	
		4.30pm	Messages to 3rd & 5rd Dist - Evacuated to C.C.S. Officers sick two Lieut B.B.B.Brooks 4 Oxf & Bucks L.I. infty Scabies. Capt L.Kerwood 48 Worcesters Dental Caries OR sick twenty OR wounded two	App 4.
			The 13th (W.) Field Ambulance took over charge of A.D.S. HEBUTERNE & D.A.S. SAILLY from the 12th (W.) Field Ambulance	
BUZ	4.1.16	8.30am	Situation unchanged. Weather rainy	
		3pm	A.D.M.S. visited all three Field Ambulances	
		4.30pm	Messages 3rd Div. & 5th Div. - Evacuated to C.C.S. Officers sick nil Major J.E. Dixon 16th Warwicks incoming OR sick nine OR wounded one	App 5

WAR DIARY or INTELLIGENCE SUMMARY.

Army Form C. 2118.

(Erase heading not required.)

Instructions regarding War Diaries and Intelligence Summaries are contained in F.S. Regs., Part II and the Staff Manual respectively. Title pages will be prepared in manuscript.

Place	Date	Hour	Summary of Events and Information	Remarks and references to Appendices
B.U.D.	5.1.16	8.30am	Situation unchanged. Weather mild.	
		1pm	ODM.I. went with ADOMS to attend funeral of an in this connection officers not reported? Demanded rest station - afterwards visited Field Ambulance.	
"		4.30pm	Evacuated to 31st & 38rd - Evacuated to C.C.S. Officers sick two Lieut J.G. FUSSELL 1/8 R.Warwicks Dental Caries. Lieut G.M. HUBBARD 1/8 R.Warwicks Dental Caries. OR sick nineteen OR wounded two. Other formations officers sick one - of Lieut A.P. PRICE-JONES R2 attached 7 Corps S'gnals Shop to tender.	App 6.
R.U.B.	6.1.16	8.00am	Lieut H.H. FAIRFAX R.A.M.C. (T.C.) reported for duty 4.1.16 Posted to 1/3rd (South Midland) Field Ambulance. Situation unchanged. Weather rainy.	App 7.
"	"	4.30pm	Evacuated to C.C.S. Officers sick Nil OR sick thirteen OR wounded four.	
B.U.D.	7.1.16	8.30am	Situation unchanged. Weather raining. Nautieno.	
"	"	11.30pm	Evacuated 2nd & 3rd Mid - Evacuated to C.C.S. Officers sick one Capt HELM. S. Chaplain 1/5 Glosters Dental Caries. OR sick sixteen OR wounded four.	App 8.
B.U.B.	8.1.16	8.30am	Situation unchanged. Weather milder.	
"	"		Received a report from O.C. 1st (S.M.) Field Ambulance of the work of the Dental Department that Ambulance since 1st inst, when it was opened. A large amount of various kinds of Dental work has been done & the Department promises to be great success. It has only been necessary to evacuate 4 of the worst cases to the C.C.S., whereas for many weeks past this has averaged 4 p.b.week.	a
"	"	11.30pm	Evacuated 2nd & 3rd Mid - Evacuated 6 C.C.S. Officers sick two Major H.E. PITMAN 1/6 R.Warwicks Pyorrhea Lieut DAVIES-MASON 3rd (S.M.) R.F.A. 2nd Warwick B.D. Pyorrhea OR sick fourteen OR wounded	App 9.

1577 Wt. W10791/1773 500,000 1/15 D.D. & L. A.D.S.S./Forms/C 2118.

WAR DIARY
or
INTELLIGENCE SUMMARY.
(Erase heading not required.)

Army Form C. 2118.

Instructions regarding War Diaries and Intelligence Summaries are contained in F. S. Regs., Part II. and the Staff Manual respectively. Title pages will be prepared in manuscript.

Place	Date	Hour	Summary of Events and Information	Remarks and references to Appendices
BUS	9.1.16	8.30 am	Situation unchanged. Weather mild, snowy.	
"		12.30 pm	O.D.Md. visits B. & the C.O.W., also all three Field Ambulances	
"		4.30 pm	Messages to D.Md. 7 Div. Evacuated to C.C.S. Officers sick two Lieut. L.H. NEVILLE 1/8 Worcesters & Symits Knee Major 7 R. HEDGES 1/8 R. Berks Quinsy. Three O.R. sick, twenty O.R. wounded. Other formations O.R. sick one.	App/o 10.
"			Weekly message rect. war office to ADMS. Officers sick 10. wounded nil. O.R. sick 111 wounded 12. (9. being an increase of 8 offrs. sick & 15 O.R. sick & 3 wounded) & last week.	
BUS	10.1.16	8.30 am	Situation unchanged. Weather variable.	
"		11.30 am	A visit with the KMed. Bishop of Birmingham visits all three Field Ambulances	
"		4.30 am	Messages to D.Md. 7 Div.Md. - Evacuated to C.C.S. Officers sick nil. O.R. wounded one.	App/o 11.
"		11 am	O.Md. VII Corps called & saw ADMed.	
BUS	11.1.16	9.30 am	Situation unchanged. Weather changeable.	
"		1.00 pm	Messages to 7 Div & D.Md. - Evacuated to C.C.S. Officers sick nil O.R. sick eleven O.R. wounded eleven.	App/o 12.
BUS	12.1.16	8.30 am	Situation unchanged. Weather variable.	
"		3.30 pm	O. Md visits Advanced dressing Station for advanced views.	
"			Lieut F.N. WALSH RAMC(T.F.) reported for duty. Posted to charge of 1/8 R.Warwicks	
"		4.30 pm	Evacuated to C.C.S. Officers sick one Capt R.W. MARSHALL 1/8 Gloster Trench feet. O.R. sick nine wounded O.R. one.	App/o 13.
BUS	13.1.16	8.30 am	Situation unchanged. Weather stormy	
"		4.30 pm	Messages to D.Md. & 7 D.Md. Evacuated to C.C.S. Officers sick nil. O.R. sick fourteen O.R. wounded one.	App/o 14.

WAR DIARY
or
INTELLIGENCE SUMMARY

Army Form C. 2118.

(Erase heading not required.)

Place	Date	Hour	Summary of Events and Information	Remarks and references to Appendices
B.u.8	14/1/16	8.30am	Situation unchanged. Weather cold & sunny	
"	"	4.30pm	Messages to 2nd & 3rd Bns - Evacuated to C.C.S. Officers nil. O.R. sick eleven. O.R. wounded three. Other ranks sick one.	App 15
"	"		Situation unchanged. Weather raining.	
B.u.8	15/1/16	8.30am	A Duel with C.R.E. visited Fonquevillers to fix site upon which shelter for wounded one to be constructed.	
"	"	12.15pm	Messages to 2nd & 3rd Bns - Officers sick nil. O.R. sick eighteen. O.R. wounded one. Other Formations Officers wounded three (Capt R. Erskine 7th R.F.C., 2nd Lieut J. Squires R.F.C. bullet wound leg, 2nd Lieut J.M. Herring 58sqd R.F.C. bullet wound trunk, 2nd Lieut R.P. Denn 58sqd R.F.C. bullet wound thigh) O.R. sick one.	App 16
"	"	4.30pm		
B.u.8	16/1/16	8.30am	Situation unchanged. Weather raining.	
"	"	4.30pm	Messages to 2nd & 3rd Bns - Evacuated to C.C.S. Officers sick one, 2/Lieut R.V. Newbury 1st R.Bucks R.F.S Suspected Diphtheria. O.R. sick nine.	App 17
"	"		Weekly average want to A.D.S. are Officers two O.R. 101. Officers wounded wounded nil, OR sick 83 wounded 1.S. being hd. Offs - 2.8 O.R. sick less compared with last week.	
"	"		A 2nd proceeds on leave to England.	
B.u.8	17/1/16	8.30am	Situation unchanged. Weather rainy.	
"	"	11.30am	2nd Mdl. interviewed the O.C.'s of the O/c 1st & 2nd Bn R. Buck R. Infy with reference to fixing site for a "Tube" Dug-out in the trenches on the extreme right of the line.	
"	"	4.30pm	I.S. Med (called) saw 2nd Mdl.	
			Messages to 2nd & 3rd Bns - Evacuated to C.C.S. Officers sick nil. O.R. sick twenty-two. OR. wounded one. Other Formations O.R. sick one.	App 18

Army Form C. 2118.

WAR DIARY
or
INTELLIGENCE SUMMARY.

Army Form C. 2118.

Instructions regarding War Diaries and Intelligence Summaries are contained in F. S. Regs., Part II. and the Staff Manual respectively. Title pages will be prepared in manuscript.

(Erase heading not required.)

Place	Date	Hour	Summary of Events and Information	Remarks and references to Appendices
B.H.Q	18.1.16	8.30am	Situation unchanged. Weather rainy	
"	"	12.30pm	A.D.M.S visited all three Fd. Ambulances.	
"	"	4.30pm	Messages to D.M.S & D.D.M.S - Evacuated to C.C.S. Officers nil, OR sick fourteen. O.R. wounded two. Other formations OR sick one.	App 19
"	"		Lieut C. Andrew-Jones RAMC (TC) reported for duty & posted to N.1 (FA) Fld Amb. Capt. H. E. McCready RAMC (TF) of N.1 Unit will be appointed to medical chge of 45th Renwick & Capt R. Kennon RAMC (TC) on relief by Capt McCready proceeds to join N.4 C.C.S. Situation unchanged. Weather rainy.	
B.H.Q.	19.1.16	8.30am	Messages to DMS & DDMS - Evacuated to CCS Officers nil Nil Reich fourteen. Other formations OR sick three.	App 20
"	"	2.30pm	Situation unchanged. Weather mild sunny	
B.H.Q	20.1.16	8.30am	Messages to DMS & DDMS - Evacuated to CCS Officers nil OR sick thirteen. Other formations OR sick one.	App 21
"	"	11.30pm	Situation unchanged. Weather mild sunny	
B.H.Q	21.1.16	8.30am	A.D.M.S with A.Dir 7 & Worcesters visited Renwick "Section 5" in extreme right line to choose site for tube Ary unit as Regimental Aid post.	
"	"	2pm	Messages to DMS & DDMS - Evacuated to CCS Officers nil Capt P.D.Bennett 1/5 R. Wenwick. superseded Oftenbirats OR sick thirteen OR wounded one.	App 22
"	"	4.30pm	Messages from A.Dir C. 8pm16 NA 2930 Clark 1/9 Worcesters. Cardio Spinal hemoptysis, to W/c R.U.D. informs. Situation unchanged. Weather mild	App 22a
B.H.Q	22.1.16	8.30pm	Messages to DMS & DDMS - Evacuated to CCS Officers nil OR sick ten. Other formations OR sick two.	App 23

WAR DIARY
or
INTELLIGENCE SUMMARY.

(Erase heading not required.)

Army Form C. 2118.

Place	Date	Hour	Summary of Events and Information	Remarks and references to Appendices
B.U.S.	23/1/16	8.30am	Situation unchanged. Weather rainy. Arrangements have been made by "Q" to send Divisional soiled underclothing to Paris, the washed Articles, first to be handed by Sanitary Section A.D. depot, to give a man a complete change of underclothing once every 17 days.	
"	"	4.30pm	Messages to D.M.S. & D.D.M.S. re casualties. C.C.S officers sick twenty five. O.R. wounded two.	App. 24.
			Weekly wastage. S.D. of Base. Officers sick one. O.R. sick 109 - O.R. wounded 8 being a decrease of 1 Officer but increase of 24 O.R. comp'd with last week.	
B.U.S	24/1/16	8.30am	Situation unchanged. Weather rainy.	
			D.D.M.S. had further conferences with "Q" re sending & washing to Paris & distribution of clean clothes to the men.	
"	"	1.30pm	D.D.M.S. again visited Qt Section of line with reference to protection of above mentioned dugout.	
B.U.S	"	4.30pm	Messages to D.M.S. & D.D.M.S - re casualties. C.C.S. officers sick two. Lieut E.L. BIRD. 1/4 Glosters trench fever Septic foot. O.R. sick twenty one. O.R. wounded two.	App. 25.
B.U.S	25/1/16	8.30am	Situation unchanged. Weather mild & sunny.	
"	"	4.30pm	Messages to D.M.S. & D.D.M.S. - re casualties. C.C.S. officers sick fifteen. O.R. wounded three.	App. 26
B.U.S	26/1/16	8.30am	Situation unchanged. Weather rainy.	
"	"	1 pm	D.D.M.S. attended conference on "Gas" delivered by Colonel A. BRIGER 2d Army. D.D.M.S. 4 Corps present.	
			A.D.M.S. returned from leave.	
"	"	4.30pm	Messages to D.M.S. & D.D.M.S - Re casualties. C.C.S. officers sick one. Lieut G.R. BRECKNOCK 1/6 Royal	App. 27.

WAR DIARY or INTELLIGENCE SUMMARY.

Army Form C. 2118.

Place	Date	Hour	Summary of Events and Information	Remarks and references to Appendices
But	27.1.16	8.30am	Warwicks Battalion relieved. OR sick eleven OR wounded two one Other Formation 78 eight	appx
		11.30am	Situation unchanged. Weather rainy	
			Adjut & D.A.D.M.S. attended lecture by Lt Col Stagnell RAMC 10th Field Ambulance, at Divisional HQ on "Experiences of Field Ambulance work in heavy fighting".	
		5.30pm	Moved to Sheet & D.D.M.S. Evacuated to C.C.S. Officers sick nil OR sick twenty two OR wounded one	app 28
		7.30pm	Alarm of "gas" was given. Later, this turned out the false. no gas having been used.	
But	28.1.16	8.30am	Situation unchanged. Weather variable.	
		4.30pm	In charge to Sheet & D.A.D. Evacuated to C.C.S. Officers sick one Lt Col E.P.Davis DSO Bucks B.S Punctured clavicle. OR sick ten OR wounded three Other Formations OR wounded one	app 29
But	29.1.16	9.30am	Situation unchanged. Weather mild, sunny	
			In anticipation of the evacuation of ARQUEVES by the Division, the A.D.M.S. with D.A.D.S. Vet.S. and O.C. 1/1st (H.C.) Field Ambulance as (usual) A.U.T.H.I.E to choose suitable buildings for that ambulance.	
		1.15pm	In charge to Sheet & D.D.M.S. Evacuated to C.C.S. Officers sick one 2/Lieut G.A. HOBBARD 1/8 R Warwick Rgt Neurasthenia OR sick ten OR wounded three Other Formations OR sick one	app 30
But	30.1.16	8.30am	Situation unchanged. Weather windy, rainy	
		4.30pm	In charge to Sheet & D.A.D. Evacuated to C.C.S. Officers sick nil OR sick sixteen OR wounded nil from Other Formation OR sick one	app 31
But	31.1.16	9am	Situation unchanged. Weather as 30th July	

Weekly Return appx 32. Four Officers sick 2 OR sick 105 OR wounded 3, 18 days in charge, 14 Officers sick, and because 2 OR sick if an index rate of 13 OR's wounded per week.

Army Form C. 2118.

WAR DIARY
or
INTELLIGENCE SUMMARY.

(Erase heading not required.)

Instructions regarding War Diaries and Intelligence Summaries are contained in F. S. Regs., Part II. and the Staff Manual respectively. Title pages will be prepared in manuscript.

Place	Date	Hour	Summary of Events and Information	Remarks and references to Appendices
B.H.Q.	31/1/16	2.45pm	D.D.M.S. called. Saw Stafford.	
		3.30pm	A.D.M.S visited H.Q. 1/1/2 & 1/3r) Field Ambulances	
		4.30pm	Arranges to stand by 1st & 2nd. - Evacuated to C.C.S. Officers and men kept to Summer HAYES (R.E.) and 2 others the Mons-Stuart D. Roftentwellen D.A. & 1 twenty aux. D.T. wounded from --- The formation was now	App/32
			The situation. The Division on matters from head of had on North. The 37th Division being on the left. 6th & 7th Division on the Right	

[signature]
COLONEL,
A.D.M.S. 46th (S.M.) DIVISION.

Feb 1916

A.O.M.S. 48ᵗʰ (S. Mᵇ. Div)

CONFIDENTIAL

War Diary
of
A.9.hd. 8th Division
from 1st Feby 1916 to 29th Feby 1916.

Vol XI

Army Form C. 2118.

WAR DIARY
or
INTELLIGENCE SUMMARY.
(Erase heading not required.)

Instructions regarding War Diaries and Intelligence Summaries are contained in F. S. Regs., Part II. and the Staff Manual respectively. Title pages will be prepared in manuscript.

Place	Date	Hour	Summary of Events and Information	Remarks and references to Appendices
Bu 6	1.2.16	8.30 a.m.	Situation unaltered. Snowfall of 30.1.16. Weather cold, dry. ADMS issued orders for the closing of the 1st (Glas) Field Ambulance at BERTRANCOURT prior to it's being moved to BERTRANCOURT. Also for an Officer from that Ambulance to proceed to No 11 Field Ambulance at that place to enquire into system of advanced posts & the personnel & equipment kept therein.	App 1
"	"	4.30 p.m.	Evacuated to 9 Fd. & 8 Fd. - Evacuated to CCS. Officers nil, OR sick fifteen one 2/Lieut R.B.O'Hara 1/7 R Warwick Bronchitis. OR sick fifteen see Other Formations Return Ann.	
Bu 2	2.2.16	8.30 a.m.	Situation unchanged. Weather cold. Evacuees from Highland C.C.S. - 149 Ptc 104 A 1/5th Lincs po artie Cerebro-Spinal Meningitis. Cultures separated & examined by OC 3rd Lab. Laboratory	App 2
"	"	4.30 p.m.	Evacuated to 9 Fd. & 8 Fd. - Evacuated to CCS. Officers nil, one efficient ADR 1/6 Gordon Bomb wound leg. OR sick seven OR wounded five. see Other formations OR sick seven. A.DMS having in Qr. arrangement for 36 DM (2nd Rhs) Field Ambulance to be attached to the various Bns in the trenches of the 81 Brigade, these men proceeded to HEBUTERNE for 12 days, when they will be replaced by another party for 12 days.	App 3
Bu 7	3.2.16	2.30 a.m.	Situation unchanged. Weather milder, snowy. O.C. 1/1st (Gl.) Field Ambulance called & drew ADMS's attention to the taking over from No 11 Field Ambulance (H Division).	
"	"	11.30 p.m.	Evacuees to 9 Fd. & 8 Fd. Evacuated to CCS Officers nil, OR sick fifteen. OR wounded nil. Other formations OR sick one.	App 4

1577 Wt. W10791/1773 500,000 1/15 D. D. & L. A.D.S.S./Forms/C. 2118.

Army Form C. 2118.

WAR DIARY
or
INTELLIGENCE SUMMARY.
(Erase heading not required.)

Instructions regarding War Diaries and Intelligence Summaries are contained in F. S. Regs., Part II. and the Staff Manual respectively. Title pages will be prepared in manuscript.

Place	Date	Hour	Summary of Events and Information	Remarks and references to Appendices
Bus	4.2.16	8.30 a.m.	Situation unchanged. Weather mild, sunny.	
"	"	4.30 p.m.	Reports to D.M.S. & D.D.M.S. Evacuated to C.C.S. Officers sick one, Capt L.W.E. Elliott R.F.A. afd 1/Y B, 9th R.F.A. empl. sick C.B.m. O.R. sick twelve. O.R. wounded one. Other formations O.R. sick five.	App. 5
"	"		1/1st (Nth) Field Ambulance move to Beatrancourt taking mess from 2.3.11 Field Amb. Lee Mess the A.D.S. at Courcelles and three posts in the trenches.	
Bus	5.2.16	8.30 a.m.	Situation unchanged. Weather mild, sunny.	
"	"	12 noon	A.D.M.S. visits 1/1st (Nth) Field Ambulance.	
"	"	4.30 p.m.	Reports to D.M.S. & D.D.M.S. Evacuated to C.C.S. Officers sick two. Lieut. P.E. Baddeley 1/8 R. Warwicks. Lieut. Stevens. Capt. J.P. Kellar 1st (Nth) Bde. R.F.A. Bronchitis. O.R. sick twenty. O.R. wounded nine. Other formations O.R. sick five.	App. 6
Bus	6.2.16	8.30 a.m.	Situation unchanged. Weather mild, windy.	
"	"	4.30 p.m.	Reports to D.M.S. & D.D.M.S. Evacuated to C.C.S. Officers sick nil. O.R. sick sixteen. O.R. wounded one. Other formations O.R. sick seven.	App. 7
"	"		Reports to D.D.M.S. Base weather not sitgd.	
Bus	7.2.16	8.30 a.m.	Situation unchanged. Weather dull & showery. Machine Guns. Evacuation wire to C.C.S. 48th Div. trench three sick, one wounded. Other Divns. Lt. Q.S. Nicholson. 25 Lndn. arm fract. Sectn. Pltchfn. other ranks	
"	"		Mortars sick, wounded two.	
Bus	8.2.16	8.30 a.m.	Situation unchanged. Weather tryggt & rather colder. - A.D.M.S. visited all 3 Field Ambulances. Wnd. Offrs & N.Y. Orvd "Evacuated to C.C.S. Lieut Lt. F. Forte 1/5 Glousters Regt. I.C.T. — other ranks, sick, nine — Other formations O.R. sick twenty. O.R. wounded three. —	

WAR DIARY or INTELLIGENCE SUMMARY

Army Form C. 2118.

Place	Date	Hour	Summary of Events and Information	Remarks and references to Appendices
BUS	9/2/16	8.30 am	Situation unchanged. Weather cold but fine. Fall of snow last night which has now melted.	
		4.30	Lieut E.V. Sullivan RAMC T.C. reported his arrival from No 21 C.C.S. to relieve Capt Finlay on O/S of Sm Bde RFA	
		5 pm	Wired DDMS & ADMS "Evacuated to CCS Officers sick nil, OR sick Thurlow, OR wounded Two, other promotions sick Two."	
10/2/16		8.30 am	Situation unchanged. Hard frost during night, weather cold & bright.	
			1st Sm Field Ambulance relieved personnel of 3rd Sm Field Ambulance at ADS Sadilley & Hebuterne	
			3rd Sm " " " " " " " " Fonquevillers	
			Capt Finlay RAMC (T) proceeded for duty with No 21 C.C.S.	
			Wired DDMS & ADMS "Evacuated to CCS Officers nil, OR sick Ten, wounded nine. Other promotions OR sick four, OR wounded four –"	
			Received report that 2nd Lt Jordan, 7th Worcester Regt had been found dead in his billet at Couvelles. Directed that the body be removed to 2nd Sm Field Ambulance at Souvement for P.M. examination. ADMS called	
11/2/16		8.30 am	Situation unchanged. Very wet & cold day, frequent sleet showers.	
			Lieut Gillott RAMC attd 17 Bde RFA, returned from Highland Caswell, Clearing Station.	
			Wired DDMS & ADMS – "Evacuated to CCS, OR sick 21, OR wounded 4 – Other from Units Off Henning and Jord, West Riding Regt, C.O. prisoner, OR sick 5, wounded 4 –"	

WAR DIARY
or
INTELLIGENCE SUMMARY.

(Erase heading not required.)

Army Form C. 2118.

Instructions regarding War Diaries and Intelligence Summaries are contained in F. S. Regs., Part II. and the Staff Manual respectively. Title pages will be prepared in manuscript.

Place	Date	Hour	Summary of Events and Information	Remarks and references to Appendices
Bus	12/2/16	8.30 am	Situation unchanged. Weather bright, after rain, somewhat cold. One section 3rd S.M. Field Ambulance moved to SOUASTRE.	
		11 a.m.	A.D.mS. visited 1st S.M. Field Ambulance at BERTRANCOURT. Also both and ADS at SAILLY. both at BAYENCOURT & provision for hospital at SOUASTRE – Also went to BIENVILLERS which is about to be occupied in part by 48th Division –	
		4.30 pm	Wire to ADmS & DmS "Evacuated to C.C.S. 26. T. Balfour 1/5th Gloster Rgt & 21 13473 Allen 1st Worcester Battery R.F.A. both "Dental Caries" and Capt. T.J. Griffin 1/1st Ox & Bucks L.I. GSW Rght arm & thigh. O.R. Sick 9 – O.R. wounded 4 – Other formations O.R. sick 5."	
Bus	13/2/16	8.30	Situation unchanged – Weather bright & mild. Routine duties.	
		4.30 pm	Wire to ADmS & DmS "Evacuated to C.C.S. Officers nil. O.R. sick 10. O.R. wounded 2. Other formations O.R. sick 6. O.R. wounded two."	
Bus	14/2/16	8.30	Situation unchanged. Weather showery & warm. Received wire from H.Q. 48th Division directing Lt Col J Young to proceed to England & report at War Office on appointment as ADmS 61st S. M. Divn. Forwarded it to him for necessary action & to report departure. ADmS visited 2nd & 3rd S.M. Field Ambulances, called at PAS to see ADmS 37th Divn, but did not meet him & afterwards visited section of 3rd S.M. Field Ambulance at SOUASTRE. Gave instructions to Capt G. S. Williamson in regards forming A.D.S at Bienvillers –	

WAR DIARY or INTELLIGENCE SUMMARY

Army Form C. 2118.

Place	Date	Hour	Summary of Events and Information	Remarks and references to Appendices
Bus (continued)	14/2/16	2.30 pm	Went to Bus & B'villers — "Evacuated to C.C.S. Mreun sick 3, 2d S.R. Prock sick 1/5 R Warw Regt. Other ranks. 2d N Church R.H. 1/8 Worcester Flat feet. 2d 21 Q.M. Achroy 4B Amb A.C. Orchitis. OR sick 17. OR wounded 3. Other formations OR sick 7. OR wounded 8 —"	
BuP	15-2-16	8.30 am	The Division extended its right, taking over that part of the line up to BIENVILLERS - MONCHY ROAD held by 112th Brigade of 37th Division	
"	"	11.30 pm	Lt Col J Young R.A.M.C (17) reports his departure to England to take up duties as Med. Officer in charge of Troops at Ryde I. of Wight. — Evacuated to C.C.S. Officers sick one Lieut D.D. Bassett # (R.S.M) 8th R.F.A. Dental Caries OR sick five wounded two. Other formations Reich Twenty one OR wounded five	
BuP	16-2-16	8.30 am	Situation as above. Weather dull raining + stormy	
"	"	4 pm	A.D.M.S visited to him 3d (Eng.) Field Ambulance at Zouastre, making arrangements with A.A & QMG for the situation & billeting of the Headquarters of the Ambulance on its arrival there. Then proceeded to BIENVILLERS, interviewing A.D.C. 143rd Brigade, proceeding after to HANNESCAMP, inspecting #1 I from 1/1st Scottish + interviewing the medical officer, also looking at extractions for an Advanced Dressing Station in BIENVILLERS. — Evacuated to C.C.S Officers sick nil. OR sick Eleven OR wounded one. Other formations OR sick two OR wounded five.	
BuP	17/2/16	8.30am	Situation unchanged. Weather stormy + wet.	
"	"	11 am	A.D.M.S with D.A & Q.M.G. + O.C. 1/2 and (Eng) Field Ambulance. Visited BARTON St for billets re for 1/2 (Eng) Field Ambulance on its arriving B'tel place	
"	"	4.30 pm	A.D.M.S. to B'villers & B'tel — Evacuated to C.C.B. Officers sick one Lieut NA GRANDAGE 2/1st (Eng) Fld Co R.E. Papilloma to liver OR sick Ten OR wounded nil. Other formations OR sick seven	

WAR DIARY
or
INTELLIGENCE SUMMARY.

Army Form C. 2118.

Instructions regarding War Diaries and Intelligence Summaries are contained in F. S. Regs., Part II. and the Staff Manual respectively. Title pages will be prepared in manuscript.

(Erase heading not required.)

Place	Date	Hour	Summary of Events and Information	Remarks and references to Appendices
B.u.f	18.2.16	9.30 a.m.	Situation unchanged. Weather stormy & cold.	
"	"	4.15 p.m.	O.P. M.d. visited 3rd (Sth) Field Ambulance to attend at SOUASTRE	
"	"	4.30 p.m.	Evacuated 8th M.d. 7 O.P. M.d. Evacuated K.C.O.B. Officers sick viz Lieut. Col 7.O. WETHERED to Queen Alex. Convalescent Home NICE. O.R. sick twenty two O.R. wounded three. O.R. formation two sick viz Alhlin O.R. wounded three.	
B.u.f	19.2.16	9.30 a.m.	Situation unchanged. (advance) Weather raining	
"	"	2.30 p.m.	A.D.M.S. visited O.C. 1.M.D. to attend to 1st K.O. Lancaders.elf in the Trenches of extreme left of the Division with reference to number of "trench foot" cases occurring in R.D. Batt.	
"	"	4.30 p.m.	Message to 2nd A.F.M.d.— Evacuated K.C.O.B. Officers sick viz A.dcoulten O.R. wounded two O.R. formation sick twelve O.R. wounded one	
B.u.f	"	5.30 p.m.	Message from Highland C.C.S. 2 x 2 S Sgt. Clark 1/S.R. Warwicks Regiment. Crabs. Grid Queenfither. A.D. informed this Office. & will proceed to them tc.	
"	20.2.16	9.30 a.m.	Situation unchanged. Weather snowy, cold	
"	"	11 a.m.	O.P. M.d. visited 1st (W) Field Ambulance at BERTRANCOURT.	
"	"	4.30 p.m.	Messengert 2nd (W) 2nd M.d. Evacuated K.C.O.B. Officers sick three Lieut. N H CLARKE 1/H Stanley Nervous Debility. Lieut. T. ROPER 1/ Warcaster Influenza. Lieut. H.B.TEED 4/R. Berks Influenza O.R. sick twenty O.R. wounded one, O.R. formation Officers sick H Lieut J.D.R CURTIS 1st K.O. Lancaders. Rgt. Pyrexia O.R. wounded one. O.R. ROACH H Nanvicum 2 and Lance Nicholas Bayonet wound shot & Staff wound O.R. sick twelve O.R. wounded two	
B.u.f	21.2.16	9.30 a.m.	Situation unchanged. Weather snowy but cold.	
"	"	12.30 a.m.	O.P. M.d. visited 1st (H) (Sth) Field Ambulance ; 2nd (W) Field Ambulance at STATON. + LOUVENCOURT	

WAR DIARY or INTELLIGENCE SUMMARY

Army Form C. 2118.

Place	Date	Hour	Summary of Events and Information	Remarks and references to Appendices
B.U.S	21/2/16		The accommodation at BARTON is małhew inadequate.	
			O.I.Mil also visited 8 Ind & 9th Corps with reference to accommodation for new cases in the 2nd (Eth) Field Ambulance.	
		4.30pm	Evacuated to 8 Ind. & 9 Ind. Evacuated to C.C.S. Officers sick one Capt C.A. LEWIS 4th Berks. influenza. O.R. sick fifteen. O.R. wounded three. Thir formation Officers sick one 2/Lieut S WATERHOUSE 2nd Essex R.gt 1 C.T. left wrist. O.R. most Officers wounded one Capt (accident - own 24 R Fancs two O.R.) and kome Zouaires staff wounds head. O.R. sick thirteen O.R. wounded twenty-two.	
B.U.S	22/2/16	8.30am	Situation unchanged. Weather cold, freezing blizzard. Instructions regarding prevention frostbite of trench feet sent to 149 Bde & all Medical Officers of 1st & 2nd Infantry Bdes.	
			No 19254 Pte JEFFERSON 1/8 R Warwick invented C.B.W. from the Highland C.C.S. Investigation. There was no communication between these cases. The one reported at 2.9.5 from Thiévres. B/5	
		4.30pm	Evacuated to 8 Ind. & 9 Ind. Evacuated to C.C.S Officers sick twelve. O.R. wounded three. Third formation Officers sick one 2/Lieut P.S. HEARD 9 K.R.O. Rans Rgt. O.R. 1 & 2 K.O. Ranners S. the chest. O.R. sick fourteen. O.R. wounded eight.	
B.U.S	23/2/16	8.13am	Situation unchanged. Weather cold & dull.	
		1 p.m.	O.I. Mil visited 2nd (4th) Field Ambulance at BARTON, & 3rd Zieb Ambulance SOUASTRE	
		4.30pm	Evacuated to 8 Ind. & 9 Ind. Evacuated to C.C.B Officers sick nil. O.R. sick fifteen. O.R. wounded two. Third formation O.R. sick thirty six O.R. wounded three	

Army Form C. 2118.

WAR DIARY
or
INTELLIGENCE SUMMARY.
(Erase heading not required.)

Instructions regarding War Diaries and Intelligence Summaries are contained in F. S. Regs., Part II. and the Staff Manual respectively. Title pages will be prepared in manuscript.

Place	Date	Hour	Summary of Events and Information	Remarks and references to Appendices
Bus	24.2.16	8.30am	Situation unchanged. Weather very cold, but sunny. Routine duties.	
"		4.30pm	Spoke to 2/Lieut. DDMS. Evacuated to CCS officers sick Lieut. Wm H Lyon 1/4 Kite Rollers Section, 2/Lieut. J Manship 4th R.Berks. Sephora OR sick twenty three OR wounded three. OR sick twenty four OR wounded three.	
Bus	25.2.16	8.30am	Situation unchanged. Weather very cold. Foggy am.	
"		12.45pm	Afield with CRS visited HEBUTERNE + chose position for erecting the "Duke" hut + made arrangements for reception (of wounded).	
"		4.30pm	Messages to 2/Lt ADMS. Evacuated to CCS officers sick Capt A W Duncan 1/5th Sussex Minute Capt W E Harper RAMC att'd M.T.R.O. Lt Fracture ARC Lt acted to machine OR wounded four am. The formation OR sick fourteen OR wounded seven.	
Bus	26.2.16	8.30am	Situation unchanged. Weather very cold. Sunny.	
"		4.30pm	ADMS with DADMS & officer Intelpeta visited AMIENS to make arrangements for sending personnel proceeding to enemies on leave to PARIS.	
"		"	Messages to DMS + DDMS. Evacuated to CCS officer wounded Lt OR sick twenty four OR wounded one. The formation OR sick am.	
Bus	27.2.16	8.30am	Situation unchanged. Weather slightly milder. Raining.	
"		4.30am	Messages to ADMS + DDMS. Evacuated to DO's officer sick Lt OR sick twenty OR sick fifteen officers sick one R/Lieut Chas Graham 1st K.O. Lancaster Regt Jaundice. OR wounded. Formation on Total Base.	

1577 Wt. W10791/1773 500,000 1/15 D. D. & L. A.D.S.S./Forms/C. 2118.

WAR DIARY
or
INTELLIGENCE SUMMARY.
(Erase heading not required.)

Army Form C. 2118.

Place	Date	Hour	Summary of Events and Information	Remarks and references to Appendices
B 4	28.2.16	8.30am	Situation unchanged. Weather cold & dull. Thawing slightly.	
		10 am	D.A.D.M.S. called at A.D.M.S. - Principally with reference to 10th B.D. to H.Q. Divisional Real Station at Mondicourt. They having been a shortage of post cards of 1921.	
		12.30 pm	A.D.M.S. visited 3rd (S.M.) Field Ambulance at Souastre. Cases from Highland C.C.S. - No 3581 Pte Yates & 1/8 R Warwick postcard 6 P.B.M.; M.O. informs all necessary precautions taken.	
		1.30 pm	D.D.M.S. visited A.D.M.S. Evacuated to C.C.S. officer sick from Lieut F.T. Wakeman 1/5 R Warwick. Influenza Lieut R.K. Blackall 1/8 R Warwick. Lieut R.O. Richards 1/6 R Warwick Debility. Reg't. V.D. summer eyes. Were able to employ bucket & defective vision OR sick transfers other formation officer sick one Capt G.C. Pepper saw Lance Cpl Trailer 1/1 Ox OR sick seventeen OR wounded from trenches unchanged. Weather milder, some rain.	
B 4	29.2.16	8.30 am	D.D.M.S. of Corps called, saw A.D.M.S.	
		12 noon	Myerscoufe D.D.M.S. & D.M.L. Evacuated to C.C.S. officers sick nil OR sick Trench & R wounded.	
		2.30 pm	Three other formations 90 OR sick & nil & neuralgia one. Sketch of division area attached hereto.	

ADMS. 48th (S.M.) DIVISION.

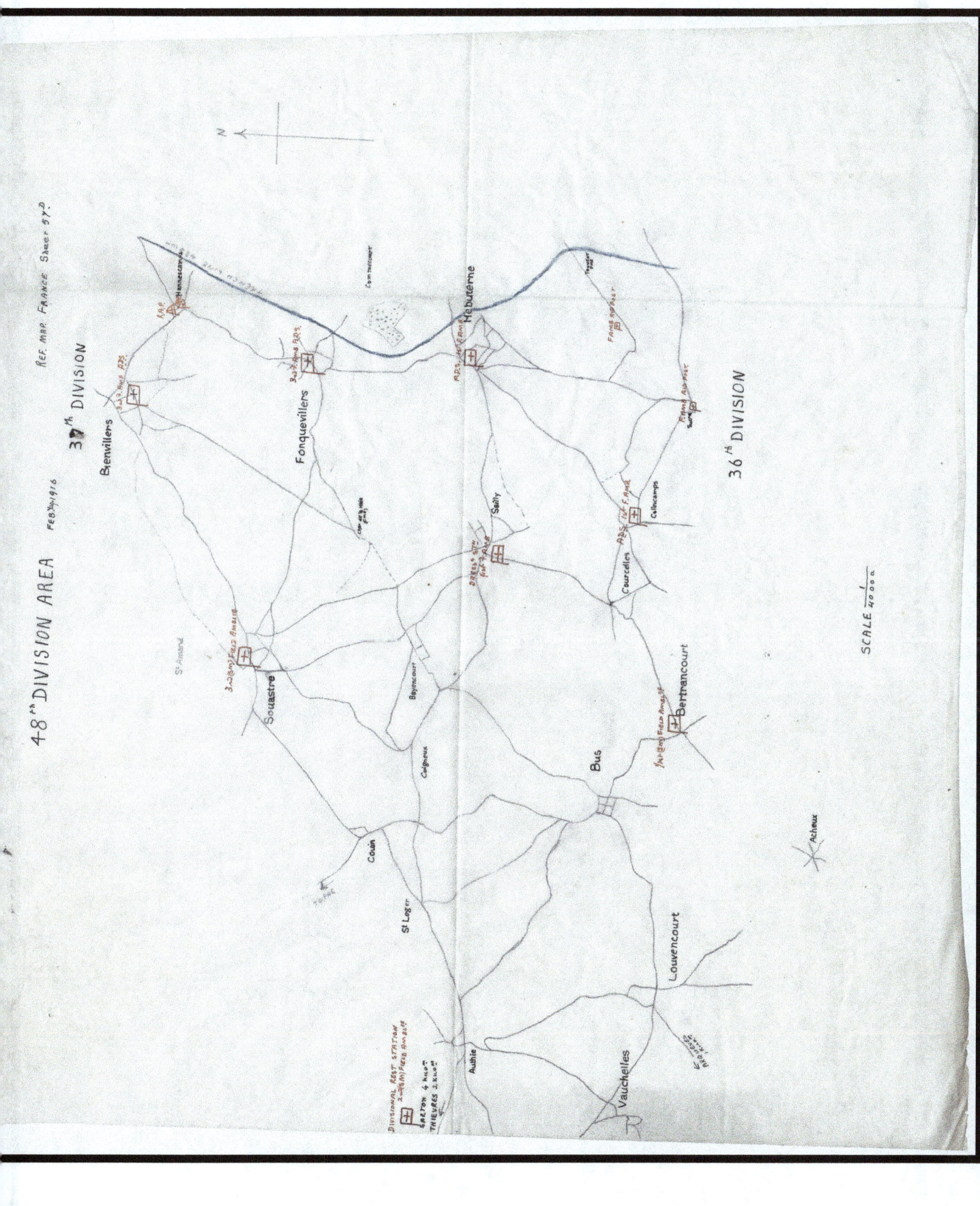

March 1916

A.D.M.S. 49th (S.M.) Div

CONFIDENTIAL

War Diary
of
A.D.P. 48th Division
from 1.3.16 - to - 31.3.16
Vol XII

Army Form C. 2118.

WAR DIARY
or
INTELLIGENCE SUMMARY.
(Erase heading not required.)

Instructions regarding War Diaries and Intelligence Summaries are contained in F. S. Regs., Part II. and the Staff Manual respectively. Title pages will be prepared in manuscript.

Place	Date	Hour	Summary of Events and Information	Remarks and references to Appendices
B.u.8	1.3.16	8.30 a.m.	Distribution as follows. The 143rd Inf:y B:de have taken over (extending their left) a small further portion of the line formerly held by the 144th Inf:y B:de. The 144th B:de have been withdrawn from the portion of the line East of HANNESCAMP and BIENVILLERS, being relieved by 37th Division. The B:de is at present billeted at BOUQUETMAISON, OCCOCHES, RUE.	
		1 p.m.	O.O. M.S. visited 3rd (W:R) Field Ambulance at BOUQUETRE, & the Advanced Dressing Station at FONQUEVILLERS.	App. 1.
		4.30 p.m.	Messages to A.M.L. & D.M.S. evacuated to C.C.S. officers nil, other ranks 5 in Que, sick 3, Inj:d —	
			B:urs:y app. 95 men at Nortes B:C:S, 143 Inf:y B:de invalids 9 suspects diphtheria. O:R:ch fifteen OR wounded on our other Formation two OR sick fourteen	
B.u.8	2.3.16	8.30 a.m.	Situation as above. Weather mild, rainy.	
		12.45 p.m.	O.O. M:L. visited A.D. M:L 10 Corps and 6th of IV Army at noon today.	
			Wire from D.D.M:L. 10 Corps that Returns are now to be rendered to B:de IV Army	App. 2.
		4.30 p.m.	Message to A.D.M:L. 10 Corps & M:d IV Army, also to D.D.M:L. 7 Corps & B:de IV Army. Evacuated to C.C.S. Officer — nil OR sick eleven OR wounded two our Other Formations Officers nil OR sick thirteen N.M.S. town and one men heavy rain. OR sick thirteen	
B.u.8	3.3.16	8.30 a.m.	Situation unchanged. Weather variable, mild.	
		11.30 a.m.	D.O. M:L. with D.D.O. & Surg. inspected billets and cover with a view to the 42 & (W) Field Ambulance moving to Batplencé from BENTANCOURT to B:U:8.	
			Instructions issued for Half (W) Field Ambulance to move from BENTANCOURT to B:U:8.	
		4.30 p.m.	Message to A.D.M:L. 10 Corps & B:de IV Army. Evacuated C.C.S. Officer sick nil OR sick twenty two OR wounded two Other Formation Officer nil OR sick eighteen OR wounded in one OR sick expected one	App. 3.

Army Form C. 2118.

WAR DIARY
or
INTELLIGENCE SUMMARY.
(Erase heading not required.)

Instructions regarding War Diaries and Intelligence Summaries are contained in F. S. Regs., Part II and the Staff Manual respectively. Title pages will be prepared in manuscript.

Place	Date	Hour	Summary of Events and Information	Remarks and references to Appendices
B.u.B	4.3.16	8.30am	Situation – during night 3/4 the 144th Inf Bde Fd Amb Hinchen held by 2nd Inf Bde 48th Division – self inoculant 2 48th Division came under 1 O. & Corps 4th Army	
			1/1 st (Nth) Field Ambulance moved into B.u.B	
		1.30 pm	In charge to 4 Ind. II Army & 2nd Med. & Corps – Evacuated to C.C.S. officers received one Lieut B.W.	App 4
			CARDEN 1/6 Gloster neurasthenia OR sick fifty OR wounded seven	
B.u.B	5.3.16	8.30am	Situation as above. Worked my cold Stypads.	
		4.30 pm	In charge to 4 Ind. IV Army & 2nd Med. & Corps – Evacuated C.C.S. officers sick one of Head	App 5
			7.B. HISSEY 1/5 R Sussex Asthma, Bronchitis OR sick seven OR wounded one	
			Messages to S.A. (Bay week) is down grid water tap - Officers sick y O.R sick 122, O.R wounded 10	
			Being an increase of Officers 1, O.R sick & compared with evening 27.2.16	
B.u.B	6.3.16	3.30 am	Situation unchanged. Weather milder, enemy fired during night.	
		4.30 pm	In charge to 2nd Ind. & D.Med. Evacuated to C.C.S. Officers nil one Capt J.L. SIMCOX 1/6	App 6
			R. Warwicks. Increased wound left knee. OR sick thirty two. OR wounded two.	
			Lieut NORIS NORRIS (T.F.) O.C. 55th Ind. Sanitary Section arrived to day to be attached to 2nd D.C	
			1/8 D Ind Sanitary Section for instructional purposes	
B.u.B	7.3.16	8.30 am	Situation unchanged. Weather milder. Enemy fired last night.	
		4.30 pm	In charge to 2nd D.Med. & 2nd Med. – Evacuated to C.C.S. Officers five Lieut N.A. INDER 1/7 R Warwick	App 7
			Influenza 2/Lt KATHSMITH 2nd (Ny) B.G., R.F.A. 3rd B.G Influenza. Lieut FORCROT 1/5 Gloster Dental (Pain)	
			Capt - L.W. VINEY 1st Bucks 8° Dislocated Cartilage knee OR sick twenty one OR wounded un -	
B.u.B	8.3.16	8.30 am	Situation much improved. Weather sunny, enemy firing day & probably night	
		1 pm	O.M. Smith A.O.O.M.S and G & O.I. visited 3rd (Nth) Field Ambulance at BOOKSTORE and 2.0 HALF FM S	

Army Form C. 2118.

WAR DIARY
or
INTELLIGENCE SUMMARY.
(Erase heading not required.)

Instructions regarding War Diaries and Intelligence Summaries are contained in F. S. Regs., Part II. and the Staff Manual respectively. Title pages will be prepared in manuscript.

Place	Date	Hour	Summary of Events and Information	Remarks and references to Appendices
BUP	8.3.16		Lieuts R BROOKES and B.C SPURGIN RAMC.T.C. reported for duty. The former posted temporarily to 1/3rd (Wm) Field Ambulance. A note was received from O/C Nº1 Boulogne Base regarding that Col Spurgin be returned unmed. reply, which motion was carried out	App 8.
"	"	4.30pm	Proceeded to Brig H. Army HQ Brid & Capt - Evacuated to C.C.S officers sick one 2/Lieut M J HOLDSWORTH 1/5 R Warwicks BY Sick nineteen OR wounded six	
BUP	9.3.16	8.30am	Situation unchanged. Weather cold & snow	
"	"	1pm	ADMS with OC Nº1 (Wm) Field Ambulance after conference of DDMS II Corps who had telephoned to ADMS to select a Lt. Col 77 for appointment of ADMS 1/1st London Div and Div. as being the selected officer & sent see him.	App 9.
"	"	4.30pm	Proceeded to Brid IV Army 8 Brid & Capt - Evacuated to C.C.S officers sick one 2/Lieut A.T. CLAYTON 1/5 Gloster PLENVIN OR sick twenty one OR wounded three	
BUP	10.3.16	8.30am	Situation unchanged. Weather frosty	
"	"	6pm	ADMS with DDx Brig visited H/Q (Wm) Field Ambulance SOUASTRE and ADS SONNEVILLERS	App 10.
"	"	5pm	Proceeded to Bred & Brig. Evacuated CCS officers sick nil OR sick fifteen	
"	"	"	ADMS issued instructions to 1/3rd (Wm) Field Ambulance to move the Headquarters of the Ambulance to the Chateau BOUIN	
BUP	11.3.16	8.30am	Situation unchanged. Weather milder, thawing	
"	"	4.30pm	Proceeded to Brid & H. Brid. - Evacuated to C.C.S officers sick from 2/Lieut R V STRATTON 6R Warwick 2/Lieut R.V STRATTON 6R Warwick Batteries began P.W. now 1/6 OR. sick killing Dugoon Smashes officer 2/Lieut N.R.S GUEST 1/7 R Warwick Batteries began P.W. now 1/6 Evacuated Dugoons Lieut R.H.ASTBURY 1/6 R Warwick carpenters OR sick fifteen OR wounded ten	App 11.
			1/3rd (Wm) Field Ambulance moved from SOUASTRE to BOUIN	

WAR DIARY
or
INTELLIGENCE SUMMARY.

(Erase heading not required.)

Army Form C. 2118.

Place	Date	Hour	Summary of Events and Information	Remarks and references to Appendices
BuB	12/3/16	8.30am	Situation unchanged. Weather continues milder.	
"	"	3pm	A.D.M.S. with O.C.No 5 C.F.A. visited all Field Ambulances except 13 and all Divisional Stations + A.D.R. Co except HEBUTERNE.	App 12
"	"	4.30pm	4 cases to Bn/H.Q. Stn. Evacuated to C.C.S. officers sick two Capt B.H. CLARKE 13 Worcester Influenza. Lieut R BROOKES 13 (Ser. Bn) Field Ambulance Bronchitis O.R. sick fifteen O.R. wounded none.	
BuB	13/3/16	8.30am	Situation unchanged. Weather warm sunny.	
"	"	2 pm	Conference with officers of H.Q. with A.D.M.S.	App 13
"	"	4.30pm	14 cases to Sn/H.Q. Stn. and Div H.Q. Evacuated to C.C.S. officers sick one Capt L.W. CROUCH R.A.M.C. R 15. Dental Caries O.R. sick twenty three O.R. wounded four.	
BuB	14/3/16	8.30am	Situation unchanged. Weather warm sunny.	
"	"	4pm	A.D.M.S. visited 132nd (No) Field Ambulance at SARTON.	App 14
"	"	4.30pm	9 cases to Stn/H.Q + B. Stn. Evacuated to C.C.S. officers sick one Lieut J.H. GOLDEN Y.&R. Bronch. Dental Caries O.R. sick twenty O.R. wounded form.	
BuB	15/3/16	8.30am	Situation unchanged. Weather warm sunny.	
"	"	1pm	A.D.M.S. visited A.D.S. FONQUEVILLERS, which had been shelled during night causing considerable damage + necessitates the evacuation in part. Also to the 1/3w (Sth) Field Ambulance at COUIN.	App 15
"	"	4.30pm	4 cases to Stn + D Stn/H. Evacuated to C.C.S. officers sick three Lieut J.W. BOSTON A.S.C. R.o.A.Coy Lieut Y.B. HALL (Y.Oxfors) Bucks Dental Caries Lieut J. GRAY 1/A Train Colonel Jaundice. O.R. sick twenty six O.R. wounded five.	
BuB	16/3/16	8.30am	Situation unchanged. Weather mild, sunny.	
"	"	12 noon	A Stnd. attend conference D.D.M.S. Corps.	App 16
"	"	4.30pm	9 cases to B Stn. + H Stn. Evacuated to C.C.S. officers one at C.C.S. Lieut H.G. WYERS	

Army Form C. 2118.

WAR DIARY
or
INTELLIGENCE SUMMARY.
(Erase heading not required.)

Instructions regarding War Diaries and Intelligence Summaries are contained in F. S. Regs., Part II. and the Staff Manual respectively. Title pages will be prepared in manuscript.

Place	Date	Hour	Summary of Events and Information	Remarks and references to Appendices
B.u.F	17/3/16	8.30am	3rd (Rif) S & R.F.A. Bronchitis Lieut W.T. WREFORD A.S.C. C.R.O. Peritonitis skull O.R. Lumbago O.R. wounded, n.y.	app 17
			Situation unchanged. Weather mild, rain at times	
		4.30pm	Proceeded to 3rd D Field Amb. Evacuated to C.C.S. Officers sick nil. O.R. sick nil. O.R. sick right. O.R. wounded 15	
B.u.F	18/3/16	8.30am	Situation unchanged. Weather warm, sunny	
		12pm	Q.M.H. visited 15th (Am) Field Ambulance	
		11.30pm	Wine to 3rd D & 3rd S.W. Proceeded to C.C.S. Officers sick one accidental wound Capt J WILLEY 3rd West Riding B. R.F.A. 7 K.B.Y. wound head from shrapnel, skull. Officers wounded 3 Capt E.F. JONES 4/6 Leicesters & 2 W. Yau Reg. O.R. sick eleven O.R. wounded ten	app 18
B.u.F.	19/3/16	3.a.m.	The enemy bombarded LA SIGNY FARM + trenches 124 & Brigade FM & medical aid sent up to COLINCAMP. of 5 stretcher squads 7 medical officers. Total casualties caused 10 killed, 38 wounded, 2 missing	
		8.30am	Situation unchanged. Weather warm, sunny	
		4.30pm	Wine to 3rd D & 3rd S.W. - Evacuated to C.C.S. officers sick three Lieut F W.R. BIRCH Div.l Cyclist Coy. Osteosclerosis 2nd Lieut W.O. DOWN 1/4 R. Berks Bronchitis 2/Lieut B WHITEMAN 1/5 R B ward debility. Officers wounded two Lieut S. BRINDLE 1/6 Glosters Shell wound Face + shoulder Capt. Young E.L. 1/6 Glosters Shell wound Face, neck, arm O.R. sick nine O.R. wounded Four.	app 19
			Wire from Q.M.G.B. R.W. 1670 Bth. GOODENOUGH 4 1/4 R. Berks Cerebro-spinal meningitis	
B.u.F	20/3/16	8.30am	Situation unchanged. Weather mild, sunny	
			A.D.M.S. issued instructions for 1 & 2nd (Am) Field Ambulance 3rd Div.l to FONCQUEVILLERS	app 20
		12.30pm	Conference with Regimental Medical officers	
		4.30pm	Proceeded to 3rd D 3rd Fd D.H.S. - Presented to C.C.S. Officers sick two Lieut E.L. CHAMBERLAIN	app 2

WAR DIARY
or
INTELLIGENCE SUMMARY

Army Form C. 2118.

Place	Date	Hour	Summary of Events and Information	Remarks and references to Appendices
B.H.Q.	20/3/16		O/C No 3 Coy Train Septic food. Left Capt E.D.A. BURBIDGE A.S.C. German measles. O.R. sick seventeen. O.R. wounded 2. Forty	
B.H.Q.	21/3/16	8.30am	Situation unchanged. Weather mild sunny	
"		11.45am	A.D.M.S. with D.A.A. & Q.M.G. also O.C. 2/nd (Lth) Field Ambulance visited FONQUEVILLERS to choose position for the Field Ambulance. Place considered unsuitable	App 22
"		4.30pm	Evac'd to No 1 & No 2 M.D.S. – Evacuated to C.C.S. Officers nil at two Capt. T.W. NOTT 1/6 Gloucesters sick Cables. Lieut 1/8 CRAWFORD 1/8 Worcesters dental. O.R's sick seven O.R's wounded five	
B.H.Q.	22/3/16	8.30am	Situation unchanged, weather dull, inclined to rain	
"		12 noon	A.D.M.S. with A.D.O.S. visited BUS to ZALEAU on the AUTHIE-FANSCHON Road with a view to placing 2/nd (Lth) Field Ambulance in huts there. A.D.M.S. also visited 43 and (Lth) Field Ambulance at SOUASTRE & COUIN.	App 23
"		11.30am	Wires to D.A.G. & D.D.M.S. – for a dentist O.C's officers sick four. O/Cpl W.F. KIDDLER 1/nd B.M.B. A. RFA. HuChishin. 2/Lieut KING 1/6 Gloster Dental Caries 143 B.GR. G Coy Lieut C.W. TIPPE N.Y.D. Lieut R.T. TERRY 1/5 R. Warwicks N.Y.D. O.R. sick ten. O.R. wounded eight. Wire received from Jn O.11th Brd 1/Bucks L.I. asking for ambulance & conveyance for a man of new draft who was probably German measles. He was conveyed into by a motor to the Highland C.C.S.	App 24
B.H.Q.	23/3/16	8.30am	Situation unchanged. Winds & weather evening A.D.M.S. visited 1/2nd (Lth) Field Ambulance at BARTON & after to a conference with D.D.M.S. IIIrd Corps	
"		12.50pm		

WAR DIARY
or
INTELLIGENCE SUMMARY.

Army Form C. 2118.

Place	Date	Hour	Summary of Events and Information	Remarks and references to Appendices
But	23.3.16	4.30 p.m.	O/bd. attends conference G.O.C. the Division. During night 22/23rd a small raid took place into the German trenches. Casualties in wounded amounted to 2 Officers & 27 O.R.	
"	"	4.30 p.m.	Wires to 8 th/J. & 9 th.N.S. – Evacuated to C.C.S. Officers sick one – Major H.F.W. BOEDDICKER 1/1st (SM) Field Ambulance Inflammation. Invalided. Officers wounded two Lieut A.H. HAYNES 3rd R.W.R. B97 R 7 9 8th Bty. Shell wound head 2/Lieut S. HOLT 1/5 R. Warwicks. G.S.W. Rt Leg Rt Neck sixteen O.R. wounded twelve.	App 25
"	"		Instructions issued to 1/2nd (SM) Field Ambulance to move into the hub in BOIS de LOCON.	
"	24.3.16	8.30 a.m.	Situation unchanged. Weather colder, rainy.	
"	"	4.30 p.m.	Wires to 8 W/J. & 9 N.M. – Evacuated to C.C.S. Officers sick one – Capt. P. PICKFORD 1/1st (SM) Field Ambulance B.U.B. Neuralgia. O.R. sick fifteen. O.R. wounded eighteen.	App 26
"	"		Instructions issued for D.R.S. to move to 1/1st (SM) Field Ambulance during the night.	
"	25.3.16	8.30 a.m.	Situation unchanged. Weather cold, heavy fall of snow during the night.	
"	"	4.30 p.m.	Messages to 8 W/J & 9 N.M. – Evacuated to C.C.S. Officers wounded one – Lieut. G. HOLMAN 1/6 Stratins G.S.W. arm. O.R. sick fifteen. O.R. wounded five.	App 27
"	26.3.16	8.30 a.m.	Situation unchanged. Weather milder, rainy.	
"	"	4.30 p.m.	Wires 8W/M/J & Corps & 2nd IV Army – Evacuated to C.C.S. Officers sick nil. O.R. sick nine. O.R. wounded five.	App 28
"	"	5 p.m.	During the day the 61st Quarter Division moves to COUIN.	

WAR DIARY or INTELLIGENCE SUMMARY

Army Form C. 2118.

Place	Date	Hour	Summary of Events and Information	Remarks and references to Appendices
COUIN	27/3/16	8.30 am	Situation unchanged. Weather rainy.	
"	"	11 am	ADMS visits 1/3 (Lon) Field Ambulance	Appx 9
"	"	2.30 pm	Bearers to 1st & 2nd/1st - Evacuated to C.C.S. officers sick three Capt F CASTLE 1/1 Staton Dental Centre Capt F WINSCOM 1/2 Bisho Benchitz Lieut S GATHORNE-HARDY 1/1 R Berks N.Y.R. OR sick twenty three OR wounded two	
"	"	5.15 pm	ADMS attends Conference G.O.C. at Headquarters	
"	"	2.30 pm	Monthly conference with Regimental Medical Officers Lieut Walter RAMC (S.R.) Regt A/Lt (T/C) of 1/1st Dublins & 31st Div arrived on command instruction + attachments Lieut ARMY (S.R.) 1/1 (S.M.) Field Ambulance	
COUIN	28/3/16	8.30 am	Situation unchanged. Weather very rainy, some rain.	
"	"	4.30 pm	Wire to ADM & DMS - Evacuated to C.C.S officers sick one Capt V.A.BEAUFORT R.Q.O R.W Kent Battalion Station Caines & Bomb Ankle OR sick eight ten OR wounded five Bearers from highland C.C.S. - 3 067 P/g J PAYNE bearer for C.B.M. M.O.1/2 R.F. infantry none for emergency taken	Appx 30
"	"			Appx 31
COUIN	29/3/16	8.30 am	Situation unchanged. Weather colder warmly ADMS visits 1/3 od (S.M.) FieldAmbulance	
"	"	11 am		
"	"	4.30 pm	Wire to ADMS + D.M.S. - Evacuated to C.C.S officers sick three Lieut-Col S. DAVENPORT 1/1 Staten Suffering from asthma. Major W.R.S. BARNE R.A. 1/8 Divl Haemorroids Lieut A.R. 3 WARREN 1/8 Worcester Someron OR sick eleven OR wounded three Wire to ADM I Corps asking if further arrangements can be made for one local own of troops at BARTON + ORVILLE as hand (1m) Field Ambulance is no onward to AUTHIE	Appx 32
"	"			Appx 33

48th DIVn AREA. April 1. 1916.

4th DIVn

REF MAP FRANCE Sheet 57D
1/100000.

Fonquevillers

Hebuterne

Souastre

Bayencourt

Sailly

Coigneux

Couin

St Leger

Famechon

Thievres

31st DIVn

Army Form C. 2118.

WAR DIARY
or
INTELLIGENCE SUMMARY.
(Erase heading not required.)

Instructions regarding War Diaries and Intelligence Summaries are contained in F. S. Regs., Part II. and the Staff Manual respectively. Title pages will be prepared in manuscript.

Place	Date	Hour	Summary of Events and Information	Remarks and references to Appendices
COUIN	30.3.16	8.30am	Situation unchanged. Weather cold + stormy.	
"	"	4.30pm	Went to 3rd IV Army + D.Med VIII Corps (the Division having joined VIII Corps night 29/30) - proceeded to CCP Officers at Ch [ ]. 14 sick, fourteen O.R. wounded three.	App 34.
"	"	6pm	Instructions received verbally for 2nd (S.M.) Field Ambulance at once from Bus. DADMS. proceeded with DAP's & A.S. to BOUSTRE to choose position for same.	
COUIN	31.3.16	8.30am	Situation unchanged. Weather milder. Raining.	
"	"	9.30am	ADMS gave instructions to O.C. 1/2nd (S.M.) Field Ambulance to move to BOUSTRE.	
"	"	3.30pm	ADMS visited A.D.G at SAILLY which is being moved another part of the village. Also visited BOUSTRE to 1/2nd (S.M.) Field Ambulance.	
"	"	4.30pm	Wires 1st Bucks Army + 2nd Med VIII Corps. Evacuated 1 O.R. officer wounded one. Official S.I. REED.	App 35.
"	"		4/4 Gloster Insomnia O.R. sick eleven O.R. wounded eight.	
			Daily sick admissions to Field Ambulances for the month = 1554. Total admissions for the month = 5012. Map of Divisional area attached.	

[signature]
COLONEL,
A.D.M.S. 48th (S.M.) DIVISION.

April/16

War Diary
of.
A.D.M.S. 49/8th Division
for.
April 1916

COMMITTEE FOR THE
MEDICAL HISTORY OF THE WAR
Date 9 - JUN. 1916

CONFIDENTIAL

Vol XIII

War Diary
of
A.D.M.S. 48th Division
from 1-4-16 to 30-4-16.

WAR DIARY
or
INTELLIGENCE SUMMARY

Army Form C. 2118.

(Erase heading not required.)

Instructions regarding War Diaries and Intelligence Summaries are contained in F. S. Regs., Part II. and the Staff Manual respectively. Title pages will be prepared in manuscript.

Place	Date	Hour	Summary of Events and Information	Remarks and references to Appendices
COUIN	1.4.16	8.30 am	Situation unchanged from that of 31.3.16. Weather warm & sunny.	
			ADMS temporarily assumed duties of DDMS VIII Corps in addition to ADMS.	
	"	4 pm	ADMS visited VIII Corps at MARIEUX	
	"	4.30 pm	1/1st (BM) Field Ambulance arrived at ROUGETRE	
			Wires to DMS IV Army & DDMS VIII Corps. Evacuated to CCS Officers sick & wound	App 1.
			R to CAREW-HUNT 1/4 Oxfords Bucks Lay regts OR sick eleven OR wounded ten.	
COUIN	2.4.16	8.30 am	Situation unchanged. Weather warm & sunny.	
	"	4.30 pm	Wires DMS IV Army & DDMS VIII Corps. Evacuated to CCS officers & sick OR sick	App 2
			Sick wastage for week ending 1st Noon 2.4.16 = .65%	
	"	8 pm	Arrangements from HQrs to detach Motor Ambulances and temporarily for duty with 29th Division	App 3.
	"	8.15 pm	Arrangements to 1/2nd (H.M.) Field Ambulance to detach 2 cars for temporary duty with ADMS 29th Div	App 4.
COUIN	3.4.16	8.30 am	Situation unchanged. Weather warm & sunny.	
	"	12 noon	ADMS visited VIII Corps	
	"	1.30 pm	DADMS attended Conference C.O.C.	
	"	2 pm	ADMS Conference with PM, O of 2nd & 3rd Co Field Ambulances	
	"	4.30 pm	Wires to DMS IV Army & DDMS – evacuated to CCS Officers sick nil OR sick twenty two OR wounded nine/ten.	App 5.

Army Form C. 2118.

WAR DIARY
or
INTELLIGENCE SUMMARY.
(Erase heading not required.)

Instructions regarding War Diaries and Intelligence Summaries are contained in F. S. Regs., Part II. and the Staff Manual respectively. Title pages will be prepared in manuscript.

Place	Date	Hour	Summary of Events and Information	Remarks and references to Appendices
COUIN	4.4.16	8.30 am	Situation unchanged. Weather warm & sunny.	
"	"	1 pm	ADMS to DDMS VIII Corps held conference of O's DsMS of VIII Corps at MARIEUX	
"	"	5 pm	ADMS attended conference SOC.	
"	"	"	Wires to and from IV Army & DMS VIII Corps. Evacuated to CCS Officers and five other ranks	app 6.
			R.F. WEBB 3rd (Ry) Bt. R.9.A. Influenza 2/Lieut A.LEIGH 1/4 R. Berks Machine Gun Section Sibia, Sciatica	
			2/Lieut W. HATWELL 1/8 R. Warwicks Dental Caries Capt G.K.ROSE 1/4 Oxford & Bucks Light Infantry	
			V. CAROL Bn Commandant Rapa app 109 K.T.M.B.G. Stone in bladder & prich hetroe & peritonitis [?]	
COUIN	5.4.16	8.30 am	Situation - Arid line now extends from B 28 a 9.9 to K 28 a 9.8. (Ref Mnp France Sheet 57 D/10000)	
			Rest of Arid area as per sketch sent with my last evening report.	
"	"	1.30 pm	AD. MS to DDMS VIII Corps attended Conference DMS IV Army.	
"	"	4.30 pm	Evacuated to C.O.S. Officers and other Ranks from DR. wounds three.	app 7.
COUIN	6.4.16	8.30 am	Situation unchanged. Weather colder.	
"	"	11.30 pm	A.DMS attended conference S.O.C.	
"	"	"	Wires to DMS, & DNMS. Officers evacuated to C.C.S. each one. Capt W.G. SAMS 1/7 R. Warwicks	app 8.
			Sarcoidosis & R.Rickliven 07 R. wounded Arm.	
COUIN	7.4.16	8.30 am	Situation unchanged. Weather cold & windy.	
"	"	1.30 pm	Wires to D.M.S. & D.DM.S. - Evacuated to C.C.S. Officers and nil OR and an Other Rank	app 9.
			wounded three	

WAR DIARY
or
INTELLIGENCE SUMMARY.

Army Form C. 2118.

Place	Date	Hour	Summary of Events and Information	Remarks and references to Appendices
COUIN	8.4.16	8.30am	Situation unchanged - Weather cold.	
		12 noon	A.D.M.S. visited 1/1 & 2/1 (S.M.) Field Ambulance & A.D.S at FONQUEVILLERS	
		4.30pm	A.D.M.S. attended conference S.A.C.	
			Wires to D.M.S. & Army & D.M.S. VIII Corps. Evacuated to C.C.S officers nil O.R sick two officers sick one O.R wounded one O.R sick. Capt W.A. CURTIS 1/5 WARWICKS & Lieut C. FARRINGTON 1/7 R WARWICKS R.A.M.C & Lieut GARRISH 1/5 R Sussex Shell shock O.R sick eighteen wounded one.	App 10
			Instructions received to select a medical officer to take charge of reinforcement where received in	
			VALHEUREUX. & No 28 Squadron R.F.C. Lieut W.D. Ewing details for this duty.	
			Wire from No 4 C.C.S - "No 9.5 Pt. MILLS 5th 4/7 WARWICKS Dragoons C.S.M." K.I.A.	
			Informed usual routine carried out.	
COUIN	9.4.16	8.30am	Situation unchanged - Weather very quiet am.	
		4.30pm	Wires to D.M.S & D.D.M.S. Evacuated to C.C.S officers sick nil O.R sick twelve wounded three	App 11
			A.D.M.S Raining all duties & D.D.M.S VIII Corps.	
COUIN	10.4.16	8.30am	Situation unchanged - Weather very cold	
		12.45pm	A.D.M.S visited Dressing Station SAILLY & A.D.S at HEBUTERNE	
		3.30pm	A.D.M.S conference with R.M.Os	
		4.30pm	Wires to D.M.S & D.D.M.S. Evacuated to C.C.S officers sick two Capt S.L. GRAHAM 1/7 R Warwick Mental Case & Lieut E.L. REED 1/4 Gloster Neurasthenia Wounded one officer Lieut AITKEN Bucks Bn S.W. Reg Rt. O.R sick twenty five O.R wounded twenty five	App 12

WAR DIARY or INTELLIGENCE SUMMARY

Army Form C. 2118.

Place	Date	Hour	Summary of Events and Information	Remarks and references to Appendices
COUIN	11.4.16	8:00am	Situation unchanged. Weather rainy.	
"		1 pm	A/Adjt attended Conference 8/Adjt VII Corps.	
"		4.30 pm	A/Adjt attended Conference S.O.C.	
"			Wires Adjt to D.Ad.S. - Evacuated to C.C.S. officers sick two 2/Lieut B.H. POWELL 1/4 Oxfords. Fractured metacarpal hand. Capt McCONNELL A.S.R. German measles R.A.M.C. 1/2nd (2nd M) Field Ambulance German measles O.R. sick seventeen O.R. wounded one 37th Division. Officers sick one Capt PUCKLE B.M. 112th & 113th Inf. Bdes.	App 13.
COUIN	12.4.16	8.30 am	Situation unchanged. Weather rainy.	
"		4.30 pm	Wires to Adjt & D.Ad.S. - Evacuated to C.C.S. officers sick two Lieut.Col. L.H. HANBURY Comdg 14. 1/7 R.Warwicks Gastritis Lieut G.P. PAINTER 1/5 R.Warwicks Scabies OR sick eight OR wounded ten	App 14.
"			Lieut A.P. FAIRLEY R.A.M.C. (T.C.) reported for duty.	
COUIN	13.4.16	8.30 am	Situation unchanged. Weather colder and rainy.	
"		4.30 pm	Wires to Adjt & D.Ad.S. - Evacuated to C.C.S. officers sick three Lieut J.V. THOMAS 1/1st (Bn.) Field Co R.E. Neurasthenia Lieut R.S. Miller 1/8 Worcesters German measles Lieut C.A. COOK 1/4 Stafford Pyrexia OR sick nine OR wounded one	App 15.
"			Wire from O/B ranch Ant 14 Op - Wire DMS 8 stating men on leave except those in special leave one with furlo'men to return by train leaving CONDON Apl 15th	App 16.
"			Wire from D.D.M.S. (and in manual) our officers from each Field Ambulance to attend IV Army Anti Gas School. (CPT. FEGRIS 1/1st F.Amb., Capt Ramsay 1/2nd F.Amb. & Capt. MOORE 1/3rd F.Amb. submitted).	App 17.

WAR DIARY or INTELLIGENCE SUMMARY

Army Form C. 2118.

Place	Date	Hour	Summary of Events and Information	Remarks and references to Appendices
COUIN	14.4.16	8.30 am	A.D.M.S. proceeded on leave. Situation unchanged. Weather cold, raining.	
"	"	2.30 pm	D.md.S 1st Army & D.md.S 8th Corps called & then inspected Main Dressing Stations and Advanced Dressing Stations of 1/1st & 1/3rd (Wx) Field Ambulances.	
"	"	4.15 pm	D.A.D.M.S. attended Conference G.O.C.	
"	"	5 pm	Evac to 34d C.C.B. — Evacuated to C.C.B. officers sick three Lieut S.J. CORNISH 1/6 Glosters.	App 18
			Brass S/R Lieut J. WILSON — CHARGE 1/8 R.Warwick, trench fever Capt D. WHEAL 1/4 Gloster. 2 lad foot & tib. fracture & R.sick twenty four on twenty four. Lieut H.P. FAIRLEY R.A.M.C.T.F. and D.F. DODSON R.A.M.C.T.C. joined for duty.	
COUIN	15.4.16	8.30 am	Situation unchanged. Weather rainy.	
"	"	4.30 pm	Visit to 34d C.C.B. Evacuated to C.C.B. officers sick two Capt R. HOMFRAY 1/7 Worcesters Capt. HBMARTINDALE R.D.C. holville Bolton Section Citens Autumn Highness RA. sick evacuation 39 evacuation delay.	App 19
COUIN	16.4.16	8.30 am	Situation unchanged. Weather sunny but windy.	
"	"	4.30 pm	Visit to 34d C.C.B. Evacuated to C.C.B. officers sick one Lieut J. MacAdam O'Brien Dwight = 77 O.R. delay evacuated 118. Sick wastage for week ending 15/4/16 one = 77 O.R. delay evacuated 118.	App 20
COUIN	17.4.16	8.30 am	Situation unchanged. Weather colder & raining.	
"	"	4.30 pm	Visit to 34d C.C.B. — Evacuated to C.C.B. officers sick two S/Lieut V.H. WILSON 1/5 R.Warwick. Ambrose Officer nine & one Lieut S.R. ARNELL 1/8 R.Warwick. S.S.W. Back & forearm left 1/R.sick twentyfive & twentythree. Lieut A.G.H. GLANVILLE R.A.M.C.T.C. reported for duty. Capt E.J. BOONE reported that Field Ambulance.	App 21

WAR DIARY
or
INTELLIGENCE SUMMARY.

(Erase heading not required.)

Army Form C. 2118.

Instructions regarding War Diaries and Intelligence Summaries are contained in F. S. Regs., Part II. and the Staff Manual respectively. Title pages will be prepared in manuscript.

Place	Date	Hour	Summary of Events and Information	Remarks and references to Appendices
COUIN	18.4.16	8.30 a.m.	Situation unchanged. Weather stormy.	
"	"	4.15 p.m.	ADMS returned from leave.	
"	"		ADMS attended conference G.O.C.	
"	"		Visits to 1st MDS, 2nd MDS, D.R.S. — Evacuated to 1 C.C.S. Officers sick two Capt H WADE 1/8 Glosters, Other Ranks sick one, OR sick fourteen, OR wounded seven.	App 22.
"	"		Capt M.H. LAXTON 1/8 Gloster Yarmouthenia OR sick fourteen OR wounded seven.	
"	"	4.30 p.m.	G.O.C.R.P. VIII Corps called, saw ADM.S.	
COUIN	19.4.16	8.30 a.m.	Situation unchanged. Weather cold. Stormy.	
"	"	4.30 p.m.	Visits to 2nd & DRS. Evacuated to C.C.S. Officers sick hit March sick two OR wounded one.	App 23.
COUIN	20.4.16	8.30 a.m.	Situation unchanged. Weather rainy.	
"	"	4.30 p.m.	Visits to 1st MDS & 2nd MDS. Evacuated to C.C.S. Officers sick one Lieut G.V. GAMBLE 1/5 R. Berks Yarmouthenia, OR sick five.	App 24.
COUIN	21.4.16	8.30 a.m.	Situation unchanged except about 500 yards on extreme Right of line have been given up to 21st Division.	
"	"		ADMS attended conference G.O.C.	
"	"	4.30 p.m.	Visits to 1st MDS, 2nd MDS. Evacuated to C.C.S. Officers sick one — Lieut H.B. CARTER 1/8 Worcesters German measles OR sick thirteen OR wounded four.	App 25.
COUIN	22.4.16	8.30 a.m.	Situation unchanged. Weather wet, cold.	
"	"	4.30 p.m.	Visits to 1st MDS & 2nd MDS. Evacuated to C.C.S. Officers sick one OR sick thirteen OR wounded three.	App 26.
"	"	7.30 p.m.	ADMS attended conference G.O.C. with reference to Divl Staff exercise.	

Army Form C. 2118.

WAR DIARY
or
INTELLIGENCE SUMMARY.
(Erase heading not required.)

Place	Date	Hour	Summary of Events and Information	Remarks and references to Appendices
COUIN	23/4/16	8.30 am	Situation unchanged. Weather milder.	
"	"	4.30 pm	Wire to D.Md. 1 D.M.S. - Evacuated to C.C.S. Officers sick two Capt. C.M. THRELFALL Lt. BROWN all 1/3 Indian Cavalry Corps Pct., Bruises inflicted Major R.O. THOMPSON 1/2 Scottish Colts Wounded one officer T.F.D. VFF 1/4R BORDR Shell wound back. O.R. sick fifteen O.R. wounded nine sick great Lt. D. NORMAN 23rd Pdr. - 777 Div. Situation unchanged. Weather improving	app. 27
COUIN	24/4/16	8.30 am	D.Md. attended conference G.O.C. on D.M.I. & Off Services	
"	"	5 pm	Wire to D.Md. & D.M.S. Evacuated to C.C.S. Officer sick two Capt. E. JONES 1/8 Worcester German measles Lieut J.W. HASKINS 1/8 R. Warwick. Two Lt. Res. R.R. sick twenty-two O.R.wounded six	app 28
COUIN	25/4/16	8.30 am	Situation unchanged. Weather warmer, sunny	
"	"	1 pm	D.Md. attended Conference D.Md. VIIIth Corps. The subject the deficiency in specialist personnel & deficient supply of medical & field ambulance by advance depot medical stores	
"	"	4.30 pm	D.Md. attended Conference TpD. V.O.C	
"	"	"	Wire to D.Md. & D.M.S. - Evacuated to A.C.C.S. Officer sick til O.R sick nineteen O.R.wounded nine	app 29
COUIN	26/4/16	8.30 am	Situation unchanged. Weather warm, sunny	
"	"	5 pm	D.Md. attended Conference S.O.C.	
"	"	"	Wires to D.Md. & D.M.S. - Evacuated to C.C.S. - Officers sick nil O.R.sick one O.Recommended nil	app 30
"	"	"	Surg: Capt. T.W. WAUGH Divnl 1/5 R.R. Survey rejoined for duty from England.	
COUIN	27/4/16	8.30 am	Situation unchanged. Weather warm sunny.	
"	"	4.30 pm	Wire to D.Md. & D.M.S. - Evacuated to C.C.S. Officers sick from Capt. L.G. PARKINSON 1/4 Glosters German	app 31

Army Form C. 2118.

WAR DIARY
or
INTELLIGENCE SUMMARY.
(Erase heading not required.)

Instructions regarding War Diaries and Intelligence Summaries are contained in F. S. Regs., Part II. and the Staff Manual respectively. Title pages will be prepared in manuscript.

Place	Date	Hour	Summary of Events and Information	Remarks and references to Appendices
COJEUL	28.4.16	8.30am	Measles Capt B LONG 14/5 B N.F. Coy German measles Lieut G.T. ROSCOE O/C app. 4/8 Worcesters. German measles 2/Lieut A.R. MONTGOMERY 1/7 Worcestershire, German measles O/R sick twenty two. Situation unchanged. Weather warm sunny.	app. 32.
		4.30pm	Wire to ADMS 48th Div. Evacuated to C.C.S. Officers nil sick two Lieut 2/M FOWLER 1/7 R Warwicks app. 4/8 Worcesters. Lieut N.P. HOUGHTON 1/5 Gloucesters German measles O/R sick ten. Evacuated ten.	
COJEUL	29.4.16	8.30am	Situation unchanged. Weather warm sunny.	
		4.30pm	Wire to ADMS 48th Div. Evacuated to C.C.S. Officers sick three Lieut K.C. BAXTER 1/7 Worcesters German measles Lieut S.C. WROTH 1/5 R Warwick German measles Capt P.R. HALL Bucks B.N. German measles Officers wounded per Lieut W. LANE 2nd Bn B.N. R.F.A. Shrapnel wound Buttock + fracture Rt g left. O/R sick nineteen O/R wounded two.	app 33.
COJEUL	30.4.16	8.30am	Situation unchanged. Weather warm sunny.	
		10.30am	Wire from Highland C.C.S. - 2379 Pte WAINE. E 1/4 Oxford fracture Rt. G.S.M. - W.O. informed. Nurses' orderlies arrived.	app/084
		4.30pm	Wire to ADMS, H.Q. Evacuated to C.C.S. Officers sick nil 2/Lieut C.D. SHARPE 1/4 R Berks Halluz Valgus.	

[signature] COLONEL,
A.D.M.S. 48th (S.M.) DIVISION.

A.D.M.S. 49th Division

May 1916

CONFIDENTIAL

Vol 14

War Diary
of
A.D.M.S. 48th Division

From 1.5.16 to 31.5.16.

WAR DIARY
INTELLIGENCE SUMMARY

Army Form C. 2118.

Place	Date	Hour	Summary of Events and Information	Remarks and references to Appendices
COUIN	1.5.16	8.30am	Situation unchanged from that of 30th April. Death of fine	
"	"	6pm	A Brief with A.D.M.S. went round new billeting area towards the Brigade of the Division are going to move – viz BEAUVAL, HEM, GEZAINCOURT, BEAUQUESNE.	App 1.
"	"		Wires to D Adj & D.A.Q. Evacuated to C.C.S. Officers sick one, Lieut WISDON H. 14/3 B.Rs.	
"	"		OR Coy German Measles. Officers wounded two Lieut T. CALDER 14/R Batts. Shell shock	
"	"		Capt. GOODWIN N.F. 47 Wounded. Private wound lg. R.O. Paid twenty eight OR wounded nine	
"	"		Major R.C. OLDHAM R.A.M.C.(T.F.) proceeds to report to A.D.M.S. having finished	
"	"		Capt. R.B. ROE R.A.M.C (T.S) proceeds on duty to No 9 C.C.S.	
COUIN	2.5.16	8.30am	Situation unchanged. Weather fine	
"	"	10.30pm	A Dnd attended Conference D Dnd VIII Corps.	
"	"	11.30pm	Wires to A Adj & D D.A.Q. - Evacuated to C.C.S. Officers sick nil OR sick ten OR wounded three	App x.
COUIN	3.5.16	8.30am	Situation unchanged. Weather fine	
"	"	11.30am	A Dnd 56th Division called & saw O Dnd with reference to medical arrangements at HEBUTERNE – Northern sub district, the 56th Div is taking over.	
"	"	4.30pm	Wires to A Dnd & D D.M.S. - Evacuated to C.C.S. Officers sick nil OR sick twenty three OR wounded two	App 3.
"	"		Instructions issued to O.C. 1/2nd (Welsh) Field Ambulance to move to BEAUVAL on 4th inst. Instructions handed to O.C. 1/2nd Field Amb.le to move A.D.S. at BAILLY to J.16.B.2. (Ref. Wood Sh. 2).	

WAR DIARY
or
INTELLIGENCE SUMMARY.

Army Form C. 2118.

(Erase heading not required.)

Place	Date	Hour	Summary of Events and Information	Remarks and references to Appendices
COUIN	4.5.16	8.30am	Situation as described below (6th inst) Weather fine	Appx 4.
		4.30pm	Wires to 2nd & 99th Fd Ambs – Evacuate to C.C.S. Officers sick nil Wounded one 2/Lieut Affleck 1/4 Oxfds. Shell wound fingers left OR wounded fifteen OR wounded three other formation officers wounded one Lieut C Jordon 86th Bde 29th Divn. Scalp wound – sent on to Base. accidental "2/ 14th Pte Smith B.C. fracture of leg Ulna" – naval precaution taken. Wires from Highland C.C.S. Wires from 1/1st (West Riding) Field Ambulance moved from SOUASTRE to BEAUVAL	Appx 5
COUIN	5.5.16	8.30am	Situation as described below (6th inst) Weather fine. A.D.M.S. visited A.D.S. Hebuterne Sailly Ref 57d B2/4000 which has been moved to Bailly Ref 57d B2/4000 also the A.D.S. Hebuterne	Appx 6.
	"	4.30pm	Wires to 2nd & 99th F.A.'s – Evacuated to C.C.S. Officers sick nil OR sick twenty OR wounded two	
COUIN	6.5.16	8.30am	Situation as follows – 46 – 56th Divisions have taken over line from FONQUEVILLERS to HEBUTERNE (PUSIEUX Road) – The 48th Divisional line extending from this point south to R 29 b 19 Ref 57d 4/40000. The 1/4th & 8th Somersets billeted in BEAUVAL & other billets in HEM.	
	"	4.30pm	Wires to 2nd & 99th F.A. – sent one to C.O.S. Officers sick one Capt M R E & 8 nch 8th German wounded OR sick thirteen OR wounded five	Appx 7
COUIN	7.5.16	8.30am	Situation as above – 143rd Bde in Bullch & Bavincourt OR sick sixty Advanced Dressing Station at Fonquevillers handed over to 5th Division	Appx 8.
	"	4.30pm	Wires to 2nd & 3rd & 1/1st W.Rg Coys – Evacuate to C.C.B. officers sick nil OR sick nineteen OR wounded two Back Wastage for week = .95 per thousand per day.	

ACKA BOEDDICKER M.D.
Wt.W10791/1773 500,000 1/15 D.D.&L. A.D.S.S./Forms/C. 2118.

WAR DIARY
or
INTELLIGENCE SUMMARY.

Army Form C. 2118.

Place	Date	Hour	Summary of Events and Information	Remarks and references to Appendices
COUIN	8.5.16	8.30am	Situation no change. Weather inclined to stormy & cold.	
		4.30pm	Wires to D.M.S. & D.D.M.S. - Evacuated to C.C.S. officers nil OR sick twenty seven OR wounded nineteen. Capt E.J. BOONE 1/1st (9.M) Field Ambulance departed from M/Laundry Chimney Station	App 9
COUIN	9.5.16	8.30am	Situation as above. Weather stormy, cold wet.	
		2.30pm	O/C Hut visited Hosp (9.M.) Field Ambulance at BEAUVAL, also to No 1 Divisional area at GEZAINCOURT, MON.	
		4.30pm	Wires to D.M.S. & D.D.M.S. - Evacuated to C.C.S. officers sick nil OR sick eight OR wounded none.	App 10
COUIN	10.5.16	8.30am	Situation as follows. Rain held as above. 8 1/4.3 W Duffy B.S. in Road 2 GEZAINCOURT.	
		4.30pm	Wires to D.M.S. & D.D.M.S. - Evacuated to C.C.S. officers sick nil OR sick thirteen	App 11
COUIN	11.5.16	8.30am	Situation as above. Weather fine.	
		4.30pm	Wires D.M.S./D.D.M.S. - Evacuated to C.C.S. officers sick two Lieut F.H. SMITH 1/4 Gloster Lieut J.E. MARIGOLD 1/5 R Warwicks Acute appendicitis OR sick nil OR wounded fine	App 12
COUIN	12.5.16	8.30am	Situation unchanged. Weather fine.	
		1pm	O/C Hut visited Advanced Dressing Station HEBUTERNE.	
		4.30pm	Wires to D.M.S. & D.D.M.S. - Evacuated to C.C.S. officer sick one 2/Lieut T.E. MATTHEWS 2/1st Field Coy R.E. Primary Syphilis OR sick sixteen	App 13

Army Form C. 2118.

WAR DIARY
or
INTELLIGENCE SUMMARY.
(Erase heading not required.)

Instructions regarding War Diaries and Intelligence Summaries are contained in F. S. Regs., Part II. and the Staff Manual respectively. Title pages will be prepared in manuscript.

Place	Date	Hour	Summary of Events and Information	Remarks and references to Appendices
COUIN	13.5.16	8.30am	Situation unchanged. Weather colder and.	
"		4.30pm	Wires to D.Art. & D.Ind. - Evacuated to C.C.S. Officers sick ten Lieut E.M.EDWARDS 48 Div train to "A" Coy. German measles. Lieut J. PASKIN 1/4th B & M.G. Coy Gastritis. for Dental treatment O.R. sick thirteen O.R. wounded five.	App 14
COUIN	14.5.16	9.30am	Situation unchanged. Weather cold moist.	
"		4.30pm	Wires to D.Art. & D.D.M.S. - Evacuated to C.C.S. officers sick nil OR sick six OR wounded one. Sick evacuation for week ending 14.5.16 = "65" ph Thousand per day.	App 15
COUIN	15.5.16	8.30am	Situation unchanged. Weather estd moist.	
"		4.30pm	Wires to D.Art. & D.Adml. - Evacuated to C.C.S. Officers sick nil OR sick fourteen	App 16
COUIN	16.5.16	8.30am	Situation unchanged. Weather warmer & fine.	
"		4.30pm	Wires to D.Adj. & D.Ind. - Evacuated to C.C.S. officers sick nil wounded one Lieut G.S. REED Stokes morts unit ?? sick twelve OR wounded forty seven. Above large number wounded owing to a raid made on "G" sector (held by 1/7th R. Bucks) on extreme right of Div.t. Front line at 12.30am 16.5.16.	App 17
COUIN	17.5.16	8.30am	Situation unchanged. Weather fine. O.D.M.T. proceeded on 9 days leave.	
"		4.30pm	Wires to D.Adml. & D.Ind. - Evacuated to C.C.S. Officers sick nil OR sick thirteen OR wounded four.	App 18

Army Form C. 2118.

WAR DIARY
or
INTELLIGENCE SUMMARY.
(Erase heading not required.)

Instructions regarding War Diaries and Intelligence Summaries are contained in F.S. Regs., Part II. and the Staff Manual respectively. Title pages will be prepared in manuscript.

Place	Date	Hour	Summary of Events and Information	Remarks and references to Appendices
COUIN	18.5.16	8.30am	Situation unchanged. Weather fine	
		4.30pm	Wires to Ad'ms D.M.S. - Evacuated to C.C.S. officers sick two Capt G. KNIGHT-ATKINS 1/4 (Glos) Clunie Dyspepsia. Lieut E.F. CHAMBERLAIN A.S.C. No3 Coy Pain & debility O.R. sick nine O.R. wounded three.	App 19
COUIN	19.5.16	8.30am	Situation unchanged. Weather fine	
		4.30pm	Wires to Ad'ms D.M.S. - Evacuated to C.C.S. officers sick three Lieut S. & CARTER 1/4 (RW) B'n R.F.A. German Measles Lieut T.P. RATE 1/8 Worc German Measles Capt E.J. HAM A.S.C. No 2 Coy Pain German Measles O.R. sick twelve O.R. wounded two	App 20
COUIN	20.5.16	8.30am	Situation unchanged. Weather fine	
		4.30pm	Wires to Ad'ms D.M.S. - Evacuated to C.C.S. officers sick two Lieut H.G. PHIPPEN 1/5 (Glos) German Measles Lieut J.B. HILL Bucks B'n German Measles O.R. sick three O.R. wounded two	App 21
COUIN	21.5.16	8.30am	Situation unchanged. Weather fine	
		12.30pm	D.M.S. in camp with the Surgical Specialist of the Army (Col Sinclair) inspected the building of Chateau at AUTHIE the mess for seriously wounded of 1/1 South Midland Heavy 1/2 and 1/3 (R&M) Field Ambulance	
		4.30pm	Wires to Ad'ms D.M.S. - Evacuated to C.C.S. officers sick nil O.R. sick one 2/Lieut H CARTER 1/8 Worc German Measles wounded Ammo O.R. sick nine	App 22

WAR DIARY
or
INTELLIGENCE SUMMARY.

(Erase heading not required.)

Army Form C. 2118.

Instructions regarding War Diaries and Intelligence Summaries are contained in F. S. Regs., Part II. and the Staff Manual respectively. Title pages will be prepared in manuscript.

Place	Date	Hour	Summary of Events and Information	Remarks and references to Appendices
COUIN	22.5.16	8.30am	Situation unchanged. Weather fine.	
"	"	5pm	D.A.D.M.S. attended conference D.H.Q. VII Corps. Then proceeded to No. 48 Div. Supply Col. at FIENVILLERS with reference to the reduction of motor cycles allotted to Field Ambulances from 3 to 2.	App 23
"	"	5.30pm	Wires to D.M.S. & D.D.M.S. Evacuated to C.C.S. Officers sick nil Other ranks sick eight O.R. wounded one.	
COUIN	23.5.16	8.30am	Situation unchanged. Weather unsettled. Cooler.	
"	"	4.30pm	Wires to D.M.S. & D.D.M.S. Evacuated to C.C.S. Officers sick two 2/Lieut R.J. HOLDSWORTH 1/5 R.Sussex German Grenade Major W. WARD 2nd Bn RFZ. (I & L) Other ranks wounded one Lieut N.O. KIRBY 1/7 R. Warwicks (S.W. Bord) O.R. sick right O.R. wounded two. An accident occurred at GEZAINCOURT with 143 B.R. Household Battery through suffering premature in Stokes Gun thereby killing 5 wounding 8.	App 24
COUIN	24.5.16	8.30am	Situation unchanged. Weather unsettled.	
"	"	1pm	D.D.M.S. with A.D. & A.Q. visited HEBUTERNE trenches to select site for 2 Elephant Dug-outs. also inspected watering points in the Trenches. Wires to D.M.S. & D.D.M.S.	
COUIN	25.5.16	8.30am	Situation unchanged. Weather raining.	
"	"	4.30pm	Wires to D.M.S. D.D.M.S. Evacuated to C.C.S. Officers sick one Lieut J.B. FULLERTON 240 & 5 R.F.A. Other ranks O.R. sick seven O.R. wounded one.	App 25.

Army Form C. 2118.

WAR DIARY
or
INTELLIGENCE SUMMARY.
(Erase heading not required.)

Instructions regarding War Diaries and Intelligence Summaries are contained in F. S. Regs., Part II. and the Staff Manual respectively. Title pages will be prepared in manuscript.

Place	Date	Hour	Summary of Events and Information	Remarks and references to Appendices
COUIN	26/5/16	8.30 am	Situation unchanged. Weather raining	
"	"	12.30 pm	A.D.M.S. accompanied D.D.M.S. VIII Corps to HEBUTERNE A.D.S. & to the trenches	
"	"	4.30 pm	Wires to D.M.S. & D.D.M.S. - Evacuated to C.C.S. officers nil O.R. sick eight O.R. wounded two. A.D.V.S. returned from leave.	App 27.
COUIN	27/5/16	8.30 am	Situation unchanged. Weather warmer, finer.	
"	"	4.30 pm	Wires to D.M.S. & D.D.M.S. - Evacuated to C.C.S. Officers sick one Lieut W. BAYLEY 48th T.M. Battery	App 28.
"	"		Trench fever O.R. sick thirteen	
COUIN	28/5/16	8.30 am	Situation unchanged. Weather fine	
"	"	4.30 pm	Wires to D.M.S. & D.D.M.S. - Evacuated to C.C.S. Officers sick nil wounded one, O.R. sick six O.R. wounded three. HICKS 114 Hy Bty, R.S.O. Shell wounds back	App 29.
"	"		Sick wastage for week = "51" per thousand per day.	
COUIN	29/5/16	8.30 am	Situation unchanged. Weather fine	
"	"	9.30 am	D.M.S. VIII Corps called, saw A.D.M.S. & Div. Sanitary Officer. Gialli Lato inspected billets in	
"	"	6 pm	AUTHIE & ST LEGER. O.D.S. returned from leave to 1/2 NM (S.M.) FIELD AMB ECE, AUTHIE	
"	"	4.30 pm	Wires to D.M.S. & D.D.M.S. - Evacuated to C.C.S. officers sick one Capt R BURLINGHAM 1/8 Worcesters Neurasthenia, O.R. sick fifteen O.R. wounded three	App 30.

Army Form C. 2118.

WAR DIARY
or
INTELLIGENCE SUMMARY.
(Erase heading not required.)

Instructions regarding War Diaries and Intelligence Summaries are contained in F. S. Regs., Part II. and the Staff Manual respectively. Title pages will be prepared in manuscript.

Place	Date	Hour	Summary of Events and Information	Remarks and references to Appendices
COUIN	30.5.16	8.30am	Situation unchanged. Weather unsettled	
		4pm	A.D.M.S. attended with Div! Sanitary Officer Conference at D.H.Q. & VIIth Corps	
		4.30pm	Visit to Medl. D.H.Q - Evacuated to C.C.S. officers sick one Lieut. Col. DAVENPORT 1/5 Yorks.	App 31
			Influenza 8 Rank seven.	
COUIN	31.5.16	8.30am	Situation unchanged. Weather fine.	
		11.00am	A.D.M.S. with D.A.D.M.S. (visits) A.D.S. BAILLY	
		4.30pm	Visit to Medl. D.D.M.S. - Evacuated to C.C.S. Officers sick one Lieut. W. DURANT 1/4th	App 32
			B 92 R.f. Cay Dental Corps O.R. sick seven O.R. wounded five	
			A.D.M.S. accompanied Medl. Is Army & Medl. VIIth Corps on a visit to 1/3rd (Nth) Field Ambulance	

[signature] COLONEL,
A.D.M.S. 48th (S.M.) DIVISION.

A.D.M.S. 46th Division

June 1916

5

CONFIDENTIAL

War Diary
of
A.D.M.S. 48th Division
from 1-6-16 to 30-6-16.

Vol 15

Army Form C. 2118.

WAR DIARY
or
INTELLIGENCE SUMMARY.
(Erase heading not required.)

Instructions regarding War Diaries and Intelligence Summaries are contained in F. S. Regs., Part II. and the Staff Manual respectively. Title pages will be prepared in manuscript.

Place	Date	Hour	Summary of Events and Information	Remarks and references to Appendices
COUIN	1.6.16	—	Inspected men of 5th, 6th & 7th R Warwick Regt reported as being unfit for duty at the front. Inspected 50 men of the 31st Salvage Company	
		3 pm	DGMS visited Officers Hospital and Divl Rest Station and expressed himself as highly pleased with all the arrangements. Evacuated 7 OR sick to CCS. Admitted 1 Officer 60 OR sick, 3 wounded – Prevailing diseases influenza & scabies.	
COUIN	2.6.16	10 am	Inspected men of 6th R Warwick Regt reported as unfit for the front. Inspected 50 more men of Divl Salvage Company.	
			Evacuated 8 OR sick. Admitted 1 Officer wounded (Lieut E V Sullivan R.A.M.C. attd 240 Bde RFA), OR 31 sick 3 wounded – Died N 7 Bateman M.A.C.	
COUIN	3.6.16	—	+ 3 OR 3/Som Yeo evad for duty with VIII Corps Cyclist Battalion at Beauquesne	
			Weather fine – Ordinary routine duties – Evacuated to CCS OR 10 sick, 2 wounded – Admitted 2 Officers sick and OR 37 sick and 13 wounded, the latter caused by shelling of our trenches by the enemy in retaliation for a raid carried out by 29th Division	
COUIN	4.6.16	—	Heavy showers of rain. Ordinary routine duties. Evacuated 2 Officers sick 21 Col Hawken Bucks Bn. Fraction of scapula & 31 Ambsy 8/R Warwicks,	
			Pyorrhea OR sick 13, wounded 8. Admitted 2 Officers 27 OR sick, 2 OR wounded Section 1/3m Fld Ambulance rcvd with 146 R.de to training area.	
COUIN	5.6.16	2.30 pm	Visited Heilbsterne with CRE to look for a site for dug out for wounded. Inspected Advanced Dressing Station & Aid Post 5/R Warwicks.	
			Evacuated OR sick 18, wounded 1. Admitted Officers 2 sick – OR 26 sick, 1 wounded.	
COUIN	6.6.16	—	Weather showery – Situation unchanged – Attended conference at R Royal VIII Corps. Captain Wrigley RAMC (TC) reported his arrival and posted for	
			temporary duty with 6th Gloucester Regt vice Capt Walker proceeding on leave. Evacuated OR sick 10. Admitted OR 26 sick, 1 wounded.	
COUIN	7.6.16	—	Weather bright with occasional showers. Evacuated OR sick 9, wounded 12. Admitted sick 1 Officer 19 OR wounded 1 Officer, 15 OR	
COUIN	8.6.16	—	Weather showery, but generally fine – Situation unchanged – Proceeded with AQ & QMG to reconnoitre site for wounded dug out. Selected	
			spot in Orchard at K.15.b.2.3. Gave instructions to OC 3/Som Yeo to arrange for digging in of 2 Elephant houses at this spot and to clear the	

WAR DIARY
or
INTELLIGENCE SUMMARY.
(Erase heading not required.)

Army Form C. 2118.

Place	Date	Hour	Summary of Events and Information	Remarks and references to Appendices
COUIN	8.6.16	—	Trench taking hit from Cemetery onwards.	
			Evacuated to No 2 Stationary Hospital, Abbeville, 1 Officer sick, Major R Hodkin, 1/4 R Warw Regt & Pucka 2 Inf officers from appendicitis — 1 Officer wounded Lieut E.C. Wyatt, 1/5 R Warw Regt. Shell wound arm right. OR sick 3, OR wounded 4.	
			Admitted sick 2 Officers Major Hodkin (noted above) & 2/H Bartlett R 2 1/7 Worcester N.Y.D, and OR 27: wounded 1 Officer 2nd Carter, E.P. 1/5 R Warw Regt and OR 3.	
COUIN	9.6.16	—	Weather fine with occasional showers. Situation unchanged. Headquarters Section 1/1 S.M Field Ambulance moved from BEAUVAL to HEM. Operating tent (35 beds) opened at Chateau AUTHIE in charge of Lt-Col Gosling 2/Sm Field Ambulance, principally for cases of abdominal injury — open to cases from VIII Corps generally. Evacuated sick, 1 Officer 2/Lt Bartlett R 2 1/7 Worcester "Nsnasthenia" OR 8; wounded, 1 Officer 2/Lt Carter EP 1/5 R Warwicks shell wound arm right OR 5. Admitted sick OR 28, wounded OR 5.	
COUIN	10.6.16	—	Situation unchanged. Weather rainy.	
			Wrist to Stud & Stud — Evacuated to C.C.S. officer sick hit OR sick seven other Formations officers sick one Lieut R.E. Wels) 4 – 4th Arm Signals att 10th & Infy 3 Os Dental.	
COUIN	11.6.16	—	Situation unchanged. Weather cold & damp.	
			R.A.M.C. — Divl. Sanitary Officer inspected latrines in "G" sector of 48th R Warwicks — also in billets & cook houses in village of HEBUTERNE. They were found in a fairly complete state.	
			Wires to Stud & S.D.M.S — Evacuated CCS officers sick one Lieut FRELDRID 145/1 T.M. Bty Inflamed Lymphaneum, OR sick seven OR wounded one.	
			Wire from 39 C.C.S. :- 109th Dn RIDGEWAY F. 1/6 Warwicks proved C.S.M — Meningococci no later.	

Army Form C. 2118.

WAR DIARY
or
INTELLIGENCE SUMMARY.
(Erase heading not required.)

Instructions regarding War Diaries and Intelligence Summaries are contained in F. S. Regs., Part II. and the Staff Manual respectively. Title pages will be prepared in manuscript.

Place	Date	Hour	Summary of Events and Information	Remarks and references to Appendices
COUIN	12.6.16	—	Situation unchanged. Weather cold with plenty of rain. Wire to DMS & DADMS. Evacuated to C.C.S. officers sick from Lieut D.F. HARRIS 1/6 Gloster Yeomanry, 2/Lieut P. EDWARDS 144th T.M. Battery, Tuned Fever. Lieut S.M. HAYES 241 at B Bty R.F.A. Amentopia, 2/Lieut G. SHEPPARD 1/1 Oxford Bucks Otitis media. O.R. sick twelve. O.R. wounded five. ADMS went to the upparts on the sanitation of the trenches & billets in HEBUTERNE occupied by 1/8 R. Warwicks. Also a circular memorandum on sanitation, regarding the dynamite that this might be circulated to all Brigade & Commanding Officers.	
COUIN	13.6.16	—	Situation unchanged. Frequent rain storms. ADMS attended Conference DMS VIII Corps. Wire to DMS & DADMS. Evacuated to C.C.S. officers sick three Lieut A. PALMER 248 TMB 13/Y Division, 2/Lieut J.C. BELL 1/6 Worcesters hand obstruction, 2/Lieut A. LESLIE 240 & 8th RFA. Dental caries. OR sick fifteen.	
COUIN	14.6.16	—	Situation unchanged. Weather dull cold. ADMS sent in scheme of medical arrangements for the forthcoming operations to the DMS VIII Corps. Wire to DMS & DADMS. Evacuated to C.C.S. officers sick one Cap.t P.N. WAUGH 1/5 R Warwicks Insomnia. Sent to Infantry Avonmore. Lieut A.D.B. BROWN Bucks Bn. GSW R.forearm. OR sick from OR wounded two.	

WAR DIARY
or
INTELLIGENCE SUMMARY.

(Erase heading not required.)

Army Form C. 2118.

Place	Date	Hour	Summary of Events and Information	Remarks and references to Appendices
COUIN	15-6-16	—	Situation unchanged. Weather cold. Dull. Wires to 2nd & 3rd F.A. - Evacuated to C.C.S. Officers sick Nil OR sick twenty-nine OR wounded one. ADMS attended conference D.O.C.	
COUIN	16-6-16	—	Situation unchanged. Weather milder. ADMS inspected work at O.D.S. HEBUTERNE. Evacuated to C.C.S. Officers sick two Capt J.W.KANE 2nd I.C. Def K malaria 2/Lieut A.A. LESLIE 2nd R.B.R.F.A. S.I.W. foot (accidental) OR sick four OR wounded six	
COUIN	17-6-16	—	Situation unchanged. Weather fine. ADMS with OC 1/(2nd) (Rly) Field Ambulance inspected ADS. BAILLY. Evacuated to C.C.S. Officers sick one Capt T.E. BOLTON 1/5 R. Sussex Pl'throis Wounded one Lieut J.M. ROLLESTON Bucks Bn. Bomb wound scalp (hand). OR sick 14 OR wounded 3.	
COUIN	18-6-16	—	Situation unchanged. Weather milder & sunny. ADMS worked F.O.C. Visited 1/(2nd) (Rly) Field Ambulance RUTHIE. Four nursing sisters arrived for duty with Operating Unit at Chateau AUTHIE. Evacuated to C.C.S. Officers sick Nil OR sick 15 OR wounded one. The formation officers wounded one Lieut DAVY R.M 16th West Yorks 31st Brit. Bullet wound abdomen & Thorax.	

Army Form C. 2118.

WAR DIARY
or
INTELLIGENCE SUMMARY.
(Erase heading not required.)

Instructions regarding War Diaries and Intelligence Summaries are contained in F. S. Regs., Part II. and the Staff Manual respectively. Title pages will be prepared in manuscript.

Place	Date	Hour	Summary of Events and Information	Remarks and references to Appendices
COUIN	19.6.16	—	Situation unchanged. Weather improving. Evacuated to C.C.S. officers sick two N.Y. (Plus Chaplain attd 1/4 Ox & Bucks) Field Ambulance Capt. Kingsley R.H., Dieulouard. Capt. PICKFORD P. 1/4 Oxf'd & Bucks L.I. Haematuria OR sick 23 OR wounded 3.	
COUIN	20.6.16	—	Situation unchanged. Warmer weather, some rain. ADMS visited ADS HEBUTERNE. Evacuated to C.C.S. officers sick one 2/Lieut ENOCK W.H. 1/4 Oxf'd 73 and R.J. L.J. Hernia OR sick 18 OR wounded two.	
COUIN	21.6.16	—	Situation unchanged. Weather fine. ADMS with GOC visited 1/3rd (Glos) Field Ambulance. Evacuated to C.C.S. officers sick one Capt. F.E. FRANCILLON 1/5 Glosters L. OR sick 27 OR wounded 1.	
COUIN	22.6.16	—	Situation unchanged. Weather fine. DADMS visits 3 y.c. R. of. Artillery (French) arrange arrangements for supplying stretchers and the latrine also providing and two hilmits, & wiring 1/2 Bn Battn. 2/Lincs R 20 & 81 R p up 54 [?] 12.30. Evacuated to C.C.S. officers nil OR sick 15 OR wounded 5.	

WAR DIARY
or
INTELLIGENCE SUMMARY

Army Form C. 2118.

Place	Date	Hour	Summary of Events and Information	Remarks and references to Appendices
COUIN	23.6.16	—	Situation unchanged. Weather warm sunny. Rain thunderstorms. O Stuff with D Staff VIII Corps visited. 1/3rd (Mh) Fd Ambulance & the operating tent. 1/1 and (Mh) Field Ambulance. Evacuated to C.C.S. Officers sick one Capt SAUNDERS RN. Cardiac weakness. OR sick 65. OR wounded 5.	
COUIN	24.6.16	—	Situation unchanged. Weather rainy. O Stuff attended Conference D Staff VIII Corps. Evacuated to C.C.S. Officers sick one Capt R J SULLIVAN RAMC (SR) at H2 1/5 London F/A. OR sick 29. OR wounded 3.	
		6 am	The bombardment of the enemy trenches starts. 6 am this morning. Number of wounded for the twenty four hours ending 6 am 25.6.16 = Officers 1. ORs 8. Capt Dawson Bd RAMC 75 wounded July. Situation unchanged. Weather fine.	
COUIN	25.6.16	—	First fairly. 1/P RAMC (TC) gift with OR duty from 3rd Bn trenches 75/75. Eva away Ev to C.C.S. Sick Nil. OR wounded seven. Weekly sick unvetape 165 = 1.45. Wounded admissions for 24 hours ending (excluding) 6 am 26.6.16. Officers 1. OR 13.	
COUIN	26.6.16	—	Situation unchanged. Weather rainy. O Staff visited 1/2 nd (Mh) Field Ambulance & A.D.S. Sailly. Evacuated C.C.B. Officers nil. OR sick thirteen. OR wounded eleven. Wounded admissions for 24 hours ending (excluding) 6 am 27.6.16. Officers 1. OR 16.	

Army Form C. 2118.

WAR DIARY
or
INTELLIGENCE SUMMARY.
(Erase heading not required.)

Place	Date	Hour	Summary of Events and Information	Remarks and references to Appendices
COUIN	27.6.16	—	Situation unchanged. Weather showery. Evacuated to C.C.S. Officers wounded two Lieut FIELD A.J. Shell wound R.hand & thigh, 2/Lt IMBER W.R. Shell wound back & arm. Both of 1/7 R. Warwicks. O.R sick 24. O.R wounded 19. Number of wounded admitted for 24 hours ending 5.45 am 28.6.16 - Officers 2 O.R. 17.	
COUIN	28.6.16	—	Situation unchanged. Weather dull & showery. Admitted wounded to No 1 (S.M.) Field Ambulance. Evacuated to C.C.S. Officers wounded one 2/Lieut MARVIN 1/5 R. Warwicks bullet wound hand & thigh. O.R sick 14 O.R wounded 15. Wounded admissions for 24 hours ending 5.45 am 29.6.16. Officers 1 O.R. 25.	
COUIN	29.6.16	—	Situation unchanged. Weather dull. Evacuated to C.C.S. Officers sick one A.Phee Chaplain Capt HINGLEY R.H. also 4/6(R.M.) Field Ambulance Chronic Diarrhoea. Wounded two 2/Lieut ALABASTER F.C. 1/5 R. Warwicks Shell wound hand. 2/Lieut HAWBRIDGE R. 1/5 R. Warwicks Shell wound feet & arms. Nine wounded three Wounded admissions for 24 hours ending 5.45 am 30.6.16 O.R 10.	
COUIN	30.6.16	—	Situation unchanged. Weather improving. Three cases of Diphtheria occurred in 1/4 R Berks billetted in COUIN also 3 suspects. Definite cases found on enquiry up to the outbreak sent to 39 C.C.S. Evacuated to C.C.S. Officers wounded four 2/Lieut CAMERON E.R. 23rd Heavy Luff. Batty. Shty. OR or J. O.R wounded five. Officers sick two	

1577 Wt.W10791/1773 500,000 1/15 D. D. & L. A.D.S.S./Forms/C. 2118.
TRAPNELL H. H/Section Pyrotin Capt HEK F.W. H/Section Albuminuria

WAR DIARY
or
INTELLIGENCE SUMMARY.
(Erase heading not required.)

Army Form C. 2118.

Place	Date	Hour	Summary of Events and Information	Remarks and references to Appendices
COUIN	30/6/16		Orders received to 1/2nd & 1/3rd (Wx) Field Ambulances and to detail one complete section to proceed with 144 & 145 Infy Brigades to MAILLY-MAILLET in rest July, in accordance with 48th Divl Order No 82 dated 30th June. Wounded admitted for the 24 hours ending 5.45am 1.7.15 — 10 officers 19 OR. Division on 48th Divl Right - 31st Divsn. On 48th Divl Left 56th Divsn. Scheme for Collection of Wounded & Medical Arrangements in the event of heavy fighting. R.A.M.C. Operation Orders by Col C.A. Young. No. 1 2 3 4.	

COLONEL,
A.D.M.S. 48th (S.M.) DIVISION.

SECRET

48th DIVISION

Refc Map
Sheet 57D
1/40000.

R.A.M.C. OPERATION ORDER NO.1.

BY COLONEL C.A.YOUNG, C.M.G., A.M.S., A.D.M.S.
18th June 1916.

1. EVACUATION.
   (a) Lying down cases will be sent to Nos. 4 and 29 Casualty Clearing Stations by No.20 Motor Ambulance Convoy.
   (b) Slight cases, sitting, from the Divisional Collecting Station to the Corps Collecting Station at ACHEUX by horse ambulance wagons, general service wagons, and the sanitary lorry.
   Slight cases, lying, may also be sent to ACHEUX in the motor ambulance wagons of Field Ambulances, The number of cases suitable for diverting to this point are to be notified to the A.D.M.S. who will arrange with O.C. Corps Collecting Station for their reception The O.C. 2nd Field Ambulance will arrange for a supply of straw to be held at the Divisional Collecting Station for flooring general service wagons etc.
   (c) Officers will, as far as possible, be sent to GEZAINCOURT but all Casualty Clearing Stations can receive them.
   (d) Infectious cases will be dealt with as at present.
   (e) Abdominal and other injuries requiring immediate operation will be sent to the Chateau at AUTHIE.
   (f) The 93rd Field Ambulance, SARTON, will be kept open during operations for the reception of sick. Cases not seriously ill will be sent to and accommodated there until they can be finally disposed of.

2. STRETCHERS.
   Each Casualty Clearing Station holds a reserve of 100 stretchers - Officers Commanding Field Ambulances requiring extra stretchers during operations will send an indent for the required number by any ambulance car taking wounded and the stretchers will be despatched by the returning car.

3. PERSONNEL FOR CASUALTY CLEARING STATIONS.
   In addition to the 25 convalescent patients which the O.C. Divisional Rest Station will send to No.4 Casualty Clearing Station, each O.C. Field Ambulance will detail 1 Officer 1 N.C.O. and 7 men (O.C. 3rd Field Ambulance 6 men) for duty at No.29 C.C.S. These moves will take place on receipt of further orders.

4. PRISONERS OF WAR.
   Wounded prisoners will have all documents removed from them at Main Dressing Stations. All such documents and identifications will be handed over to the A.P.M.

Officers Commanding Medical Units will pay special attention to the instructions and regulations on this subject and take such steps as will enable them to trace any articles should reports of loss be made subsequently.

6. REPORT OF WOUNDED.
The following messages are required from Divisional Collecting Station and Main Dressing Stations - as soon after 8 a.m., noon, and 9 p.m. as possible as regards numbers of WOUNDED ONLY.
(a) Admitted in the intervals between 8 a.m. and noon; noon and 9 p.m.; 9 p.m. and 6 a.m. Officers French troops, and prisoners of war to be distinguished
(b) Remaining when messages are sent, distinguishing between "lying down" and "sitting" cases.

   (specimen message) Admitted since 6 a.m. Officers 10, O.R. 120, French 2, Germans 3, aaa Remaining lying 40 sitting 95 aaa xx S.M.Field Ambulance.
Officers names are not required.

7. The foregoing arrangements will come into operation on the commencement of the bombardment unless otherwise ordered.

            (signed) C.A.YOUNG, Colonel

                    A.D.M.S. 48th Divn.

SECRET.

R.A.M.C. OPERATION ORDER No.2.
BY COLONEL C.A.YOUNG, A.M.S., C.M.G., A.D.M.S.
20th June 1916.

----

1. REPORTS.   Patients admitted to the Divisional Collecting Station will be shewn as admissions to the Field Ambulance whose personnel establish the Collecting Station. Before being sent to the Corps Collecting Station at ACHEUX a note will be made on the "Tally" of each case to the effect that they are "TRANSFERS".

The Corps Collecting Station (89th Field Ambulance) will not record cases as fresh admissions which have already been thus "tallied" at Divisional Collecting Stations, but when reporting them on telegrams and other returns, will be careful to distinguish such cases as TRANSFERS.

(signed) C.A.YOUNG, Colonel.
A.D.M.S. 48th Divn.

48th DIVISION.

R.A.M.C. OPERATION ORDER No.3.
By COLONEL C.A.YOUNG C.M.G., A.M.S., A.D.M.S.
23rd June 1916.

1. EVACUATION.
   No.20 Motor Ambulance Convoy will evacuate lying down cases to No 4 Casualty Clearing Station, DOULLENS, only; all other lying down cases will be evacuated by light railway to No.29 Casualty Clearing Station, GEZAINCOURT.
   Sitting up cases will be evacuated by light railway or Motor Ambulance Convoy to No 29 Casualty Clearing Station only.
   48th Division R.A.M.C. Operation Order No 1 of 18th June para 1 should be amended accordingly.

2. SPECIAL CASES.
   The O.C. 1/2nd S.M.Field Ambulance will notify A.DS.M.S. Divisions direct should his accommodation become full.

3. "SICK" and "WOUNDED"
   (a) The Divisional Rest Station will be kept open for the reception of all SICK of the Division. They will be admitted direct and will not be shewn as "transferred" from other Field Ambulances.
   The 3rd S.M. Field Ambulance will not take in sick.
   (b) Wounded from the A.D.S. at SAILLY will be sent to the 2nd S.M.Field Ambulance.
   Wounded from the A.D.S. at HEBUTERNE will be sent to the 3rd S.M.Field Ambulance.
   They will be shewn as <u>Admissions</u> to their respective units.
   Abdominal and other serious injuries will all be admitted to the 2nd S.M.Field Ambulance.
   (c) All cases now in Field Ambulances will be evacuated to Casualty Clearing Stations by the end of this week, except
   (1) Men who will be fit for duty in 48 hours.
   (2) Men who can be employed at light duty in the Division as "Temporarily unfit".
   (3) The 25 men for duty at No.4 C.C.S.

                          (signed) C.A.YOUNG, Colonel,
                                   A.D.M.S. 48th Divn.

48th Division.

R.A.M.C. Operation Order No. 4.
by Colonel C.A. Young, C.M.G, A.M.S, A.D.M.S.
30th June 1916.

1. **Move.**

The Officers Commanding 1/2nd and 1/3rd S.M. Field Ambulances will each detail One Section to be in readiness to march to P.18.a., S.W. of MAILLY MAILLET at half an hour's notice any time after 8 a.m tomorrow 1st July.

On arrival at MAILLY MAILLET the section 1/2nd S.M. Field Ambulance will be attached to the 144th Infantry Brigade, and the section 1/3rd S.M. Field Ambulance to the 145th Infantry Brigade.   Packs and greatcoats will be taken.

A.D.M.S. 48th Divn.

Secret.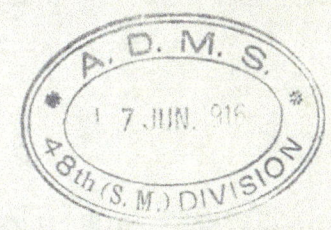

48th DIVISION.

SCHEME OF MEDICAL ARRANGEMENTS IN THE EVENT OF HEAVY FIGHTING.

Reference Map Sheet 57D.

1. **LINE HELD.** From Trench K.17/10 exclusive North to K.23/1 exclusive South. This line is held by two battalions.

2. **ADVANCED DRESSING STATIONS.**
   (a) HEBUTERNE - 1 Tent Subdivision, 3rd S.M. Field Ambulance.
   1 Bearer Subdivision, 3rd S.M. Field Ambulance.
   (these bearers will be for duty in the trenches, and will be reinforced by bearers from the Advanced Dressing Station at J.16.d.8.7. if necessary).
   (b) W. of SAILLY at J.16.d.8.7. - 1 Tent Subdivision, 2nd S.M. Field Ambulance.
   1 Bearer Subdivision, 2nd S.M. Field Ambulance.
   (will reinforce bearers at HEBUTERNE if necessary).

3. **MAIN DRESSING STATIONS**
   (a) COUIN - 2 Tent Subdivisions, 3rd S.M. Field Ambulance.
   (b) N. of AUTHIE at I.10.c.6.6.) 2 Tent Subdivisions, 2nd
       CHATEAU, AUTHIE.   ) S.M. Field Ambulance.

4. **DIVISIONAL COLLECTING STATION.** W. of SAILLY at J.16.d.8.7. - Found by personnel of 2nd S.M. Field Ambulance forming Advanced Dressing Station at this point.

5. **IN RESERVE.** 2 Bearer Subdivisions n 2nd S.M. Field Ambulance.
   2 Bearer Subdivisions - 3rd S.M. Field Ambulance.

6. **SICK TRANSPORT.** The Motor Ambulance Wagons of the 2nd and 3rd S.Mid. Field Ambulances will be parked in the vicinity of the Advanced Dressing Station at J.16.d.8.7. and will be used as required for the transport of wounded from HEBUTERNE and SAILLY to the Main Dressing Stations at COUIN and AUTHIE.
   The route to COUIN will be via the Valley Road through COIGNEUX and up the COUIN HILL to the Main Dressing Station; empty ambulances returning to HEBUTERNE across D.26. from S.W. to N.E. through SOUASTRE - BAYENCOURT & SAILLY.
   The route to AUTHIE will be the Valley Road via COIGNEUX and ST. LEGER; empty cars returning via HENU - SOUASTRE & BAYENCOURT - SAILLY.
   The Horse Ambulance Wagons of the 2nd and 3rd S.Mid. Field Ambulances will be parked at the Divisional Collecting Station, and will be at the disposal of the Officer i/c for the conveyance of slightly wounded men to ACHEUX for evacuation by rail, in accordance with para. 10.

7. **EQUIPMENT.** 100 stretchers will be kept at each Advanced Dressing Station, as well as an ample supply of blankets (2 per stretcher), splints, bandages, tallies, shell and other dressings, anti-tetanic serum, anti-gangrene vaccine, medicaments for treating burns, oxygen cylinders and ammonia ampoules for treating "gas" cases, rations and medical comforts. The fact that dressings will be required not only for use at the Advanced Dressing Stations but for the replenishment of the stocks of Regimental Medical Officers in Aid Posts must not be lost sight of, and an ample reserve must therefore be maintained.

8. **EQUIPMENT for the DIVISIONAL COLLECTING STATION.** An Admission and Discharge Book, tallies, bandages, dressings, anti-tetanic serum, medical comforts, and a supply of rations, cooking appliances, etc.

9. **EVACUATION OF SERIOUSLY WOUNDED.** Regimental Stretcher Bearers will convey the wounded to the Regimental Aid Posts. From these they will be carried or assisted to the Advanced Dressing Stations by R.A.M.C. bearers who will be detailed for duty at the regimental aid posts by the Officer i/c Advanced Dressing Station in accord--ance with requirements. As circumstances permit the motor ambulances will be brought up and will convey the wounded to the Main Dressing Stations, by the routes previously mentioned From the Main Dressing Stations evacuations to the Casualty Clearing Stations will be carried out by the Motor Ambulance Convoys.

10. **DIVISIONAL COLLECTING STATION & EVACUATION OF SLIGHTLY WOUNDED.**
    (a) Slightly wounded men able to walk and who do not require sick transport will be collected into parties of ten (or other convenient number) and marched in charge of an N.C.O. or R.A.M.C. orderly to the Divisional Collecting Station W. of SAILLY at J.16.d.8.7.
    (b) The route to this from HEBUTERNE will be through SAILLY and along the R.AUTHIE Valley Road; these routes will be indicated by directing posts, for the erection of which the O.C. 3rd S.Mid. Field Ambulance will be responsible.
    (c) From the Divisional Collecting Station casualties requiring evacuation will proceed to the entraining station at ACHEUX (P.18.a.2.5.) those who are able to walk will march under the command of a wounded Officer or N.C.O. those who are unable to walk, in the Horse Ambulance Wagons which will be collected at the Divisional Collecting Station in accordance with these instructions. The very slightly wounded not requiring evacuation after being treated, fed, and rested will be returned to their units.
    The names of all men who receive attention at the Divisional Collecting Station will be entered in the Admission and Discharge Book and a note will be made as to their disposal, i.e. whether evacuated to rail or returned to unit.
    All men evacuated will be furnished with a tally.

(signed) G.A.YOUNG, Colonel.
A.D.M.S. 48th DIVISION.

CONFIDENTIAL

War Diary
of
A.D.M.S. 48th Division
from 1st July to 31st July 1916

Vol 16

July 1916
51

COMMITTEE FOR THE
MEDICAL HISTORY OF THE WAR
Date 13 SEP. 1915

Army Form C. 2118.

WAR DIARY
or
INTELLIGENCE SUMMARY.
(Erase heading not required.)

Instructions regarding War Diaries and Intelligence Summaries are contained in F. S. Regs., Part II. and the Staff Manual respectively. Title pages will be prepared in manuscript.

Place	Date	Hour	Summary of Events and Information	Remarks and references to Appendices
COUIN	1.7.16	8.30 a.m.	Situation unchanged	
		10 a.m.	Divisional Advanced Headquarters opened at Mailly-Maillet. D.D.M.S. proceeding there.	
		11.30 a.m.	144th Infy Bde arrived at P.18.a (Ref map France sheet 57d 1/40,000) D.W. of Mailly-Maillet, with a section of the 1/2nd (S.M.) Field Ambulance attached to it.	
		12.30 p.m.	The 1/1/5th & Infy Bde also arrived at same place with a section of 1/2 (S.M.) Field Ambulance attached to it.	
			Staff notified arrival of these Brigades, & section of the Field Ambulances attached thereto to O.Bn/1 4th Division. Also got in contact with the Advanced Dressing Station of 4th Division & of 29th Division – both situated in Mailly-Maillet.	
		4 p.m.	A.D.M.S. arrived at Advanced Divisional Headquarters.	
			Evacuated to C.C.S. – Officers sick two Capt MASTERS T.A.S. 1/5 R Sussex Debility, Capt HALL P.P. Bucks Bn. O.C. Townellets. O.R. sick nil O.R. wounded 18.	
			Admissions from 9.5 p.m. 1.7.16 to 5.45 a.m. 2.7.16. Wounded. Officers 8 O.R. 56.	
MAILLY-MAILLET	2.7.16	–	Situation Divisional Advanced Headquarters, 144th & 145th Infy Brigades + sections of 1/2nd & 1/3rd (S.M.) Field Ambulances as above, situated at Mailly-Maillet on VIII Corps Reserve.	
		–	Upon receipt of operation orders from "G" for above Brigade to attack from R. ANCRE to Y' RAVINE (Ref Map France sheet 1/15 57d S.E.) A.D.M.S. consulted A.D.M.S. 29th & 4th Division & made arrangements	

WAR DIARY or INTELLIGENCE SUMMARY

Army Form C. 2118.

Place	Date	Hour	Summary of Events and Information	Remarks and references to Appendices
Continued			for taking over the O.P.B. of 29th Division at "KNIGHTSBRIDGE" & the A.D.S. of 36th Division at HAMEL. O.Bn.L then proceeded to VIII Corps Collecting Station at ACHEUX where he saw O.Bn.L VIII Corps.	
MAILLY-MAILLET	2/7/16	—	O.Bn.L visited 1/2nd (S.M.) Field Ambulance AUTHIE & Bn. (S.M.) Field Ambulance COUIN arranging for extra personnel, stretchers & ambulance cars to be sent to the Section with the 1/4th + 1/5th & Infy Bde.	
		6 pm	O.Bn.L received R.A.M.C. operation Order No.5 dealing with scheme for evacn of wounded from KNIGHTSBRIDGE & HAMEL to the Dressing Station of 29th Division at VITERMONT.	
		9 pm	D.A.D.M.S. proceeded to HAMEL A.D.S. but on calling at 1/5 & B'de H.Qrs. at MESNIL was informed that at 11.30 pm instructions had been received for the Brigade to march back to the Bivouacs at MAILLY-MAILLET. That above operation orders were cancelled. Lieut-Col (T. Maching) + Capt H.D. THOMASON (1/4th (S.M.) Field Ambulance (wounded) Section of Field Ambulances attached to 1/4th & 1/5th B'des returned to MAILLY MAILLY from HAMEL + VITERMONT.	*
MAILLY-MAILLET	3/7/16	3.30 am	Situation as on 2nd inst. Weather overcast & rainy	
		5.30 pm	O.Bn.L visited COUIN + 1/3rd (S.M.) Field Ambulances Divisional Headquarters + Infy B. B'de returned to COUIN area.	

* Evacuated to C.C.S. Officers wounded Lieut HOWATT. J. 1/5 Bn R.E. of Lan. Head (slight) Lieut GROVE P.A. 1/5 R. Warwicks Shell wounded O.R. sick 32 O.R. wounded 8. Wounded admissions for 24 hours ending 8.45 am 3/7/16. Officers — O.R. sick 5 — O.R. w. 6.

Army Form C. 2118.

WAR DIARY
or
INTELLIGENCE SUMMARY.
(Erase heading not required.)

Instructions regarding War Diaries and Intelligence Summaries are contained in F. S. Regs., Part II. and the Staff Manual respectively. Title pages will be prepared in manuscript.

Place	Date	Hour	Summary of Events and Information	Remarks and references to Appendices
COUIN	3/7/16	—	Evacuated to C.C.S. - Officers sick one. Majors WILSON T.A. Debility & Alimentation. Officers wounded two 2/Lieut PINE H.H. 1/5 R. Warwicks Shell Shock. 2/Lieut BAGSHAW E.C. No 4 Coy 5th Bn Special Bn. R.E. Shell Shock. Number of wounded admitted for 24 hours ending 5.45 am 4/7/16 Officers 1. O.R. 13. Situation as on 3rd inst.	
COUIN	4/7/16	—	S.D.M.S. called. Saw A.D.M.S. afterwards. 148th Div taking over trenches COLINCAMP sector from 31st Div. Wire from D.D.M.S. that 1/4 (Glos) Field Ambulance is to report 148th Division forthwith. A.D.M.S. issued instructions to 1/1 (South Midland) Field Amb. to send 1 Off'r & 12 O.R. to COLINCAMP A.D.S.; 1 Off'r & 12 O.R. to "EUZTON" & 1 N.C.O. & O.R. to "ECZEMA AVE" Appts. to take over from 31st Div Field Ambulances at present working these Posts on morning 5th inst. Wire to D.D.M.S. 29th Division saying 148th Div will require one bearer sub-division (unknown) ? opening as remainder when convenient. Capt. W.J.A.B. WISHART R.A.M.C. (T.C.) reported on duty with operating unit. Lieut B.J. COURTNEY R.A.M.C. (T.C.) reported for duty. Evacuated to C.C.S. - Officers hit O.R. sick 11. Wounded admission for 24 hours ending 5.45 am 5/7/16 O.R. 3.	App 1. App 2.

Army Form C. 2118.

WAR DIARY
or
INTELLIGENCE SUMMARY.
(Erase heading not required.)

Place	Date	Hour	Summary of Events and Information	Remarks and references to Appendices
COUIN	5.7.16		Situation-during night 4/5/4 the 144 & B₂ took over trenches held by 3rd Division on H₁ Division Right. 4/5/(5hr) Field Ambulance took over Advanced Dressing Station COUIN AND the Collecting Posts at "EUSTON" on the trenches (ECZEMA AVE) A.D.M.S. visited A.D.S. at 9/114 & 144 H.B. Headquarters. Evacuated to C.C.S. Officers sick one 2/Lieut SQUIRES D.C. 1/5 R Warwicks. Acc⁴. 82 Wound. OR sick 2 Wounds H. Wounded Admissions for 24 hours ending 5.45 am 6.7.16 OR 3. Major H.W. BOEDDIKER MC(Fife)(5hr) Field Ambulance evacuated sick - fractured Fibula Situation unchanged. Weather wet.	
COUIN	6.7.16	12noon	A.D.M.S. attended Conference 2/Hghs VIII Corps & visited 4/of (8hr) Field Ambulance giving directions for advance. Billeting Party to proceed to THIEVRES VIII Corps comes under Administration of "Reserve Army". Evacuated to C.C.S. Officers Sick one Capt RICHARDSON S.B. 1/5 R Sussex Occ: of 440 Highl. Scothn. OR sick thirteen Wounded admissions for 24 hrs ending 5.45 am 7.9.16 = OR 32.	

WAR DIARY
or
INTELLIGENCE SUMMARY.
(Erase heading not required.)

Army Form C. 2118.

Place	Date	Hour	Summary of Events and Information	Remarks and references to Appendices
COUIN	7/7/16	—	Situation unchanged. Weather very stormy and wet. Routine work. Evacuated to C.C.S. officers sick one Capt F.H. SPRAGUE RAMC. attd 2D.O's Bn, Officers wounded Lieut A.G. TUCKER Shrapnel wound, Lieut G.A.P. MONTAGUE (Canadian) attd W. RID Shrapnel wound. Lieut A.G. TUCKER Shrapnel wound. attd 4/6 Gordons Lieut A. FOWNE 10 R Scots w. attd 1/4/6 Gordons Bruised foot (Shell Shock) OR sick 6. OR wounded 29. Wife from W RID saying the only army wound a concussion no bones broken.	
COUIN	8/7/16	—	Situation unchanged. Weather improving. Q.M.G. visited VIII Division. Lieut A.DUTHIE 4/1 Ld (Rh) Field Ambulance, which has come to THIEVRES. Evacuated to C.C.S. officers sick two Lieut R. SOUTHAM 14th 5th R.f. Cy Debility Lieut M. RESTCOURT 48 R.A.C. Scabies. Wounded one. Lieut G.W. LEWIS 1/8 Worcester Shell Shock. OR sick 13 OR wounded 8. Wire recd from 2 2 & 8. I continue numbers to furnish to admitted.	
COUIN	9/7/16	—	Situation unchanged. Weather fine. Routine work. Evacuated to C.C.S. officers sick two Capt A.E. PENNY 2/1 Ld 5 Rn R.G.A. Kaso she Capt S.R. KELLAR 2/1 Ld 6 Rn R.G.A. Diphtheria. OR sick 13. OR wounded 11. Lichnowsky furnace riding 9.7.16 Officers sick 8. OR sick 47. Officers wounded 3. OR 74. Sick wastage pr 1000 fr day '63.	

Army Form C. 2118.

WAR DIARY
or
INTELLIGENCE SUMMARY.
(Erase heading not required.)

Instructions regarding War Diaries and Intelligence Summaries are contained in F. S. Regs., Part II. and the Staff Manual respectively. Title pages will be prepared in manuscript.

Place	Date	Hour	Summary of Events and Information	Remarks and references to Appendices
COUIN	10.7.16	—	Situation unchanged. Weather fine. O.Ps/And. made arrangements for receiving Dental work within the Division. Evacuated to C.C.S. Offficio sick one 2/Lieut DURRANT D.G. 1/5 Border Dental Carries. T.R. sick four T.R. wounded seven. Wound(s) admissions for 24 hours ending 5.45am 10.7.16 = O.R. 17.	
COUIN	11.7.16	—	Situation unchanged. Weather fine (but cool). O.And. visited 1/3rd (Rly) Field Ambulance. Evacuated to C.C.S. Officers sick two Lieut WALDRON F. 1/8 Worcesters Rheumatism, 2/Lieut PAGE H.R. 1/6 Glosters Rheumatism. O.R. sick 5. O.R. wounded 11. Wound(s) admissions for 24 hours ending 5.45 am 12.7.16 = 13 O.R.	
COUIN	12.7.16	—	Situation unchanged. Weather dry (but cool). And. held a conference with O.C.s of the Field Ambulances as regards the nursing of sick Field Ambulance in mobility (Field) work. Evacuated to C.C.B. Officers sick two Lieut MURPHY W.E. 1/7 R Warwicks Dental Carries, Capt GREGG O.M. 1/7 R Warwicks Dental Carries. O.R. sick 6. Wounded Y. Wound(s) admissions for 24 hours ending 5.45am 13.7.16 = 12 O.R. Capt ENJ O'FARRELL RAMC (T.C.) reports for duty.	

Army Form C. 2118.

WAR DIARY
or
INTELLIGENCE SUMMARY.
(Erase heading not required.)

Instructions regarding War Diaries and Intelligence Summaries are contained in F. S. Regs., Part II. and the Staff Manual respectively. Title pages will be prepared in manuscript.

Place	Date	Hour	Summary of Events and Information	Remarks and references to Appendices
COUIN	13/7/16	—	Situation unchanged. Weather dull.	
		6 p.m.	DDMS visited DDs of VIII Corps. Also 1/2nd (Wx) Field Ambulance. And gave instructions for 1/1st (Wx) Field Ambulance to send 1 Bearer Subdivision & 7 ambulance cars to report to DDMS X Corps at SENLIS.	App 1.
			1/43rd Infy Brigade moves to BOUZINCOURT & joins X Corps.	App 2.
		6.55 p.m.	Message from DMS VIII Corps — Bearers of 1/1st (Wx) Field Ambulance and 7 ambulance cars will proceed today to report to 10th Corps. 1/1st (Wx) Field Amb. instructed accordingly.	App 3.
		8.40 p.m.	Wire from X Corps — That "Bearer Divn & ambulance wagons of Field Ambulance will march to BOUZINCOURT tonight & remainder of Field Amb. to CONTAY tomorrow." Instructions issued to 1/1st (Wx) Field Ambulance accordingly.	App 4.
		—	CAPT. LEWIS R. R.A.M.C.(T.C.) 1/2nd (Wx) Field Ambulance evacuated sick — Switched about. Evacuated to C.C.S. Officer sick was Capt Byrne JK RAMC (TF) att 1/6 R Warwicks. Total Cases D.R. sick nine D.R. wounded six. 2 Officers wounded for 24 hours ending 5.45am 14/7/16 — DR 1.	
COUIN	14/7/16	—	Situation as before.	
		12.9am	Wire from DDMS 10th Corps — "36 Bearers & 5 MT Ambulances have arrived BENUS and the Bearer Sub Division & 2 MT Ambulances (will proceed) to BENUS & att BOUZINCOURT tomorrow". Instructions issued. DDMS 10th Corps informed.	App 5, 6, 7, 8.

WAR DIARY
or
INTELLIGENCE SUMMARY.
(Erase heading not required.)

Army Form C. 2118.

Place	Date	Hour	Summary of Events and Information	Remarks and references to Appendices
COUIN	14.7.16		ODMS visited 1/2nd & 1/3rd (SM) Field Ambulance, instructing these Ambulances to prepare for a move. 1/1st (SM) Field Ambulance moved to CONTAY.	
			3rd Reserve Army visited 1/3rd (SM) Field Ambulance with ADMS. Wire from 8th Corps that 1/1st, 2nd Coy & 1/1st H.Q. of 15-, & 1/3rd (SM) Field Ambulances to move to CONTAY on 15-.	App 9
			DA DMS 38th Division called & saw ODMS with reference to taking over from this Division. The 129th Field Ambulance 38th Division relieved 1/2nd (SM) Field Ambulance at COUIN. Operation Order (RAMC) just received from DMS 10th Corps with this object for one Field Ambulance 38th Division to relieve 1/1st Field Ambulance 32nd Division at BOUZINCOURT commencing 9 am on 15 inst. Instructions issued to 1/1st (SM) Field Ambulance accordingly.	App 10
			Evacuated to C.C.S. officers sick two Capt C.W MARTIN 1/8 R Warwick Rheumatism. 2/Lieut C.J. RICHARDS 1/8 R Warwick Influenza. Wounded one Lieut N D HOUGHTON 1/5 Glos.	
			1 Ptc left am OR sick 43. OR wounds 3.	
			Wounded admissions for 24 hours ending 5.43 am 15 7 16 Offr in 2 OR 25.	
			Capt J.R. KENION RAMC(T) reported for duty.	

Army Form C. 2118.

WAR DIARY
or
INTELLIGENCE SUMMARY.
(Erase heading not required.)

Instructions regarding War Diaries and Intelligence Summaries are contained in F. S. Regs., Part II. and the Staff Manual respectively. Title pages will be prepared in manuscript.

Place	Date	Hour	Summary of Events and Information	Remarks and references to Appendices
LOUIN	15/7/16	—	Situation unchanged.	
			1/1st (Wx) Field Ambulance took over from 91st Field Ambulance 32nd Division at BOUZINCOURT with the Collecting Posts at CRUCIFIX POST W.12.c.1.1., DONNET POST W.12.a.7.6., BOUILLERS POST W.18.d.3.3.	
			1/3rd (Wx) Field Ambulance moved to WARLOY, a took over from 90th Field Ambulance 3rd Division.	
			14th Infy Bde — 02 Battalions in 5 Buffy Bar moved to FORCEVILLE in X Corps Area.	
			D.D.M.S. proceeded to BOUZINCOURT to arrange taking over from 32nd Division A.D.M.S.	
			Evacuates to C.C.S. Officers sick two Lieut FOWLIE J.M. 1/6 Cheshire Septic arm Lieut E. NORRETT 48th Bn 2.am Debility — Wounded one Lieut HANCOCK R.B. 9/3 Worcesters Shell wound R/g [illeg.]	
			O.R. sick 41 O.R. wounded 23	
		1.30	28th Brigade took over line formerly held by 32nd Division at present South & East and of DIVIDERS at — X.28.5. & X.8.a.0.2.	
LOUIN	16/7/16	8.30 am	Situation as above.	
			D.D.M.S. issued instructions for 1 Section of 1/2nd (Wx) Field Ambulance to proceed WARLOY.	
		12 noon	48th Division took over area from 32nd Division & line above, & 1/4 Gommecourt to BOUZINCOURT.	
			1/2nd (Wx) arrived at BOUZINCOURT.	
		3 pm	D.D.M.S. visited 1/3rd (Wx) Field Ambulance at WARLOY, & issued instructions re the taking of 1/2nd (Wx) Field Ambulance at the place to join the X Corps operating South & under a ambulance.	
			Evacuated to C.C.S. Officers sick nil. O.R. sick 10 O.R. wounded 21.	

WAR DIARY or INTELLIGENCE SUMMARY

Army Form C. 2118.

Place	Date	Hour	Summary of Events and Information	Remarks and references to Appendices
BOUZINCOURT	17/7/16	—	Situation as above. ADMS visited DDMS X Corps & ADMS 25th Division with reference to taking over Field Amble & Collecting Posts of 25th Division, then proceeded to WARLOY & issued instructions to O.C. 1/3 (Wm) Field Ambulance to move to MILLENCOURT & take over from 76th Field Amble the collecting post at NORTH CHIMNEY, ALBERT, & at BAPAUME POST. ADMS then issued Operation Order No 6 dealing with allowances & Relaying 1/2nd (Wm) Field Amble to take over X Corps operating Unit & to relieve 76th Field Ambulance 25th Division, both at WARLOY. The 1/1st & 1/3rd (Wm) Field Ambulances each to send 1 tent subdivision to take on the "lightly wounded" Dressing Station & BRB from 77th Field Ambulance at VADENCOURT. Operation Order No 6 dated 17/7/16 & copies from DDMS & Corps, which also directs Drossing Station at MILLENCOURT to be handed over to III Corps by noon 19th inst. Instructions to O.C. 1/2nd (Wm) Field Ambulance accordingly. Absence from Duty Capt Q.S.Danns & Capt HODGES WC RAMC (T.F.) & Capt MASON J.B. RAMC (a reported for duty. Evacuated a Dunkirk from 6 am 17.7.16 to 5.55 am 18.7.16. O.R. 4. Wounded admitted to C.C.B. Officers his Officers one. 145th Infy Brigade moved to BOUZINCOURT.	App 11.
BOUZINCOURT	18/7/16		Situation generally, as above. ADMS visited 1/2nd (Wm) Field Ambulance at WARLOY & DRS at VADENCOURT	

WAR DIARY
or
INTELLIGENCE SUMMARY.

Army Form C. 2118.

Place	Date	Hour	Summary of Events and Information	Remarks and references to Appendices
BOUZINCOURT	10/7/16		DADMS with O/c Collecting post at BARAUME POST (W24c73 Ref Sheet France Blvd 57 d SE 20000) to ascertain if it were possible to establish a Collecting Post in BOISELLE. Ground conditions disagreeable at present, but (9000) 34 wheeled stretcher carriers at South and entrance Millets & visited 111th Brigade Headquarters informing the S.O.C. as to the arrangements for collection of wounded. Evacuated to C.C.S. Officers Wounded 8 O.R. Wounded 48. Other Formations Officers wounded 1 O.R. sick 2 O.R. wounded 15. Wounded & Sickness for 24 hours ending 5.55 am 19/7/16. Officers 6. O.R. 216. German 18.	
BOUZINCOURT	19/7/16		Situation generally unchanged. A.D.M.S. visited Collecting Posts at NORTH CHIMNEY, ALBERT, & at BARAUME POST. D.D.M.S. visited Field Ambulances at WARLOY & VADENCOURT. Messages from D.D.M.S. & C of S that 1st Australian Division taking over from 34 & Div on 12 Div Right. & (but situation for them had to be found) at N.CHIMNEY & they also take BARAUME POST O 4c BARAUME POST & N.CHIMNEY in the Casualty and ½ of the building at N.CHIMNEY (and) Vic 1st Australian Division. Field Ambulance at MALENCOURT handed over to 3rd Corps & 15th (Kelly) Field Ambulance moved back to VADENCOURT Evacuated to C.C.S Officers wounded 6 O.R. sick 2 wounded 170. Other Formations Officers sick one wounded 1 O.R. sick 12 wounded 42. Wounded & Sickness for 24 hours ending 5:55 am 20/7/16. Officers 6 O.R 232. German 10.	

WAR DIARY or INTELLIGENCE SUMMARY

Army Form C. 2118.

Place	Date	Hour	Summary of Events and Information	Remarks and references to Appendices
BOUZINCOURT	20.7.16	-	Situation unchanged. Everything fine. O.&n.l. visited D.S.L. & X Coys. Also Collecting Posts at CRUCIFIX CORNER, DONNET POST, OFFICERS POST. A large number of casualties occurred from gassing among the 1/8 Worcesters (who were in support party between LA BOISSELLE & POZIERES rd) due to the enemy shelling this road with 5.9's 7.7mm. gas shells between hours of 11.10pm & 1.00am night 19/20. Of these there were 2 Officers & 5 O.R.'s NY injury was certain. The battalion marched back to BOUZINCOURT about 1.30am reaching billets about 4am. Shortly after symptoms (8 sneezing) began to appear among the men. Severe approximately five cases up to the present. (6pm) Symptoms appeared the mucous cases, spasms & difficulty breathing, later colic, vomiting, headache. Some had lachrymation resembling lydite. Some also said that the smell (of the smell of gas entered gas entered lethal) was like lilac. & the shells, other described gas as well as smell. There were also 15 cases (gassing among Cornwall (1/3 S.R. 2 O.R.s? 3 Lincs. Evacuated to C.C.S. Officers wounded 1, 3 R. sick 5, OR wounded 79, other Armston Officers wounded 1. OR sick 19, OR wounded 25. Wounded & Immersion for 24 hours ending 5.55am 21.7.16 Officers 3 OR wounded 79 German 2.	
BOUZINCOURT	21.7.16		Situation unchanged. O.&n.l. visited 1/8 Worcestershire Regt. interviewed Medical Officer & some men who had been gassed on night 19/20.8. The majority of those gassed are still unfit for duty & will probably be so for at least a week. Forwarded report of this effect to Headquarters 144 I.B.	

Army Form C. 2118.

WAR DIARY
or
INTELLIGENCE SUMMARY.
(Erase heading not required.)

Instructions regarding War Diaries and Intelligence Summaries are contained in F. S. Regs., Part II. and the Staff Manual respectively. Title pages will be prepared in manuscript.

Place	Date	Hour	Summary of Events and Information	Remarks and references to Appendices
BOUZINCOURT	31.7.16	CPD	Evacuated to C.C.S. Officers sick one wounded 2. O.R. sick 12 Wounded 216. Other ranks wounded officers sick one wounded one. O.R. sick 33 wounded 117. Wounded admissions for 24 hours ending 5.55 am 22.7.16 Officers 12. O.R. 380. Capt. SAVAGE RAMC temporarily in charge 25 H.Q. duty group pending his return to his field ambulance 32nd Division	
BOUZINCOURT	22.7.16		Situation unchanged. 1 Brit. visited H.Q.(?) Field Ambulances at WARLOY & VADENCOURT. Also inspected VBC vicinity [?] men very heavy. Am only fit and fit order ability. S/Sgt M.[?] visited Collecting Post at N. CHIMNEY - BAPAUME POST. Evacuated sick Officers nil wounded 3 O.R. sick 1 Wounded 30. Other Ranks also Officers sick 2 wounded 3. O.R. sick 2 wounded 53. Wounded admissions for 24 hours ending 5.55 am 23.7.16 Officers 6 O.R. 150	
BOUZINCOURT	23.7.16		Situation generally unchanged. (A Brit) visited Collecting Post at CRUCIFIX CORNER (WIDELL Rfl Kapt Franc. SYD BE (2000). Also visited Collecting Post at N. Chimney HEBERT & BAPAUME POST (W24C14). Evacuated to C.C.S. Officers sick 1. Wounded 10. O.R. sick 12 Wounded 211. Other Ranks also O.R. sick 16 wounded 245. Wounded admissions for 24 hours ending 5.55 am 24.7.16 Officers 30 O.R. 577.	

1577 Wt. W10791/1773 500,000 1/15 D. D. & L. A.D.S.S./Forms/C. 2118.

2151

Army Form C. 2118.

WAR DIARY
or
INTELLIGENCE SUMMARY.
(Erase heading not required.)

2161

Place	Date	Hour	Summary of Events and Information	Remarks and references to Appendices
BOUZINCOURT	24/7/16		Situation unchanged. Went thro' old Bot. Hq. D.A.A. & L Corps with 8. D.V. & 2nd Corps Collec'r saw O'Neil.	
		12 noon	II Corps took me from X Corps & 18th Division came under II Corps. O'Neil made Collecting post at N.E. Corner ALBERT & BAPAUME POST. Evacuated to C.C.P. Officers wounded fifteen. O.R. sick 27 O.R. wounded 413. Other Formations Officers wounded 6. O.R. sick 16 wounded 91.	
			Wounded admissions for 24 hours ending 5.55 am 25/7/16. Officers 9 O.R. 240. Genuar O.R. 3. Capt. G. MOORE 9/3rd (HC) Field Ambulance evacuated. Afraw alibi. Situation generally unchanged. General advance by our Infantry at South end of	
			POZIERES.	
BOUZINCOURT	25/7/16		A third went (4) Field Ambulances at WARLOY & VADENCOURT. Bathed II Corps & OA Hut 12 L Dorsen Coll'n W) arranged with O'Neil for a Field Ambulance the 1st Division to relieve 96th (H.C.) Field Ambulance at BOUZINCOURT on the & inventory allow'd by 12 th Dan. Wire from O'Neil 1/3 th Division that 34th & Field Ambulances will move to BOUZINCOURT.	app. 12
			Evacuated to C.C.P. Officers wounded 9 & O.R. sick 18 wounded 273. Other Formations Officers wounded 3 O.R. sick 5 wounded 50.	
			Wounded admissions for 24 hours ending 5.55 am 26/7/16. Officers nine O.R. 185- French 1 German 4.	

WAR DIARY
INTELLIGENCE SUMMARY

Army Form C. 2118.

Place	Date	Hour	Summary of Events and Information	Remarks and references to Appendices
BOUZINCOURT	26/7/16		Situation generally unchanged. A.D.M.S. attended Conference S.D.M.S. II Corps. 1/1st (5th) Field Ambulance moved to DONART AREA. Evacuated to C.C.S. Officers sick 1 wounded 3. O.R. sick 26 wounded 126. Other formations Officers wounded 2. O.R. sick 13 wounded 52. Wounded admissions for 24 hours ending 5.55 am 27.7.16 Officers 3. O.R. 105. German O.R. 8.	
BOUZINCOURT	27/7/16		Situation unchanged. A.D.M.S. visited S.D.M.S. II Corps. Also Field Ambulances at WARLOY & VADENCOURT. Instructions received from D.D.M.S. II Corps that 1/2nd (6th) Field Ambulance is to remain behind at WARLOY when Division moves back. Evacuated to C.C.S. Officers sick one O.R. sick 36 wounded 80. Other formations Officers wounded 2. O.R. sick 18 wounded 49.	
BOUZINCOURT	28/7/16	8 am	Situation unchanged. Weather hot.	
		10 am	48th Div. Head quarters moved to LE PLOUY (near DOMAQVEUX) 144th Infy Bde proceeding to DOMART Area. Evacuated to C.C.S. Officers wounded 3. O.R. sick 26 wounded 52. Other formations O.R. sick 11 wounded 58.	
LE PLOUY	29/7/16		All Infantry Brigades arriving in DOMART AREA. Artillery in STOUEN Area. S.D.M.S. II Corps called and lunched.	

2171.

Army Form C. 2118.

WAR DIARY
or
INTELLIGENCE SUMMARY.
(Erase heading not required.)

Instructions regarding War Diaries and Intelligence Summaries are contained in F. S. Regs., Part II. and the Staff Manual respectively. Title pages will be prepared in manuscript.

Place	Date	Hour	Summary of Events and Information	Remarks and references to Appendices
LE PLOUY	29/7/16		O.O. and visited 1/8 Worcesters.	
LE PLOUY	30/7/16		1/1st (H) 2/Cy Ambulance arrived & opened DOM QUEUR for reception of the sick of the Division. Evacuated to C.C.S. full. Situation — 2/8th Division in "Rest" about DOM ART AEP. O/Crd examined men of Salvage Coy for return to duty. Routine. Evacuated to C.C.S. OR. "AXL".	
LE PLOUY	31/7/16		1/3rd (H) Field Ambulance arrived at FRANQUEVILLE. Situation remains another hot. O.O and visited 1/8 Worcesters. Division bathes started at DOM QUEUR. Evacuated to C.C.B. OR sick form. Attached are Appendices 1-12, & RAMC Operation Orders 5 & 6.	2181

Army Ordered about 40 men

R.A.M.C. Operation Order No 5
by Colonel C.A. Young Ch.f. A.m. S. A.D.M.S 48th Division

2nd July 1916.

Ref Map France 57D 1/40000.

1. One Tent Subdivision and 1½ Bearer Subdivisions 1/3rd S.M. Field Ambulance will accompany the 145th Infantry Brigade.
   The Tent Subdivision will form an Advanced Dressing Station at HAMEL. Walking cases will be evacuated to the 29th Division A.D.S at MESNIL, via "JACOBS LADDER". Lying cases will be kept till nightfall and will be evacuated by M/ Stn Ambulance cars via "COOKERS POST" Q 29 b.4.2. - AVELUY WOOD - W 10.d.9.6. and MARTINSART to A.D.S at VITERMONT.

2. One Tent Subdivision and 1½ Bearer Subdivisions will accompany the 144th Infantry Brigade.
   The Tent Subdivision (less 2 Medical Officers) will report to the O/c A.D.S at "KNIGHTSBRIDGE" (Q 16.d.2.3.) and remain there for duty.
   Two Medical officers will report for duty at the A.D.S. at VITERMONT.
   All wounded will be sent to the A.D.S at KNIGHTSBRIDGE.

3. All transport will proceed to A.D.S at VITERMONT for duty as required.

(Sgd) C.C. Young
Colonel
A.D.M.S 48th Division

48th DIVISION.   17th July 1916.

R.A.M.C OPERATION ORDER NO 6 by COLONEL YOUNG, C.M.G., A.M.S., A.D.M.S.

1. The Main Dressing Station at MILLENCOURT will be handed over to the IIIrd Corps by 12 noon 19th July.

2. On completion of handing over, the 3rd South Midland Field Ambulance will withdraw and take over VADENCOURT (Lightly Wounded Station and D.R.S) leaving a Tent Sub-division as A.D.S. at North Chimney Corner, ALBERT, and a Collecting Post at BAPAUME POST.

3. The evacuation route from North Chimney, ALBERT, will be via MILLENCOURT, LAVIEVILLE? HENENCOURT to WARLOY or VADENCOURT according to the Traffic Control Map (Operations) Fourth Army.

4. The Tent Subdivision of the 1st South Midland Field Ambulance at present doing duty at VADENCOURT will be attached to the 2nd South Midland Field Ambulance at WARLOY; the tent subdivision of the 49th Division Field Ambulance will return to its unit.

5. The extra Mobilization equipment, Medical stores, extra rations etc. in excess of establishment held at MILLENCOURT will be handed over to the incoming Field Ambulance IIIrd Corps.

6. All moves to be completed by 12 noon on 19th July.

7. The Motor Lorry (Xth Corps Siege Park) at present doing duty at MILLENCOURT will be stationed at North Chimney, ALBERT for conveyance of Lightly Wounded cases to Vadencourt.

(sd)   C.A. YOUNG, Colonel,
                A.D.M.S. 48th Division.

Copy Aug 1916.

War Diary
of
ADMS 48th Division
from 1.8.16 to 31.8.16.

Vol 17

COMMITTEE FOR THE
MEDICAL HISTORY OF THE WAR
Date -5 OCT 1916

WAR DIARY
or
INTELLIGENCE SUMMARY.

(Erase heading not required.)

Army Form C. 2118.

Place	Date	Hour	Summary of Events and Information	Remarks and references to Appendices
LE PLOUY	1.8.16	—	Situation — 48th Division in "Rest" around DOMART area.	
		12 noon	O/Ried visited No.1 (Sth) Field Ambulance DOMQUEUR & 1/3rd (Sth) Field Ambulance FRANQUEVILLE 48th Division transferred to IX Corps.	
			Evacuated to C.C.S. Officers sick one Lieut W.K. BRASHER 48th Signal Coy Pyrexia, wounded one 2/Lieut L.R. BANFORD 1/8 Worcesters, Effective 10 OR sick 30 wounded 7 (Effect 1/6s)	
LE PLOUY	2.8.16	—	Situation unchanged.	
			O/Ried inspected men of 1/8 Worcesters. Also visited 143rd (Sth) Field Ambulance, which had moved to LONGVILLERS. & 141st (Sth) Field Ambulance.	
			Evacuated to C.C.S. Officers sick one Lieut PRIDMORE R.M. X H.6 TM. Battery Pyrexia. O/Rank 9. Officers wounded nil able to attend a long journey	App 1.
			We received from D.D.M.S. IX Corps to evacuate all Officers considered not able to attend a long journey	App 2.
			Wire received from D.D.M.S. IX Corps cancelling above	
LE PLOUY	3.8.16	—	Situation unchanged	
			O/Ried visited D.D.M.S. IX Corps	
			The 1/8 Worcesters were recommended by the O/Ried to be sent to the sea side for the week to recover from the effects of recent Pyrexia in night of 19/20 July.	
			Evacuated to C.C.S. Officers sick two 2/Lieut M.L. HARCOURT 1/5 R. Warwicks Pyrexia of front	

WAR DIARY or INTELLIGENCE SUMMARY

Army Form C. 2118.

Place	Date	Hour	Summary of Events and Information	Remarks and references to Appendices
LE PLOUY	3.8.16	—	J. CHALCRAFT 1/4 R. Shorthands att 1/6 R. Warwicks dysentery. known tr. Raid 11. Wounded 21 (field cases).	
LE PLOUY	4.8.16	—	Situation unchanged. Weather not seasonable. O.C. Med. visits 1/1st (Rh) Field Ambulance 2/1st (Rh) Field Ambulance 1/2nd (Rh) Field Ambulance arrived & located at RODERIE FARM. Evacuated to C.C.S. tr Raid 13.	
LE PLOUY	5.8.16	—	Situation unchanged. Weather fine. Sanitary Section returned from Divisional Headquarters for inoculation to the present with a/Lieut OXBERRY F.C. 1/4 R. Warwicks Pyrexia, Capt A.T. MITCHIESON M.O. att 1/6 R. Warwicks att Rifle Bgde Pyrexia.	
LE PLOUY	6.8.16	—	Situation unchanged. Weather improving. Evacuated to C.C.S. Micro sick three. Lt. Col. MACEFARLANE E.S. 1/8 R. Warwicks – Emphysema Capt. H.B. BEVAN 1/4 Gloster Pyrexia. Capt M.B. BORZAGE 1/44 R.I.G. Coy. Pyrexia. Trench form. Situation unchanged.	
LE PLOUY	7.8.16	—	O.C. Med. visits 48 to ascertain with A.D.M.S. Wires received from Halgarties that wired of fol direction to the wounded is approved.	App. 3.
			O.C. Med. with Asst. Sanitary Officer visits Warwicks to arrange for Field Laundry.	

WAR DIARY
or
INTELLIGENCE SUMMARY.
(Erase heading not required.)

Army Form C. 2118.

Place	Date	Hour	Summary of Events and Information	Remarks and references to Appendices
LE PLOUY	7.8.16		Evacuated to C.C.S. O.R. sick 8.	
LE PLOUY	8.8.16	—	Situation unchanged. Weather fine. A.D.M.S. visits all Field Ambulances	
			Evacuated to C.C.S. Officers sick one Lieut Dixon T.6. 1/7 Worcesters Pyrexia O.R. sick 30.	
LE PLOUY	9.8.16	8am	Division on move	
		11am	Divisional Headquarters opened here	
BEAUVAL		3pm	All Field Ambulances arrived BEAUVAL. Hosp (Cly) Field Ambulance Opens temporary	
			Evacuated to C.C.S. Officers sick 7 Capt ROYLE & 1/4 R. Berks Fractured rib. Lieut R.T. HAWKINS 1/4 R. Berks	
			Pyrexia. Capt HOMFRAY R. 1/7 Worcesters Pyrexia 2/Lieut W.A. WAGNER 1/4 R. Berkshire Pyrexia 2/Lieut NEVILLE 2	
			1/8 Worcs R/R Bomb. wound Face (A.S.) 2/Lieut MOLLOY H.E. Bucks 8/E. Bombardment Face (A.S.)	
			Capt D.D. MACKAY 1/3rd (SM) Field Ambulance R.A.M.C. Pyrexia O.R. 63	
BEAUVAL	10.8.16	—	Division in move.	
			1/1st (SM) Field Ambulance arrived at VARENNES; 1/2nd & 1/3rd (SM) Field Ambulances arrived at RAINCHEVRE.	
			A.D.M.S. visits 1/2nd & 1/3rd (SM) Field Ambulances	
			Evacuated to C.C.S. O.R. sick 93 O.R. wounded 3 (passed from 1/8 Worcesters)	
			Instructions issued for Capt J. SIMPSON R.A.M.C. T.F. of 1/1st (SM) Field Ambulance & upon fortnight with 37th Field Ambulance to follow Capt R. KENNION Field M. Unit who will join 1/1st (SM) Field Ambulance.	

T.J.134. Wt. W708-776. 500000. 4/15. Sir J. C. & S.

WAR DIARY
or
INTELLIGENCE SUMMARY.

Army Form C. 2118.

(Erase heading not required.)

Instructions regarding War Diaries and Intelligence Summaries are contained in F. S. Regs., Part II. and the Staff Manual respectively. Title pages will be prepared in manuscript.

Place	Date	Hour	Summary of Events and Information	Remarks and references to Appendices
BEAUVAL	11.8.16	—	Division en route to concentrate in II Corps Reserve Army. ADMS visited DDMS II Corps with reference to physical arrangements on taking over line from 12th Division in BOUZINCOURT area. Also visited DMS Reserve Army. ADMS visited 4/1 (Highld) Field Ambulance at VARENNES, 3 1/2 and 1/3rd (Rlry) Field Ambce RAINCHEVAL. Wire sent to ADMS 12th Division asking if 12 noon 13th inst. will suit to take over Field Ambs. at BOUZINCOURT, VARENNES, & LOUVENCOURT. Evacuated to CCS No. 1 — from the Field Ambulances of this Division which went forward.	app. A.
BEAUVAL	12.8.16		Division moving. Wire from ADMS 12 Division – Reserve Div. relieved Div. into his line to-morrow, making of 13th inst. Letter from O Board 12th Div. that 13th inst. names and will suit for taking over at BOUZINCOURT, VARENNES & LOUVENCOURT. ADMS issued instructions to the Field Ambulances of this Division accordingly.	app. B.
BEAUVAL	13.8.16	10 am	Division moving. 4/1 (Highld) Field Ambulance took over from 37th Field Ambulance at BOUZINCOURT. 1/2 and (Rlry) Field Ambulance took over VARENNES & CLAIRFAYE. 1/3rd took over LOUVENCOURT.	

WAR DIARY
or
INTELLIGENCE SUMMARY.

(Erase heading not required.)

Army Form C. 2118.

Instructions regarding War Diaries and Intelligence Summaries are contained in F. S. Regs., Part II. and the Staff Manual respectively. Title pages will be prepared in manuscript.

Place	Date	Hour	Summary of Events and Information	Remarks and references to Appendices
BOUZINCOURT	13-8-16	12 noon	Divisional Headquarters arrived here.	
		3 pm	48th Division took over line from 12th Division	
		8.30 pm	Wire from 3rd Reserve Army – 2 Lt. V.B. BUTLER R.A.M.C. under military Service Act –	Apx 6
		10.30 pm	Wire 13th April – As 2 Lt BUTLER is domiciled in IRELAND presumably he cannot come under military service act	Apx 7
BOUZINCOURT	14.8.16		Situation as above.	
			A.D.M.S. visited H.Q. (R.H.) Field Ambulance in BOUZINCOURT, 1/2 m (R.H) Field Ambulance VARENNES, and 1/3 2/1 (Rh) Field Ambulance LOUVENCOURT.	
			A.D.M.S. with O.C. 1/2 Nl (Rh) Field Ambulance visited Advanced Dressing Station at CRUCIFIX CORNER.	
			Collecting Post at VILLERS at X.8.C.4.6, and X.8.d.7.6 (Ref Map France 57D 1/20000) the latter being a dugout in bye-rd nearly the germans formerly as a pyramidal (R.A.P.)	
			Evacuated to A.C.C.S. Officers sick 1 wounded 1 O Ranks wounded 10 minor officers sick 2 wounded 11 Rank & file 52	
			Wastage for week ending 13.8.16 m.m. OR sick 194	
			(Wounded Admissions from 0am 13.8.16 – 11.55 am 14.8.16 Officers H. OR 9.9.)	

WAR DIARY
or
INTELLIGENCE SUMMARY.
(Erase heading not required.)

Army Form C. 2118.

Instructions regarding War Diaries and Intelligence Summaries are contained in F. S. Regs., Part II. and the Staff Manual respectively. Title pages will be prepared in manuscript.

Place	Date	Hour	Summary of Events and Information	Remarks and references to Appendices
BOUZINCOURT	15.8.16		Situation generally unchanged. Abdul issues Scheme for Burial Arrangements. Lieut R. Younger Reuc to appointed Adjt. Evacuated to C.C.S. Officers sick 1 Wounded 6, O.R. sick 11 Wounded 92. Other Formations Officers sick 2 wounded 1, O.R. sick wounded 34. (Wounded) admissions for 24hrs ending 5.55am 15.8.16. Officers 5 OR 166 German OR 1.	
BOUZINCOURT	16.8.16		Situation unchanged. Abdul attends Conference 3 Abdul R Corps. Evacuated to C.C.S. Officers sick 1, Wounded 8, O.R. sick 10 Wounded 114. Other Formation Officers sick 2 wounded 1 one O.R. sick 23 Wounded 128. (Wounded) admissions for 24 hrs ending 5.55am 16.8.16. Officers 13 OR 230.	
BOUZINCOURT	17.8.16		Situation unchanged. Abdul visited all Field Ambulances. Evacuated to C.C.S. Officers sick kld, wounded 1, O.R. sick 28 Wounded 132. Other Formations Officers sick 2 Wounded nil, OR sick 16 Wounded 20. Wounded Admissions for 24 hrs ending 5.55am 17.8.16. Officers 13 OR 250.	

WAR DIARY
or
INTELLIGENCE SUMMARY.
(Erase heading not required.)

Army Form C. 2118.

Place	Date	Hour	Summary of Events and Information	Remarks and references to Appendices
BOUZINCOURT	18.8.16	—	Situation unchanged. A.D.M.S. visited all Field Ambulances — making arrangements for the attack on permanent line this evening to the hand of Officers about X2a, X2b (Ryburgh 54th France Hardy) Evacuated to C.C.S. Officers wounded 1. O.R. sick 26 wounded 55. 9the Permature Officers sick 4. O.R. sick 23 wounded 22. 29. (Capt. N.G. TUSSNEY & T. FERGUSON (T.C.) appts. for duty. Wounded admissions to 26 am. 21 Aug 5.35 am 18.8.16 Officers 3 O.R. 115	
BOUZINCOURT	19.8.16	—	Situation unchanged except for some slight advance held [illegible] during morning 1st Evacuated to C.C.S. Officers sick 1. Wounded 12 O.R. sick 25 Wounded 124 Other formations Officers wounded 2 O.R. sick 7 wounded 10. Wounded admissions for 24 hrs ending 5.35 am 19/8/16 Officers 5 O.R. 40. Situation generally unchanged. P. Wratten Slevvey	
BOUZINCOURT	20.8.16		A.D.M.S. visited all Field Ambulances. Evacuated to C.C.S. Officers sick 3 Wounded 2 O.R. sick 9 Wounded 159. Other formations Officers sick 2 O.R. sick 9 Wounded 19 — Wounded admissions for 24 hrs ending 5.35 am 20.8.16 Officers 15 O.R. 322 German Officer 1 O.R. 43	

WAR DIARY or INTELLIGENCE SUMMARY

Army Form C. 2118.

Place	Date	Hour	Summary of Events and Information	Remarks and references to Appendices
BOUZINCOURT	21/8/16	—	Situation generally unchanged. Bttn. worked Collecting Posts at RAPAUME POST & IV CHIMNEY ALBERT. Evacuated to C.C.S. Officers wounded 5. OR sick 15. Wounded 126. Other Evacuation Officers sick 1. OR sick 7 wounded 12. Wounded & prisoners for preceding 5 days 21. 8/16 Officers 2 OR 60 figures FR 6.	
BOUZINCOURT	22/8/16		Situation generally unchanged. Have advance cadre N.W. of ouvrers. Evacuated to C.C.S. Officers sick 3 wounded 1. OR sick 9 wounded 54. Other Evacuation Officers sick nil OR sick nine wounded eight. Wounded & missing from preceding 5 22. 8/m. 22. 8/16 Officers 5 OR n/a German O.R. 1.	
BOUZINCOURT	23/8/16	—	Situation unchanged. Weather fine. B.H.Q. attended Conference of Lt. Col. D Capper. Then proceeded to visit the Brigadier when a Medical Board was assembled — Major T.A. Greer R.A.M.C. 47 President, Capts C.E.K. Horsfall & R.B. Williams R.A.M.C. (T.F.) members — to enquire into the state of health of the members had been frozen on night July 19/6/. These men were all OR found unfit. Evacuated to C.C.S. Officer wounded 1 one OR sick & wounded 45. Other Evacuation Officers sick 1. OR sick 23 wounded 29.	

Army Form C. 2118.

WAR DIARY
or
INTELLIGENCE SUMMARY.
(Erase heading not required.)

Instructions regarding War Diaries and Intelligence Summaries are contained in F. S. Regs., Part II. and the Staff Manual respectively. Title pages will be prepared in manuscript.

Place	Date	Hour	Summary of Events and Information	Remarks and references to Appendices
BOUZINCOURT	23.8.16		Wounded admissions for 24 hours ending 5.55am 23.8.16. OR 203. Iceman 16	
BOUZINCOURT	24.8.16	—	Situation unchanged. Evacuated to C.C.S. Officers sick 1. Wounded 4. O Rank 26 Wounded 114 Sick Branches. Officers sick 2 O R sick 6 wounded 11. Wounded Admissions for 24 hours ending 5.55 am 24.8.16. Officers 2 OR 116. Iceman IR 2.	
BOUZINCOURT	25.8.16		Situation unchanged. O/C 1 & 6th Divisions called saw DDMS with reference to taking over FedAmbulant BERTRANCOURT when 144 Inf'y R'l's joins that Division on 27th. Later 39th Division taking over advanced dressing stations & collecting posts around MAILLY-MAILLET, ACHONVILLERS &c. O Ind visited DDMS II Corps. O Ind issued instructions for 1/3 W (WHY) Field Ambulance on being relieved by 77th Field Ambulance 25th Division to take over at BERTRANCOURT. Wire from O Ind 6th Div. that 39th Div. Did intend to collect from 144th Inf. B'de. above. Being timed for relief of 116th, 117th & 7 Amb'c post by 2 Div'n as Intaugable to burn 26th. on own present station BERTRANCOURT &c 27th. O Ind 25th Division called, saw O Ind	app. 8.

T.2134. Wt. W708—776. 500000. 4/15. Sir J. C. & S.

Army Form C. 2118.

WAR DIARY
or
INTELLIGENCE SUMMARY.
(Erase heading not required.)

Instructions regarding War Diaries and Intelligence Summaries are contained in F. S. Regs., Part II. and the Staff Manual respectively. Title pages will be prepared in manuscript.

Place	Date	Hour	Summary of Events and Information	Remarks and references to Appendices
BOUZINCOURT	25/8/16	—	Evacuated to C.C.S. Officers sick 4 wounded two OR sick 25 wounded 96 Other Formation. Officers sick one wounded two OR sick 4 wounded 15. Wounded admissions for 24 hours ending 5.55am 25/8/16 Officers 3. OR 113.	
BOUZINCOURT	26/8/16	—	Situation unchanged. ADMS visited all Field Ambulances. ADMS interviewed DDMS V Corps with reference to nursing the ambulances of the Division into V Corps Area. Evacuated to C.C.S. Officers sick 2 wounded 1. OR sick (wounded) 37. Other formations Officers wounded 1. OR sick 2 wounded 22. Wounded admissions for 24 hours ending 5.55am 26/8/16 Officers 3 OR 76.	
BOUZINCOURT	27/8/16	noon	Situation unchanged. 70th Field Ambulance 25th Division took over dressing Station at BOUZINCOURT & the advanced collecting posts. 113 (ALY) Field Ambulance took over Field Ambulance at BERTRANCOURT from R 2 Ambulance. ADMS made arrangements for hand. Rle Field Ambulance to up Vouchers. Evacuated sick Officers wounded 1. OR sick 4 wounded 26 Other formations Officers sick (wounded) 47.	

T.J.134. Wt. W708—776. 500000. 4/15. Sir J. C. & S.

WAR DIARY or INTELLIGENCE SUMMARY

Army Form C. 2118.

Place	Date	Hour	Summary of Events and Information	Remarks and references to Appendices
BOUZINCOURT	27.8.16		Wounded admissions for 24 hrs. Sitting 55, lying 27 8/C Officers 1 OR 71 Gunmen 1	
BOUZINCOURT	28.8.16	8.30am	Situation unchanged generally.	
			Division moved to BERTRANCOURT & Corps reserve. V Corps. Nothenbrine K34d73 to Q12a4.3	
		10am	1/2nd (H) Field Ambulance moved to VAUCHELLES. 1/1st (H) Field Ambulance to BUS & receiving the sick of the Division.	
			DDMS visited 1/1st, 1/2nd, 2/1st Field Ambulances.	
			Lieut B.L. COURTNEY R.A.M.C. att'd. 1/1 R.Warwicks wounded, reported Capt.R.P.McCONNELL	
			Evacuated to C.C.S. Officers 1 wounded, O.Ranks 112 wounded, 32 Other formations	
			Officers 1 wounded, OR 1 wounded 6.	
			Wounded admissions for 24 hrs ending 28.8.16 Officers 3 OR 13 Gunmen 2	
BERTRANCOURT	29.8.16		Situation as above.	
			ADMS visited 1/1st, 1/2nd Field Ambulances. Also DUTHIE with reference to starting Baths	
			100 men from 1/1 Dunster firing Sanitary Section for Duty	
			Lieut V.H.L. MACSWINEY R.A.M.C. joined for duty.	
			Evacuated to C.C.S. OR wounded 6. Other formations OR sick 4 wounded 6.	

WAR DIARY
or
INTELLIGENCE SUMMARY.
(Erase heading not required.)

Army Form C. 2118.

Instructions regarding War Diaries and Intelligence Summaries are contained in F. S. Regs., Part II. and the Staff Manual respectively. Title pages will be prepared in manuscript.

Place	Date	Hour	Summary of Events and Information	Remarks and references to Appendices
BERTRANCOURT	30.8.16		Situation unchanged. Weather very stormy for this time of year. A.D.M.S. attended Conference D.D.S. & Cofs. Also visited 2/2nd & 2/3rd S.M. Field Ambulances. Evacuated to C.C.S. Officers sick 2, wounded 3. Other ranks sick 113, wounded 2 Officers.	
BERTRANCOURT	31.8.16		Situation unchanged. Weather warmer. Evacuated to C.C.S. O.R. sick 6 wounded 3. Other formations Officers wounded 2, O.Ranks wounded 30. Attached Scheme Medical Arrangements during Period 13.8.16 to 28.8.16.	

[signature]
COLONEL,
A.D.M.S. 48th (S.M.) DIVISION.

48th DIVISION.

SCHEME OF MEDICAL ARRANGEMENTS DURING ACTIVE OPERATIONS
Refce Sheet 57D. S.E. 1/20,000.

1. All wounded will be evacuated to the Advanced Dressing Station at BOUZINCOURT, either via the Collecting Post at CRUCIFIX CORNER or that at NORTH CHIMNEY, ALBERT.
   At BOUZINCOURT they will be sorted out and despatched to destination as follows -
   (a) Abdominal wounds, cases of haemorrhage and those suffering from severe collapse to the II corps Operating Station at WARLOY.
   (b) All other seriously wounded to VARENNES;
   (c) All lightly wounded to Clairfaye Farm.

2. There are Main Collecting Posts at CRUCIFIX CORNER (W.12.c.11.) and at NORTH CHIMNEY, ALBERT (W.28.b.1.8).

3. There are subsidiary Medical Posts for the Left Sector at DONNET POST (W.18.b.5.7), OVILLERS POST (W.18.b.4.3), CAB RANK (X.8.c.4.6), POINT 27 (X.8.b.3.7), and for the Right Sector at GERMAN POST (X.8.b.7.5) and BAPAUME POST (W.24.c.9.3) where R.A.M.C. bearers are stationed.

4. Motor Ambulance wagons are kept at Chateau AVELUY, CAB RANK, LA BOISSELLE, North Chimney Albert, and BOUZINCOURT.

5. All applications for Medical Assistance, stretchers, blankets, medical comforts, etc, should be sent to CRUCIFIX CORNER or NORTH CHIMNEY, ALBERT.

6. The entrances of Aid Posts and Collecting Posts should be efficiently protected with blanket doors, and should have Vermorel Sprayers and a supply of spraying solution in readiness in case of gas attacks. A Small reserve of Gas helmets should be kept.

C. A. YOUNG, Colonel.

15.8.16.   A.D.M.S., 48th Division.

Vol 18

CONFIDENTIAL.

War Diary
of
ADMS 48th Division
from 1-9-16 to 30-9-16.

COMMITTEE FOR THE
MEDICAL HISTORY OF THE WAR
Date 26 OCT 1916

WAR DIARY or INTELLIGENCE SUMMARY

Army Form C. 2118.

Place	Date	Hour	Summary of Events and Information	Remarks and references to Appendices
BERTRANCOURT	1.9.16	—	Situation unchanged. Remainder of 3rd Bn. arrived 1916. Capt. F.E. Williamson RAMC T.F. /3 1 H/C Fd. Ambulance proceeded to report to O.C. 3rd HAVRE under orders from 4th Reserve Army for duty as Bacteriologist. Evacuated to C.C.S. Officers sick 1. OR sick 4 wounded 10. Other Formations Officers sick 1 wounded 2. OR sick 7 wounded 6.	
BERTRANCOURT	2.9.16		Situation unchanged. Capt. J.D. CARROL RAMC T.C. started for duty. Capt. K.D. BENN RAMC T.R. returned to duty from civil leave. Evacuated to C.C.S. OR sick 6 wounded 4. Other Formations OR sick 6 wounded 6.	
BERTRANCOURT	3.9.16	3.30 am	Situation unchanged. Bde Headquarters moved to REDOUBT. Brigade concentrating in Reel around AUTHIE, BERTON, BUS except 144th Brigade which is in the line AUCHONVILLERS sector.	
		10 am	The Medical Inspection Staff inspected men of B Wiltshire rendered unfit by the gas-attack on night July 17/20 "extremely" numbering 380. Evacuated to C.C.S. Officers sick 1. OR sick 2. Other Formations Officers sick 1. OR sick 3 wounded 3. Sick in our lines sick Sunday 3.9.16 Officers 6 wounded 3. OR sick 19 wounded 58.	

Army Form C. 2118.

WAR DIARY
or
INTELLIGENCE SUMMARY.
(Erase heading not required.)

Instructions regarding War Diaries and Intelligence Summaries are contained in F. S. Regs., Part II. and the Staff Manual respectively. Title pages will be prepared in manuscript.

Place	Date	Hour	Summary of Events and Information	Remarks and references to Appendices
BEAUVAL	4.9.16	—	Situation as above. Weather stormy. General routine. Evacuated to C.C.S. Officers Nil. Rank & file (sick & wounded) 14. Other formations (Rank & file wounded) 3.	
BEAUVAL	5.9.16	—	Situation unchanged. Weather cold & showery. General routine. Capt. S. HARRISON R.A.M.C. T.F. attached to Infy. Bde. 148th Field Amby. Evacuated - Officers Nil. Rank & file sick & wounded 15. Other formations O.R. sick & wounded 10.	
BEAUVAL	6.9.16	—	Situation unchanged. A.Med. Staff D.D. Conference D.Med.S. Corps. Discussed all Field Ambulances with regard to their moving on foot of the 1st Line being taken over by 39 D. Evacuated to C.C.S. O.R. sick 21 wounded 10. Other formations O.R. sick & wounded 4.	
BEAUVAL	7.9.16	—	Situation unchanged, except that 29 D. Division took over half Line Brigades Artillery. D.Med. held a special Board on 6 men "P.B." of V.I Corps attached BEAUVAL & MARIEU. 1/3rd (Her) Field Ambulance left us from 1/Capt Field Ambulance at 5 a.m. 1/1st 7th And ambces. to BARTON & 1/2nd Hen Field Ambulance moved to BOIS DE WARNIMONT. Evacuated to C.C.S. Officers Nil. O.R. sick & wounded 2. Other formations O.R. sick & wounded H.	

Army Form C. 2118.

WAR DIARY
or
INTELLIGENCE SUMMARY.
(Erase heading not required.)

Instructions regarding War Diaries and Intelligence Summaries are contained in F. S. Regs., Part II. and the Staff Manual respectively. Title pages will be prepared in manuscript.

Place	Date	Hour	Summary of Events and Information	Remarks and references to Appendices
BEAUVAL	8.9.16	—	Situation unchanged. O/Cmd inspected 25 men of 1/5 R Warwick for transfer to the Base as unfit for duty at the front. Also visited all Field Ambulances. Evacuated to C.C.S. Officers sick 1. OR sick 3. Other formation OR sick 1.	
BEAUVAL	9.9.16	—	Situation unchanged. Routine. Capt S.C. BOUTTER RAMC T.C. reported for duty. Evacuated to C.C.S. OR sick 9. Other formation OR sick 2.	
BEAUVAL	10.9.16	—	Situation unchanged. Weather warm & sunny. Evacuated to C.C.S. OR sick 9 wounded 1. Other formation Nil. Evacuation week endg. Officers sick 8. OR sick 46. OR wounded 21. Sick average p/1000 = .46	
BEAUVAL	11.9.16	8.30am	Situation unchanged. O/Cmd visited Divl Baths at GEZAINCOURT.	
		6pm	1st & 2nd Field Ambulances moved to GEZAINCOURT. 1/2 and 3/2 Field Ambulance to BEAUVAL. 143rd (Infy) moved to SEZAINCOURT. 145 Infy B.9. to BEAUVAL. Evacuated to C.C.S. OR sick 21. OR wounded 2. Other formation Nil.	

T.2134. Wt. W708-776. 500000. 4/15. Sir J. C. & S.

Army Form C. 2118.

WAR DIARY
or
INTELLIGENCE SUMMARY.
(Erase heading not required.)

Instructions regarding War Diaries and Intelligence Summaries are contained in F. S. Regs., Part II. and the Staff Manual respectively. Title pages will be prepared in manuscript.

Place	Date	Hour	Summary of Events and Information	Remarks and references to Appendices
BEAUVAL	12/9/16	—	Situation as above except that 144th F.A. 9s came out of line ordered to area of BOIS DE WARNIMONT. O.Shed visited 141st Sth Field Ambulance GEZAINCOURT & 1/2 with Field Ambulance BEAUVAL. Evacuated to C.C.S. 2R sick 15.	
BEAUVAL	13/9/16	—	Situation unchanged except that 144th safety A.9. moved to MARLIER. 1/3rd Sth. Field Ambulance moved to MARLIER. O.Shed attended Conference of Med. & Corps. Evacuated to C.C.S 96 francs sick 2. 2R sick 46.	
BEAUVAL	14/9/16	—	Situation — Division in Rest. G.O.C. inspected 1/9 and Sth Field Ambulance Evacuated to C.C.S Officers sick 2 2R sick 3	
BEAUVAL	15/9/16	—	Situation unchanged. O.Shed attended Conference of O.C. O.Shed visited all Field Ambulances giving instructions is used of a substance. Evacuated S.C.C.7. 2R sick 14	

T.1134. Wt. W708—776. 50C000. 4/15. Sir J. C. & S.

WAR DIARY
or
INTELLIGENCE SUMMARY.
(Erase heading not required.)

Army Form C. 2118.

Place	Date	Hour	Summary of Events and Information	Remarks and references to Appendices
BEAUVAL	16.9.16	—	Situation unchanged. O & md with A.D.M.S. visited Bird Dressing St AMIENS Lieut Col J.S. BARING ROUTLETT departed to 8 Rest ETAPES for duty. Major A.A. KINGSTON assumed command of 42 and 5th Field Ambulance. Major N.P.W. BOEDDICKER rejoined ynd 5th Field Ambulance from Sick leave. Evacuated to C.C.S. Officers sick 1. O.R. sick 1.	
BEAUVAL	17.9.16	—	Situation unchanged. O & md visited all Field Ambulances. Evacuated to C.C.S. Officers sick 1. O.R. sick 8.	
BEAUVAL	18.9.16	8.30 am	Situation unchanged. Divl Headquarters moved to BERNAVILLE — Brigades Field Ambulances remaining to DOMPIERRE.	
		11 am	1/1st 5th Field Ambulance arrived at ST HILAIRE, 42 and 5th Field Ambulances at FIENVILLERS and	
		6 pm	1/3rd 5th Field Ambulance arrived MONTPLAISIR. Evacuated to C.C.S. Officers sick 3. O.R. sick 24.	
BERNAVILLE	19.9.16	—	Division in Rest as above, except 2nd Artillery which is still in action. Instructions given for anti inoculation against Enteric Fever issued.	

Army Form C. 2118.

WAR DIARY
or
INTELLIGENCE SUMMARY.
(Erase heading not required.)

Instructions regarding War Diaries and Intelligence Summaries are contained in F. S. Regs., Part II. and the Staff Manual respectively. Title pages will be prepared in manuscript.

Place	Date	Hour	Summary of Events and Information	Remarks and references to Appendices
BERNAVILLE	19/9/16		A.D.M.S visited 9th Field Ambulance re-opened ST HILAIRE	
BERNAVILLE	20/9/16		Evacuated B.C.C.S. & R.R.I.C.H.Y. Situation unchanged. Routine work. Evacuated to C.C.S. J.R. 14	
"	21/9/16	9.30am	Conference at Divl Headquarters attended by A.D.M.S & D.A.D.M.S. - D.A.D.M.S proceeded to England on leave - Capt Sheridan 1st Wore heavy injured 1/7 Worcester from the Base, Capt Wrigley injured 1/3 S.M. Field Ambulance - Evacuated 15 C.C.S. 2 Officers and 15 other ranks.	
"	22/9/16		Situation unchanged. Weather bright and fine - Routine work - Evacuated to C.C.S. 3 Officers and 20 other ranks	
"	23/9/16		Situation unchanged - A.D.M.S visited 2nd & 3rd S.M. Field Ambulances. 1st S.M. Field Ambulance moved from ST HILAIRE to RIBEAUCOURT & BARLETTE. Under instructions from A.D.M.S. XIII Corps. Just Mace Survey detailed to 25th Amn. Sn. Park. 5 cases of diarrhoea admitted - 1 case of Diphtheria (Sgt Hunt 1st / 10th R. Berks Regt.) sent to 2/1 S.M. C.C.S yesterday - 1 Officer and 13 other ranks evacuated.	
"	24/9/16		Situation as before. Weather fine. A.D.M.S visited 1st S.M. Field Ambulance and A.D.M.S XIII Corps. Evacuated 6 other ranks	
"	25/9/16		A.D.M.S visited 1/1 S.M. Field Ambulance and arranged for Ambul departmental to be opened at BARLETTE - Evacuated to C.C.S. 5 Officers & 11 other ranks	

Army Form C. 2118.

WAR DIARY
or
INTELLIGENCE SUMMARY.
(Erase heading not required.)

Instructions regarding War Diaries and Intelligence Summaries are contained in F. S. Regs., Part II. and the Staff Manual respectively. Title pages will be prepared in manuscript.

Place	Date	Hour	Summary of Events and Information	Remarks and references to Appendices
BERNAVILLE	26/9/16		A.D.M.S. attended medical services carried out by 143rd Inf. Bde. and inspected the field work of 1/1st S.M. Field Ambulance. Bivouacked 1 officer & 6 other ranks	
"	27/9/16		A.D.M.S. visited 1/3 S.M. Field Ambulance — Under instructions from D.D.M.S. XIII Corps, 2 officers and 29 other ranks sent to various C.C.S.'s for temporary duty. Evacuated 1 officer and 8 men.	
"	28/9/16		Situation unchanged — Weather has changed and has become very showery, but much milder — Evacuated 1 officer & 5 other ranks.	
"	29/9/16		Orders received for the Division to move to another area — 143rd and 145th Inf. Bdes. marched at 10 am & 11.30 am respectively. 1/1 S.M. Field Ambulance moved from BEAUCOURT to CANDAS in anticipation of further move tomorrow — being to hook up if hospital accommodation 1 officer & 49 other ranks evacuated, & 6 sent to duty. One car of German wounded from 1/1 units and 1 case of Diphtheria from 1/6th Berks sent to 2/1 Sou. C.C.S.	
BERNAVILLE	30/9/16	8.30 a.m.	Situation as above & Division on the move. Divisional Headquarters arrived at HÉNU	
HÉNU	30/9/16		1/1st S.M. Field Ambulance arrived at GAUDIEMPRE; 1/2nd S.M. Field Ambulance at VAUCHELLES & 1/3rd S.M. Field Ambulance at IVERGNY 46th Division is now under VII Corps, III Army.	
		2 p.m.	Evacuated — 2 officers, 85 O.R.	

A.D.M.S. 46th (S. M.) Division
COLONEL

P.T.O.

Army Form C. 2118.

WAR DIARY
or
INTELLIGENCE SUMMARY.
(Erase heading not required.)

Instructions regarding War Diaries and Intelligence Summaries are contained in F. S. Regs., Part II. and the Staff Manual respectively. Title pages will be prepared in manuscript.

Place	Date	Hour	Summary of Events and Information	Remarks and references to Appendices
			Attached - RAMC 28th Division Operation Order No 7.	

48th Division.
Royal Army Medical Corps, Order 7
by Colonel C. A. Young, C.M.G., A.D.M.S.

1. The O.C. 1/3rd S. Mid. Field Ambulance will hand over the Main Dressing Station at BERTRANCOURT, the Advanced Dressing Station at MAILLY MAILLET, (F.12.d.9.7), and the Collecting Post at Q.10.c.4.3. to a Field Ambulance of the 39th Division tomorrow, 7th inst. before noon. He will still retain the Advanced Dressing Station at "Red House", and the Collecting Posts north of Broadway, and will be responsible for the evacuation of all sick and wounded of the 48th Division occupying the line and in MAILLY MAILLET and BUS. After handing over at BERTRANCOURT, the 1/3rd S. Mid. Field Ambulance will proceed to BUS, and will take over from the 1/1st S. Mid. Field Ambulance.

2. On being relieved by the 1/3rd S. Mid. Field Ambulance tomorrow, 7th inst. the 1/1st S. Mid. Field Ambulance will proceed to SARTON, and will open there for the reception of the sick of the remainder of the Division.

3. The 1/2nd S. Mid. Field Ambulance will move from VAUCHELLES to WARNIMONT WOOD tomorrow, 7th inst.

4. Reports of completion of the above moves to be reported to this office.

6.9.16.

A.D.M.S. 48th Division.

CONFIDENTIAL

War Diary
of
A.D.M.S. 48th Division
from 1-10-16 to 31-10-16

Vol 19
140/1783

WAR DIARY
or
INTELLIGENCE SUMMARY.
(Erase heading not required.)

Army Form C. 2118.

Place	Date	Hour	Summary of Events and Information	Remarks and references to Appendices
XENU	1.10.16		Division moving off again MONDICOURT, SOUASTRE, WARLINCOURT. 1/1st Lth Field Ambulance arrived at ST AMAND; 2nd Lth Field Ambulance bivd over from Ambulance at D 26 Central (Ref. Map 1/40 000 5J) between COUIN & SOUASTRE. 1/3rd Lth Field Ambulance arrived at GRENAS. A Div'l Winter H'qt's 1/3rd Lth Field Ambulance. Evacuation nil.	
HENU	2.10.16		Division moving, 143 B'g'd took over trenches in front of HEBUTERNE. Weather very wet. A 8 Div'l Winter 1/2nd Lth Field Ambulance & Advanced Dressing Station at FONQUEVILLERS. Lieut Col. HOSKINS arrived back from England & resumed command of Lth Field Amb'ce. Evacuated OR sick two.	
HENU	3.10.16		Division completely arrived in above area. 1/3rd Lth Field Ambulance took over MONDICOURT, & forms Div'l D.R.S. Lieut I.M.ED'S reported for duty. Posted to 240 B. 3 & R.F.A. A.D.Med (Sanitation) called. Saw A.D.Med. Div'l Sanitary Officer. Also Lieut Col Garsland, 51st Field Ambulance, 17th Division reported, as his unit is arriving	

WAR DIARY
or
INTELLIGENCE SUMMARY.
(Erase heading not required.)

Army Form C. 2118.

Instructions regarding War Diaries and Intelligence Summaries are contained in F. S. Regs, Part II. and the Staff Manual respectively. Title pages will be prepared in manuscript.

Place	Date	Hour	Summary of Events and Information	Remarks and references to Appendices
HENU	3.10.16	a.m.	under 48th Division for Administration (temporarily). Staff of VII Corps called. Said D.D.M.S. with reference to the situation. 11/1st Lth Field Ambulance withdrew A.D.S. at FONQUEVILLERS. Evacuated to C.C.S. Officers sick 2, O.R sick 8.	
HENU	4.10.16	—	Lieut. T.B. ROTIER RAMC T.C. reported on 4 sup trains proceeding in advance of Contract. Situation unchanged. 5/1st Army B.S. & 151st Field Amb.Co. came under administration of 48th Div. A.D.M.S. visited all three ambulances. Evacuated. O.R sick 6 wounded 1.	
HENU	5.10.16	—	Situation unchanged. A.D.M.S. attended Conference C.O.C. Evacuated — Officers sick 1. O.R sick 9 wounded 3.	
HENU	6.10.16	—	Situation unchanged. Weather unkind. A.D.M.S. visited 1/1st Rly Fld Ambulance. Attended Conference D.D.M.S. VIIth Corps. Evacuated to C.C.S. – Officers sick 1. Major J.A. Beaumontayes RAMC a/AD.M.S of 2nd Div.wounded. O.R sick 8 wounded 17.	

WAR DIARY
or
INTELLIGENCE SUMMARY.
(Erase heading not required.)

Army Form C. 2118.

Place	Date	Hour	Summary of Events and Information	Remarks and references to Appendices
HENU	7/10/16	—	Situation unchanged. Weather very wet.	
		9 p.m.	ADMS attended Conference.	
			Evacuated to C.C.S. Officers sick 1. wounded 1. OR sick 7. wounded 5.	
HENU	8/10/16	—	Situation unchanged.	
			ADMS with D.D.M.S. VII Corps visited sites from MERVITERNE to FONQUEVILLERS with a view to selecting Advanced Posts & routes of evacuation for wounded. Also visited A.D.S. at FONQUEVILLERS. Capt HOBBES returned to duty & Lieut for duty from WARLOY	
			Evacuated — Officers sick 2. OR sick 11. wounded 3. G.	
HENU	9/10/16	—	Situation unchanged.	
			ADMS attended Conference 4th 3rd Army.	
			Evacuated - Officers sick 1. OR sick 25. wounded 3. kil	
HENU	10/10/16	—	Situation unchanged.	
			ADMS visited all Field Ambulances.	
			Evacuated - Officers sick 1. OR sick 20.	

WAR DIARY
or
INTELLIGENCE SUMMARY.
(Erase heading not required.)

Army Form C. 2118.

Instructions regarding War Diaries and Intelligence Summaries are contained in F. S. Regs., Part II. and the Staff Manual respectively. Title pages will be prepared in manuscript.

Place	Date	Hour	Summary of Events and Information	Remarks and references to Appendices
HENU	11.10.16	—	Situation unchanged.	
			ADMS held a conference of Regimental Medical Officers with reference to evacuation of wounded during forthcoming operations.	
			Evacuated – OR sick 67 Wounded 2.	
			ADMS called on & informed ADMS that 1/3rd Nth Fld Ambulance was to move from MONDICOURT.	
			Wire from ADMS 14th Division – Preparing sending advanced party tomorrow to take over at MONDICOURT remainder of 53rd F Amb'ly to complete takingover by Friday 13th inst.	app 1.
			Wire to ADMS 14th Div. saying there fats well suit.	app 2.
HENU	12.10.16	—	Situation unchanged	
			Routine work.	
			Wire of 1/3rd Nth Fld Ambulance postponed to 14th inst.	
			Evacuated – OR sick 37.	
			Three cases of Typhoid + three cases of Paratyphoid have been notified, occurring in Back R. 1st, 1/4th Oxf and Bucks, 1/5 Gordons, 1/5 Warwicks, 2/10 Worcesters. All cases being investigated.	

WAR DIARY
or
INTELLIGENCE SUMMARY.
(Erase heading not required.)

Army Form C. 2118.

Place	Date	Hour	Summary of Events and Information	Remarks and references to Appendices
HENU	13/10/16	—	Situation unchanged. A.D.M.S. visited D.M.S. VII Corps with reference to evacuation of wounded. Scheme of medical arrangements sent to Headquarters & copies for Brigades. About 8 sick & evacuated to C.C.S. O.R. sick 57. O.R. wounded 7.	
HENU	14/10/16		Situation unchanged. 1/3rd S.M. Field Ambulance moved to HENU, remaining closed, but take over A.D.S. at FONQUEVILLERS from 1/1st S.M. Field Ambulance. A.D.M.S. visited above A.D.S. also with O.C. 1/3rd S.M. F. Amb. visited "JUNCTION KEEP" (Ref. Map France 57D.NE 1/20000) with reference to setting up an Advanced Dressing Station for walking wounded. Evacuated — Officers sick 2. O.R. sick 46. wounded 4.	
HENU	15/10/16		Situation unchanged. Routine work. Evacuated — Officers sick 1. O.R. sick 21. wounded.	

Army Form C. 2118.

WAR DIARY
or
INTELLIGENCE SUMMARY.
(Erase heading not required.)

Instructions regarding War Diaries and Intelligence Summaries are contained in F. S. Regs., Part II. and the Staff Manual respectively. Title pages will be prepared in manuscript.

Place	Date	Hour	Summary of Events and Information	Remarks and references to Appendices
HENU	16.10.16	—	Situation unchanged. A.D.M.S. visited HEBUTERNE to select a position for an Advanced Dressing Station for the wounded of this Division. Evacuated: — Officers sick 1. OR sick 14 wounded 2.	
HENU	17.10.16	—	Situation unchanged. Capt (K.D.) WILKINSON R.A.M.C. departs for duty with 38 C.C.S. under authority from D.G.M.S. Evacuated: — OR sick 14.	
HENU	18.10.16	—	Situation unchanged. A.D.M.S. 14th Division saw A.D.M.S. with reference to taking over Corps D.R.S. at MONDICOURT & the Field Ambulance at D.26 with A.D.S. at HEBUTERNE. Evacuated to C.C.S. Officers sick 1. OR sick 10.	
HENU	19.10.16	—	Situation unchanged. Weather very wet. 1/3rd Sy Field Ambulance moved to D 26 Central. A Staff with Q.A. & Q.M.I. visited area in which Division is going through (Billet) arranged with A.D.M.S. of 14th & 49th Divisions about relief of the various Field Ambulances. Evacuated: Officers sick 1. OR sick 16.	

WAR DIARY
or
INTELLIGENCE SUMMARY.

Army Form C. 2118.

Place	Date	Hour	Summary of Events and Information	Remarks and references to Appendices
HENU	20.10.16	-	During night 19/20 Infy Bde relieved from trenches by 29th Inf Bde. 1/3rd Fld Ambulance marched to GRAND RULLECOURT. Instructions issued to the 1/1st & 1/2nd Fld Ambulances with regard to moves. A.D.M.S. visited 1/1st Fld Ambulance. Capt Boorda evacuated sick.	
HENU	21.10.16	-	Divrs moving to new area around COUTERELLE. Divisional Headquarters opened at DOULLENS.	
DOULLENS	-	11 am	1/3rd Fld Ambulance tented as field Ambulance at COUTERELLE. 1/1st Fld Ambulance tented as field Ambulance at SAUDIEMPRE, but changing places with Hd Q & Divrs and remaining ambulance. A.D.M.S. with A.D.M.S. visited Divisional Laundry AMIENS. Evacuated to C.C.S. Officers sick 1. O.R. sick 3. wounded 1. Divrs moving	
DOULLENS	22.10.16	-	1/2nd Fld Ambulance moved to BEAUVAL. Div. Hd Headquarters for 1/3rd Fld Ambulance to HALLOY. A.D.M.S. visited 1/2nd Fld Ambulance at BEAUVAL. Also gave instructions to O.C. 1/1st Fld Ambulance tents as Bn O.C. has Brigade Drs. when the latter move down with BAZZEAUX area. Evacuated. A Divl Assistant Director Conference of O.C.	app 3

Army Form C. 2118.

WAR DIARY
or
INTELLIGENCE SUMMARY.
(Erase heading not required.)

Instructions regarding War Diaries and Intelligence Summaries are contained in F.S. Regs., Part II. and the Staff Manual respectively. Title pages will be prepared in manuscript.

Place	Date	Hour	Summary of Events and Information	Remarks and references to Appendices
BAIZIEUX	23.10.16	12noon	Divisional Headquarters arrived here. Brigades to Hérissart & this area. Evacuated – OP sick 14.	
BAIZEUX	24.10.16		Division resting. 1/2nd Sth Field Ambulance arrived at BEHENCOURT. 145th & 8th arrived same place. O.Ethel visited & Sth 1 III Corps. Evacuated off sick TR106 sick.	
BAZIEUX	25/10/16 12·1 am		Division orders number 19 Army 2 III Corps. A.Ethel issued various Orders & confirmation received from 4th Army & III Corps & the Field Ambulances. 1/2nd Sth Field Ambulances arrived at FRANVILLERS. 1/3rd Sth Field Ambulance arrived at BRESLE. 1/2nd Sth Field Ambulance sent 2 tent subdivisions to take over at BOTTOM WOOD not necessary 9 to to. Two received from & Sthd for Field Ambulance to take over Copshed & to RETURNT as 26 inst. -- 1/3rd Sth Field Ambulance detailed. Evacuated OP sick 15. 1/1st Sth Field Ambulance details found & sent to Divisional Hdqrs not necessary & adm REOUNT station	App 425

Army Form C. 2118.

WAR DIARY
or
INTELLIGENCE SUMMARY.
(Erase heading not required.)

Instructions regarding War Diaries and Intelligence Summaries are contained in F. S. Regs., Part II. and the Staff Manual respectively. Title pages will be prepared in manuscript.

Place	Date	Hour	Summary of Events and Information	Remarks and references to Appendices
BAIZIEUX	26.10.16	—	Division moving. Three officers 21 DR deto sho to Hot KM CCS for duty. Capt. G THORNLEY RAMC evacuated to CCS with burns. Orthol visited all Field Ambulances. Also attended conference 9.30ad W Corps Evacuated — OR sick 2 OR sick 15	
BAIZIEUX	27.10.16		Division moving. ADMS visited Special Hospital WARLOY with reference to death of Capt. SHARPIN (re. Office) & Bucks NS. In burnt power Receipt (Field Hospitals). Then visited No.1 Aus Field Ambulance MILLENCOURT and 9 and No. Field Ambulance FRANVILLERS. Also Ambulance at LAVIEVILLE. Was from W Corps on 25 mfor Bearer subdivision of Field Ambs at FRANVILLERS sta over from 27th Field Amb at BAIZIEUX, and a Bearer subdivision of the Field Amb to at MILLENCOURT to take over from the S.A. Field Amb to at LAVIEVILLE. This area was 26 areal. W.O. No Field Ambulance took over W Corps Red Station at BECOURT X 25 c. (Rly. hoop) Source sheet continued ALBERT (4000D) Evacuated OR sick 2	app 6

Army Form C. 2118.

WAR DIARY
or
INTELLIGENCE SUMMARY.
(Erase heading not required.)

Place	Date	Hour	Summary of Events and Information	Remarks and references to Appendices
ENTRETEUX	29/10	—	Reconnoitring 143 B[de] & 1/3 Corps areas in MAMETZ WOOD area.	
			O.C./f. visited the hospitals & by Ist echelon of 7 am 4th Field Ambce at BAIZIEUX	
			the army being necessary to a inspection term & leaving for said	
			evacuates 2 off sick, O.R. 5 sick	
ENTRETEUX	29/10	—	Genl. found for hour the same body	
			Cadre sick	
			evacuated Nervo sick 2, March 1.	
BAIZIEUX	30/10/16	—	Strength generally — 143 Infy. B., 144 R.D.a MAMETZ WOOD area, 144 R.D. a ALBERT area & 145th Infy	
			B[de] in BÉHENCOURT	
			O.C./f. with D.D.M.S. visited D. Corps Rest Station run by 139 [?] Field Amb[ce].	
			evacuates OR sick 2.	
BAIZIEUX	31-10-16	—	Situation unchanged	
		12 Noon	Divl HQrs moved to Corps H.A 2nd MILLENCOURT-ALBERT road on side MILLENCOURT	
			ADMS with D.D.M.S visited 1st heavy dressing Station REFOURT chateau & to a side	
MILLENCOURT	" "		Dressing Station BOTTOM WOOD	
			Evacuated OR sick 3.	

[signed] Colonel,
A.D.M.S. 48th (S.M.) DIVISION.

Brixton
Vol 20

War Diary
of
A D M S 48th Division
from 1-11-16 to 30-11-16.

15

Nov 1916

CONFIDENTIAL

COMMITTEE FOR THE
MEDICAL HISTORY OF THE WAR
Date −3 JAN. 1917

Army Form C. 2118.

WAR DIARY
or
INTELLIGENCE SUMMARY.
(Erase heading not required.)

Instructions regarding War Diaries and Intelligence Summaries are contained in F. S. Regs., Part II. and the Staff Manual respectively. Title pages will be prepared in manuscript.

Place	Date	Hour	Summary of Events and Information	Remarks and references to Appendices
MILLENCOURT	1.11.16	—	Situation as above. ADMS visited 93rd & 4th Field Ambulances. ODMS 15th Division called with reference to this division taking over. Orders were issued for 142 Bde Field Ambulance to move to Contalmaison taking over from 45th Field Ambulance, the Advanced Dressing Station. Evacuated — Officers 10 OR sick.	
MILLENCOURT	2.11.16	—	Situation — Division moving. ADMS attended Conference 9.30 AM III Corps. ADMS 15th Division called — saw DADMS & SA DMS. Evacuated — Officers sick 2. OR sick 2.	
LOZENGE WOOD	3.11.16	9 a.m.	Division took over from 15th Division. Remainder of Division moving off into the line in front of LE SARS. 50th Division on Right — Canadians on Left. Evacuated — Officers sick 1. OR sick 16. Lieut H SPATEL proceeded to join No 6 Stationary Hospital. Divl Sanitary Officer arrived at BAIZIEUX under Corps arrangements as Sanitary Officer to the Div area.	

Army Form C. 2118.

WAR DIARY
or
INTELLIGENCE SUMMARY.
(Erase heading not required.)

Instructions regarding War Diaries and Intelligence Summaries are contained in F. S. Regs., Part II. and the Staff Manual respectively. Title pages will be prepared in manuscript.

Place	Date	Hour	Summary of Events and Information	Remarks and references to Appendices
LOZENGE WOOD	4-11-16	—	Situation as above	
			A Maj. vacated 1/1st and 1/2nd Lth Field Ambulances	
			Evacuated Marshal OR sick 15	
LOZENGE WOOD	5-11-16	—	Situation unchanged	
			2. OR W.B. wanted support trenches (twenty park avenue + Spence trench) and MARTINPUCH cliff. Absence fromy RKth	
				Evacuated OR sick 22
			reference to scheme for evacuation of wounded	
LOZENGE WOOD	6-11-16	—	Situation unchanged	
			Routine work	
			Evacuated — Officers sick 1, OR sick 45.	
LOZENGE WOOD	7-11-16	—	Situation unchanged	
			Routine work. Scheme for evacuation of wounded sent to F.a.e. for approval	Appx.
			Evacuated Off hld OR sick 23	
			Lieut R Edwards R.A.M.C.T.C. reported for duty - Posted Hd 2th Field Ambulance	
LOZENGE WOOD	8-11-16	—	Situation unchanged	
			Routine work	
			Evacuated - Off hld OR sick 44.	

WAR DIARY
or
INTELLIGENCE SUMMARY.

(Erase heading not required.)

Army Form C. 2118.

Place	Date	Hour	Summary of Events and Information	Remarks and references to Appendices
LOZENGE WOOD	9.11.16	—	Situation unchanged. Weather rainy. A.D.M.S. visited 3/10 & 13th Fd Field Ambulances. Evacuated Officers sick 1. O.R. sick 91	
LOZENGE WOOD	10.11.16	—	Situation unchanged - no rain. A.D.M.S visited 3/10 Fd Amb & 1/1st Wm Field Ambulance. Capt L. BALL RAMC TF reported for duty with 1/1st Wm Field Ambulance. Evacuated Officers sick 1. O.R. sick 46	
LOZENGE WOOD	11.11.16	—	Situation unchanged - weather windy - no rain. O.But visited D.D.M.S III Corps. Also III Corps Rest Station. Lieut H.M. FAIRFAX RAMC (T) departed for LONDON on application for Contract on H. Fleet. Evacuated - Off sick OR sick 36	
LOZENGE WOOD	12.11.16	—	Situation unchanged. Weather dull misty. A.But with D.Dr.S III Corps visited LANGUARD CIRCUS S & L.O.O. (Refuge Trones Contour Sheet ALBERT (HOOD) with reference to situation of a Corps Collecting Station for walking wounded. Also visited 1/1st Wm Field Ambulance. Capt SMYTHE 1/3 Wm Field Ambulance evacuated sick 10.11.16. Evacuated Officers sick 1, O.R. sick 32	

Army Form C. 2118.

WAR DIARY
or
INTELLIGENCE SUMMARY.
(Erase heading not required.)

Instructions regarding War Diaries and Intelligence Summaries are contained in F. S. Regs., Part II. and the Staff Manual respectively. Title pages will be prepared in manuscript.

Place	Date	Hour	Summary of Events and Information	Remarks and references to Appendices
LOZENGE WOOD	13-11-16	—	Situation unchanged. Weather dry but misty. Headquarters informed that the number of latrines in the various camps are magnificent. Evacuated Officers sick 3 OR sick 43.	
LOZENGE WOOD	14-11-16	—	Situation unchanged. A.D.M.S. with O.C. 1/2 Ldn Field Ambulance visited O.D.S. MARTINPUICH & inspected advance pool Aid Collecting Station for walking wounded in that village. Evacuated OR sick 36	
"	"			
LOZENGE WOOD	15-11-16		Situation unchanged - Weather cold & dry. Routine work. Officers sick 1, OR sick 32. Evacuated.	
LOZENGE WOOD	16-11-16	—	A.D.M.S. attended Conference D.D.M.S. III Corps. Visited Div Clothes Store ALBERT and 452 Ldn Field Ambulance. Evacuated Officers sick 2 OR sick 4 on active.	
LOZENGE WOOD	17-11-16	—	Situation unchanged - Weather cold & dry. Routine work. Evacuated - Officers sick Nil OR sick 28	

Army Form C. 2118.

WAR DIARY
or
INTELLIGENCE SUMMARY.
(Erase heading not required.)

Instructions regarding War Diaries and Intelligence Summaries are contained in F. S. Regs., Part II. and the Staff Manual respectively. Title pages will be prepared in manuscript.

Place	Date	Hour	Summary of Events and Information	Remarks and references to Appendices
LOZENGE WOOD	18.11.16	—	Situation unchanged. Weather cold, snow turning to rain.	
			O/Ord with ADMS (visit) Div¹ Laundry at AMIENS	
			Evacuated. — OR sick 19	
LOZENGE WOOD	19.11.16	—	Situation unchanged	
			Routine work.	
			Evacuated — OR sick 28. Capt. ANDERSON RAMC evacuated sick to Base	
LOZENGE WOOD	20.11.16	—	Division extended slightly to the right. Section we could part of Line formerly held by "A" Division.	
			The ADP at QUARRY POST M.22.d.4.3. taken over by 1/at S.M. Field Ambulance	
			Evacuated officers one OR sick 36	
LOZENGE WOOD	21.11.16	—	Situation unchanged. Weather cold misty.	
			Routine work.	
			Capt.s MURRAY & McCONNELL rejoined from Sth. Field Ambulance from No 2 M.D.S.	
			Evacuated — OR sick 26.	
LOZENGE WOOD	22.11.16	—	Situation unchanged. Weather misty.	
			ADMS visited 1/5 Gordons inspecting the sanitation &c of the Unit. Also visited H.Q. 4th Sth. F. Amb.	
			Conference with A.D.O.S. with reference to Recel Instructions regarding Officers Shell Shock W.	
			Evacuated — OR sick 51.	

T.2134. Wt. W708–776. 500000. 4/16. Sir J. C. & S.

Army Form C. 2118.

WAR DIARY
or
INTELLIGENCE SUMMARY.
(Erase heading not required.)

Instructions regarding War Diaries and Intelligence Summaries are contained in F. S. Regs., Part II. and the Staff Manual respectively. Title pages will be prepared in manuscript.

Place	Date	Hour	Summary of Events and Information	Remarks and references to Appendices
LOZENGE WOOD	23.11.16	—	Situation unchanged. Weather cold & misty. O.R.S. attended Conference 9th & 3rd Corps. Visits paid the Field Ambulances & gave instructions for Field Units to proceed to WARLOY. Evacuated Officers sick 2 O.R. sick 34. Capt W. BOWATER returned from sick leave in England.	
LOZENGE WOOD	24.11.16	—	Situation unchanged. Weather misty. Routine work. Evacuated Officers sick 2 O.R. sick 48.	
LOZENGE WOOD	25.11.16	—	Situation unchanged. Weather stormy & much rain. Routine work. Evacuated Officers sick 1 O.R. sick 66.	
LOZENGE WOOD	26.11.16	—	Situation unchanged. Weather very misty. Routine work. O.R.S. visited 11th Div. Field Ambulance. Evacuated O.R. sick 35.	
LOZENGE WOOD	27.11.16	—	Situation unchanged. Weather very wet. O.R.S. visited 4/1 Lth. Field Ambulance, Div. Laundry the ALBERT & 1/5 & 1/6 Lth. Field Ambulance. Evacuated Officers sick one O.R. sick 23. Detailed personnel returned & then units 1/1 & 1/2 Lth. Field Ambulances from C.C.S.	

T2134. Wt. W708—776. 500000. 4/15. Sir J. C. & S.

Army Form C. 2118.

WAR DIARY
or
INTELLIGENCE SUMMARY.

(Erase heading not required.)

Instructions regarding War Diaries and Intelligence Summaries are contained in F. S. Regs., Part II. and the Staff Manual respectively. Title pages will be prepared in manuscript.

Place	Date	Hour	Summary of Events and Information	Remarks and references to Appendices
LOZENGE WOOD	28.11.16	—	Situation unchanged. Weather cold, sky cloudy. A. DMS visited 1/3rd Sth Fld. Ambulance, WARLOY. Evacuated officers sick 1, troops 29.	
LOZENGE WOOD	29.11.16	—	Situation unchanged. Weather cold & damp. A. DMS held a Medical Board under directions received from 3rd 4th Army on Major +4 Q. O'SULLIVAN, B.I. (Robins) R.I.F. Cheshire Regt. Relvd. 1/3rd Sth. Fld. Amb.- at BECOURT. Evacuated officers sick one 07R sick 28. Lieut M. Sr C. Hamilton R.A.M.C. BR. reported for duty.	
LOZENGE WOOD	30.11.16	—	Situation unchanged. Weather colder, dry misty. Routine work. A. DMS proceeded on 10 days leave. Evacuated officers sick 2, OR 80. 1st Division on Right, 51st Division on Left.	

J.W. Beckton
D.M.S.
A.D.M.S. 6th (38th) DIVISION.

CONFIDENTIAL

Vol 21

War Diary
of
A.D.M.S. 48th Division
from 1-12-16 to 31-12-16.

COMMITTEE FOR THE
MEDICAL HISTORY OF THE WAR
Date 31 JAN.1917

Army Form C.

WAR DIARY
or
INTELLIGENCE SUMMARY.
(Erase heading not required.)

Instructions regarding War Diaries and Intelligence Summaries are contained in F. S. Regs., Part II. and the Staff Manual respectively. Title pages will be prepared in manuscript.

Place	Date	Hour	Summary of Events and Information	Remarks and references to Appendices
LOZENGE WOOD	1.12.16	—	Situation unaltered from that of 30th inst. 1st Devons on Right. 51st Division on Left.	
			Reinforcements.	
			Evacuated officers sick. One OR sick 38.	
LOZENGE WOOD	2.12.16	—	Situation unchanged. Weather very cold. Approx frost.	
			Routine work.	
			Evacuated OR sick 29.	
LOZENGE WOOD	3.12.16	—	Situation unchanged. Weather milder & rain.	
			Evacuated Officers sick 1. OR sick 24. 50 Cases of trench foot were admitted (32 from 1/5 Warwicks)	
LOZENGE WOOD	4.12.16	—	Situation unchanged. Weather milder, rain & much.	
			Evacuated Officers sick 3. OR sick 22.	
LOZENGE WOOD	5.12.16	—	Situation unchanged. Weather – warm wet much rain &	
			Evacuated Officers sick 2. OR sick 31.	
			Wire from 8th & 143 Inf Bde III Corps – LO/H.D. & Chief. Evacuate all wounded & wounded sick kind to C.C.S. – (This evening the Chateau BECOURT being shelled(?))	Appx 1.
LOZENGE WOOD	6.12.16	—	Situation unchanged. Weather misty	
			Evacuated OR sick 42. Lieut G. PLATTER R.A.M.C. departs on permanent transfer & attached	

Army Form C.

WAR DIARY
or
INTELLIGENCE SUMMARY.
(Erase heading not required.)

Instructions regarding War Diaries and Intelligence Summaries are contained in F. S. Regs., Part II. and the Staff Manual respectively. Title pages will be prepared in manuscript.

Place	Date	Hour	Summary of Events and Information	Remarks and references to Appendices
LOZENGE WOOD	7.12.16	—	Situation unchanged. Weather unsettled. Evacuated officers sick, OR sick 31	
LOZENGE WOOD	8.12.16	—	Situation unchanged. Weather unsettled. Wire received from Record – Lt R.B.B. reported fr wounds duty only. Lieut E. ASHBY RAMC T.C. reported for duty in relief of Capt WICKS ordered to report to D.D.M.S.	App 2.
			BOULOGNE BASE for duty. Evacuated Officers wounded 1, OR sick 19	
LOZENGE WOOD	9.12.16	—	Situation unchanged. Weather milder & cleaner. Evacuated OR sick 23	
LOZENGE WOOD	10.12.16	—	Situation unchanged. Weather colder, snow front. Evacuated OR sick 28	
LOZENGE WOOD	11.12.16	—	Situation unchanged. Weather unsettled. Evacuated OR sick 41	
LOZENGE WOOD	12.12.16	—	Situation unchanged. Weather very severe, snow & sleet. Evacuated OR sick #49	
			O But returned from leave. D.D.M.S. visited Unit. Lt Field Ambulance. Capt WICKS reported for duty at BOULOGNE BASE	

Army Form C. 2118.

Instructions regarding War Diaries and Intelligence Summaries are contained in F. S. Regs., Part II. and the Staff Manual respectively. Title pages will be prepared in manuscript.

WAR DIARY
or
INTELLIGENCE SUMMARY.
(Erase heading not required.)

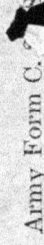

Place	Date	Hour	Summary of Events and Information	Remarks and references to Appendices
LOZENGE WOOD	13.12.16	—	Situation unchanged. Weather dull overcast. Routine work. Evacuated IR sick 20.	
LOZENGE WOOD	14.12.16	—	Division being relieved by 15th Div. Divisions 145th B. Infy. 82d moved to RECOURT. Weather unsettled. A.D.M.S. attended Conference D.D.M.S. III Corps. Evacuated — Officer sick 1 IR sick 29	
" "	15/12/16		Advanced Dressing Station at MARTIN PUICH and QUARRY POST taken over by 45th Field Ambulance. 15th Division, who also took over the Surg. Hutchison at VILLA STATION and near MARTIN PUICH. ADMS proceeded to England on 10 days leave. Total admissions 79. Officer 23 Trench feet, other chiefly P.U.O. Evacuations 30—	
ALBERT	16/12/16		Fine morning very wet afternoon. Headquarters moved from Fricourt Wood Camp to Albert. 1st S.M. Field Ambulance moved from CONTALMAISON on 14th by 45th F.A. 15th Diva. Headquarters of unit went to BAISIEUX, 1 section under Major A'Cull taking over L'ECOLE SUPERIEURE ALBERT for treatment of local sick — Admissions 52. Trench feet 11 — Evacuations 67	
"	17/12/16		Rain, cold & foggy. ADMS inspected the School house at ALBERT opposite L'ECOLE SUPERIEUR by order of DDMS IInd Corps to ascertain if suitable for a Field Ambulance. It has sufficient accommodation but after certain repairs a good deal of repair. 1st S.m Field Ambulance ordered to take it over tomorrow & put in a guard — Total admissions 78 — less administration. Trench feet — Evacuations 38.	

T2134. Wt. W708—776. 500090. 4/15. Sir J. C. & S.

Army Form C. 2118.

WAR DIARY
or
INTELLIGENCE SUMMARY.
(Erase heading not required.)

Instructions regarding War Diaries and Intelligence Summaries are contained in F. S. Regs., Part II. and the Staff Manual respectively. Title pages will be prepared in manuscript.

Place	Date	Hour	Summary of Events and Information	Remarks and references to Appendices
ALBERT	18/12/16		Fine but cold. ADMS visited 2/3rd Field Ambulance at NARLOY with DDMS VIII Corps. OC directed to take over buildings and equipment at Civil Hospital temporarily. Arranged with Town Major, ALBERT, for a site for the housing of the 3/3rd Field Ambulance then found standing being unsatisfactory. Admissions 52 - Trench feet 3 - Evacuations 34.	
"	19/12/16		Very hard frost Snowy night - ADMS visited camps of the Battalions of 145 Inf Bde at RECOURT & interviewed M.O. Also visited 3rd S.M. Field Ambulance - 1 Section of 3rd S.M. Fd moved from Becourt Hill to Schoolroom, Albert. Admission 45. Evacuations 51.	
"	20/12/16		Fine, hard and cold. Visited Sections of 1/1 S.M. Fd & 1/3 S.M. Fd at ALBERT. Total admissions 38 - Evacuations 20 -	
"	21/12/16		Fine and bright - ADMS attended DDMS' conference at HENENCOURT - Admissions 38 - Evacuations 41.	
"	22/12/16		Wet and stormy - Medical Board on Captain Ratcliff RAMC - Admissions 46 - Evacuations 29 -	
"	23/12/16		Fine - ADMS called and visited the Sections of the 1st & 3rd S.M. Field Ambulances at ALBERT - Admissions 40 - Evacuations 20 with ADMS	
"	24/12/16		Fine but cold. ADMS visited 1st S.M. Field Ambulance at BAISIEUX Admissions 42. Evacuations 35.	
"	25/12/16		Cold wet & foggy. ADMS visited 1st S.M. Field Ambulance at ALBERT - Admissions 23. Evacuations 20 - Captain Allium reported his departure en route for England on expiration of contract. Capt J.N. Long posted to charge of 1/8 Worcester.	
"	26/12/16		Fine but cold - ADMS visited 3/S.M. Field Ambulance at WARLOY. Admissions 14. Evacuations 10.	
"	27/12/16		Fine. ADMS visited 3/S.M. Fd Ambulance at Becourt Hill. Admissions 58. Evacuations 41. DADMS returned from leave.	
"	28.12.16		Fine, hard cold. ADMS attended Conference D.D.M.S. Lt. Col. Ware KCI Main Dressing Station BECOURT CHATEAU from	

Army Form C. 2118.

WAR DIARY
or
INTELLIGENCE SUMMARY.
(Erase heading not required.)

Instructions regarding War Diaries and Intelligence Summaries are contained in F. S. Regs., Part II. and the Staff Manual respectively. Title pages will be prepared in manuscript.

Place	Date	Hour	Summary of Events and Information.	Remarks and references to Appendices
ALBERT	28.12.16	—	46th Field Ambulance, which Ambulance relieved the section of the 1/1st R.M. Field Ambulance at ECOLE SUPERIOR, ALBERT, opening its Headquarters. Evacuated O.R. sick 63	
ALBERT	29.12.16		Winter remained - Evacuated O.R. sick 36	
ALBERT	30.12.16		Showery. A.D.M.S. visited First Kennedy AMIENS - Representative opening supply of materials made to Headquarters. A.D.M.S. visited Bucks B.B., being in that 2 cases of Diphtheria in that B., from seen (no suspicious) having occurred within last week. Asked O.C. Buck mobile (Back) Laboratory asked to assist in investigation of these cases. Evacuated - O.R. sick 25	
ALBERT	31.12.16		Weather fine. A.D.M.S. inspected men of 1/5 R.Nurses reported unfit. also visited 1/3rd L.M. field Ambulance 9 1/1st L.M. Field Ambulance at No.1 M.D.S. A.D.M.S. opened 1/3rd L.M. Field Amb. to bel. at 10/P. A.D.C.O.s. 736 men for temporary attachment to 1/1st Rly Field Ambulance. Evacuated O.R. sick 34	

[signature] COLONEL,
A.D.M.S. 48th (S.M.) DIVISION.

140/19/41

Vol 22

CONFIDENTIAL

War Diary

of

ADMS 48th Division

from 1st January 1917 to 31st January 1917

COMMITTEE FOR THE
MEDICAL HISTORY OF THE WAR
Date 13 MAR. 1917

Jany 1917

51

Army Form C. 2118.

WAR DIARY
or
INTELLIGENCE SUMMARY.
(Erase heading not required.)

Instructions regarding War Diaries and Intelligence Summaries are contained in F. S. Regs., Part II. and the Staff Manual respectively. Title pages will be prepared in manuscript.

Place	Date	Hour	Summary of Events and Information	Remarks and references to Appendices
BAIZEUX	1.1.17	9 a.m	Divl H.Q. & orderlies opened here. Brigades moved back to WARLOY, CONTAY, BAIZEUX. 1/3rd Nth Fld Ambulance moved to BEHOC HOUSE ALBERT. Evacuated. Capt. J.H.ENGLISH R.A.M.C. reported for duty. He rejoins EDI8.	
BAIZEUX	2.1.17		Snow in a.m. Weather dull. A.D.M.S. attended S Conference J.O.C. Routine. Evacuated. RenR CHAPLAINS F and HEUT BOYLORE left. Temp staff of duty.	
BAIZEUX	3.1.17		Dull, fine rain. A.D.M.S. visited 42nd Fld. Field Ambulance WARLOY. Evacuated.	
BAIZEUX	4.1.17		Rain; Cold; fine towards evening. A.D.M.S. attended Conference D.H.Q. It was arranged for Capt. LENNON R.A.M.C. to go with D.D.M.S. & see localities of Dressed Posts in French Artillery Brigade. Lieut J.M.EDIS R.A.M.C. departed for duty at BOULOGNE BASE. Evacuated.	
BAIZEUX	5.1.17		Fine & sunny. A.D.M.S. attended Conference of O.C. A'mbulances D.H.Q. attend with H.Q. with regard to moving of the Field Ambulance when Division proceed to training area further West. Arranged for Section from 1/3rd Nth Field Ambulance to relieve with a Section from 1/3rd Nth Field Ambulance to accompany the Division. Also Sanitary Section & also the O.C.	

Army Form C. 2118.

WAR DIARY
or
INTELLIGENCE SUMMARY.
(Erase heading not required.)

Instructions regarding War Diaries and Intelligence Summaries are contained in F.S. Regs., Part II. and the Staff Manual respectively. Title pages will be prepared in manuscript.

Place	Date	Hour	Summary of Events and Information	Remarks and references to Appendices
BAIZEUX	6.1.17		Rainy - O.Ond visited D.Md with reference to cures of Ambulance down to bus Area. Units detailed as an stwalth. go confirmed Evacuated	
BAIZEUX	7.1.17		Une bit cold. Further orders received regarding these. Evacuated	
BAIZEUX	8.1.17	8.30 am	Rainy. Arrow moving to bus Area	
		11 am	D.M.S Evacuation opened at HALLENCOURT.	
		1 pm	2 Sections of A.T.B arrived at PONT-REMY - "A" Section proceeded to ARAINES and "B" Section to HUPPY. Weather turned very cold, hail & snow	
HALLENCOURT	9.1.17		Rainy, snow. A.Md visited FRUCOURT unable to site for "B" Section. Used old field Amb to.	
"	10.1.17		Arrangements made for Divisional Clothing Store at HALLENCOURT. DADMS made a reconnaissance of the villages of LIMEUX, LIMERCOURT & BAILLEUL with a view to finding a Field Ambulance site in case it should be necessary to move "B" Section 3/S.M.T.a from HUPPY - None suitable found. Ensigns Mumford-Hannay, G.a. Staff, + D.A Divn transferred to ABBEVILLE suffering from Laryngitis (?) - Too spacious to be hopeful - Weather wet & cold.	
"	11.1.17		Capt. Rushton R.A.M.C. DADMS, transferred to ABBEVILLE suffering from a sprained ankle. applied to retain of Capt. Dale, Ind. Sanitary Officer, now performing army duty at the Fourth Army School of Sanitation, or for another sanitarian	

T2134. Wt. W708—776. 500000. 4/15. Str J. C. & S.

Army Form C. 2118.

WAR DIARY
or
INTELLIGENCE SUMMARY.
(Erase heading not required.)

Instructions regarding War Diaries and Intelligence Summaries are contained in F. S. Regs., Part II. and the Staff Manual respectively. Title pages will be prepared in manuscript.

Place	Date	Hour	Summary of Events and Information	Remarks and references to Appendices
HALLENCOURT	11/1/17	—	Employed officers on sanitation in area as mentioned & there is much to be done — Applied for permission to march patient to BOSEVILLE instead of to LE TREPORT which is twice the distance — 23 admissions, 1 evacuated —	
"	12/1/17		A.D.M.S. visited 3/Sou Fd a at AIRAINES & section of 2/Sou Fd a at FRUCOURT — Received orders from III rd Corps for 2/Sou Fd a at WARLOY to hand over to an Australian F.A. & proceed to No. 5 Area — Captain Shiel N.Z.m.C. arrived from Army S.of I. with Ord N.C. & was detached for duty with 4th R.Bks giving advice on leave of Capt. Bearse. 21 admitted, 2 evacuated.	
"	13/1/17		A.D.M.S. inspected Divisional Laundry at AMIENS — Received & transmitted orders for 2/Sou Fd a to entrain at FRECHENCOURT at 12 noon on 14th & to detrain at LONGPRE; transport to come by road — a 2 days march. 29 admitted, 21 evacuated. Weather cold & wet.	
"	14/1/17		A.D.M.S. visited section of 3/Sou Fd a at HUPPY — Issued orders for Capt Harrison R.A.M.C. attached 1/6th Gloster and Lt. Hamilton R.A.M.C. attached 1/5th Gloster to attend Fourth Army School of Sanitation at ALBERT on 15th–18th and arranged for their journey by ambulance car. 13 admitted, 2 evacuated.	
"	15/1/17		Arranged for personnel of 33rd Fd Ambul now in HALLENCOURT who attended by M.O./c Amb. Train. Transport and personnel of 2/Sou Fd a arrived at FRUCOURT. 23 admitted, evacuated nil	
"	16/1/17		A.D.M.S. visited 2/Sou Fd a at FRUCOURT — Directed O.C. 2/Sou Fd a to detail a medical officer for temporary medical charge of 1/5th Sussex Hut Wnd O.C. 1/Sou Fd a to send a medical officer daily to visit R.A. troops lines near Albert. 24 admissions, 24 evacuations	
"	17/1/17		Heavy fall of snow during night & still continuing. Lt & Qm Wright 2/Sou Fd a reported his arrival from leave. 29 admissions, 23 evacuated.	

T.2134. Wt. W708—776. 500000. 4/15. Sir J. C. & S.

Army Form C. 2118.

WAR DIARY
or
INTELLIGENCE SUMMARY.
(Erase heading not required.)

Instructions regarding War Diaries and Intelligence
Summaries are contained in F. S. Regs., Part II.
and the Staff Manual respectively. Title pages
will be prepared in manuscript.

Place	Date	Hour	Summary of Events and Information	Remarks and references to Appendices
HALLENCOURT	18/1/17		ADMS visited 2/5m FA at FRUCOURT & ordered 1/3 Sm FA to reconnoitre Village of FRUCOURT with a view to finding better accommodation for patients than in the barns they are at present occupying. Capt Hamilton & Lt Hamilton rejoined their unit from Fourth Army School of Sanitation. Admitted 18. Evacuated nil	
"	19/1/17		ADMS attended Conference at ADMS' office at Corps Headquarters. Notified by DDMS that Fourth Army School of Sanitation are about to further order. Directed OC 1/3 Sm FA to send Vivd Nackards 1/5 N Warwicks to APM's office at AMIENS by 10 am tomorrow. Admission 26 Evacuated 23	
"	20/1/17		ADMS visited the Divl Laundry at Salens & paid employés in absence of Capt Drake Officer i/c Baths & Laundry who is ill in hospital. Admitted to hospital 22. Evacuated 11. Hand park has been provided but 2 bags & still continues. Heating keeps very satisfactory.	
"	21/1/17		ADMS issued to OC 1/3 Sm FA to attach Capt Borrodi to Divl Headquarters forthwith with the Miniaride heretofore as Div Gas Capt. Borrodi reported his arrival about 5 pm. Directed OC 2/5 Sm FA to detail an officer for medical charge of 1/8 Worcester during absence on leave of Capt Davy. Admitted 18. Evacuated 27.	
"	22/1/17		Hand park continues. Routine work. Admitted 13. Evacuated nil. Arranged with S.S.O to get in supply of anti trench foot materials.	
"	23/1/17		" " Capt Smith DMC reported his arrival from Essex. Admitted 39. Evacuated 24.	
"	24/1/17		Weather very cold, dry & bright. 7 reinforcements arrived from base. Also brought & ration lorries for Field Ambulances. Received report from OC 1/1 Sm Field Ambulance to forward medical arrangements in the new area which the Divn is about to take over. Admitted 27. Evacuated 17 -	

T.2134. Wt. W708—776. 500000. 4/16. Sir J. C. & S.

Army Form C. 2118.

WAR DIARY
or
INTELLIGENCE SUMMARY.
(Erase heading not required.)

Instructions regarding War Diaries and Intelligence Summaries are contained in F. S. Regs., Part II. and the Staff Manual respectively. Title pages will be prepared in manuscript.

Place	Date	Hour	Summary of Events and Information	Remarks and references to Appendices
HALLENCOURT	25/1/17		Issued instructions to Medical units for move to new area in accordance with orders received from Division Headquarters	
"	26/1/17	2.30 pm	ADMS attended conference at Divisional Headquarters. Lt Col Houghton reported his arrival from leave. Admitted 31. Evacuated 25"	
			ADMS visited column of 3/1 Sm Field Ambulance at HUPPY and AIRANES and the 2/1 Sm F.A. at FROCOURT. DADMS returned from No. 2 Stationary Hospital ABBEVILLE. Capt Carroll No 1/3 Warwicks reported his arrival from leave.	
			Transport of "A" Section 3/1 Sm F.A. began its march to new area accompanying that of 143rd Inf. Bde. Admitted 28 evacuated 36	
HALLENCOURT	27/1/17		"A" Section 1/3rd Sthn Field Ambulance entrained for MERICOURT SUR-SOMME.	
			Transport of 2/1 Sthn Field Ambulance began to march to new area marching with that of the 145th B Bde Infantry Brigade	
			Divisional Headquarters arrived here	
MERICOURT-SUR-SOMME.	28/1/17	noon	"B" Section of 1/3rd Sthn FieldAmbulance arrived at CERISY GAILLY. The 1/1st Sthn Field Ambulance Railway train 62 c.r.p. 1/10000	
			Ambulance reported the Divisional Train arrived at MERICOURT.	
			ADMS accompanied the French Field Ambulance at CAPPY	
MERICOURT	29/1/17		ADMS visited 1/3rd Sthn Field Ambulance MERICOURT & 1/1st Sthn Field Ambulance, MERICOURT.	
			Also Officers of "B" Section 1/3rd S.Amb to report to Headquarters.	
			ADMS visited the Medicin-Chef of 152nd Division (French) at HERBECOURT with reference to the taking over of the French Field Ambulance into a nett arrangements for Medical affairs from the Sthn Field Amb to proceed on 1st Feby for the purpose of	

WAR DIARY
or
INTELLIGENCE SUMMARY.
(Erase heading not required.)

Army Form C. 2118.

Instructions regarding War Diaries and Intelligence Summaries are contained in F. S. Regs., Part II. and the Staff Manual respectively. Title pages will be prepared in manuscript.

Place	Date	Hour	Summary of Events and Information	Remarks and references to Appendices
	29.11.17		reconnoitring the area	
MERICOURT	30.11.17		12 and 1/4 Field Ambles arrived at HAMEL. ADMS visited 4 and III Corps at VILLERS-BRETTONEUX, and 1/2 and 1/4 Field Ambulances at HAMEL. D.D.M.S. called - saw A.D.M.S. - afterwards taking over from the 2nd & 4th Field Ambulances. Orders issued for 1/2 & 1/4 Field Ambulances to Field Dist. Battalions. FOUILLOY will not to-day take over the north of the advanced Posts but to be responsible for the collection of sick returning from the advanced Front.	
MERICOURT	31.11.17		Conference with A. generals of divisions held by A.D.M.S., at which preparatory measures against Trench Foot was discussed, & subsequently detailed instructions on this subject were issued to all F.A.s.	

[signature] COLONEL,
A.D.M.S. 48th (S.M.) DIVISION.

140/QP6

Vol 23

CONFIDENTIAL

War Diary
of
A/DMS 48th Division
from 1-2-17 to 28-2-17.

COMMITTEE FOR THE
MEDICAL HISTORY OF THE WAR
Date 4— APR.1917

WAR DIARY
or
INTELLIGENCE SUMMARY.

Army Form C. 2118.

Place	Date	Hour	Summary of Events and Information	Remarks and references to Appendices
MERICOURT SUR-SOMME	1-3-17		Weather cold, snow and wind. 1/3/17 7th Field Ambulance took over from Second Field Ambulance at ECLUSIER & the advanced posts thereof. O.R. battle 9 officers & 2 O.Rs. Instructions issued to O.C. 7th Field Ambulance regarding care of sick Captains YOUNGER R.A.M.C. 15 Hussars, BEAN, & Lieut. 4th R. Berks and FERGUSON R.A.M.C. 1/7 Bucks Bn. returned from leave. Admitted to hosp. W/2 O.R.s. Evacuated to hosp. Off. 2 O.R.s.	
MERICOURT	2-3-17		Weather very cold, sunny. A/Dir'd visited 7/2 and 8th Field Ambulances ECLUSIER & with O.C. visited forage Requisition & French Division at Cursed Quarry by ride. This did not appear to be suited to the purpose of Field Ambulances of this Division. A/Dir'd also visited French Field Ambulance at CAPPY MARNÉ where 7/4 R.A. Field Ambulance had arrived and drawn to-night in full. (1/94 examined & L/C DRYSDALE HYDROIDS attached 145 T.M. Battery as to his health. Captain .... (mbd to Hosp) 7th Field Ambulance 1 more temporarily ECLUSIER. Admitted sick OR 58/2. To guard ...... Sick OR20. Weather very cold, sunny. Today we from French Division in line	
CAPPY	3-2-17	10 a.m.		

Army Form C. 2118.

WAR DIARY
or
INTELLIGENCE SUMMARY.
(Erase heading not required.)

Instructions regarding War Diaries and Intelligence Summaries are contained in F. S. Regs., Part II. and the Staff Manual respectively. Title pages will be prepared in manuscript.

Place	Date	Hour	Summary of Events and Information	Remarks and references to Appendices
CAPPY	3-2-17		1/2 and 3/4 Fd. Ambulances moved to ECLUSIER. General enquiry into the state of the men very unsatisfactory. There is enough flu in the area to justify us giving up a tent to them. To improve it. Men are very depressed. Admitted Sick OR 37. Wounded OR 7. Weather very cold but sunny & dry.	
CAPPY	4-2-17		A Thed visited 1/2 and 3/4 Fd. Ambulance which is not opened to receiving sick. Evacuated Sick 1 off. 7 OR. Wounded 6 OR. Admitted 9 Sick off. 1 OR 36. Wounded OR 4. Weather continues cold but sunny.	
CAPPY	5-2-17		Every morning at 8 every case for embolic is viewed and admitted 96 admits. Lieut Col RAWLINGSTON R.C. 1/2 and 1/2 Fd Ambulance proceeded on paid leave to England.	
CAPPY	6-2-17		Orders issued to move 1/2 and 1/3 Fd. Ambulance by 8.8 Admitted OR Sick 57. OR wounded 22. Evacuated sick OR 13. off. 3 wounded OR. Weather very cold. Day snowed. Dry.	
CAPPY	7-2-17		A Thed visited 1/2 and 1/3 Fd. Field Ambulances. 1/2 and 1/3 the Field Ambulances taken over from the Passed Field Ambulance 2 nd 19 P.Y. Evacuated Sick 3 Officers. 32 OR. Wounded 34 OR. Admitted Sick Off. 3 OR 42. Wounded OR 35. Situation unchanged. Weather very cold. Sunny day. A Thed visited 1/2 and 1/3 Fd Ambulance Eva evacuated Sick 30 ff. 20 OR. Wounded 4 OR. Admitted Sick OR 43. Wounded OR 65. Wounded to OR C.	

Army Form C. 2118.

WAR DIARY
or
INTELLIGENCE SUMMARY.
(Erase heading not required.)

Instructions regarding War Diaries and Intelligence Summaries are contained in F. S. Regs., Part II. and the Staff Manual respectively. Title pages will be prepared in manuscript.

Place	Date	Hour	Summary of Events and Information	Remarks and references to Appendices
CAPPY	8.2.17		Situation unchanged. Weather very cold. Enemy quiet.	
			O.C. visited 137 & 1/4 Field Ambulance.	
			O.C. attended Conference 2/Lieut III Corps.	
			A report sent to HQ signed by O.C. that the sand and salt treatment has come to a standstill owing to lack of materials	
			1/2 en the Field Ambulance sent an advanced party to the French Field Ambulance at CAPPY SUD. Our CHAUSSEURS and preparing & taking over. Evacuated sick OR 25. Wounded 58	
CAPPY	9.2.17		Situation unchanged. Weather very cold. Enemy quiet.	
			About fifty of all three Field Ambulances	Evacuated sick off 7 OR... wounded 2 off 18 OR
			moved to CAPPY SUD.	
CAPPY	10.2.17		Situation unchanged. Weather very cold enemy.	
			O.C. visited Camp at MAY/B Master at MAPPY CAMP (Rfl.) - all Field Ambulances.	Ref App. 62 passed.
			Evacuated OR sick 13. Wounded OR 1. Died of wounds off 1 OR 54. Wounded OR 2.	
CAPPY	11.2.17		Weather very cold. Dull, slight snow.	
			O.D.M.S. visited all three Field Ambulances. Drowned Bath started at CAPPY.	
			Evacuated sick 11 Officers 60 OR. Wounded 1 Officers. Admitted sick 10 Officers...	

WAR DIARY
or
INTELLIGENCE SUMMARY.
(Erase heading not required.)

Army Form C. 2118.

Place	Date	Hour	Summary of Events and Information	Remarks and references to Appendices
CAPPY	12.2.17		Situation unchanged. Right evacuated the sick. Weather milder, slight thaw. ADMS visited all three Ambulances & Camp 52, two later with reference to installation of ablution hut (improvement in unit treatment for Trench Foot). Capt STIEL RAMC proceeds on usual leave to England. Evacuated 1 (Rank 34, Wounded) 1 Off., 2 OR, Wounded Officers 2, Wounded Off. 1 OR 6.	
CAPPY	13.2.17		Situation unchanged. Weather milder. Snowing. ADMS called & visited ADMS visited all three Field Ambulances. Lieut Col. HOWKINS OC yesterday 1/1 Field Ambulance reported D on leave. Evacuated Sick 1 Officer, 10 OR Wounded 3 OR, Admitted Officers Sick Off. Wounded Off. 2. Situation unchanged. Weather milder, thawing, sunny.	
CAPPY	14.2.17		ADMS visited Camp 52 + Baths at ECLUSIER. Also Met 1/3rd Sth. Field Ambulance Wounded 1 Off, Sick 1 Officer, 18 OR, Wounded OR 5. Lieut ASHBY evacuated sick Admitted Sick Off. 1 & 2g. Wounded Off. 1 OR.	
CAPPY	15.2.17		Situation unchanged. Weather milder. ADMS visited 1/3rd Sth. Field Ambulance and ADS. FLAUCOURT. Evacuated Sick 1 Officer 7 OR. Wounded form Admitted Sick Off. 1 OR 33, Wounded Off. 1 OR 6.	

WAR DIARY or INTELLIGENCE SUMMARY

Army Form C. 2118.

Place	Date	Hour	Summary of Events and Information	Remarks and references to Appendices
CAPPY	16-2-17		Situation unchanged. Weather mild, thawing. Divisional headquarters moved to CAMP OLYMPE (63299 Sh.62c France) ¼ map. O.C. Unit I.O.M. visited No 2 Sn Field Ambulance. Evacuated O.R. sick 13. O.Rwounded 1. O.Munt holt offt. T.R.35. Wound 7.	
CAPPY	17-2-17		Situation unchanged. Thawing. O.C. Unit visited all three Field Ambulances. Evacuated sick offers 2. O.R.14. Wounded O.R.4. O.M.Hotchkiss 12.O.R no wounds 1902.	
CAPPY	18-2-17		Situation unchanged. Synchs milder – rain – Scheme for the evacuation of wounded was prepared and copies forwarded to O.C. Unit & Headquarters Div. Evacuated offers sick 3. O.R.3. officer wounded 0. O.R.17 wounded 1.	
CAPPY	19-2-17		Situation unchanged. Thaw continues, weather misty. O.C. Unit visited HERBECOURT to select site for a Divisional Collecting Station. Then visited all the Ambulances, arranging with the 4/2nd & 4th Field Ambulances to establish a Divisional Collecting Station at HERBECOURT. Evacuated offers sick 3. O.R sick 8. Wounded 3. Officer wounded 1. offer Hotchkiss S.R.35. wounded offers 3.	

T.J.134. Wt. W708–776. 500000. 4/15. Sir J. C. & S.

WAR DIARY
or
INTELLIGENCE SUMMARY.

Army Form C. 2118.

Place	Date	Hour	Summary of Events and Information	Remarks and references to Appendices
CAPPY	20.2.17		Situation much as yesterday. Some rain. A/Maj visited all three Field Ambulances	
CAPPY	21.2.17	—	Evacuated Sick - Officers 2 O.R. 9 Wounded 1 O.R. Admitted Sick Offs. 1 O.R. 5 Wounded Offs 1. Weather rainy & misty. A/Maj visited 1/3rd & 1/2 nd Sth. Mid. Field Ambulances. Evacuated Sick Officers 0 O.R. Admitted Sick Officers 1 O.R. Wounded Offs. O.R. Hill reported for duty. Situation unchanged. Weather rainy. Trenches falling in much and men very exhausted the working parties of the trenches & on relief of S.B. Ambulances sent to HERBECOURT to help when coming out on relief of S.B. Ambulances. Given men very exhausted to bring the nine exhausted men back to their Camp. A.D.M.S. attended Conference D.M.S. III Corps.	
CAPPY	22.2.17		Evacuated Sick Off. 1 O.R.9. Admitted Sick Off. O.R. Wounded O.R. 9 Situation unchanged. Weather very much dumps. A/Maj visited Dvl. Collecting Station HERBECOURT, & the Soup Kitchen there. Visited all three Field Ambulances. Lieutt. F. Cuco French Int. A. on Mil. Off. the 24 hours ending 12 noon to-day. Capt VIDALE returned from CPL. MARTIN	

WAR DIARY or INTELLIGENCE SUMMARY

Army Form C. 2118.

Place	Date	Hour	Summary of Events and Information	Remarks and references to Appendices
CAPPY	24.2.17		Situation unchanged. Weather very cold & damp. Sixty seven cases of Trench Foot were admitted. A Shed in camp any north West used as the Ambulance when there - and the cases admitted on previous day - in all 94 - were being transferred unfit to Depots. The majority of the cases were of a mild description and probably be fit for full gentle in a fortnight. AD.M.S. visited & found nothing but in Camps 56 found the arrangements satisfactory. A Report on the prophylactic measures being employed for Trench Foot was submitted to Divisional Head Quarters. Capt. D.D. MACKAY R.A.M.C. T.F. joined for duty. Posted 9/5, 1/3rd B.S. Field Ambulance. Admitted Offs.1. O.R.139 - Evacuated Offs. act 1. O.R.25.	
CAPPY	25.2.17		Situation unchanged. Sixty-seven cases. Report submitted to D.M.S. H. Army on the second trial of Campbell Stark Grip and late treatment of Pent as a prophylactic measure for trench foot (incidence) worth an evaluation. O.9.2.8 evacd. 2/A.D.S.Offs. & Invalid MARY Camp. A.Director Offs.1. OR.62. Wounded 0.R.26. Evacuated to field 1 off. OR.45. Wounded O.R.20.	

A5834 Wt. W4973 M687 750,000 8/16 D. D. & L. Ltd. Forms/C.2118/13.

WAR DIARY or INTELLIGENCE SUMMARY

Army Form C. 2118.

Place	Date	Hour	Summary of Events and Information	Remarks and references to Appendices
CAPPY	26.2.17		Situation unchanged. Everything will enemy. O.P.A.S visited all three Field Ambulances. Arranged with Ordnance for the supply of stoves and buckets for the foot washing places in forward area. Lieut Col Hoskins returned from leave. Capt G. 87612 RAMC T.C. directed to report for duty at No.5 Stationary Hospital. Admitted OR sick 49. Evacuated 9. Evacuated OR sick 9. OR wounded 5.	
CAPPY	27.2.17		Situation unchanged. Weather mild, sunny. A.D.M.S visited all three Field Ambulances. Orders issued for relief of personnel of 45th A.M Field Ambulance by 148th Field Ambulance at the (Advanced) Dressing Station & Posts on 1st prox. Capt McMAHON R.A.M.C. T.C. Bacteriologist to IV Army visited this area & took samples from water points for testing purposes. Admitted HQ sick Officers 1. OR 69. Wounded Officers 1. OR 3. Evacuated Officers 1. OR 20. Wounded Officers 1. OR 2.	

WAR DIARY
or
INTELLIGENCE SUMMARY.

Army Form C. 2118.

Place	Date	Hour	Summary of Events and Information	Remarks and references to Appendices
CAPPY	28/2/17		Situation unchanged. Weather dull. ADMS visited Divisional Collecting Station HERBECOURT and 1/2nd & 2/3rd Wly Field Amb. 2 MO's & 20 OR of 2nd Wly Field Ambulance reported to III Corps Rest Station CERISY in relief of a similar party at present there. Admitted sick off: 1 OR 42 Wounded Off: 1 OR 3. Evacuated Officers: nil OR: 8. Division on Right is 1st Division, on Left N. of River SOMME is 33rd Division, XV Corps. Sketch & extension of Field Ambulances is attached.	

MOYNIHAN
COLONEL,
A.D.M.S. 48th (S.M.) Division

Appendix A

SECRET   48th Division.

SCHEME OF MEDICAL ARRANGEMENTS IN THE EVENT OF HEAVY FIGHTING.

Ref. Map Sheet 62 C.

1. **LINE HELD.** The 48th Division holds the northern sector of the IIIrd Corps front, its line extending from H.12.a.9.1. on the right to BIACHES on the left with outlying posts as far north as SORMONT FARM. This front is held by 4 battalions with 2 battalions in support.

2. **REGIMENTAL AID POSTS.**
   Left Battalion,   H.30.d.3.2.)
   Left Centre Battn,   H.30.c.3.1.)   Left Sector.
   Left Support Battn,   H.21.a.9.4.)

   Right Support Battn.   N.5.a.9.7.)
   Right Centre Battn,   N.6.d.3.3.)   Right Sector.
   Right Battalion,   N.3.b.3.9.)

                                                                        Lying down accommodation.

3. **FIELD AMBULANCE POSTS.**
   DESIRÉ POST,   -   H.36.c.2.6.)   20 Stretcher cases
   ACHILLE POST,   -   N.5.a.7.7.)   12 cases
   GUERRIER POST, -   H.29.b.8.1.)   2 cases

4. **ADVANCED DRESSING STATION.**
   FLAUCOURT,   -   H.4.a.3.3.)   25 cases.

5. **MAIN DRESSING STATIONS.**
                                                                        Accommodation
   1/3rd S.M.Fd.Ambce, ECLUSIER, G.15.c.2.4.   400 lying cases
   1/1st S.M.Fd.Ambce, CAPPY MAIRIE, G.25.b.3.5. 300   "   "
   1/2nd S.M.Fd.Ambce, CAPPY SUD, G.25.d.2.4.   300   "   "

   Temporary accommodation for 2000 sitting cases can be found in the village of CAPPY in close proximity to the 1/1st S.Mid. Field Ambulance at CAPPY MAIRIE.

6. **DISPOSITION OF R.A.M.C. PERSONNEL.** In addition to the R.A.M.C. Personnel at the R.A.M.C. Posts, Advanced Dressing Station, and Divisional Collecting Station, the following R.A.M.C. bearers will be allotted:-
   (a) Each Regimental Aid Post will have 10 bearers.
   (b) 100 bearers will work between the Regimental Aid Posts, the R.A.M.C. Posts, and the Advanced Dressing Stations.

7. **EVACUATION OF SERIOUSLY WOUNDED TO ADVANCED DRESSING STATION.** The R.A.M.C. bearers at Regimental Aid Posts will assist the regimental bearers to bring the wounded in from the forward area to the Regimental Aid Posts. Here they will be taken over by relay bearers, taken to the R.A.M.C. Posts, taken over by a fresh set of bearers, and so on to the Advanced Dressing Station.
   It will be possible to use stretcher carriers to a large extent along the roads from the R.A.M.C. Posts to the Advanced Dressing Station, and at night the ambulance cars can go up to these Posts.

8. **FURTHER EVACUATION.** From the Advanced Dressing Station at FLAUCOURT wounded will be evacuated in the motor ambulance cars of Field Ambulances to the Main Dressing Station at G.15.c.2.4. via HERBECOURT and ECLUSIER. In the event of the Main

Dressing Station becoming congested and unable to take in further casualties, the cars will take wounded on to the 1/2nd S.Mid. Field Ambulance at CAPPY SUD. All cars will return to FLAUCOURT along the CAPPY CHATEAU - HERBECOURT Road.

9. DIVISIONAL COLLECTING STATION.   HERBECOURT, H.32.a.1.9.   1 Tent Sub-division. Slightly wounded cases able to walk will be directed to proceed through the main communication trenches and by road to this post, the route to which will be marked out by directing notices which the Officer i/c Advanced Dressing Station will be responsible for erecting.

10. EVACUATION OF SLIGHTLY WOUNDED.   From the Divisional Collecting Station the slightly wounded will be conveyed to the Field Ambulance at CAPPY MAIRIE by horse ambulances and motor lorries.

                                          C.A. YOUNG, Colonel,
3-3-17.   A.D.M.S. 48th Division.

48

140/2031 Vol 24

CONFIDENTIAL

War Diary
of
A.D.M.S. 48th Division
from 1.3.17 to 31.3.17.

COMMITTEE FOR THE
MEDICAL HISTORY OF THE WAR
Date 11 MAY 1917

Vol XXIV

WAR DIARY or INTELLIGENCE SUMMARY

Army Form C. 2118.

Place	Date	Hour	Summary of Events and Information	Remarks and references to Appendices
CAPPY	1.3.17	—	Situation unchanged from that of 28th Feby. Weather fair. A.D.M.S. attended Conference D.D.M.S. III Corps. W/O. 68th Field Ambulance relieved B.O. 5th Div. Zillebeke in forward area. Admitted Officers sick 4. O.R. 64. Wounded Off. 1. O.R. 14. Evacuated Off. 4. O.R. 13. Wounded Off. 1. O.R. 10.	
CAPPY	2.3.17	—	Situation unchanged. Weather fair. A.D.M.S. visited all three Field Ambulances. Admitted Officers sick 2. O.R. 60. Wounded O.R. 14. Evac – Lt-t- Off. 2. O.R. 20. Wounded O.R. 9.	Appendix A
CAPPY	3.3.17	—	Situation unchanged. Weather cold. Foggy. A.D.M.S. mounted H.Q. Scheme for evacuation (forward). Admitted Sick – Off. 1. O.R. 53. Wounded Off. 1. O.R. 11. Evacuated Sick Off. 1. O.R. 19. Wounded Off. 1. O.R. 12.	
CAPPY	4.3.17	—	Situation unchanged. Weather continues cold. A.D.M.S. visited all three Field Ambulances, A.D.S. FLAUCOURT & the Advanced Bn. Admitted Sick Off. 2. O.R. 53. Wounded Off. 1. O.R. 22. Evacuated Sick Off. 2. O.R. 57. Wounded Off. 1. O.R. 25.	
CAPPY	5.3.17	—	Situation unchanged. Cold & raining. Much snow during night 4-5th. A.D.M.S. visited No. 1 & No. 2 Field Ambulances. Admitted O.R. sick 33. Wounded O.R. 7. Evacuated O.R. 26 sick. O.R. Wounded 9.	

Army Form C. 2118.

WAR DIARY
or
INTELLIGENCE SUMMARY.
(Erase heading not required.)

Instructions regarding War Diaries and Intelligence Summaries are contained in F.S. Regs., Part II. and the Staff Manual respectively. Title pages will be prepared in manuscript.

Place	Date	Hour	Summary of Events and Information	Remarks and references to Appendices
CAPPY	6.3.17		Situation unchanged. Weather colder & dryer wind. Admd/vacted all three Field Ambulances and MARLY CAMP. Capt. R.B. BRODERICK RAMC T.F. appointed to Temporary Command of South Field Ambulance. Admitted sick – Offrs 1. OR 27. Wounded OR 1. Evacuated sick OR 25. Wounded 2.	
CAPPY	7.3.17		Situation unchanged. Weather continues cold. Admd/vacted 3rd & 1st Cdn Field Ambulances and MARLY CAMP. Admitted sick Offrs 1. OR 47. Wounded OR 5. Evacuated sick Offr 1. OR 21.	
CAPPY	8.3.17		Situation unchanged. Weather & colder. Freezing. Adm/vacted 1/3rd 1/1/ & 2/1 Field Ambulances. Admitted sick Offr 1. OR 63. Wounded OR 3. Evacuated Offr 1. OR 21. Wounded 8 IR 4.	
CAPPY	9.3.17		Situation unchanged. Weather cold. Some snow turning to sleet & rain. Admd/vacted all three Field Ambulances. Admitted sick Offrs 2. OR 24. Wounded OR 32. Evacuated sick Offrs 2. OR 13. Wounded OR 29.	
CAPPY	10.3.17		Situation unchanged. Weather colder – windy. Admd/vacted all three Field Ambulances. Admitted sick Offrs 3. OR 42. Wounded OR 13. Evacuated Offrs 3. OR 10. Wounded OR 8.	

Army Form C. 2118.

WAR DIARY
or
INTELLIGENCE SUMMARY.
(Erase heading not required.)

Instructions regarding War Diaries and Intelligence Summaries are contained in F. S. Regs., Part II. and the Staff Manual respectively. Title pages will be prepared in manuscript.

Place	Date	Hour	Summary of Events and Information	Remarks and references to Appendices
CAPPY	11/3/17	—	Situation unchanged. Weather warm & sunny. ADMS visited all three Field Ambulances. Then with O.J.md visited 1/1st R.H. & 1/3rd R.H. Field Ambulances. ADMS Held Sick Offr 1. O.R. 40. Wounded O.R. 6. Evacuated sick offr. O.R. 14. Wounded O.R. 5.	
CAPPY	12/3/17	—	Situation unchanged. Weather mild. ADMS with A.D.Vet.S. visited HERBECOURT & inspected the arrangements & buying from Govt constructed there. Also O.J.md visited 1/1st 8th Field Ambulance. O.J.md attended Conference of O.C. Ambulances Sick Offr 1. O.R. 52. Wounded O.R. 4. Evacuated sick off. O.R. 18. Wounded O.R. 5.	
CAPPY	13/3/17	—	Situation unchanged. Weather mild & misty. O.J.md attended Conference. O.J.md at (?) Corps. ADMS Held Sick Off 2. O.R. 63. Wounded O.R. 9. Evacuated sick off. 2. O.R. 29. Wounded O.R. 3.	
CAPPY	14/3/17	—	Situation unchanged. Weather – rain. ADMS visited all three Field Ambulances. Capt. MEEK R.A.M.C.⁰ joined for duty. Capt. I. DALE R.A.M.C. T.F. Anti-Sanitary Officer Appointed IV Army. Capt. D.O.V. CHARLTON being appointed in his place ADMS Held Sick Off 2. O.R. 82. Wounded O.R. 6. Evacuated sick off. 2. O.R. 16. Wounded O.R. 3.	

Army Form C. 2118.

WAR DIARY
or
INTELLIGENCE SUMMARY.
(Erase heading not required.)

Instructions regarding War Diaries and Intelligence Summaries are contained in F. S. Regs. Part II. and the Staff Manual respectively. Title pages will be prepared in manuscript.

Place	Date	Hour	Summary of Events and Information	Remarks and references to Appendices
CAPPY	15.3.17	—	Situation unchanged. Weather mild. A Stud visited 1/4th, 1/2nd & 1/3rd Field Ambulances. Admitted 0 Offs. OR Sick Wounded Offs. 2 OR 1. Evacuated sick OR 25. Wounded Offs. 2 OR 3.	
CAPPY	16.3.17	—	Situation unchanged. Weather mild & dry. Routine work. Lt. Col. proceeded on leave to England. Lt. Col. Hawkins appointed Acting A.D.M.S. Admitted sick Offs. 2 OR 37. Wounded OR 5. Evacuated sick Offs. OR 24. Wounded OR 1. Inkild.	
CAPPY	17.3.17	—	Situation unchanged. Weather mild & dry. Routine. Admitted sick Off. 1. OR 28. Wounded Offs. 2 OR 2. Evacuated sick M/1 OR 8 wounded Off. 1 OR 2.	
CAPPY	18.3.17	—	Situation. Patrols entered Mt ST QUENTIN, PERONNE, LA MAISONETTE. Wants enemy by. Routine. An advanced Dressing Station established in BIACHE. Admitted sick Off. 2 OR 30. Wounded Offs 5 OR 19. Evacuated sick Off 1 OR 21. Wounded Offs 3 OR 21 (figures)	
CAPPY	19.3.17	—	Situation. Patrols pushing on, occupying DOIGNY, LE MESNIL. Weather enemy small. Lieut Col. Hawkins & DADMS reconnoitred GARDEN FARM, LA CHAPELLETTE & PERONNE with a view to establishing Advanced Dressing Stations. Visited A.D.S. BIACHE. Admitted sick Offs 3 OR 52. Evacuated sick Off 4 OR 15. Wounded Offs 1 OR 3.	

WAR DIARY or INTELLIGENCE SUMMARY

Army Form C. 2118.

Place	Date	Hour	Summary of Events and Information	Remarks and references to Appendices
CAPPY	20-3-17	—	Situation - Work & hits blown (formed of 2 Battalions, Section R.2, 2 Batteries R.G.A. &c.) moved. One Section 4/3 of 8th Field Ambulance detailed to accompany this force. 8/3rd moved 4/ol Bn. Field Ambulance & proceeded with O.C. to PERONNE. Advanced Dressing Station established at PERONNE & GARDEN FARM (Ref. 62c. 1/40000) by H.Q. & 8th Field Ambulance. Admitted sick Offr 1. O.R. 30. wounded 3. Evacuated Offr Wnd 1. O.R. wounded O.R.2. Capt. T. FERGUSON A/MC to deputize for Land Curtis at Officer.	
CAPPY	21-3-17	—	Situation as above. Weather fine. A.D.M.S. visited PERONNE A.D.S. and also accompanied the visit by BIACHE & SAILEUR. Admitted sick Offr 3. O.R. 52. Evacuated sick Offr 3. O.R. 46 wounded O.R. 2.	
CAPPY	22-3-17	—	Situation as above. Weather very cold. Snow storms &c. Capt DAVIES-JONES detailed for duty in connection with French front inhabitants (refugees) left behind in TINCOURT (the number 500) by the enemy. Admitted sick Offr 1. O.R. 34. wounded 5. Evacuated sick Offr 1. O.R. 43. wounded O.R. 5.	
CAPPY	23-3-17	—	Situation as above. Patrols out further East. Weather cold & stormy. C Section 1/1st Bn. Field Ambulance sent to PERONNE A.D.S. Admitted O.R. sick 44. wounded O.R. 1. Evacuated sick O.R. 44. wounded 2.	

WAR DIARY
or
INTELLIGENCE SUMMARY.
(Erase heading not required.)

Army Form C. 2118.

Place	Date	Hour	Summary of Events and Information	Remarks and references to Appendices
CAPPY	24/3/17	—	Situation as above. Weather cold & dull. BARLEUX taken into Divisional area Routine. The wells in PERONNE, HALLE, LACHAPELETTE, 5 good ones found in HALLE, 1 in PERONNE, 4 in LA CHAPELETTE – water from that one disapproved from metallic pipes & have been notified in a discharge. Admitted sick Off 3 OR 34. Wounded OR 1. Evacuated sick Off 3 OR 19. Wounded OR 2.	
CAPPY	25/3/17	—	8 Itch taken in. H.Q. Division moving to R. BONNE. Deaths Off 2 East wing Fontaine. The wells at BARLEUX which was reported unsafe by Capt. D. BUCHANAN Ass't. Sanitary Officer, who obtained a specimen of the water which he carefully examined. No arsenic or other chemical was found by him after testing. Admitted sick Off 3 OR 35. Wounded OR 1. Evacuated sick Off 1 OR 11.	
LERPY	26/3/17	—	Div H.Qrs Advance moving to QUINCONCE. I 21 Central. WeeB Col Ordnance & change of Dorin's Force AUSTR. with annexe 2 guns, 1 Section 42. Admitted sick Off 1 OR 38. Wounded Off 2 OR 1 OR 35. Wounded OR 9. Evacuated sick Off 1 OR 33.	
QUINCONCE	27/3/17	—	Division practically all at R BONNE. Weather improved cold. 1/1st Fld. Amb. still arrived in PERONNE. Advanced Dressing Stations formed at BUSSU by "B" Section of 1/3rd Fld. Field Ambulance and at BUIRE by detachment from 1/1st Fld. Field Ambulance. Sanitary Section arrived in PERONNE. Admitted sick Off 3 OR 39. Wounded Off 1 OR 19. Evacuated Off 1 OR French, wounded Off 1 OR 17.	

WAR DIARY
or
INTELLIGENCE SUMMARY.

(Erase heading not required.)

Army Form C. 2118.

Instructions regarding War Diaries and Intelligence Summaries are contained in F. S. Regs., Part II. and the Staff Manual respectively. Title pages will be prepared in manuscript.

Place	Date	Hour	Summary of Events and Information	Remarks and references to Appendices
QUINCONCE	28.3.17	—	Divisional boundaries E(ROISEL - K3 Central - E14CEN GAVESNES - E20Central - E19a. Weather very cold, snow, bitter. Advanced Dressing Station moved from BUIRE to TINCOURT, & one established at TEMPLEUX-LA-FOSSE. 1/3 2/8, Field Ambulance arrived at DOINGT. A.D.M.S. returned from leave. Admitted sick Officers 1, O.R. 34. Wounded Off. 1, O.R. 2. Evacuated sick Off. 1, O.R. 24. Wounded Off. 1, O.R. 3.	
QUINCONCE	29.3.17	—	Situation as above. Weather wet. A.D.M.S. visited 1/1 and 2/8 Field Ambulances, 1/3 2/8 Field Ambulance and the A.D.S. at TINCOURT. Also inspected Offs. Kitchen at BUIRE. Admitted sick Off. 1, O.R. 31. Evacuated sick Off. 1 O.R. Attack.	
QUINCONCE	30.3.17	—	Situation unaltered. Weather wet. A.D.M.S. visited 1/1 and 1/3 2/8 Field Ambulances.	
		4.15 pm	A.D.M.S. visited A.D.S. TINCOURT with reference to the collection of prevention during & covering the attack on village of ST EMILIE. Which village was captured at 5 p.m. Admitted sick Off. 1, O.R. 37. Wounded Off. 7. Evacuated sick Off. 5, O.R. 25. Wounded O.R. 10.	
QUINCONCE	31.3.17	—	Situation as above. Weather wet. A.D.M.S. visited 1/1 and 1/3 2/8 Field Ambulance. Divisional Headquarters moved to TINCOURT BOUCLY. Admitted sick Off. 1, O.R. 24. Wounded Off. 6, O.R. 28. Evacuated sick Off. 9, O.R. Wounded Off. 1, O.R. 14.	

P.T.O.

O. M. Powell
COLONEL,
A.D.M.S. 48th (S.M.) DIVISION.

Army Form C. 2118.

WAR DIARY
or
INTELLIGENCE SUMMARY.
(Erase heading not required.)

Instructions regarding War Diaries and Intelligence Summaries are contained in F. S. Regs., Part II. and the Staff Manual respectively. Title pages will be prepared in manuscript.

Place	Date	Hour	Summary of Events and Information	Remarks and references to Appendices
QUINCONCE	31/8/17	—	69th Division on Right and 8th Division on Left.	

CONFIDENTIAL

War Diary
of
A.D.M.S. 48th Division
from 1-4-17 to 30-4-17.

Vol XXV

COMMITTEE FOR THE
MEDICAL HISTORY OF THE WAR
Date -6 JUN. 1917

Army Form C. 2118.

WAR DIARY
or
INTELLIGENCE SUMMARY.
(Erase heading not required.)

Instructions regarding War Diaries and Intelligence Summaries are contained in F. S. Regs., Part II. and the Staff Manual respectively. Title pages will be prepared in manuscript.

Place	Date	Hour	Summary of Events and Information	Remarks and references to Appendices
TINCOURT	1-4-17	5 a.m.	The villages of EPEHY & PEZIERES occupied. Weather wet, cold. A.D.M.S. visited A.D.S. TEMPLEUX-LA-FOSSE. A.D.M.S. visited 1/3 L'pool Bn. Field Ambulances. A/Lt. Col. R.A. Broderick returned from leave. Admitted sick officers 0 R.55. Wounded 0 R.11. Evacuated sick off 5 O.R. 29. Wounded off 4 O.R. 22.	
TINCOURT	2-4-17		Situation unchanged. Weather wet & windy. A.D.M.S. visited 1/ol & 3rd Bn. Field Ambulances. Also visited A.D.S at TEMPLEUX, and to LONGAVESNES. The wells in all the villages of the Divisional Area have now been examined. The majority are all filled in and destroyed, but there are one or two in each village that contain water which is fit for drinking after chlorination. All the wells in TINCOURT are intact. No poisons have been found in any of the wells. Admitted sick off 2 O.R. 49. Wounded off 1 O.R. 90. Evacuated sick 1 R.10. Wounded off 1 O.R. 57.	
TINCOURT	3-4-17		Situation as above. Weather improving. Day. O.Ral. visited VILLERS-FANCON & LONGAVESNES with reference to the evacuation of wounded & established an A.D.S at the former place. Also visited ADS at TEMPLEUX. Admitted sick O R.45. Wounded off 2 O R.5. Evacuated sick off 2 O R.23. Wounded off 1 O R.24.	

WAR DIARY
or
INTELLIGENCE SUMMARY.

Army Form C. 2118.

Place	Date	Hour	Summary of Events and Information	Remarks and references to Appendices
TINCOURT	4-4-17	—	Situation unaltered. Severe snowstorm. O.D.M.S. visited 1/3rd & 2/1st S.M. Field Ambulances. An Advanced Dressing Station established at VILLERS-FAUCON, with R.M.O. in detail by 1/3rd S.M. Amb. '5' Section, 1/3 and 2/1 field Ambulance took over A.D.S. TINCOURT from 1/2 field ambulance. Nominal roll of Offs. ORs wounded & ORs evacuated and OR 16 wounded OR 3.	App "A" App Supp 62 1/10,000
TINCOURT	5-4-17	6 a.m.	Villages of RONSSOY to LEMPIRE taken & the high ground in F28 to S.E. of RONSSOY. Weather fine. O.D.M.S. visited A.D.S. TINCOURT and proceed to the Temporary Collecting Post established at K12.d.14. to deal with cases coming down from the Brigade attack up the Right. A.C.P. F2B. Also visited A.D.Ss. at VILLERS FAUCON and TEMPLEUX. An. Recd. OS 6 NCOs 1/3rd S.M. Field Ambulance. Lieut. Davidson R.A.M.C. T.F. proceed to Temporary Duty with 39.C.C.S. in accordance with Division Committee sick Off, 0R 34, wound OR 4. Evacd. sick 4 Offs 0R 253 wound Offs 2 OR 9. Divisional Outpost line as follows - F22 Central - Eastern outskirts of RONSSOY - Eastern outskirts of LEMPIRE - ENFER WOOD - MAZISSE FARM - F20.7.9. - F22.1.8. - W29.c.49 - W25a Central. Weather fine. Capt. B.C.O Sheridan R.A.M.C. S.R. proceed to 1/3rd S.M. Field Ambulance. Capt. Meek R.A.M.C. T.C. Whitfield on leave having been wounded on 30th March. Adm. N.C.o sick Offs, OR 42 wound Off 1 ADR 142. Evacd. sick Offs, OR 35 wound OR 3 Offs OR 105.	
TINCOURT	7-4-17		Situation as above. Weather wet & cold. O.D.M.S. visited No 1 S.M. Field Ambulance with reference R.T.Q establishing on operating Centre there the 8th. Visited 1/3 M. Field Ambulance + R.V.S at TEMPLEUX-LA-FOSSE. Adm. sick 143 OR 27, wound 1 OR 8. Evacd. sick & Offs 3 OR 13. wounded OR 4.	

Army Form C. 2118.

WAR DIARY
or
INTELLIGENCE SUMMARY.
(Erase heading not required.)

Instructions regarding War Diaries and Intelligence Summaries are contained in F.S. Regs., Part II. and the Staff Manual respectively. Title pages will be prepared in manuscript.

Place	Date	Hour	Summary of Events and Information	Remarks and references to Appendices
TINCOURT	8.4.17	—	Situation unaltered. Weather fine. O.Rh.S. visited A.D.M.S. Tincourt. Paraday Tyler became Army Troops. Admitted sick Off 2 OR 65 Wounded Off 2 OR 18 Evacuated sick Off 1 OR 21 Wounded OR 8.	
TINCOURT	9.4.17	—	Situation unchanged. Weather wet + cold. O.Rh. visited 11ed. Fld. Field Ambulance. New Methea site at PERONNE. Admitted sick Off 3 OR 34 Wounded 3 OR 3 Evacuated sick Off 3 OR 24 Wounded Off 1 OR 3.	
TINCOURT	10.4.17	—	Situation unchanged. Very severe blizzard. very cold. O.Rh. visited Dir. Methea Stores Baths at TINCOURT. Capt R J Doeer RAMC TF reported for duty. Admitted sick Off 1 OR 42 Wounded Off 1 OR 10. Evacuated Off 1 OR 25 Wounded Off 1 OR 2.	
TINCOURT.	11.4.17	—	Situation unchanged. Weather fine. O.Rh.S. reported that the Field Ambulance, to which an operating unit has been attached. Also visited 113 W. Fld. Field Ambulance. Admitted sick Off 3 OR 31 Wounded 9 OR H. Evacuated sick Off 1 OR 10 Wounded OR 4.	
TINCOURT	12.4.17	—	Situation unchanged. Severe blizzard. Cold. A bird attached Cyferne S.D.C. Lt Col C H Morris RAMC TF reported & took up duties of O.Rh. 61st Division Field Ambulance. accumed command of the 14th Fld. Field Ambulance. Admitted sick Off 1 OR 62 Wounded OR 6 Evacuated sick Off 5 OR 16 Wounded OR 6. Capts J R Syms RAMC TF and D Aird reported for duty.	

A.5834 Wt. W.4973 M.687 750,000 8/16 D.D. & L. Ltd. Forms/C.2118/13.

Army Form C. 2118.

WAR DIARY
or
INTELLIGENCE SUMMARY.
(Erase heading not required.)

Instructions regarding War Diaries and Intelligence Summaries are contained in F. S. Regs., Part II. and the Staff Manual respectively. Title pages will be prepared in manuscript.

Place	Date	Hour	Summary of Events and Information	Remarks and references to Appendices
TINCOURT	13-4-17	—	Situation unchanged. Weather warm & sunny. A.D.M.S. visited G.O.Bn at TEMPLEUX and VILLERS-FAUCON. A.D.V.S. called here 10am. A.D.M.S. visited H.Q. of 2/R. Field Ambulance at PERONNE. Wounded & sick Off 4 OR 12, sick Wounded ORS Evacuated Off 4 OR 50.	
TINCOURT	14-4-17		Divisional line now being moved up going with X29 — X23 — X17, then via QUEUCHETTES WOOD — SART FARM — N° 2 COPSE and copse at X27C6.7 — X27A4.1 — X26A8.6. Weather mild & sunny. A.D.M.S. visited H.Q. of 2/Rn. Field Ambulance. Admitted Off 3 OR 39, Wounded Off 1 OR 46. Evacuated and Off 3 OR 74, Wounded Off 1, OR 30. Died OR 1.	
TINCOURT	15-4-17		Situation unaltered. Weather wet. A.D.M.S. visited A.D.Ss at VILLERS-FAUCON and TEMPLEUX-LA-FOSSE. Also Mot S.B. Field Ambulance. Admitted sick Off 1 OR 37, Wounded OR 3. Evacuated Off 2 OR 3 sick, Wounded OR 16.	
TINCOURT	16-4-17	2 am	Divisional outpost line pushed further forward to line TOMBOIS FARM — PETIT PRIEL FARM & towards VILLERS-GUISLAIN. Weather very wet & stormy. A.D.M.S. with D.A.Q.M.G visited Divisional Dumping at BUSSU. Also Hot met Off H2 Wounded OR 2. Evacuated and OR 16 Wounded OR 2.	
TINCOURT	17-4-17		Situation unchanged. Weather wet & cold. A.D.M.S. visited B N°2 D.B. TEMPLEUX. Also Hot met Off 3 OR 33. Evacuated and Off 1 OR 12 Wounded Off 1, OR 5. Wounded sick Off 5 OR 44 Wounded OR 11 OR 3 OR 33.	

WAR DIARY
or
INTELLIGENCE SUMMARY.
(Erase heading not required.)

Army Form C. 2118.

Instructions regarding War Diaries and Intelligence Summaries are contained in F.S. Regs., Part II. and the Staff Manual respectively. Title pages will be prepared in manuscript.

Place	Date	Hour	Summary of Events and Information	Remarks and references to Appendices
TINCOURT	21.4.17	—	Situation unchanged. Weather mild. O.D.R. reverted that the Field Ambulance at Hyro Offrand Other Field Ambulance at Doignt N.T. Lieut C Royer R.A.M.C. O in C. 14 Offrand 2 Ranks. N.D. places In Arrest. Capt. T. Ferguson appointed in his place. Admitted sick Offr 1 OR 35. Wounded Offr 1 OR 34. Evacuated sick Offr 1 OR 36. Wounded Offr 1 OR 27.	Ref App 62 c 4/4/3/1033
TINCOURT	22.4.17	8 am	Situation unchanged. Weather fine.	
		11 am	Visit Hea Dquartes moved to Queeny at K11a79. O.D.R. visited all three Field Ambulances. Admitted sick Offr 8 OR 45. Evacuated Offr 1 OR 9. Wounded Offr 1 OR 6. Evacuated sick OR 36.	
K11a79	22.4.17	—	Situation medical. Weather fine & dry. O.D.R. visited A D Bs at TINCOURT and VILLERS-FAUCON & TEMPLEUX. 1/3-3 Br. Field Ambulance moved to TEMPLEUX-LA-FOSSE. O.D.R. visited A.D.R. 8 III Corps. Admitted sick Offr 4 OR 60. Evacuated sick Offr 1 OR 17. 19. Wounded Offr 1 OR 2.	
K11a79.	23.4.17	—	Situation moved except from the line. During the night 23/24 an attack was made on GUILLEMONT FARM & ground to the N. by the 8th Tank armour later but rested in a counter attack. 1/3 L. Located Collecting Post at RONSSOY ST EMILIE 9 M/3 at VILLERS-FAUCON. A Wd.2 and 3 and at PERONNE. Admitted sick Offr 4/w 3 d. LH. Field Ambulance. Admitted sick Offr 4 OR 42. Wounded Off 1 OR 1. Evacuated sick Offr 2 OR 22. Wounded Offr 1 OR 5.	

A S814   Wt. W.4973 M687. 750,000 8/16 D. D. & L. Ltd. Forms/C.2118/13.

WAR DIARY or INTELLIGENCE SUMMARY

Army Form C. 2118.

Place	Date	Hour	Summary of Events and Information	Remarks and references to Appendices
TINCOURT	12.4.17	—	Situation unchanged. Weather until dawn. A.D.M.S. instructed O.C. 1/3rd S.M. Field Ambulance to move the A.D.S. at VILLERS-FAUCON from the house unto tents, owing to the fact that it appears that owing to the house still standing false signs may not be portrayed on enemy. Capt. E. HARRISON R.A.M.C. T.F. (together with all headquarters staff of 1/6 8th (North Staff)) killed by heavy blown up in one of the afore said dug outs. A.D.M.S. visited Nr 2 M.M.R. Wounded Off. 6 O.R. 102. Evacuated Off. 3 O.R. 17, Wounded Off. 5 O.R. 114.	
TINCOURT	19.4.17	—	Situation unchanged. Weather mild & fine. O. Still visited O.D.B. TEMPENY & No.1 the Field Ambulance. Also visited A.D.R.S. & various devans near at PERONNE. 1/2 and 8th Field Ambulance — Headquarters Section — moved to DOIGNT. & to No.1 C/O Evacuated Station. "C" Section now arrived at CAPPY. Sub to run the Anti Rail Station. Admitted sick Off. 3 O.R. 33. To wounded 5 O.R.5. Evacuated sick Off. 1 O.R. 5. Wounded 2 O.R.4.	
TINCOURT	20.4.17	—	Situation unchanged. Weather mild & sunny. A.D.M.S. visited 1/1st 2/6 & 8th Field Ambulances. Also the Headquarters Section Nr 2 and 8th Field Ambulance at DOIGNT. Capt. J. FERGUSON R.A.M.C. T.C. reported for duty. Admitted 9 and OR 41. Wounded Off. 1 OR. Evacuated sick Off. 20. Wounded Off. 2 OR. 22. Capt. D. MACKAY R.A.M.C. T.C. temp. for R. Berks. plus a 9 in Orient. Capt. L. ROSS R.A.M.C. T.F. appointed O.D. hospitan.	

WAR DIARY or INTELLIGENCE SUMMARY

Army Form C. 2118

Place	Date	Hour	Summary of Events and Information	Remarks and references to Appendices
K11c 7.9.	25/4/17	—	During night 24/25 a second attack launched on GILLEMONT FARM & KNOLL ground little. Weather fine but colder. ADMS visited 9DB VILLERS. Also two of 2½ Field Ambulances. Capt J.B. MITTON R.A.M.C. reported for duty. Capt RAKERR rejoined from hospital. Admitted sick Off. 1 O.R. 47 Wounded Off. 1 O.R. 150. Evacuated sick Off. 23 Wounded Off. 6 O.R. 119	
K11c 7.9.	26/4/17	—	Situation as above. Weather mild & dry. ADMS assumed duties of DDMS III Corps during absence on leave of D.D.M.S. Capt J.S. Williamson R.A.M.C. T.R. reported to A.D.M.S. for duty no 2 to 2/2nd S.M. Field Ambulance. Admitted sick Off. 1 O.R. 27 Wounded Off. 2 O.R. 133. Evacuated sick Off. 3 O.R. 114 Wounded Off. 3 O.R. 136.	
K11c 7.9	27/4/17	—	Situation unchanged. Weather warm & sunny. ABMS visited ADS at VILLERS & TEMPLEUX. Also part of 2/2nd S.M. Field Ambulance. Admitted sick Off. O.R. 10. Evacuated Off. 1 O.R.M. Evacuated sick Off. 1 O.R. 8. Wounded O.R. 21	
K11c 7.9	28/4/17	—	Situation unchanged. Weather fine. D.D.H.S. L visited LJD&D Off of III Corps Lieut F. Andrews R.A.M.C. Off. admitted to Hospital Cpl M.A. HIBBS admitted to hospital as sick O.R. 1/8 Worcesters. Admitted sick Off. 1 O.R. 31. Wounded Off. 1 O.R. 9. Evacuated sick Off. 1 O.R. 16. Wounded Off. 1 O.R. 16	

WAR DIARY
or
INTELLIGENCE SUMMARY.

Army Form C. 2118.

Place	Date	Hour	Summary of Events and Information	Remarks and references to Appendices
K11a 7.9	29.4.17		Situation unchanged. Weather dry but warm. A.D.M.S. worked O.D. at miners & B.sd. (Inspect 9/4/24) Rtly. Field South lances. Admitted sick Off 2 ORs Wounded Off. To or a total of Off 1 OR 8. Wounded OR 3.	
K11a 7.9	30.4.17		Situation much as yesterday. Weather warmer. becoming crazy. Routine work. A.Dmitted sick 8 OR 1 Wounded 2 ORs. Evacuated sick O Rs 7.	

Menzies
COLONEL,
A.D.M.S. 43D.(?)

Office

48th Division

MEDICAL ARRANGEMENTS FOR EVACUATION OF SICK & WOUNDED FROM PRESENT LINE.

1. **R.A.M.C. POSTS.**
   R.A.M.C. Posts are established at -
   EPEHY -   E,1,c,8,6. - 3 Bearer Squads and 3 Wheeled Stretchers
   STE. EMILIE,- E.18,d,2-8- -2 Bearer Squads and 2 Wheeled Stretch
   STE. EMILIE - E.23,d,1,0.- 2 Bearer Squads and 2 Wheeled Stretch

2. **ADVANCED DRESSING STATIONS**
   Advanced Dressing Stations are established at -
   VILLERS FAUCON - E.28,b,1,8, (Billet 215).
   TEMPLEUX LA FOSSE - D,28,d,4,2.
   TINCOURT,-   J,24,a,9,6.

3. **EVACUATION OF CASUALTIES.**
   Casualties from the line EPEHY - STE. EMILIE - and eastward will be evacuated by wheeled stretchers as far as the R.A.M.C. Post at STE. EMILIE, E.23,d,1,0, thence by ambulance wagons to A.D.S. at VILLERS FAUCON. Casualties from SAULCOURT, LONGAVESNES and area between these will be evacuated by ambulance wagon to A.D.S. at TEMPLEUX LA FOSSE. Casualties South of the LONGAVESNES - VILLERS FAUCON Road will be evacuated by ambulance wagon to A.D.S. at TINCOURT.

4. **MOTOR AMBULANCES.**
   Two motor ambulances will be kept at TEMPLEUX LA FOSSE, two at LONGAVESNES, and two at VILLERS FAUCON. These will be worked on the 'block' system. One motor ambulance will be kept at SAULCOURT and one at TINCOURT.

5. **MEDICAL ASSISTANCE.**
   All demands for medical assistance, transport, stretchers, dressings, bearers, etc. are to be made on the Advanced Dressing Stations and when necessary a guide is to be sent.

3-4-17.

C.A.YOUNG, Colonel,
A.D.M.S. 48th Division.

140/2152

A.D.M.S., 48th Division

COMMITTEE FOR THE
MEDICAL HISTORY OF THE WAR
Date   10 JUL. 1917

Vol #26

CONFIDENTIAL

War Diary
of
A. Dn.L. 48th Divn.
from 1.5.17 to 31.5.17.

Vol XXVI

Army Form C. 2118.

WAR DIARY
or
INTELLIGENCE SUMMARY.
(Erase heading not required.)

Instructions regarding War Diaries and Intelligence Summaries are contained in F. S. Regs., Part II. and the Staff Manual respectively. Title pages will be prepared in manuscript.

Place	Date	Hour	Summary of Events and Information	Remarks and references to Appendices
K11a79	1.5.17		Division moving out of line. 42nd Division taking over. 143 Infy Bde at FRISE & 145 Infy Bde at PERONNE. Located HQ 144 Infy Bde - enclosed at F21a55. Weather warm & sunny. ADMS & ADVS inspected the Sanitary Conditions of the area of 59th Division (on Rt of 42nd Division). Interviewed O.C's of 59th Division Issued orders for 1/3 S.M. Field Ambulance to proceed from TEMPEUX LA FOSSE to CAPPY and there to open for treatment of sick of 143rd Inf Bde. Section 1/2 S.M. Field Ambulance to hand over ADS at TINCOURT to a Field Ambulance of the 42nd Division & open Headquarters at DOINGT	Ref Appx 62 Ref App L/Instrn
Flammicourt	3.5.17		Divl Headquarters moved to new Headquarters camp at FLAMMICOURT. Orders for move of 3/ S.M. Field Ambulance to CAPPY cancelled in accordance with instructions from Divl Headquarters & unit moved to HALLE & to Main Dressing Station in lieu as follows 1/1 S.M. Field Ambulance Main Dressing Station at PERONNE - 2 Sections 1/S.M. Field Ambulance opening Corps Scabies Station at DOINGT & 1 Section at D.R.S. CAPPY - 3/ S.M. Field Ambulance closed at HALLE - Weather fine and hot	
"	4.5.17		ADMS visited 3/ S.M. Field Ambulance at HALLE and inspected proposed site for new D.R.S. that at CAPPY being 2/ far under forward circumstances. Issued orders to Regimental Medical Officers briefly and chiefly through the should use be as regard the sick in of their units	
"	5.5.17		ADMS inspected camp of 1/5 Glosters and 1/8 R.Regt, also Corps Scabies Station, Corps Mul Station (forming) and 1/ A.M. Field Ambulance. Attended Divl Conference in afternoon. Also went to carry on ADMS work at Ypres III rd Corps Headquarter. Issued orders re impuritation of Toothbrush Division in in Marve. Recommended to Divl HQ that water from Cologne River be not used for drinking -	

WAR DIARY or INTELLIGENCE SUMMARY

Army Form C. 2118.

Place	Date	Hour	Summary of Events and Information	Remarks and references to Appendices
FLAMICOURT	6.5.17		Situation unchanged. ADMS visited 1st Sth Field Ambulance and 3rd Sth Field Ambulance at HALLE	
	7.5.17		ADMS visited 2nd Sth Field Ambulance, operating Corps Scabies Station, at DOINGT. Afterwards proceeded to HAMEL and inspected the lines of the 1/1/7th Worcesters and 1/6th Gloster. Send in report to 143rd Inf. Brigade regarding the unsatisfactory condition of the latrines of above units.	
	8.5.17		General Court Martial consulted for the trial of Capt. A.D. Mackay, 1/7 Wo.C (T) late M.O. 1/4 D.York Regt on a charge of "absence from his post" and part of "neglect of duty" and of Lieut. E. Bayley, 1/4 A.W.C (T.C) on a charge of "drunkenness". ADMS visited 3/Sth Field Ambulance at HALLE and 2nd Sth F.A. at DOINGT.	
	9.5.17		ADMS visited 3/Sth Fd Amb at HALLE and conferred with O.C. regarding the arrangements for the establishment of a D.R.S. at that place. Arranged with "Q" for lorries to be sent to Edrewin to bring up Nissen huts.	
	10.5.17		Personally attended Court Martial proceedings in the case of Lieut Bayley. Finding "guilty". Sentence. To be informed in orders. — Visited three Officers for duty with 1st Sth Field Ambulance & reported fact of investigation to A.D.M.S, also suggesting that it was undesirable for these Officers to be removed to another sphere of duty. A.D.M.S visited 2/Sth F.A. and 3/Sth F.A.	
	11.5.17		Information received that 143rd Inf. Brun. is to proceed forthwith to relieve 11th Division in LE TRANSLOY - ROCQUIGNY area. Received copy of Divl Operation orders from "A" Branch. Issued Memoe orders. 2/Sth F.A. at DOINGT to hand over Corps Scabies Station to 3rd S.D. Field Amb. and make billets & proceed tomorrow with 143 Inf. Brigade Group. 3/Sth F.A. at HALLE to proceed tomorrow to same area with 145th Inf. Bde. Group. Visited all Field Ambulances & issued verbal instructions in all points. Section 2/Inf.FA. at CAPPY S.v.D. to close D.R.S. there tomorrow, preparations to join unit in new area. Lieut Challion returned to duty from hospital	

WAR DIARY or INTELLIGENCE SUMMARY

Army Form C. 2118.

Place	Date	Hour	Summary of Events and Information	Remarks and references to Appendices
FLAMICOURT	12/5/17	—	1/3rd Sth Field Ambulance proceeded by march route to new area with 145 Inf Bde Group, and 2 Sections of 2nd S.M. F. Ambulance that debussed with 143 Inf Bde Group – Directed OC 3/Sm Field Ambulance on arrival in new area to call upon ADMS 11th Divn. arrange details of relief & move the necessary orders. He reported in evening that he had done so and had debussed 2/Sm Field Ambulance to relieve medical units of 11th Divn in right section of new line. Issued orders for action of 2/Sm F.A. at CAPPY to proceed tomorrow to COMBLES & there await further orders; also for 1/1 Sm F.A. to march tomorrow with 144 Inf Bgde Group en route to new area.	
"	13/5/17		Went to BEAULENCOURT & visited ADMS 11th Divn. (Col Shanahan) Arranged with him for 2 Officers & 30 men 1/1 S.M. Field Amb. to remain temporarily at M.D.S. BEUGNY so as to take over F.A. [forth] each tomorrow morning. The main body 1/1 Sm FA being in the march cannot arrive at BEUGNY till tomorrow. Arranged scheme of medical arrangements in new line to all concerned. 1/1 Sm FA with head quarters at BEUGNY to be responsible for the clearing of the left sector; 1/2 Sm FA with head quarters at LEBUCQUIÈRE to clear the right sector – 1/3rd Sm FA arrived at N.11.C (Sheet 57 C) about 11:30 am & took over hospital site from an Anzac Field Ambd near 61 then temporarily all the sick of the Division will be treated – Visited 1/1 Sm FA at COMBLES & gave them necessary orders re reliefs.	
"	14/5/17		The A.D.S. at BEUGNY was advanced took left sector taken over by 1/1 Sm FA – The medical situation in new area is now as follows 1/1 Sm FA H.Q. headquarters at M.D.S. BEUGNY & is responsible for evacuation of left sector 1/2 Sm FA has it headquarters at A.D.S. LEBUCQUIÈRE and is in charge of evacuation of right sector. 1/3 Sm FA has its headquarters in camp at N.11.C. and in billets in the rear of the Divn. But DDMS but of equipment & stores kept at CAPPY by 2/Sm FA and asked for instructions as to their disposal. DDMS returned him leave	

WAR DIARY
or
INTELLIGENCE SUMMARY.

Army Form C. 2118.

Place	Date	Hour	Summary of Events and Information	Remarks and references to Appendices
N.11.c.	15.5.17	8:30am	Field Ambulance moving to about ½ mile NW of BEAUVENCOURT, 1.2. NHR. & convoy sent for 1st Anzac Corps, 5th Army. O. Ph. l. visited DDMS 5th Army	Ref: Appx "A" 15/5/00
N.11.c.	16.5.17		Situation as above. Weather cold & overcast. O.Ph.l. visited DDMS 1st Anzac Corps. Two Bearer Sub Divisions with Medical Officers detailed & proceeded on temporary duty with R.B. Australian Field Ambulance from 1/3rd & 1/1st Field Ambulances. Capt J.B.MATTHEWS RAMC.T. joined for duty.	
N.11.c.	17.5.17		Situation unchanged. Weather cold & damp. A.Ph.l. visited Hqrs 2 S.R. Field Ambulance BEUGNY. 1/2nd & 1/1st Field Ambulance Lev 11.c. Baths at VELU.	
N.11.c.	18.5.17		Situation unchanged. Weather fine, warm. Marquees now received by 1/3rd S.R. Field Ambulance as Hql thro Directorate from a Divisional Rest Station of N.11.c.	
N.11.c.	19.5.17		Situation unchanged. Weather warm & sunny. O.Ph.l. with DMS 5th Army visited 1/1st & 1/2 and R.h. Field Ambulances LEBUCQUIERE and Bnl	

WAR DIARY
or
INTELLIGENCE SUMMARY

Army Form C. 2118.

Place	Date	Hour	Summary of Events and Information	Remarks and references to Appendices
N.11.C.	20/5/17	—	Situation unchanged. Weather variable & close. A.D.M.S. in company with 9 D.M.S. 1st Anzac Corps visited all three Field Ambulances. O.C. unit visited 75th & 76th Field Ambulance & the Retaining Point at BAPAUME.	
N.11.C.	21/5/17	—	Situation unchanged. Weather warm & sunny. Routine work.	
N.11.C.	22/5/17	—	Situation unchanged. Weather warm & sunny. The Boden Lorry Drivers to & from VILLERS au FLOS Divisional trains back to VELU. Drivers & tourers on account of the shelling of the former place.	
N.11.C.	23/5/17	—	Situation unchanged. Weather warm & fine. O.C. unit visited Reinforcement Camp at BAPAUME. Also visited 2nd & 5th Army Troops Ambulances Posts attending to Railhead. Pms 2.3 C.C.S. No.29 Field Amb & unit.	
N.11.C.	24/5/17	—	Situation unchanged. Weather fine & sunny. A.D.M.S. visited all three Field Ambulances. Lieut Sullivan detached for temporary duty with No.3 C.C.S. from No.7th Field Amb. Capt A.P.R.E. Bunnell 19n Field Amb proceeded U.K. on leave.	
134.a.2.5	25/5/17	9am	General situation unchanged. Field Headquarters moved to locality pencilled in margin. A.D.M.S. & Major O.J. the sanitation F. without HAPPINCOURT & found it very dirty. Major HARDMAN X.I.T.ORER reported for duty with the 75th & took over 25th Field Amb duties for Major J Lee of Ind.	
132.a.2.5	26/5/17	—	A.D.M.S. visited Nos 1, 2, 75a the Field Control armies Lieut Bayner Robins, T.C. reported for duty to 2th Field Amb.	

WAR DIARY or INTELLIGENCE SUMMARY

Army Form C. 2118.

Place	Date	Hour	Summary of Events and Information	Remarks and references to Appendices
I.34.a.2.5.	27.5.17	—	Situation unchanged. Weather fine. A.D.M.S. visited Water-point at HARLINCOURT. Later on in the day interviewed O.C. 5th Australian Sanitary Section with reference to the overchlorination of the water at this Point. Lieut. Col. A.D. HINGSTON and 5th Field Ambl'ce reported for duty.	
I.34.a.2.5.	28.5.17	—	Situation unchanged. Weather fine. A.D.M.S. visited Reinforcement Camp, BAPAUME. Then proceeded to D.D.M.S. IV Corps. Discussed 1/3rd S.A. Field Ambl'ce who had D.D.M.S. discussed the arrangements regarding its present station.	
I.34.a.2.5.	29.5.17	—	Situation unchanged. Weather fine. Routine work.	
I.34.a.2.5.	30.5.17	—	Situation unchanged. Weather clear & damp after heavy rain. A.D.M.S. visited 1/1st & 1/2nd S.A. Field Ambulances. Attended G.O.C. Conference 9 a.m. IV Corps. Fresh arrangements for Medical P. & O. to be held at 4 p.m. 1/3rd S.A. Field Ambul'ce for purpose of examining all men supposed extra-regimentally "classing them in Categories A¹ A² B¹ B² & C" to send those men to report to Officer i/c each by Divisional Employment Corps.	

WAR DIARY
or
INTELLIGENCE SUMMARY.

Army Form C. 2118.

Place	Date	Hour	Summary of Events and Information	Remarks and references to Appendices
13 A.2.5.	31/5/19	—	Situation unchanged. Weather cooler, cloudy. A.D.M.S. visited 93rd B.R. Field Ambulance. Total Admissions for month - sick 1016. wounded 69. Total evacuations, sick 506, wounded 80. Divisions on Right & Left are 42nd & 20th respectively. Sketch of Divisional Area attached.	

Chumul
COLONEL,
A.D.M.S. 46th (S.M.) DIVISION.

CONFIDENTIAL

War Diary
of
A.D.M.S. 48th Division
from 1-6-17 to 30-6-17.

Vol. XVII

COMMITTEE FOR THE
MEDICAL HISTORY OF THE WAR
Date -7 AUG. 1917

Army Form C. 2118.

WAR DIARY
or
INTELLIGENCE SUMMARY.
(Erase heading not required.)

Instructions regarding War Diaries and Intelligence Summaries are contained in F. S. Regs., Part II. and the Staff Manual respectively. Title pages will be prepared in manuscript.

Place	Date	Hour	Summary of Events and Information	Remarks and references to Appendices
I34a25	1.6.17	—	Situation unaltered from that of 31.5.17. Weather fine. A.A. O.R.2 attended presence of B.C. Casualties Officers sick 1 O.R. died 29. Wounded Off 1 O.R. 4. Evacuated sick Off 1 O.R. 14. Wounded Officers 1 O.R. 4.	
I34a25	2.6.17	—	Situation unchanged. Weather hot. A Stock party of 8th Field Amb'y at BECOURT and 2/1st 1st Amb at LOUCOURT. Wounded sick Off 1 O.R. 26. Wounded O.R. 2. Evacuated sick Off 1 O.R. 11. Wounded O.R. 6. Capt of Staves to Rouen proceeded on leave.	
I34a25	3.6.17	—	Situation unchanged. Weather hot. A third howitzer '/329 B.F. Field Amb: at N 11 c. During night 2/3rd enemy aeroplanes dropped 3 bombs in rear of 12nd Dn Field Ambulance. Capt R.R. Cox of Nth Dn. Inf on 2 mths U.S. Casualties sick Off 2 O.R. 25. Wounded Off 1 (above) O.R.2. Evacuated sick Off 2 O.R. 20. Wounded Off 1 O.R. 2.	Ref Rep 517
I34a25	4.6.17	—	Situation unchanged. Weather hot. Reinforcement 2 b, 8 other ranks D.S.M.B. Capt R. Ruxnan returning from leave. Casualties sick Off 1 O.R. 26. Wounded Off 1 O.R. 9. Evacuated sick Off 1 O.R. 19. Wounded Off 1 O.R. 9.	

Army Form C. 2118.

WAR DIARY
or
INTELLIGENCE SUMMARY.
(Erase heading not required.)

Instructions regarding War Diaries and Intelligence Summaries are contained in F. S. Regs., Part II. and the Staff Manual respectively. Title pages will be prepared in manuscript.

Place	Date	Hour	Summary of Events and Information	Remarks and references to Appendices
T34a.2.5	5.6.17	—	Situation unchanged. Weather My hot. A.D.M.S. visited 1/2 and 2/2 Field Ambulance. Admitted sick Offr 2 OR 28 Wounded OR 7. Evacuated Offs 2 OR 12 Wounded 7.	
T34a.2.5	6.6.17	—	Situation unchanged. Very hot. A.D.M.S. visited 1/3 D.S.M. Field Ambulance and O.C. 5th Australian Sanitary Section. Admitted sick Offs. OR 53. Evacuated Offrs No 3 OR 17 sick. Wounded nil	
T34a.2.5	7.6.17	—	Situation unchanged. Weather hot. A.D.M.S. visited 1/2 and 3/2 and 8th Field Ambulance. Also Baths at BERGNY & HAPLINCOURT. Admitted sick Off 2 OR 29 Wounded OR 1. Evacuated Off 2 OR 14. Wounded 9 m	
T34a.2.5	8.6.17	—	Situation unchanged. Hot. A.D.M.S. visited 9 and 10th Field Ambulance. Admitted sick Off 2 (Lieut Milligan RAMCT.) OR 19. Wd OR 10. Evacuated off 2 OR 15 Wounded 9.	
T34a.2.5	9.6.17	—	Situation unchanged. Hot. Admitted sick OR 29 Wounded 6. Evacuated OR 14 Wounded 6.	
T34a.2.5	10.6.17	—	Situation unchanged. Do do. A.D.M.S. attended Conference G.O.C. Contintial held on Capt D. McKAY RAMCTc Major J.O. SUMMERHAYES RAMCTc reporting on duty from England. Lieut J. MACARTHUR RAMCTc proceeded on duty. Admitted sick Off 3 OR 25. Wounded R 3 Evacuated sick Off 3 OR 16 Wounded 2. Capt LAIRD RAMCTc reported for duty with 17th Division	

Army Form C. 2118.

WAR DIARY
or
INTELLIGENCE SUMMARY.
(Erase heading not required.)

Place	Date	Hour	Summary of Events and Information	Remarks and references to Appendices
I.34.a.2.5.	11.6.17	—	Situation unchanged. Severe Hun[?] bombardment. Stin[?] fire, occasional cases. A.D.M.S. visited 1/3rd Shr Field Ambulance. Admitted sick O.R. 24. Evacuated sick O.R. 16. —	
I.34.a.2.5.	12.6.17	—	Situation unchanged. Weather clear, hot. A.D.M.S. visited 1/2nd Lh Field Ambulance & Advanced Post at BEAUMETZ. Also visited 1/3rd Lh Field Ambulance. Admitted sick O.R. 26. Wounded O.R. 1. Evacuated sick & 1. O.R. 8. Wounded O.R. 1.	
I.34.a.2.5.	13.6.17	—	Situation unchanged. Weather hot. A.D.M.S. visited 1/2nd & 1/3rd Lh Field Ambulance. Admitted sick Off. 2. O.R. 39. Wounded O.R. 3. Evacuated sick Off. 2. O.R. 11. Wounded O.R. 3.	
I.34.a.2.5.	14.6.17	—	O Reg. 8. visited 1/2nd & 1/3rd Fd Cav[?] coating[?] & the 8 killing Bom[?] & Kerman[?] am[?] Sgt copying it[?]. Admitted sick O.R. 27. Wounded O.R. 3. Evacuated O.R. 3. Wounded O.R. 5.	
I.34.a.2.5.	15.6.17	—	Situation unchanged. D.R. A.D.M.S. visited 1/2nd 1/3rd Lh Field Ambulance. Admitted Officer sick 2. O.R. 39. Wounded 2. Evacuated sick Off. 2. O.R. 13. Wounded R 2.	
I.34.a.2.5.	16.6.17	—	Routine. A.D.M.S. visited. – O.R. 20. Wounded S.I.S. Evacuated sick – O.R. 12. Wounded 8.	

A 5834 Wt. W4973 M687. 750,000 8/16 D. D. & L. Ltd. Forms/C.2118/13.

WAR DIARY or INTELLIGENCE SUMMARY.

Army Form C. 2118.

(Erase heading not required.)

Instructions regarding War Diaries and Intelligence Summaries are contained in F. S. Regs., Part II. and the Staff Manual respectively. Title pages will be prepared in manuscript.

Place	Date	Hour	Summary of Events and Information	Remarks and references to Appendices
I 34.a.2.5	19.6.17	—	Situation unchanged. Nil. Lt MILLIGAN reported from Hospital. Capt DACRE rejoined from leave. Capt C.A. BOWMAN RAMC rejoined for duty vice Capt. AID. Admitted sick OR 30. Evacuated sick OR 14.	
I 34.a.2.5	18.6.17	—	Situation unchanged. Thunderstorms. O.P.R. S. visited 1/3rd R.R. Field Ambulance. Also 1/1st + 1/2nd Rh. Field Ambulances. Admitted sick 19 Wounded 1. Evacuated OR sick 8. OR wounded 1.	
I 34.a.2.5	19.6.17	—	Situation unchanged. Weather cloudy. hot + thunderstorms. O.P.R.S. visited O.1/2 and R.R. Field Ambulance. Admitted Officers sick 1 OR 25 Wounded Offs 3 OR 32. Evacuated sick Officers OR 8 Wounded Off 3 OR 30. Number Wounded 9 fire + many members of party + men who was over weight.	
I 34.a.2.5	20.6.17	—	Situation unchanged. weather cloudy + rain. Surg¹-Genl IRWIN. DMS. III Army visited all Field Ambulances in company with DDMS IV Corps. And expressed his entire satisfaction with all arrangements. Admitted sick — Off 2 OR 21 Wounded OR 2 Evacuated sick Off 2 OR 7. Wounded 2.	
I 34.a.2.5	21.6.17	—	Situation unchanged. Rainy. O.P.R.S. visited 1/1st 1/2nd 1/3rd 2nd Ph. Field Ambulances. Admitted sick — OR 2 Wounded 9. D.C. Evacuated sick — OR 12. Wounded 1.	

A 58.34 Wt. W4973 M687. 750,000 8/16 D. D. & L. Ltd. Forms/C.2118/13.

Army Form C. 2118.

WAR DIARY
or
INTELLIGENCE SUMMARY.
(Erase heading not required.)

Instructions regarding War Diaries and Intelligence Summaries are contained in F. S. Regs., Part II. and the Staff Manual respectively. Title pages will be prepared in manuscript.

Place	Date	Hour	Summary of Events and Information	Remarks and references to Appendices
T34a 2.5	22.6.17	—	Situation unchanged. Weather unsettled. Routine work. Admitted sick Off 1 OR 26. Wounded OR 7. Evacuated sick Off 3 Wounded OR 7.	
T34a 2.5	23.6.17	—	Situation unchanged. Weather improving. Attack attended Conference DDMS IV Corps. Then visited 75th & 76th Field Ambulances. Wounded OR 9. Admitted sick Off 2 OR 31. Evacuated sick Off 2 OR 14 Wounded OR 9. Sick from Wounds Off 1.	
T34a 2.5	24.6.17	—	Situation unchanged. Weather fine. ADMS visited 76th, 74st & 8th Field Ambulance. DDR Scalted Sanitation. Admitted sick Off 2 OR 18. OR wounded 2. Evacuated Off 2 OR 10 Wounded OR 1.	
T34a 2.6	25.6.17	—	Situation unchanged. Fine. ADMS visited 75 & 8 R. Field Ambulance. Admitted sick Off 1 OR 23. Evacuated sick Off 1 OR 7.	
T34a 2.5	26.6.17	—	ADMS visited 75 & 8th Field Ambulance. Admitted sick OR 27. Wounded OR 5. Evacuated OR 8. Wounded 5.	
T34a 2.5	27.6.17	—	ADMS visited 75 & 8th Field Ambulance. Wire sent to ADMS 3rd Division asking if an Advance Party may travel & take on IV Corps Rest Station. Reg 297 K.I. Admitted sick Off 1 OR 12 Wounded OR 3. Evacuated sick Off 1 OR 8. Wounded OR 3.	

Army Form C. 2118.

WAR DIARY
or
INTELLIGENCE SUMMARY.
(Erase heading not required.)

Instructions regarding War Diaries and Intelligence Summaries are contained in F. S. Regs. Part II. and the Staff Manual respectively. Title pages will be prepared in manuscript.

Place	Date	Hour	Summary of Events and Information	Remarks and references to Appendices
I.34 a 2.5.	28.6.17	—	Situation unchanged. Fine. A/DMS visited 1/2 and 1/3 M Field Ambulances. O/M.S. attended Conference F.O.C. Admitted sick O.R. 21. Wounded O.R. 6. Evacuated Offrs 4. Wounded O.R. 24.	
I.34 a 2.5.	29.6.17	—	Situation unchanged. Fine. A/D.M.S. visited 2/3 Division 1/2 D.M.S. 62nd Div. D called & was A/DMS with reference to making arrangements for taking over the Field Ambulances & Advanced Posts of 39th Division (attached) O/officer 1/1 M. Field Ambulance Admitted sick O.R. 22. Wounded 2. Evacuated sick O.R. 0. Wounded O.R. 2.	
I.34 a 2.5.	30.6.17	—	Situation unchanged. Fine. Resettlement work. Admitted sick Offr 1. O.R 20. Wounded 2. Evacuated sick Offr 1. O.R 4. Wounded 2.	

[signature]
COLONEL,
A.D.M.S. 49th (S.M.) DIVISION.

SECRET.

RELIEF OF 48th DIVISION BY 3rd DIVISION&

R.A.M.C. ORDERS BY COLONEL C.A.YOUNG, C.M.G., A.H.S.,
A.D.M.S. 48th Division,
June 29th 1917,

1. The 48th Division (less Artillery) will be relieved by 3rd Division commencing on June 30th and ending on July 4th. After relief the Division will concentrate in Brigade Groups in the GOMIECOURT - ACHIET-LE-PETIT - BIHUCOURT Area preparatory to moving by rail to XVIII Corps Area under orders to be issued later.

2. One Section, 1/3rd S.Mid. Field Ambulance, will proceed to GOMIECOURT tomorrow, 30th inst. starting at 2 p.m., and on arrival will come under the command of and be allotted billets by the G.O.C. 143rd Infantry Brigade.

3. The 7th Field Ambulance, 3rd Division, will take over the IV Corps Rest Station and Decauville Detraining Centre from the 3rd S.Mid. Field Ambulance by Noon on 2nd prox. and on relief the latter unit will proceed by march route to GOMIECOURT.

4. The 8th Field Ambulance, 3rd Division, will take over the Advanced Posts of the Left Sector on the night of 1st/2nd prox. and the Main Dressing Station at BEUGNY by Noon on 2nd prox. On relief the 1/1st S.Mid. Field Ambulance will proceed by march route to ACHIET-LE-PETIT Area, where it will come under the command of and be allotted billets by the G.O.C. 144th Infantry Brigade.

5. The 142nd Field Ambulance will take over the Advanced Posts of the Right Sector on the night of the 2nd/3rd prox. and the Advanced Dressing Station at LEBUCQUIERE by Noon on the 3rd prox. On relief the 1/2nd S.Mid. Field Ambulance will proceed by march route to BIHUCOURT Area, where it will come under the command of and be allotted billets by the G.O.C. 145th Infantry Brigade.

6. The Tent Sub-divisions of the 1/1st and 1/2nd S.Mid. Field Ambulances now doing duty at Nos. 3 and 29 Casualty Clearing Stations respectively, will be relieved by Tent Sub-divisions of Field Ambulances of the 3rd Division on the morning of the 4th prox. and on relief will rejoin their units in the ACHIET-LE-PETIT and BIHUCOURT Areas.

7. On the march fair weather tracks will be used as far as possible and the regulation 10 minutes halts will be observed.

8. Field Ambulances will take with them only their Mobilization Stores and equipment. All surplus stores and equipment will be handed over to the incoming units, and receipts obtained for them. A list of non-expendable medical stores and equipment handed over will be submitted to this office for transmission to the D.D.M.S. IV Corps.

9. Completion of reliefs will be reported to this office by wire.

10. The office of the A.D.M.S. will close at I,34,a, at 10 a.m. on 4th July, and re-open at the same hour at ACHIET-LE-PETIT.

C.A.YOUNG, Colonel,
A.D.M.S. 48th Division,

Distribution,-
H.Q."A" & "G" 48 Div.
Os,C,1/1,1/2,1/3 S.M.Fd Ambs.
H.Q.143,144,145 Inf.Bdes.
C.R.A.,& C.R.E.48 Div.
D.D.M.S.IV Corps,
D.D.M.S. V Corps,
D.D.M.S.XVIII Corps,
48 Div Trn. 48 Div Signals,
A.D.M.S.3rd Division,

Vol 28

CONFIDENTIAL

War Diary
of
ADMS 48th Division
from 1-7-17 to 31-7-17.

COMMITTEE FOR THE
MEDICAL HISTORY OF THE WAR
Date 10 SEP. 1917

B.E.F.

SUMMARY OF MEDICAL WAR DIARIES OF 48th Div. 18th Corps.

5th ARMY. from 22.7.17

Western Front Operations July - Sept. 1917.

A.D.M.S.   Colonel C.A. Young, C.M.G.
A.D.M.S.   Col.R. Pickard from 24th July.

D.A.D.M.S. Capt. J.J.H. Becton.

SUMMARISED UNDER THE FOLLOWING HEADINGS :-

Phase "D" 1.   Passchendaele Operations "July - Nov. 1917."

(a) - Operations commencing 1/7/17.

Army Form C. 2118.

WAR DIARY
or
INTELLIGENCE SUMMARY.
(Erase heading not required.)

Instructions regarding War Diaries and Intelligence Summaries are contained in F. S. Regs., Part II. and the Staff Manual respectively. Title pages will be prepared in manuscript.

Place	Date	Hour	Summary of Events and Information	Remarks and references to Appendices
F3h a.24.2.	1.7.17	—	Situation unchanged from that of 30.6.17. Weather fine. Hot. A Dn. B provided Divine. Lieut. Col. Green R.A.M.C. o/c A.B.&B. Admitted O.R.26. Evacuated 01. Wounded at Duty 01.	
F3h a.2	2.7.17	—	Situation unchanged. Fine. D.A.D.M.S. visited new area & Dhuib VII Corps. Orders received for move of the Field Ambulance. Admitted Off. nil. (O.R. 14 to more Regt 077) O.R.14. Evacuated Officers 1 (Capt. Davis) O.Ruck 10.	See attached App 1
F3h a. 2	3.7.17	—	Dupes Day relieved by 3rd Division. 143 Infy Brigade moving to POMMIER area. 1/1 Th Field Ambulance moving to GOUDECOURT where it will open for reception of sick of the Division with h'n Section. 1 Section going to RANSART. 2 Battalions of 144 Infy Brigade moving to ADINFER area. 143rd Fn. 2 cold. Ambulance moving to BIENVILLERS. Admitted sick Off 2. OR 13. OR more. 9.2. Evacuated sick Off 1. OR 1. Wound 9.2.	Rd Lufe LENS Sheet
F3h a. 2	4.7.17	9 am	Divisional Hd. Qrs. moving to ADINFER WOOD. 145 Infy Brigade moving to BASSEUR area. 146 Th Field Ambulance on way to BELLACOURT. Finding of the (court martial on Capt. D.P. MACKAY R.A.M.C. to promulgated. Found guilty under (Sec.40) Act. Not guilty under 1st charge, held, the 6000 to be admonished. Sent to see to be duty. Relief of 1000 Colon F Division Sewing to be completed 1000 tomorrow on the 5/7/17. Admitted sick 1. OR 54. Evacuated each OR 2.	

A3834 Wt. W4973/M687 750,000 8/16 D. D. & L. Ltd. Forms/C.2118/13.

Army Form C. 2118.

WAR DIARY
or
INTELLIGENCE SUMMARY.
(Erase heading not required.)

Instructions regarding War Diaries and Intelligence Summaries are contained in F. S. Regs., Part II. and the Staff Manual respectively. Title pages will be prepared in manuscript.

Place	Date	Hour	Summary of Events and Information	Remarks and references to Appendices
ABINFER WOOD	5/7/17	—	O/C Wing attended S.O.C. Conference on Divisional Training. Admitted sick O.R. 27. Evacuated sick O.R. 2.	
ABINFER WOOD	6/7/17		Divisional Service in which all three Field Ambulances are taking part. Capt. C. Morris returned from leave. Admitted sick 1 Off. 6 Wounded O.R. 1. Evacuated sick O.R. 2 Wounded O.R. 1.	
ABINFER WOOD	7/7/17		O.C. Wing & O.C. attended Conference 9 May B XVIII Corps at LA LOVIE (nr POPERINGHE) with reference to the scheme of evacuation. Wounded O.R. 9c. Admitted O.R. B. 34 Wounded Admitted sick Off. 2 O.R. 30. Evacuated sick O.R. 4.	
ABINFER WOOD	8/7/17, 9/7/17, 10/7/17		Routine work. Admitted Off. 1 O.R. 14. Evacuated sick O.R. 6. Admitted Off. 1 O.R. 21. Evacuated sick 1 Off. O.R. 4. Admitted sick O.R. 12. Evacuated O.R. 3.	
ABINFER WOOD	11/7/17	—	Routine work. Admitted sick Off. 2 O.R. 3. Evacuated sick O.R. 4.	
ABINFER WOOD	12/7/17		O.C. B returned from leave. Admitted sick O.R. 25. Evacuated sick 1 Off. O.R. 4.	

A 5834 Wt. W 4973 M 687 750,000 8/16 D. D. & L. Ltd. Forms/C-2118/13.

Army Form C. 2118.

WAR DIARY
or
INTELLIGENCE SUMMARY.
(Erase heading not required.)

Instructions regarding War Diaries and Intelligence Summaries are contained in F. S. Regs., Part II. and the Staff Manual respectively. Title pages will be prepared in manuscript.

Place	Date	Hour	Summary of Events and Information	Remarks and references to Appendices
ADINFER WOOD	13.7.17	—	A DMS visited DDMS VII Corps & all three Field Ambulances. Admitted sick O.R.9. Evacuated sick O.R.6.	
ADINFER WOOD	14.7.17	—	Routine work. Lieut J.C. HALLAM'S R.A.M.C. joined On Tour. Admitted sick Off. 1 O.R. 8. Evacuated sick N.R.1.	
ADINFER WOOD	15.7.17	—	Routine. Admitted sick O.R. 13. Evacuated sick O.R. 0	
ADINFER WOOD	16.7.17	—	Wire received from 3 Off. & 2 Bomb. Subaltern us to proceed to join 39th Division in advance of the Division. A DMS issued Orders accordingly. A DMS visited all three Field Ambulances. Admitted sick O.R.9. Evacuated sick O.R.2	App 2/5
ADINFER WOOD	17.7.17	—	A DMS inspected a draft of reinforcements 16 Officers & recruits that they were up to the average of the reinforcement now arriving. Visited No 10 Field Ambulance. 3 Offs & Bomb Subalterns of 1/5 N. Staffords & Aust. L.H. as proceeded to join 39th Division, XVIII Corps. Admitted sick 1 Off 2 OR 26. Evacuated sick Off. 1 OR 3.	
ADINFER WOOD	18.7.17	—	Routine. Admitted sick OR 26. Evacuated sick OR 6.	
ADINFER WOOD	19.7.17	—	A DMS attended Conference G.O.C. Admitted sick OR 16. Evacuated sick OR 7.	

A3834 Wt. W4973 M687. 750,000 8/16 D. D. & L. Ltd. Forms/C.2118/13.

Army Form C. 2118.

WAR DIARY
or
INTELLIGENCE SUMMARY.
(Erase heading not required.)

Instructions regarding War Diaries and Intelligence Summaries are contained in F. S. Regs., Part II. and the Staff Manual respectively. Title pages will be prepared in manuscript.

Place	Date	Hour	Summary of Events and Information	Remarks and references to Appendices
ADINFER WD	20/11/17	—	A Amb received instructions to proceed to tct Corps 30 Div H.Q. A Amb issued orders regarding moves of the Field Ambulances. For the Field Ambulance moved to HALLOY AREA with 143rd Infy Bde. Admitted sick OR 18. Evacuated sick OR 9.	App 4.
ADINFER WOOD	21/11/17	—	A Amb moved to B Amb of 2 Corps. Also from 5th Field Ambulance Admitted sick Off 1 OR 40. Evacuated Off 1 OR 35 sick.	
ADINFER WOOD	22/11/17	—	Division arriving to new Area A Amb departed to join 1st Corps	
Borden Camp CAMP "D" A30 C.	22/11/17	10.30am	Divisional Headquarters opened. Division came under administration of 5th Army 9 XVIII Corps Capt G. MOORE 1/3rd Lh Field Ambulance evacuated sick.	Ref Map Sheet 27 Belgium 1/40000
"D" Camp	23/11/17	—	1/1st the Field Ambulance arrived at GWENT FARM A28 a 2 6. (Res) tent sub division which was left to look after sick of 143rd Infy in POPERINGHE AREA 1/2nd Lh Field Ambulance arrived at HOOTKERQUE with 145 Infy B. 1/3rd the Field Ambulance arrived at A23 c 2 9. (Res) tent ambulance off in aid collecting 143 Infy B. at B7 JAN TER BIEZEN	App. 5 Ref Map Sheet 27 Belgium 1/40000 Sheet 28.

Army Form C. 2118.

WAR DIARY
or
INTELLIGENCE SUMMARY.
(Erase heading not required.)

Instructions regarding War Diaries and Intelligence Summaries are contained in F. S. Regs., Part II. and the Staff Manual respectively. Title pages will be prepared in manuscript.

Place	Date	Hour	Summary of Events and Information	Remarks and references to Appendices
"D" Camp	23/7/17	—	D.A. Staff visited all three Field Ambulances & D.Hq.S. × VIII Corps.	
"D" Camp	24/7/17	—	Situation as above. 1/1 Sent Subdivision attached to No 12 C.C.S. from 1/1 Lth Field Ambulance. 1 Sent Subdivision sent to No 3 Canadian C.C.S. from 1/2 Lth Field Ambulance. 6 Clerks sent to Corps Train Dressing Station for duty. H.Q. 2 Lth Field Ambulance removed to F.9.d.5.9 (Lens / Tent Subdivision left for collection and 1/1 St Jaffy R.D. at HOOTHOEKE. Col. R. PICKARD RAMC arrived to take up duties of A. Staff 28 Division. Capt. MACARTHUR RAMC T.C. detached to C.M.S.R. for temporary duty.	Sheet 27 1/40,000
"D" Camp	25/7/17	—	A. Staff visited D.Hq.S. × VIII Corps & 1/2nd Lth Field Ambulance — also visited A. Staff 39th Division. Also the wounded (the others) of the Field Ambulances sent to 39th Division on loan temporarily. 1 No C.O. & 2 Pros sent to × VIII Corps Reinforcement Depot for temporary duty. Also CAPT BRENNAN RAMC.	
"D" Camp	26/7/17	—	A. Staff visited DUHALLOW Advanced Dressing Station (C.25.d.3.1 Sheet 28.) also the trenches of 39 RAM. & visited 1/1st & 1/3rd Lth Field Ambulances. 30 O.R. sent to A.Hq.S. 39 & Division for temporary duty.	

Army Form C. 2118.

WAR DIARY
or
INTELLIGENCE SUMMARY.
(Erase heading not required.)

Instructions regarding War Diaries and Intelligence Summaries are contained in F. S. Regs., Part II. and the Staff Manual respectively. Title pages will be prepared in manuscript.

Place	Date	Hour	Summary of Events and Information	Remarks and references to Appendices
"D" Camp	28/4/17	—	Situation unaltered. O.C.M.S held Conference with O.C. the Field Ambulance. 5 Officers detached for temporary duty with 39 Division. Lt. Col. W.M. Cock returned from leave. 2 Clerks sent to Corps Rest Station for temporary duty.	
"D" Camp	28/4/17		Routine work.	
"D" Camp	29/4/17	—	O.C.M.S held a Conference with all the Regimental Medical Officers. Visited 1/5th Field Ambulance. O.C.M.S visited 4th C.C.S with reference to sick cases.	
"D" Camp	30/4/17	—	The Scheme of Field Ambulances with their act stretcher nypoko upon Unit Headquarters. A.D.M.S issued S.A.R.O. Orders regarding the forthcoming Operations.	App 6. App 7. App 8.
"D" Camp	31/7/17	—	A.D.M.S issued Instructions- Memorandum- to O.C. Field Ambulances with regard to forthcoming Operations. O.D.M.S. visited A.D.M.S 39th Division. Also A.D.S at Canal Bank (DUNHALLOW) & 39th D.S.A Collecting Post	

R Michens Col.
A.D.M.S. 46 F. Divn.

B.E.F.

1.

<u>48th Div. 18th Corps. 5th ARMY.</u>   Western Front.
July-Aug.1917.
<u>A.D.M.S. Colonel C.A. Young, C.M.G.</u>

<u>Col. R. Pickard to A.D.M.S. from 24th July.</u>

PHASE "D" 1. <u>Passchendaele Operations, "July-Nov. 1917."</u>

(a) - <u>Operations commencing July-Sept. 1917.</u>

<u>Headquarters at Border Camp.</u>   A.30 b. (28).

July 22nd.	<u>Transfer, and Moves.</u> 48th Division transferred from 7th Corps 3rd Army to 18th Corps, 5th Army, and moved to Border Camp.	
23rd.	<u>Locations F.A.</u>) App. 5. (attached). *Put back into Diary* <u>Med. Arrangements.</u>)	
24th.	<u>Moves. F.A. Detachments.</u>	1 T.S.D. of 1/1st S.M.F.A. to 12th C.C.S.
		1 T.S.D. of 1/2nd S.M.F.A. to 3rd Can. C.C.S.
	<u>Appointment.</u> Col. R. Pickard to A.D.M.S. 48th Div.	
30th-31st.	<u>Military Situation.</u>) App. 6. paras 1.,2.,3.,4. (attach <u>Medical Arrangements.</u>) *Put back into Diary*	
	<u>Appendices.</u> 5. R.A.M.C. Order 185 dated 20/7/17. 6. 48th Div. Op. Order 1. dated 30/7/17.	

B.E.F.

1.

48th Div. 18th Corps. 5th ARMY. Western Front.
A.D.M.S. Colonel C.A. Young, C.M.G. July-/Aug. 1917.
Col. R. Pickard to A.D.M.S. from 24th July.

PHASE "D" 1. Passchendaele Operations, "July-Nov. 1917."

   (a) - Operations commencing July-Sept. 1917.

Headquarters at Border Camp. A.30 b. (23).

July 22nd.	Transfer, and Moves.	48th Division transferred from 7th Corps 3rd Army to 18th Corps, 5th Army, and moved to Border Camp.
23rd.	Locations F.A.) Med. Arrangements.)	App. 5. (attached).
24th.	Moves. F.A. Detachments.	1 T.S.D. of 1/1st S.M.F.A. to 12th C.C.S.
		1 T.S.D. of 1/2nd S.M.F.A. to 3rd Can. C.C.S.
	Appointment.	Col. R. Pickard to A.D.M.S. 48th Div.
30th-31st.	Military Situation.) Medical Arrangements.)	App. 6. paras 1.,2.,3.,4. (attached)
	Appendices.	5. R.A.M.C. Order 185 dated 20/7/17.
		6. 48th Div. Op. Order 1. dated 30/7/17.

SECRET.   No.184.

                        48th Division,

    R.A.M.C.ORDERS BY COLONEL C.A.YOUNG, C.M.G.,A.M.S.
R   A.D.M.S.48th Division,
                                    19th July 1917,

    Ref.Map 1/100,000 Sheet 11,LENS, Sheet 5A HAZEBROUCK.
        1/40,000, Sheet 28.

1. The Division (less Units and details which proceeded in advance
   and Supply Column which will proceed by road) will move by rail
   to XVIII Corps area in accordance with 48th Division Order.No 205/19-7-17
2. The 1/3rd S.Mid. Field Ambulance will proceed from BIENVILLERS to
   HALLOY area on 20th inst. under the orders of the B.G.C. 143rd Inf.
   Bde.   It will entrain on 22nd inst. at AUTHIEULE, arriving there
   at 3.48 p.m. and departing at 6.48 p.m. It will detrain at PROVEN.
3. The 1/1st S.Mid. Field Ambulance (less 4 G.S.Waggons) will proceed
   on 22nd inst. from GAUDIEMPRE to MONDICOURT (arriving there at
   4.32 p.m.), will entrain, and will depart at 7.32 p.m. It will
   detrain at GODEWAERSWELDE.
   This unit will be attached to the 145th Inf. Bde. Group for the
   move, on detraining it will rejoin the 144th Inf.Bde. Group at
   POPERINGHE.
4. The 1/2nd S.Mid. Field Ambulance will proceed on 22nd inst. from
   BELLACOURT to MONDICOURT (arriving there at 4.32 p,m), will entrain
   and will depart at 7.32 p.m. It will detrain at GODEWAERSWELDE.
   On the march to MONDICOURT the main road from LARBRET to ARRAS will
   not be used.
5. The O.C.1/1st S.M.Field Ambulance will send one G.S.Waggon to report
   to the Transport Officer of each of the Battalions of the 144th Inf.
   Bde. at 6 p.m. on 20th inst. for conveyance to new area.
   These will be detrained at HOPOUTRE and will rejoin 1/1st S.Mid.
   Field Ambulance at POPERINGHE.
6. All units will entrain rationed up to and including 23rd inst.
   Rations for consumption on 24th inst. will be issued in new area.
7. The O.C.1/1st S.Mid. Field Ambulance will arrange to transfer all
   sick to VII Corps Rest Station or to Casualty Clearing Station on
   or before 21st inst., and will hand over the hospital buildings and
   equipment at GAUDIEMPRE to a guard which will be detailed to take
   them over by D.D.M.S.VII Corps.
8. The Motor ambulance cars of the above units will proceed by road to
   new area on 22nd inst. and will rejoin their respective units on
   23rd inst.
9. The office of the A.D.M.S. will close at ADINFER WOOD at 10 a,m, on
   22nd July, and will reopen at BORDER CAMP (A.30,b,Sheet 28) at the
   same hour.

                                        C.A.YOUNG, Colonel,
                                          A.D.M.S.48th Division.
Copies to,-
    Os.C.1/1,1/2,1/3,S.M.F.Ambs.
    H.Q. "G" & "A".
     " 143,144,145 Inf.Bdes,
    48 Div.Train, 48 Div Signals,
    D.D.M.S.VII Corps,
    D.D.M.S.XVIII Corps,
    A.D.M.S.39th Divn,

No 182, Ref.Map Sheet 57D,
& " 51C

R.A.M.C.ORDERS BY LIEUT-COLONEL T.A.GREEN, R.A.M.C.(T),

a/A.D.M.S. 48th Division,

2nd July 1917,

1. The two Sections of the 1/1st S.M.Field Ambulance marching with 2 Battalions of the 144th Infantry Brigade on the 3rd instant will proceed to GUADIEMPRE and take over the Ambulance Site at D.2,c,2,5, where they will open up for the reception of sick from the Division.
The Section marching with the remainder of the 144th Infantry Brigade on the 4th instant will proceed to RANSART.

2. Officers' Commanding Field Ambulances will arrange for the collection of sick from the respective Brigade Areas and send them direct to 1/1st S.M.Field Ambulance. All cases except urgent ones should arrive at 1/1st S.M.Field Ambulance not later than 12 noon.

3. Instructions as regards evacuation etc. will be issued to 1/1st S.M.Field Ambulance as soon as available.

4. The 1/2nd and 1/3rd S.M.Field Ambulances will romain closed until further orders.

5. The office of the A.D.M.S.will close at I,34,a,at 10 a,m,4th July & reopen at same hour at ADINFER WOOD,X,26,a,5,5.
5. ACKNOWLEDGE. (Sheet 51C)

T.A.Green
Lieut-Colonel,
a/A.D.M.S. 48th Division,

Copies to,-
    OsC, 1/1,1/2,1/3,SdM.Fd Ambces,
    All Regtl.M.Os.
    H.Q. 143,144,145,Inf.Bdes,
    "   "A" & "C",
    D.D.M.S.VII Corps,
    D.D.M.S.XVIII Corps,

SECRET.   No 1,

O.C.
    1/2nd S.M.Field Ambulance,

With reference to R.A.M.C. Orders regarding relief of 48th
Division, and 48th Divisional Order No 202;
Two Sections complete, of your Ambulance, will proceed with
the 2 Battalions and Details of 145th Infantry Brigade
marching on July 4th to the BASSEUX Area from the BIHUCOURT
Area.
One Section complete will march with the 2 Battalions of
145th Infantry Brigade proceeding to the BASSEUX Area on
July 5th.
The necessary details to be arranged direct with the 145th
Indantry Brigade and the Battalions concerned.
ACKNOWLEDGE.

                                              Lieut-Colonel,
2nd July 1917,   a/A.D.M.S. 48th Division,

Copies to,-
    H.Q. "A",
     "   "G",
     " 145 Inf. Bde,
    48 Div Signals,
    CRE

SECRET.   No 1.

O.C.
    1/1st S.M.Field Ambulance,

With reference to R.A.M.C.Orders regarding relief of 48th
Division, and 48th Divisional Order No 202;
Two Sections complete, of your Ambulance, will proceed with
the 2 Battalions and Details of 144th Infantry Brigade
marching on July 3rd to the ADINFER Area from ACHIET-LE-PETIT
Area.
One Section complete will march with the 2 Battalions of
144th Infantry Brigade proceeding to the ADINFER Area on
July 4th.
The necessary details to be arranged direct with the 144th
Infantry Brigade and the Battalions concerned.
acknowledge

                                              Lieut-Colonel,
2nd July 1917,   a/A.D.M.S. 48th Division,

Copies to,-
    H.Q. "A"
     "   "G"
     " 144 Inf. Bde,
    48 Div Signals,
    CRE

Two Bearer Sub div-ns
leave BEAUMETZ 14 hrs
advance party report
1½ hrs beforehand. To
be rationed for the 18th

Capt White
11.30 p
16.7.17.

"C" Form.
MESSAGES AND SIGNALS.
Army Form C. 2123.

Prefix	Code	Words	Received.	Sent, or sent out	Office Stamp.
Charges to collect	£ s. d.		From	At	YDH 17.VII.17 ARMY TELEGRAPHS
Service Instructions.			By	To	
			ACO 7 Corps	By	

Handed in at _____ Office _____ m. Received _____ m.

TO 48th Divn

Sender's Number	Day of Month	In reply to Number	AAA
Q459	16/7/17		

2 bearers subsections of 1/2nd Field Ambulance of SYLVIA will proceed by Supply Train leaving BOSTON at 14 hrs 17th inst aaa Destination Shaw aaa Strength 3 Officers 75 ORs aaa Movement order should be issued and rations for consumption 18th will be taken aaa Party will report on arrival to 134 FA at A23c2.9 sheet 28 1/40000 aaa Added 48 Divn sept-A 12 Corps 3rd Army Q ADMS and RTO Beaumetz Copy to ADMS

FROM 7th Corps Q
PLACE & TIME

* This line should be erased if not required.
(6334). Wt. W7196/M857. 500,000 Pads. 10/16. D, D, & L. (E 489). Forms C/2123/3.

"A" Form. Army Form C. 2121.
MESSAGES AND SIGNALS. No. of Message..........

TO: OC Auxilux 42nd Stn Field

Sender's Number: M.S.224   Day of Month: 17.   AAA

Your bearer subdivisions will leave BEAUMETZ at 14 hours today for 18th Div. Take rations.

From: 48 Div
Time: 7.45am

J.J.O. Beckh
Capt

SECRET.   No 183

48th Division.

R.A.M.C. ORDERS BY COLONEL C.A.YOUNG, C.M.G., A.M.S.

A.D.M.S. 48th Division,

16th July 1917,

Reference Move of 48th Division into XVIII Corps Area.

In accordance with XVIII Corps No.G.S./47/228 and 48th Division G.52,S, and under instructions from D.D.M.S. XVIII Corps, 2 Bearer Sub-divisions 1/2nd S.Mid. Field Ambulance, with 3 Officers, will proceed tomorrow by Motor bus to XVIII Corps area, starting from BELLACOURT at 8 a.m.
On arrival in XVIII Corps area this party will proceed to A.23.c.2.9. Sheet 28, 1/40,000, and will report for duty to O.C. 134 Field Ambulance for work in connection with medical arrangements.
Completion of move to be reported to this office by wire.

C.A.YOUNG, Colonel,
A.D.M.S. 48th Division,

Copies to,-
Os.C.1/1, 1/2, 1/3, S.M.F.Ambces,
D.D.M.S. VII Corps,
D.D.M.S. XVIII Corps
H.Q. "G" 48 Divn.
   " "A"   "
48th Divl Signals,
     "   Train, A.S.C.

Appendix (3)

SECRET.   No 185

48th Division.

R.A.M.C. ORDERS BY COLONEL C.A.YOUNG,C.M.G.,A.M.S.
                                    A.D.M.S.48th Divn.
                                    20th July 1917,

Ref. Map 1/40,000 Sheets 27 & 28.

MOVE OF 48th DIVISION TO XVIII CORPS AREA.

1. On arrival in XVIII Corps Area Field Ambulances will proceed
   direct from detraining Stations to following locations,-

   1/1st S.M.Field Ambulance.

1 Tent Sub-Division (with 2 motor ambulance cars) to 144th Inf.
Bde. area at POPERINGHE to attend to the sick of the Brigade.
Remainder of Unit to Field Ambulance site A.28.a.2.65.Sheet 28.

   1/2nd S.M.Field Ambulance.

1 Tent Sub-Division (with 2 motor ambulance cars) to 145th Inf.
Bde. area at HOUTKERQUE to attend to the sick of the Brigade.
1 Tent Sub-Division to XVIII Corps Rest Station at D.10.c.0.9.
Sheet 27.
Remainder of unit to F.29.d.5.9. Sheet 27.

   1/3rd S.Mid. Field Ambulance.

1 Tent Sub-Division (with 2 motor ambulance cars) to 143rd Inf.
Bde. area at ST JAN DE BIEZEN to attend to the sick of the Bde.
Remainder of unit to XVIII Corps Main Dressing Station at
A.23.c.2.9. Sheet 28.

2. The 2 Bearer Sub-Divisions 1/2nd S.Mid. Field Ambulance now in
XVIII Corps Area will rejoin their unit under orders which will
be issued later on.

                                    C.A.YOUNG, Colonel,
                                    A.D.M.S.48th Division.

Copies to,-
    Os.C. 1/1,1/2,1/3,S.M.F.Ambs.
    H.Q. "G" & "A",
    "   143,144,145,Inf. Bdes,
    48 Div. Train, 48 Div Signals,
    D.D.M.S.XVIII Corps,
    A.D.M.S.39th Divn.
    A.D.M.S.11th Divn.
    A.D.M.S.51st Divn.

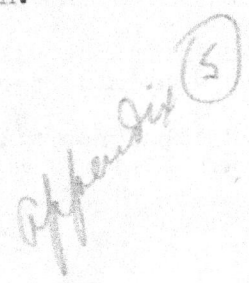

SECRET.

R.A.M.C. 48th DIVISION OPERATION ORDER No 1

Ref.Maps Sheet 27,1/40,000
" 28,1/40,000

30th July 1917.

With reference to 48th Division Order No 206 dated 28th July 1917,-

1. The Infantry Brigades of the Division are moving as follows,-

Brigade	From	To	Date.
143 Inf.Bde. (less 1st line Transport & M.G.Coy.)	"F" Bde Group area ST JAN TER BIEZEN	"A" Bde.Group area N.E.of POPERINGHE.	30/31 July, To start 11 p.m.
145 Inf.Bde. (less 1st line Transport & M.G.Coy)	HOUTKERQUE.	"F" Bde.Group area ST JAN TER BIEZEN	30/31 July March to be completed by 5 a.m. 31 July.
144 Inf.Bde. (less 1st line Transport & M.G.Coy.)	POPERINGHE & Camps,	"C" Bde.Group area N.E.of POPERINGHE,	31 July, Not to leave POPERINGHE before 6 am.

2. The Sections of the Field Ambulances attached to above Brigades will move as follows,-

	From-	To-	Date.
1/3 S.M.F.Ambce;	ST JAN TER BIEZEN,	Unit Headquarters at G.23,c,2.9.	30/31 July *
1/2 S.M.F.Ambce;	HOUTKERQUE,	Unit A Headquarters at F.29,d.5.9. (Sheet 27)	30/31 July, *
1/1 S.M.F.Ambce;	POPERINGHE & Camps,	Unit Headquarters at M.28.c.2.6. A	31 July, *

* Times to be obtained from Brigades.

3. COLLECTION OF SICK & WOUNDED.
   (a) The Tent Subdivisions now attached to Brigades will arrange to collect the sick of their respective Brigades before starting.
   (b) On arrival in the new areas the collection will be made as follows:-
   The O.C.1/1st S.M.Fd Ambulance will collect the sick and wounded of the 143 & 144 Inf. Bdes. at 9 a.m. daily or when required.
   The O.C.1/2nd S.M.Fd Ambulance will collect the sick of the 145 Inf. Bde. at 9 a.m. daily, or when required.

4. AMBULANCE CARS.

All ambulance cars will be parked at L'ABBE FARM by noon on July 30th less the undermentioned,-

  1/1st S.M.Fd Ambce,   1 Talbot,
             1 Ford,

  1/2nd S.M.Fd Ambce,   1 Talbot,
             1 Ford (attached to
                 12 Sanitary Secn)

  1/3rd S.M.Fd Ambce,   1 Talbot,
             1 Ford,

5. ACKNOWLEDGE.

              R R Pickard

             Colonel,
          A.D.M.S. 48th Division

Copies to,-
  H.Q. "G" & "A"
  D.D.M.S. XVIII Corps
  143, 144, 145 Inf. Bdes,
  O.Cs. 1/1, 1/2, 1/3, S.M.F. Amb.

INSTRUCTIONS TO MEDICAL OFFICERS DURING OPERATIONS.

1. **SUPPLIES.** i.e.
   (a) Dressings: Each M.O. will indent on the nearest Field Ambulance for dressings required as an initial supply. This will include 100 Shell Dressings in addition to those carried in haversacks. Subsequent supplies during operations will be obtained from the A.D.S. on requisition.
   (b) Each M.O. will indent for 2 Thomas' Splints and 2 Suspension Bars forthwith, and a sufficiency of other splints.
   (c) Stretchers. He will draw 8 stretchers, in addition to those already carried, from the A.D.S. or Divisional M.D.S. on moving forward.
   (d) Blankets. He will draw from the same source 16 blankets.
   (e) Water. 2 Petrol tins of water will be provided by the Field Ambulance for each Regimental Aid Post. If the M.O. requires more than this he must provide the petrol tins. For fresh supplies of water he must return the empty tins.

2. **POSITION OF MEDICAL POSTS UNCERTAIN.**
   Probably Main Dressing Station at C.25.a.4.4. Sheet 28,
   Advanced Dressing Station C.21.c.4.3.   "   29,

3. **R.A.Ps.** It is considered that the M.O. should not move forward till his Battalion H.Q. moves forward.
   The R.A.P. should be situate as near the line of evacuation of wounded as possible.
   The M.Os. of battalions taking furthest objectives should, if possible, arrange a line of evacuation through or near to the R.A.Ps. of the battalions taking the earlier objective.

4. **COMMUNICATION.**
   2 Runners per battalion will be provided from the Field Ambulance working behind the Brigade in which the battalion is placed. They are not to be used for stretcher-bearing. Their main employment is to keep up communication between the Regimental M.O. and Field Ambulance Officers.

5. **MORPHIA.** The dose of Morphia and method of administration must be clearly marked on the tallies.

6. **EVACUATION OF CASES.** All cases must be evacuated as quickly as possible. The main duty of stretcher bearers is to carry the cases to the R.A.P., but there is no objection to a few of them being specially detailed for dressing patients only.
   Gassed cases must be removed from the gassed area as soon as possible.

7. **ADDITIONAL STRETCHER BEARERS.** The Field Ambulance stretcher bearers are not to be employed in front of R.A.Ps. If circumstances urgently demand this, permission must first be obtained from the Field Ambulance Bearer Officer in whose charge the men are, who will not give it unless the reserve combatant bearers are not obtainable within a reasonable time.

8. **RESERVE BEARERS.** Reserve Bearers will, under Divisional arrangements, be placed at the disposal of the A.D.M.S. If extra bearers are required by the R.M.Os. they should, unless urgent circumstances as above detailed exist, communicate with the A.D.M.S. with a view to his sending up reserve bearers to them.

R. Pickard
Colonel,

CONFIDENTIAL.

48th Division, R.A.M.C. CIRCULAR MEMORANDUM No.2,- 31-7-17,

INSTRUCTIONS FOR OPERATIONS.

1. **GENERAL.** M.D.S. - By this is meant either C.M.D.S. or Divisional M.D.S. as the case may be.

    POOLING of Stretchers, blankets, and other stores may be necessary, requests for loans of this kind should be arranged without reference to the A.D.M.S. if there is any urgency.

    HANDING OVER, of all stores surplus to mobilisation will be carried out by the Field Ambulances in the line to their succeeding Field Ambulances.

2. **SUPPLIES.**
    (a) Stretchers. Reserves of these to be maintained at each post. 100 or more to be kept at the most advanced Station. At least 700 stretchers in all should be available at Divisional M.D.S. and forward posts.
    (b) Blankets. Same scale as stretchers.
    (c) Rations for patients to be obtained on a scale as below from S.S.O. 48th Division, on wiring,- Authority D.D.H.&T. Fifth Army S/55, Q.R.931.

Tea	20 lbs.
Sugar	100 "
Bread	500 "
Jam	150 :
Condensed Milk,	1 case,

    (d) Water,- 60 petrol tins issued for use at Advanced Posts, at present 40 of these are with the 1/2nd, & 20 with the 1/3rd Field Ambulances. These must be carefully conserved.

3. **PACK SADDLES.** Six have been issued by the Division for R.A.M.C.use, they are at present held by the 1/2nd Fd Ambce, but are for the use of R.A.M.C.Units having A.D.Ss or other advanced posts. Field Ambs must improvise others & prepare water tin crates.

4. **Regimental M.Os.** Instructions in Circular Memo. No 1 of 30-7-17, from this office will be followed by Field Ambulances as far as this concerns the latter.
    Runners for Regtl. M.Os. - O.Cs. Field Ambulances will arrange for these direct with the M.Os. concerned.

5. **DIRECTING BOARDS** A supply to be made and maintained by each Field Ambulance; the Field Ambulance in the line will collect and place these as far as the Divl. M.D.S. or A.D.S. as the case may be.

6. **LAMPS.** Candle lamps, improvised from tins and gauze or jaconet, should be used at night if circumstances permit, being placed on the ground, the light not turned towards the enemy.

7. **EXPLOSIVES.** Should be removed from patients at first Field Ambulance post.

8. **TREATMENT OF PATIENTS.**
    (a) Essential dressings only to be done. Thomas' Splints to be applied at the earliest possible time. Circle to be placed on the envelope of the Field Medical Card if redressing is not required.
    (b) Operations,- urgent amputations and arrest of haemorrhage only to be undertaken.

8. (continued)

    (c) Tourniquets, must be removed at the earliest possible moment, and the bleeding arrested either by ligature, clamping with forceps which are left on, ~~washing~~ plugging of wound after opening it ~~as well up well~~.

    (d) Anaesthetics not to be given unless absolutely necessary.

    (e) Morphia dose and time of administration to be recorded.

    (f) Anti-tetanic serum to be given at A.D.S. to all cases sent direct to C.C.S. and the cases returned to duty; other cases at M.D.S.

    (g) Food; all walking cases to be fed, lying cases when ordered by M.O.

    (h) Moribund. Obviously moribund cases not to be sent to C.M.D.S. or C.C.S.

    (i) Special cases direct to C.C.S., see No 3169, d/d 27-7-17, from this office.

    (k) Gassed cases to go lying down. Clothing to be changed as soon as possible in lachrymatory gas cases.

9. **SHELTERS.** Ground sheets to be used in wet weather for stretcher cases. Trench shelters to be used for cases which cannot be accommodated otherwise.

10. **FIELD MEDICAL CARDS.** Patient's name and unit in BLOCK LETTERS. Number of Field Ambulance to be stamped on card. M.O. to sign card and add rank.

11. **EFFECTS etc. Officers & Other Ranks.** See, for Officers, G.R.Os. 1387 & 1320.
    " for O.Ranks, " 1388 & 1782.

12. **EVACUATION.** Speed is essential. Cars must have full loads except for very urgent cases going direct to C.C.S.

13. **EXCHANGE** of Splints, Stretchers etc. is to be effected at C.C.S. or C.M.D.S. when these are sent with patients.

14. **D.M.S.** Fifth Army, No 21/32 of 12-6-17 must be adhered to as far as possible.

15. **DEAD.** Cases dying at the A.D.S. or in transit to it or the M.D.S. must have particulars taken for the A & D Books.
    DEAD, non-identified. Particulars of any marks, or other particulars which might lead to identification, must be taken down. A report must be made to this office in triplicate.

16. **PARTICULARS** (1) of patients sent direct from A.D.S. to C.C.S., and
    (2) of patients treated and returned to duty, must be sent to M.D.S.

17. **BEARER DIVISIONS** must consist of 3 Officers and 90 Other ranks at least. If it is considered that 3 Officers are not available then this office must be notified.

J.H. Beckton
Capt.

Colonel,
A.D.M.S. 48th Division.

CONFIDENTIAL

War Diary
of
A.D.M.S. 48th Division
from 1-8-17 to 31-8-17.

Vol XXIX

Army Form C. 2118.

WAR DIARY
or
INTELLIGENCE SUMMARY.
(Erase heading not required.)

Instructions regarding War Diaries and Intelligence Summaries are contained in F. S. Regs., Part II. and the Staff Manual respectively. Title pages will be prepared in manuscript.

Place	Date	Hour	Summary of Events and Information	Remarks and references to Appendices
"D" Camp A.30 Br. Inf Bde 8 Proven Belgium	1.8.17	—	Situation unaltered from 31 July. A/DM/S held conference with O.C. Field Ambulances.	
	2.8.17	—	A.D.M.S. visited Consol O.D.S. 39 & Advd D.D.P. Proceeded to reconnoitre roads in front of our forward front line up to O.G.1. Routine and weather very wet.	
"D" Camp	3.8.17	—		
D Camp	4.2.17	—	A.D.M.S. visited Cpr Booin Dressing Station. Conference held with O.C.'s Field Ambulances regarding taking over from 39 Division. A.D.M.S. visited Rtour 38 & 39 Divisions O.M. D.S. in connection with 8am situation on active operations by enemy's frame.	App I App II
D Camp	5.8.17	—	3 Div. D.A.D.M.S. to conference 9 Dm. g 13 Cpr. 1/2 th Field Ambulance took over [Perrus?] Dressing Station (Burgomn) 1/1 Lth Fd Field Ambulance " " Bourmond Collecting Post at Harrons Corner 1/1 6th Field Ambulance took over from 134 Field Ambulance at Oppodaan Dressing Station.	See Apps 2 " "
D Camp	6.8.17	—	Evac. R.S. & on line from 39 Division nightly from C11A to C.1 pA. A.D.M.S visited advanced Dressing Station & Divisional Collecting Post.	Ref March C/o Belgium 20 B.W 12000 " "
D Camp	7.8.17	— 11am	Divisional Headquarters moved from D Camp to "E" Camp A30C7.2. O.Y.C. D.O.P. establishes 4 Relay Posts at C16cl 2.3. C22a22. C22a28. C22b7.1. A/D/M/S covers the above 22nd July 2 killed 13 wounded sdl	Ref March Q/o Belgium 20 B.W 12000 " Ref Jul March Belgium 21 W 10000 1/10 0000

Army Form C. 2118.

WAR DIARY
or
INTELLIGENCE SUMMARY.
(Erase heading not required.)

Instructions regarding War Diaries and Intelligence Summaries are contained in F. S. Regs., Part II. and the Staff Manual respectively. Title pages will be prepared in manuscript.

Place	Date	Hour	Summary of Events and Information	Remarks and references to Appendices
"E" Camp	8-8-17	—	Situation unaltered. Weather raining. A.D.M.S. attended Conference 9.30 a.m. 8. XVIII Corps. Visited Advanced Dressing Station DUHALLOW, and Divisional Collecting Post with reference to moving the D.C.P. to O.G.1.	
"C" Camp	9-8-17	—	Situation unchanged. A.D.M.S. held a Conference with O.C's Field Ambulances. Capt. C.B. DAVIES-JONES R.A.M.C. T.C. reported to replace Lt. REDLAND contracted jaundice.	
"C" Camp	10-8-17	—	A.D.M.S. visited Advanced Dressing Station, Divisional Collecting Post, Relay Post. Lieut. R.P. BURPEE United States Medical Service reported for duty with this Division, posted to N° 2 Field Ambulance. A.D.M.S. had a conference with R.M.O's of N°5 Infy Bde. which has just come up the line.	
"C" Camp	11-8-17	—	Situation unchanged. Weather dull raining. A.D.M.S. held a Conference with O.C's Field Ambulances. R.A.M.C. operation order N°3 issued for the forthcoming events	app/3.
"C" Camp	12-8-17	—	Situation unaltered. Rain. A.D.M.S. visited A.D.S., D.C.P. and Relay Posts	
"C" Camp	13-8-17	—	Situation unaltered. Weather fine.	

WAR DIARY
or
INTELLIGENCE SUMMARY

(Erase heading not required.)

Army Form C. 2118.

Place	Date	Hour	Summary of Events and Information	Remarks and references to Appendices
"C" Camp	14.8.17	10 am	A.D.M.S. visited 1/2nd S.M. Field Ambulance	
		2 pm	A.D.M.S. visited Advanced Dressing Station, DUHALLOW, Divisional Collecting Post & Relay Posts	
"C" Camp	15.8.17		Situation unaltered. A.D.M.S. attended Conference 9 D.M.S. XVIII Corps	
"C" Camp	16.8.17	4.45 am	At this hour the Division attacked the German line opposite its own front, as part of the general attack, on a three Battalion front. Regimental A.D. Posts were established at ALBERTA FARM – C.14.d.5.0., New ST JULIEN C.13.c.33 and at VEN HEULE FARM C.17.d.2.6 with Field Ambulance Relay Posts in the rear as in Operation Order No. 102. The arrangements worked smoothly at the Main A.D.S. which could be got in to this R.A.P. where we were created. The condition of the ground on the left – necessitated carrying the whole way – on the right wheeled stretchers were employed from VEN HEULE FARM to the D.C.P. in CALIFORNIA TR. C.22.B.7.1. and to Relay Posts in C.22.C.5.5; etc. It was found the R.A.P. had to be carried to the Divisional Post at C.21.C.4.2 owing to the bad condition of the road. This carry was the longest & caused more fatigue to the bearers than the forward carry – not only owing to the bad condition of the road, but also owing to the congested state of the road with transport, although there was not there any delay in getting the wounded back.	App. 3.

Army Form C. 2118.

WAR DIARY
or
INTELLIGENCE SUMMARY.
(Erase heading not required.)

Instructions regarding War Diaries and Intelligence Summaries are contained in F. S. Regs., Part II. and the Staff Manual respectively. Title pages will be prepared in manuscript.

Place	Date	Hour	Summary of Events and Information	Remarks and references to Appendices
"C" Camp	17.8.17		For numbers of wounded see Appendix.	
"C" Camp	18.8.17		Operations continued. The evacuation of wounded continued smoothly. The H/2 Company of Infantry was relieved by 100 other Infantry & the R.A.M.C. Bearers in the main forward posts changed by three bearer squads. Supervising M.O. & 4 R/Boy Posts unchanged. Reinforced only during the day. The weather during this period has been fine & dry.	
"C" Camp	19.8.17		No operations are taking place. All Infantry bearers being relieved by R.A.M.C. Bearers. The Bearer Post at C.21.C.4.3 moved to C.20.d.8.5 owing to the former position having been heavily shelled. This post was surrounded by batteries firing barrages — 1 R.A.M.C. (casualty of light) received during this shelling. Few wounded arriving. The route of evacuation is now — Outwards — from O.P.s. & Bn Sig H, Morteau Farm — Burnt Farm — C.20.d.35 (new bearer post) Return — C.20.d.5 — Zouave Villa — Pittsburg — Bridge 2 — R.D.S. walking cases go by duck boards from this road at C.20.d.35 + canal Bridge 3 = bank of canal to Bridge 2a + with A.D.S.	
			Situation unchanged. Weather pin fine. A.D.M.S. & visited Dunlbow A.D.S.	
"C" Camp	20.8.17		Situation unchanged. Weather fine. O.D.m.S. visited Advanced Dressing Station, Divisional Collecting Post & Relay Post.	

Army Form C. 2118.

WAR DIARY
or
INTELLIGENCE SUMMARY.
(Erase heading not required.)

Instructions regarding War Diaries and Intelligence Summaries are contained in F. S. Regs., Part II. and the Staff Manual respectively. Title pages will be prepared in manuscript.

Place	Date	Hour	Summary of Events and Information	Remarks and references to Appendices
"C" Camp	21.8.17	—	Situation unchanged. Weather fine. A.D.M.S. inspected Sanitation of DAMBRECAMP (B.27.d) A.D.M.S. attended Conference D.D.M.S. XVIII Corps	A.D.M.S. Return dated 21.8.17 14.8am
"C" Camp	22.8.17	4.45am	Situation slightly advanced toward VANCOUVER-SPRINGFIELD-WINNIPEG Road. Casualties not numerous & conveyed to A.D.S. as previous operations; and of these evacuated at night. It being possible to use wheeled stretcher carriers down from ST JULIEN, they were emptied nearly clear.	Map ST JULIEN 1/10,000
		7 am	A.D.M.S. visited A.D.S. and D.C.P. The Bearers from 23rd Division were returned to their unit – 69 & 8 Field Ambulance	
		5 pm	A.D.M.S. visited O.D.S.	
"C" Camp	23.8.17	—	Situation as above. Weather fine. A.D.M.S. visited Advanced Dressing Station DUHALLOW. A.D.M.S. visited 93rd & 2bn Field Ambulance.	
"C" Camp	24.8.17	—	Situation unaltered. Weather fine. A.D.M.S. inspected Sanitation of REIGERSBURG Camps near BRIELEN. A.D.M.S. visited Advanced Dressing Station.	

WAR DIARY
or
INTELLIGENCE SUMMARY

Army Form C. 2118.

Place	Date	Hour	Summary of Events and Information	Remarks and references to Appendices
"C" Camp	25.8.17	—	Situation unchanged. Weather fine. A.D.M.S. visited Advanced Dressing Station & Divisional Collecting Post. A.D.M.S. 58th Division (Mr Duncan) worked with two Divisions called round A.Dk.S. with reference to Medical Arrangements in front line &c. A.D.M.S. visited Advance Dinkelstofen at 87 VAN TER BIEZEN to report return of 3 horse ambulance cars which had been sent there for repairs	
"C" Camp	26.8.17	9.30 am	Situation unchanged. Weather fine. A.D.M.S. visited A.D.S. & D.C.P. and 1/3 Ldn Field Ambulance	
		8 pm	Weather wet	
"C" Camp	27.8.17	8.30 am	Situation unchanged. Weather very wet	
		1.55 pm	Division (in conjunction with formations on Lt & Rt) attacked. The Medical arrangements were the same as in the attack of 16 instant & all evacuation proceeded smoothly, although the forward roads were in bad state & the carrying very difficult. Some slight advance was made by left Bde of the Division	
"C" Camp	28.8.17	—	Situation as above. Weather wet very wet. Evacuation proceeded being carried out & most of those nearly in to Dutch houses cleared	

A 5834 Wt. W4973/MG57 750,000 8/16 D. D. & L. Ltd. (Forms/C.2118/13

Army Form C. 2118.

WAR DIARY
or
INTELLIGENCE SUMMARY.
(Erase heading not required.)

Place	Date	Hour	Summary of Events and Information	Remarks and references to Appendices
	28.8.17	5 p.m.	in the bringing in of wounded. The Infantry Bearers relieved by 6 Platoons from 11th D.L.I. B Coy. By this time practically all the wounded had been brought in. A/DMS made arrangements with A/DMS 58 Division to leave behind 20 st. Royal Army Medical Corps to replace deficiencies in that Division until reinforcement arrived A/DMS issued Operation Order No. 4 with regard to moving Divisional Office Line on relief by 58th Division	App. 4
WORMHOUDT	29.8.17		A/DMS Office opened at WORMHOUDT. Division moving. Headquarters arrived here 1/1st Lt. Dy. Field Ambulance moved to GWENT FARM. 1/2nd " " " " L'EBBE FARM. 1/3rd " " " " ST JAN TER BIEZEN	
WORMHOUDT	30.8.17		Brigades moved into Camps in neighbourhood of ST JAN TER BIEZEN A/DMS visited all three Field Ambulances A/DMS visited D.D. & XVIIIth Corps	

Army Form C. 2118.

WAR DIARY
or
INTELLIGENCE SUMMARY.
(Erase heading not required.)

Place	Date	Hour	Summary of Events and Information	Remarks and references to Appendices
WORMHOUDT	31-8-17	—	Instruction as above. Weather showery. ADMS attended Corps A Conference with ADs DsM. Attached chart showing Sick evacuated admissions for the month.	

R. Richew Col

Instructions regarding War Diaries and Intelligence Summaries are contained in F. S. Regs., Part II. and the Staff Manual respectively. Title pages will be prepared in manuscript.

B.E.F.

SUMMARY OF MEDICAL WAR DIARIES OF 48th Div. 18th Corps.

5th ARMY.

Western Front Operations Aug. 1917.

A.D.M.S. Colonel C.A. Young, C.M.G.
A.D.M.S. Col. R. Pickard from 24th July.

D.A.D.M.S. Capt. J.J.H. Becton.

SUMMARISED UNDER THE FOLLOWING HEADINGS :-

Phase "D" 1. Passchendaele Operations "July - Nov. 1917."

(a) - Operations commencing 1/7/17.

August 6th.	Military Situation.	Took over line from 39th Div. roughly C11a. to C18a.
7th.	Moves.	To "C" Camp A.30.c. 7.2.
	Casualties R.A.M.C.	Since 22nd July 0 & 2 killed. 0 & 18 wd.
16th.	Ops. Medical Arrangements. Evacuation.	Division attacked German line opposite its own front at 4.45 a.m., as part of a general attack.

App. 3. marked portions (attached). (Put back into Diary)

The arrangements for evacuation worked smoothly, but owing to the condition of the ground on the left it necessitated carrying the whole way.
App. chart marked 1. (attached). (Put back into Diary)

B.E.F.

48th Div. 18th Corps. 5th ARMY.   Western Front.
A.D.M.S. Col. R. Pickard.   Aug.-Sept. 1917.

PHASE "D" 1. Passchendaele Operations, "July-Nov. 1917."
(a) - Operations commencing July -Sept. 1917.

Headquarters at "C" Camp A.30.c.7.2.

Aug. 27th.   Ops.   ) Division attacked in conjunction with
              Med. Arr.)
              Evac.   ) formations on its right and left. Some slight
              advance was made by the left brigade. The medical
              arrangements were similar to those on the 16th. Evacua-
              tions of wounded were smoothly carried out, although
              the bad state of the ground and roads made carrying very
              difficult.

   28th.   Moves. To Wormhoudt.
              Appendices.

                     Chart wounded admissions by Units.
                     Chart sick   "   "   "

                  1. Op. Order No.6. D.D.M.S. 18th Corps d. 3/8/17.
                  2. "   "   48th Div. dated 4/8/17.
                  3. "   "   48th Div. dated 11/8/17.
                  4. "   "   48th Div. dated 27/8/17.
                  5. D.D.M.S. Op. Order No. 10. dated 25/8/17.

August 6th.	Military Situation.	Took over line from 3oth Div. roughly C11a. to C18a.
7th.	Moves.	To "C" Camp A.30.c. 7.2.
	Casualties R.A.M.C.	Since 22nd July 0 & 2 killed. 0 & 18 wd.
16th.	Ops.) Medical Arrangements.) Evacuation.)	Division attacked German line opposite its own front at 4.45 a.m.,

as part of a general attack.

          App. 3. marked portions (attached).

       The arrangements for evacuation work-
-ed smoothly, but owing to the condition of the ground
on the left it necessitated carrying the whole way.
App. chart marked 1. (attached).

B.E.F.

48th Div. 18th Corps. 5th ARMY.   Western Front.
A.D.M.S. Col. R. Pickard.   Aug.-Sept.1917.

PHASE "D" 1. Passchendaele Operations, "July-Nov. 1917.

(a) - Operations commencing July -Sept. 1917.

Headquarters at "C" Camp A.30.c.7.2.

Aug. 27th. Ops.   ) Division attacked in conjunction with
            Med. Arr.)
            Evac.   ) formations on its right and left. Some slight advance was made by the left brigade. The medical arrangements were similar to those on the 16th. Evacuations of wounded were smoothly carried out, although the bad state of the ground and roads made carrying very difficult.

28th.   Moves. To Wormhoudt.

            Appendices.

                Chart wounded admissions by Units.
                Chart sick   "   "   "

                1. Op. Order No.6. D.D.M.S. 18th Corps d. 3/8/17.
                2. "   "   48th Div. dated 4/8/17.
                3. "   "   48th Div. dated 11/8/17.
                4. "   "   48th Div. dated 27/8/17.
                5. D.D.M.S. Op. Order No. 10. dated 25/8/17.

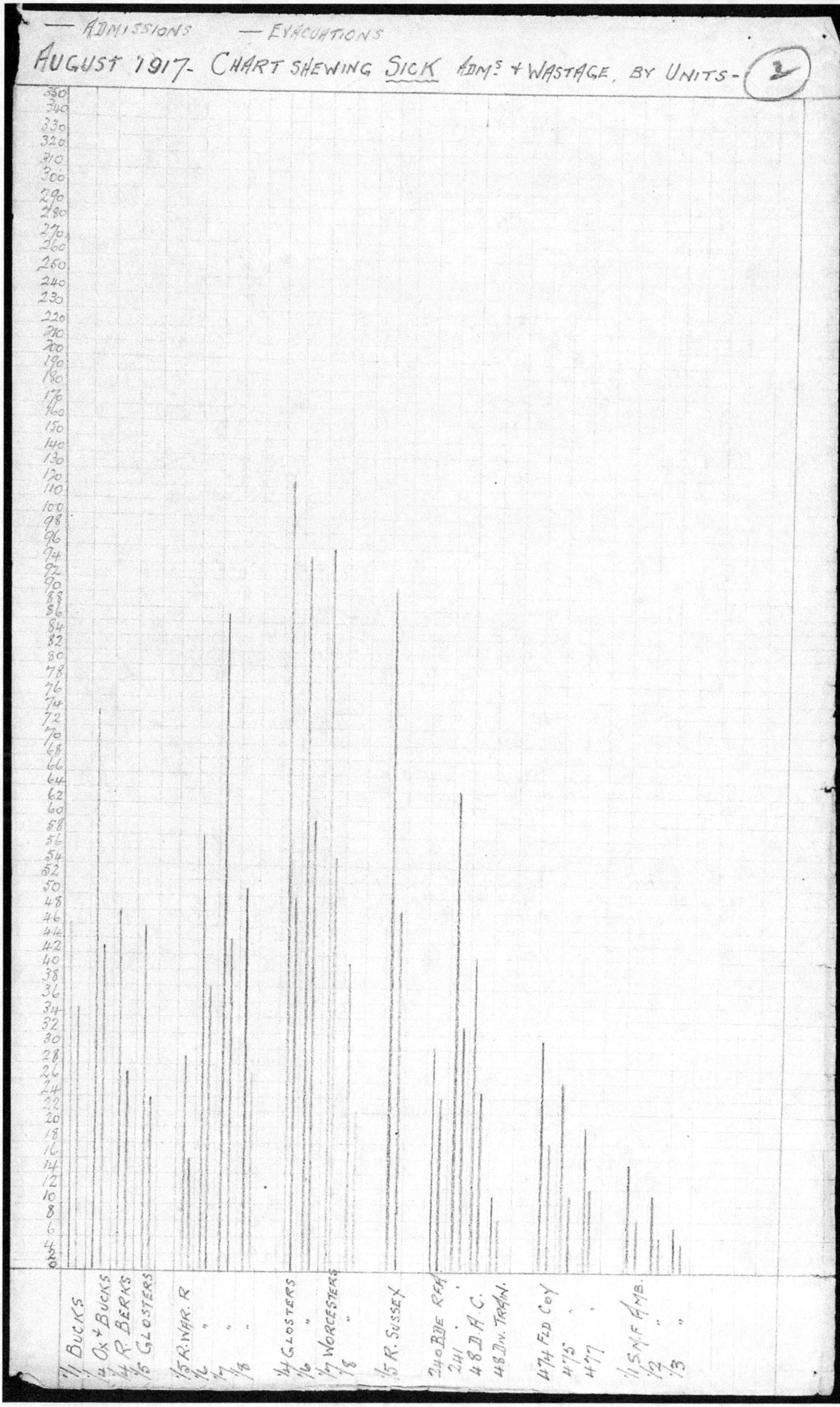

— ADMISSIONS — EVACUATIONS
AUGUST 1917 - CHART SHEWING SICK ADMS + WASTAGE, BY UNITS -
2
1/1 BUCKS
1/4 OX + BUCKS
1/4 R. BERKS
1/5 GLOSTERS
1/5 R. WAR. R
1/6 "
1/7 "
1/8 "
1/4 GLOSTERS
1/6 "
1/7 WORCESTERS
1/8 "
1/5 R. SUSSEX
240 BDE RFA
241 "
48 D.A.C.
48 DIV. TRAIN.
474 FLD COY
475 "
477 "
1/1 S.M.F AMB.
1/2 "
1/3 "

War Diary Duplicate

SECRET.
Copy No ...19....

OPERATION ORDER No 6.

D.D.M.S. XVIII Corps.

Ref. Maps:-

1/40,000 Sheet 28.
1/100,000 Sheet 5.A.

3rd August, 1917.

1. The 48th (South Midland) Division will relieve the 39th Division in the line on the night 5/6th August, 1917 and field ambulances on relief will accompany their respective brigades into the EPERLECQUES area.

2. All details of relief in connection with advanced aid posts etc will be arranged between the two divisions concerned.

3. The A.D.M.S. 39th Division will leave a sufficient number of R.A.M.C. Other ranks of his division for temporary duty with the 48th Division to make the latter up to war establishment until reinforcements for that division arrive.

4. The XVIII Corps Main Dressing Station will continue to be commanded by Lieutenant-Colonel H.C. HILDRETH, D.S.O., R.A.M.C. until further orders.

5. A Field Ambulance of the 48th Division, to be detailed by the A.D.M.S., will take over charge of the Corps Main Dressing Station for the purpose of compiling Corps return and statistics, from No 134 Field Ambulance. The latter unit will, on relief, rejoin its Division.

6. The tent sub division of No 132 Field Ambulance at the Walking Wounded Collecting Post will be relieved by a tent sub division of a field ambulance of the 48th Division, to be detailed by the A.D.M.S., but the Walking Wounded Collecting Post will remain under the command of Major G.F. WHYTE, R.A.M.C.T.F. until further notice.

7. Field Ambulances of the 39th Division on being relieved will only take away with them their approved mobilization equipment. All Sector stores, reserve of blankets and stretchers etc at present in possession of the 39th Division in the front area will be handed over to the 48th Division on relief and receipts taken.

8. Completion of the above reliefs etc to be reported to this office.

9. ACKNOWLEDGE.

Colonel, A.M.S.
D.M.D.M.S. XVIII Corps.

Headquarters.
3rd August, 1917.
Issued to Signals at 10-35.p.m.
Distribution:-

Copy No 1 to D.M.S. Fifth Army.	Copy Nos 10-11-12-13 A.D.M.S.	11 Div.
Cop No 2 to "G" XVIII Corps.	.. .. 14-15-16-17 ..	39 ..
Copy No 3 to "A"	.. .. 18-19-20-21 ..	48 ..
Copy No 4 to "A.P.M." ..	.. .. 22-23-24-25 ..	51 ..
Copy No 5 to G.O.C. R.A. ..	.. .. 26 O.C. 24 M.A.C.	
Copy No 6 to G.O.C. H.A. ..	.. .. 27 C.S.C.S.	
Copy No 7 to O.C. C.M.D.S.	.. .. 28-29 War Diary.	
Copy No 8 to O.C. W.W.C.M.P.	.. .. 30-31 File.	
Copy No 9 to O.C. C.R.S.		

SECRET.

R.A.M.C. 48th DIVISION OPERATION ORDER No 2.

Ref. Maps Sheet 28, 1/40000,

4th Aug. 1917.

1. The 48th Division will relieve the 39th Division in the line on the night of 5th/6th August 1917.

2. Locations of Medical Posts)
   1. DIVISIONAL COLLECTING POST, C.21.c.4.2.
   2. ADVANCED DRESSING STATION, (DUHALLOW) C.25.d.3.0.
   3. CORPS WALKING WOUNDED COLLECTING POST, H.3.d.5.8.
   4. CORPS MAIN DRESSING STATION, A.23.c.2.9.

3. MOVES. (a) The 1/1st S.Mid. Field Ambulance will take over GWENT FARM (A.23.a.5.5.) from 133rd Field Ambulance. The 1/1st S.Mid. Field Ambulance will take over A.D.S. at DUHALLOW on August 5th by 4.0 p.m. from 133rd Field Ambulance.
   The Bearer Division and Transport will remain at GWENT FARM.
   (b) The 1/2nd S.Mid. Field Ambulance will take over the Divisional Collecting Post and relay posts from 133rd Field Ambulance by 4.0 p.m. on Aug.5th. One Tent Sub-division will report for duty at Corps Walking Wounded Collecting Post on Aug. 5th at noon.
   The 1/2nd S.Mid. Field Ambulance Transport will move to field near GWENT FARM on August 5th.
   (c) The 1/3rd S.Mid. Field Ambulance will send the Tent Sub-division to Corps Main Dressing Station on August 5th to replace 134th Field Ambulance. Time to be arranged by Officers Commanding concerned. The Bearer Division will report at Advanced Dressing Station on August 5th at 4.0 p.m. for duty under O.C. 1/2nd S.Mid. Field Ambulance on line of evacuation.
   Advance parties will be detailed to take over stores etc. Completion of moves to be reported to this office.

4. DUTIES OF OFFICERS COMMANDING FIELD AMBS.
   (1) The O.C. 1/1st S.Mid Field Ambulance will be in charge of Advanced Dressing Station,- Personnel,- 2 Tent Sub-divisions.
   (2) The O.C. 1/2nd S.Mid. Field Ambulance will be in charge of Divisional Collecting Post and the evacuation of sick and wounded from Regimental Aid Posts East of YSER CANAL to the Advanced Dressing Station.
   Personnel,- 1 Tent Sub-division,
   Bearers of 1/2nd S.M.Fd Amboo,
   Bearers of 1/3rd S.M.Fd Arbce, &
   Bearers of 1/1st S.M.Fd Amboo
   when required.
   (3) The O.C. 1/3rd S.Mid. Field Ambulance will be in charge of his Tent Division working at Corps Main Dressing Station.

5. EVACUATION   (a) <u>Lying & Sitting cases</u>; By horse ambulance
   EAST OF CANAL.   wagons, Ford cars, wheeled stretchers,
                         or hand carriage to Advanced Dressing
                         Station. These to be pooled under
                         O.C.1/2nd S.Mid. Field Ambulance. The
                         evacuation from Advanced Dressing Station
                         to Corps Main Dressing Station is under-
                         taken by the Motor Ambulance Convoy.
                     (b) <u>Walking cases</u>,- Across tracks to the
                         Walking Wounded Collecting Post.
                     (c) <u>Special cases</u>,- See A.D.M.S.48th Divn.
                         No.3139 d/d 29-7-17.

6. EVACUATION OF   (a) The O.C. 1/3rd S.Mid. Field Ambulance will
   SICK WEST OF   arrange for collection of sick from the
   CANAL.   Units in DAMBRE CAMP and vicinity at
                      11 a.m. daily.
                  (b) The O.C.1/1st S.Mid. Field Ambulance will
                      arrange for the collection of sick from
                      REIGERSBURG CAMP & vicinity at 11 a.m.daily.

7. RETURNS etc.   The O.C.1/1st S.Mid. Field Ambulance will send to
                  C.M.D.S particulars for A & D Book of the following
                  groups,- (a) those returned to duty;
                           (b) those sent direct to C.C.S.
                           (c) those dying in charge of Field
                               Ambulances East of Canal.

8. RESERVE BEARERS. The A.D.M.S. will have at his disposal
                    extra bearers. These will be detailed
                    as required.

9. WATER POINTS. The following Water points have been or are
                 being established,-
                    Zero,   I.2.d.3.8.
                    Zero + 1,   (C.27.a.3.0.
                                   (C.21.c.5.7.
                    Zero + 2,   C.15.c.10.30.

10. REPORTS OF   All R.A.M.C.casualties will be notified to this
    CASUALTIES   office as soon as possible.
    POSITIONS &c. Any alteration in situation of posts will be
                  immediately notified to this office.

11. DIRECTING   The O.Cs. 1/2nd & 1/1st S.Mid Field Ambulances
    POSTS.   will be responsible for placing directing
                  posts for the walking wounded to find their
                  way back easily.

12.   ACKNOWLEDGE.

                                           R.Pickard
                                           Colonel,
                                           A.D.M.S.48th Division

TO,- H.Q. "A" & "G"
     D.D.M.S.XVIII Corps,
     1/1,1/2,1/3,S.M.F.Ambs.
     A.D.M.S.51st Divn.
     All R.M.Os, & M.Os.Bdes.RFA.
     H.Q.143,144,145 Inf.Bdes.
     A.D.M.S. 11 Div.
     O.C. 48 Div Signals.

SECRET.

R.A.M.C. 48th DIVISION OPERATION ORDER No 3.

11th August 1917.

Ref.Map, Trench Map BELGIUM, 28.N.W.2,
1/10,000.

1. The 48th Division will attack at a day and time to be afterwards communicated.

2. LOCATION OF
   MEDICAL POSTS.

   Regimental Aid Posts, Right,   C.17.c.7.0. & after advance
                                  move to C.12.c.3.3.

                         Left,   C.10.d.6.5. & after the advance
                                  this R.A.P. will move to
                                  C.11.d.0.5.

   Relay Posts, Right,   C.22.c.5.5.
                (after the advance)   C.17.b.40.20.
                ("   ")   C.17.c.7.0.

                Left,   C.16.d.2.3.
                                              C.22.a.1.2.
                (after the advance)   C.17.a.45.60.

   Divisional Collecting Post,   C.22.b.7.1.

   Bearer Post,   C.21.c.4.2.

   Advanced Dressing Station (DUHALLOW)   C.25.d.3.0.

   Corps Walking Wounded Collecting Post,   H.3.d.5.3.

   Corps Main Dressing Station,   A.23.c.2.9.

3. DUTIES OF   (1) The O.C. 1/1st S.Mid.Field Ambulance will be in
   OFFICERS   charge of Advanced Dressing Station,-
   COMMANDING   Personnel, 2 Tent Sub-divisions, (1/1st)
   FIELD AMBS: (2) The O.C. 1/2nd S.Mid.Field Ambulance will be in
                    charge of Divisional Collecting Post and the
                    evacuation of sick and wounded from Regimental
                    Aid Posts East of YSER CANAL to the Advanced
                    Dressing Station;
                        Personnel,- 1 Tent Sub-division, (1/2nd):
                                    Bearers of 1/2nd S.Mid.Fd Ambce,
                                    Bearers of 1/3rd S.Mid.Fd Ambce,
                                    Bearers of 1/1st S.Mid.Fd Ambce,
                                    5 Platoons Reserve Bearers.
               (3) The O.C.1/3rd S.Mid.Fd Ambulance will be in
                    charge of his Tent Division working at Corps
                    Main Dressing Station.

4. DISTRIBUTION
   OF PERSONNEL. See attached Diagram.

5. **EVACUATION EAST OF CANAL.**
    (a) <u>Lying & Sitting cases</u>,- If cars can go to the Divisional Collecting Post those cases will be loaded there; if not, then at Relay Post C.22.c.5.5., or at Bearer Post C.21.c.4.2.
    (b) <u>Walking Wounded</u>,- If lorries are available at or near the Divisional Collecting Post cases will be loaded there; if not, they will proceed to Bearer Post, dressed if necessary, and walk by the Duck-board track to Advanced Dressing Station, and so to the Corps Walking Wounded Collecting Post, being fed at WILSONS FARM en route.
    (c) Two Ford motor cars will be available from 23rd Division.
    (d) <u>Special cases</u> are to be sent from Advanced Dressing Station direct,- See No.3169 d/d 29-7-17, A.D.M.S. 48th Division.

6. **RETURNS etc.** The O.C. 1/1st S.Mid.Field Ambulance will send to Corps Main Dressing Station particulars for A & D Book of the following groups,-
    (a) those returned to duty;
    (b) those sent direct to C.C.S;
    (c) Those dying in charge of Field Ambulances East of CANAL.

7. **RESERVE BEARERS.** One and a half companies of Infantry will report at Advanced Dressing Station on Y day at 4 p.m. They will bring rations for Z and Z + 1 days, and will afterwards be rationed by 1/1st S.Mid.Field Ambulance. The O.C. 1/2nd S.Mid.Field Ambulance will arrange their distribution as per attached diagram. The Reserve Bearers will be provided at the A.D.S. with 1 stretcher per squad of 4 men and an "S.B" armlet per man, before proceeding forward.

8. **REPORTS OF CASUALTIES POSITIONS &c** All R.A.M.C. casualties will be notified to this office as soon as possible.
Estimates of R.A.M.C. casualties & other points affecting the Medical Situation must also be reported.
Any alteration in situation of posts will be immediately notified to this office.

9. **DIRECTING POSTS.** The O.Cs. 1/2nd & 1/1st S.Mid. Field Ambulances will be responsible for placing directing posts for the walking wounded to find their way back easily.

10. **DOCUMENTS OF PRISONERS.** The documents of walking wounded German prisoners will be removed from them at the Divisional Collecting Post, stored, & handed over to a representative from 48th Divisional Headquarters when asked for.

11.   ACKNOWLEDGE.

R. Pickard.
Colonel,
A.D.M.S. 48th Divn.

TO,- H.Q."A"
D.D.M.S.XVIII Corps,
1/1-1/2-1/3-S.M.F.Ambs.
A.D.M.S.23rd Divn.
All R.M.Os,& M.Os.Bdes.RFA.

ALTERATIONS, R.A.M.C. 48th Division OPERATION ORDER
No 3 dated 11th Aug.1917,

Section 5, Alteration,-

    (b) For "and so to the Corps Walking Wounded Collecting Post" substitute "thence to Corps Walking Wounded Collecting Post in lorries. O.C., A.D.S. will detail a loading party and provide ladders."

Section 6. Substitute "O.C.,A.D.S." for "O.C.,1/1st S.M.Fd Ambulance, etc".

    Add, "O.C., D.C.P. will send these particulars when necessary through O.C.,A.D.S."

                                            Colonel,
                                 A.D.M.S.48th Divn.

14-8-17,

To accompany 48th Division R.A.M.C. Operation Order
No 3. of 11th August 1917.

SCHEME OF EVACUATION, PERSONNEL etc.

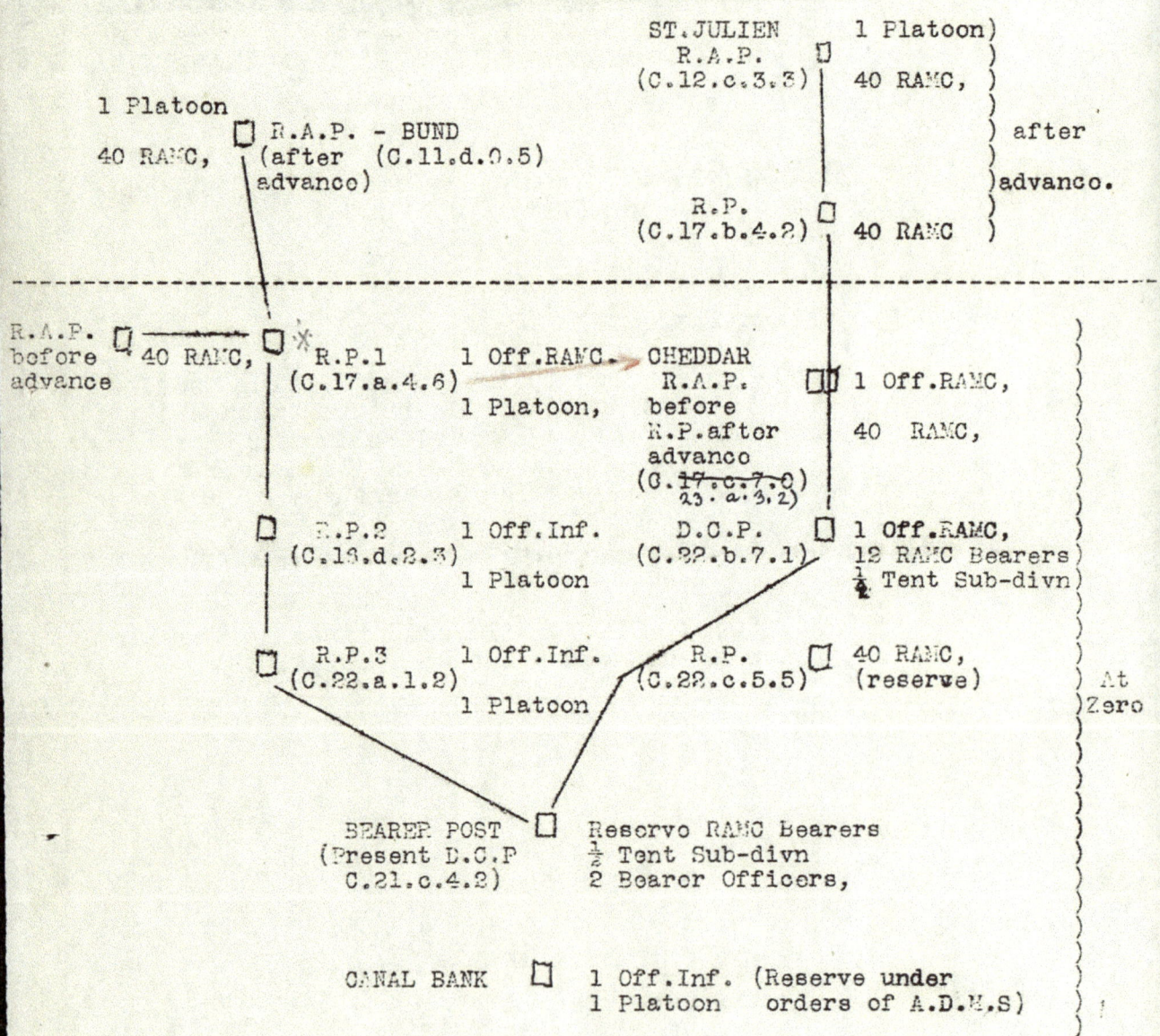

Note,- If cases can be evacuated from R.P.1 to CHEDDAR (see red arrow) 1 Platoon could be moved from R.P.3 to CHEDDAR and the Platoon at R.P.2 divided between it and R.P.3.

Rec'd. 4.15 P.M.

SECRET.

48th Division, R.A.M.C. CIRCULAR MEMORANDUM No 3.

9th Aug. 1917,

MEDICAL ARRANGEMENTS.   Ref. Map Sheet 28, 1/40,000,

1. POSITION OF MEDICAL POSTS.

RELAY POSTS,-	Right Half,	C.22.c.5.5,
	Left Half,	C.16.d.2.3.
		C.22.a.1.2.
DIVISIONAL COLLECTING POST,		C.22.b.7.1.
BEARER POST,		C.21.c.4.2.
ADVANCED DRESSING STATION,		C.25.d.3.0.
CORPS WALKING WOUNDED COLLECTING POST		H.3.d.5.8.
CORPS MAIN DRESSING STATION,		A.23.c.2.9.

2. REGIMENTAL AID POSTS.

Positions to be notified by Medical Officers to Officer in charge Divisional Collecting Post.
Cases to be taken over at Regimental Aid Posts by Field Ambulance Bearers.

3. LINES OF EVACUATION.   Right Half, Road through CHEDDAR VILLA (C.17.c.7.0) to DIVISIONAL COLLECTING POST.

Left Half, Duck-board track to BUFFS ROAD and BEARER POST (C.21.c.4.2).
WALKING WOUNDED, from ~~DIVISIONAL COLLECTING~~ Bearer POST by Duck-board track to ADVANCED DRESSING STATION, or by lorries from DIVISIONAL COLLECTING POST if these are available.

4. EXTRA BEARERS.   One and a half Infantry Companies will be required, with their Officers. They will report to the ADVANCED DRESSING STATION (C.25.d.3.0).

Colonel,
A.D.M.S. 48th Division.

SECRET.

48th Division, R.A.M.C. CIRCULAR MEMORANDUM No 3.

9th Aug. 1917,

Ref. Map Sheet 28,1/40,000

1. POSITION OF MEDICAL POSTS.

  RELAY POSTS,- Right Half, C.22.b.7.1.
             C.22.c.5.5.

        Left Half, C.16.d.2.3.
             C.22.a.1.2.

  DIVISIONAL   )
  COLLECTING POST) C.21.c.4.2.

  ADVANCED DRESSING)
    STATION,   ) C.25.d.3.0.

  CORPS WALKING WOUNDED)
    COLLECTING POST) H.3.d.5.8.

  CORPS MAIN DRESSING)
    STATION,   ) A.23.c.2.9.

2. LINES OF EVACUATION.

    Right Half, Road through CHEDDAR VILLA
          (C.17.c.7.0.) by BUFFS ROAD
          to DIVISIONAL COLLECTING POST.

    Left Half, Duck-board track to BUFFS ROAD
         and DIVISIONAL COLLECTING POST.

         from
        Walking Wounded/Divisional
        Collecting Post by Duck-board
        to ADVANCED DRESSING STATION.

              Colonel,
          A.D.M.S. 48th Division.

H.Q. "G",
  48th Divn,

SECRET.

R.A.M.C. 48th Division, OPERATION ORDER No. 4.

27th Aug. 1917,

Ref.Maps 1/40000 Sheet 28,& 27,
1/100000 " 5A

1. **NEW AREA.** The 48th Division will be relieved by the 58th Division on the night 28th/29th inst. and will move to areas as follows,-
   48th Divl.H.Q. at WORMHOUDT,
   ROAD CAMP   F.25.c.   Sheet 27,
   TUNNELLING CAMP, F.27.a.   do
   SCHOOL CAMP L.3.c.   do.
   BROWN CAMP   A.23.a.   Sheet 28,
                & A.22.d.

2. D.D.M.S. Operation Order No.10 will be carried out by the Field Ambulances of the 48th Division. Receipts and notifications under Paras. 11 & 16 will be carried out through this office.

3. O.C. 1/1st S.Mid. Field Ambulance will hand over the Advanced Dressing Station to the 2/2nd H.C.Field Ambulance by 11 a.m. on the 29th inst.
   He will move his personnel to GWENT FARM where the 1/1st S.Mid. Field Ambulance will be stationed.

4. O.C. 1/2nd S.Mid. Field Ambulance will hand over the posts East of the Canal to the 2/1st H.C.Field Ambulance move to be completed by 11 a.m. on 29th inst.
   In the event of casualties of the 48th Division remaining to be collected he will leave as many Bearers and Officers behind as are necessary to collect them, reporting numbers of bearers and units to this office and the O.Cs concerned.
   He will arrange to leave behind a party of Bearers, an equal number from each Field Ambulance, to bring up the 58th Division to *mobilisation* strength, the number to be notified later.
   He will move the 1/2nd S.Mid. Field Ambulance to L'EBBE FARM (F.29.d.5.9. Sheet 27) this to be completed by noon on 30th inst.

5. The O.C. 1/3rd S.Mid. Field Ambulance will withdraw his Tent Division from Corps Main Dressing Station and move the 1/3rd S.Mid. Field Ambulance to ST JAN TER BIEZEN (Sheet 27, L.2.d.7.4.) move to be completed by 6 p.m. on the 29th inst.

6. Sick etc. of Division: These will be collected by the Field Ambulance at ST JAN TER BIEZEN at 10 a.m. daily. All the cases which will recover in 48 hours will be detained if possible. Other cases will be sent to Corps Sick Collecting Station.

7. ACKNOWLEDGE.

R. Pickard
Colonel,
A.D.M.S. 48th Divn.

TO H.Q. "A",
D.D.M.S. 18 Corps,
Os.C.1/1, 1/2, 1/3 S.M.F.Ambs.
A.D.M.S. 58th Divn,
   "   51st "
   "   11th "

5. **EVACUATION EAST OF CANAL.**
   (a) <u>Lying & Sitting cases</u>,- If cars can go to the Divisional Collecting Post those cases will be loaded there; if not, then at Relay Post C.22.c.5.5., or at Bearer Post C.21.c.4.2.
   (b) <u>Walking Wounded</u>,- If lorries are available at or near the Divisional Collecting Post cases will be loaded there; if not, they will proceed to Bearer Post, dressed if necessary, and walk by the Duck-board track to Advanced Dressing Station, and so thence to the Corps Walking Wounded Collecting Post, being fed at WILSONS FARM en route.
   (c) Two Ford motor cars will be available from 23rd Division.
   (d) <u>Special cases</u> are to be sent from Advanced Dressing Station direct,- See No.Z169 d/d 29-7-17, A.D.M.S. 48th Division.

6. **RETURNS etc.** The O.C. 1/1st S.Mid.Field Ambulance will send to Corps Main Dressing Station particulars for A & D Book of the following groups,-
   (a) those returned to duty;
   (b) those sent direct to C.C.S;
   (c) Those dying in charge of Field Ambulances East of CANAL.

   The O.C. & C.P. will send these particulars when necessary

7. **RESERVE BEARERS.** One and a half companies of Infantry will report at Advanced Dressing Station on Y day at 4 p.m. They will bring rations for Z and Z + 1 days, and will afterwards be rationed by 1/1st S.Mid.Field Ambulance. The O.C. 1/2nd S.Mid.Field Ambulance will arrange their distribution as per attached diagram. The Reserve Bearers will be provided at the A.D.S. with 1 stretcher per squad of 4 men and an "S.B" armlet per man, before proceeding forward.

8. **REPORTS OF CASUALTIES POSITIONS &c** All R.A.M.C. casualties will be notified to this office as soon as possible.
   Estimates of R.A.M.C. casualties & other points affecting the Medical Situation must also be reported.
   Any alteration in situation of posts will be immediately notified to this office.

9. **DIRECTING POSTS.** The O.Cs. 1/2nd & 1/1st S.Mid. Field Ambulances will be responsible for placing directing posts for the walking wounded to find their way back easily.

10. **DOCUMENTS OF PRISONERS.** The documents of walking wounded German prisoners will be removed from them at the Divisional Collecting Post, stored, & handed over to a representative from 48th Divisional Headquarters when asked for.

11. ACKNOWLEDGE.

R. Pickard
Colonel,
A.D.M.S. 48th Divn.

TO,- H.Q."A"
D.D.M.S. XVIII Corps,
1/1-1/2-1/3-S.M.F.Ambs.
A.D.M.S. 23rd Divn.
All R.M.Os,& M.Os.Bdes.RFA.

PROVISIONAL. * To be brought into force by a wire from this office.
SECRET.
Copy No....16...

Ref.Maps:-
1/40000 Sheet 28.
1/100000 " 5A.

OPERATION ORDER NO 10.

D.D.M.S. XVIII Corps.

Re. XVIII Corps Medical Arrangements dated 10/7/17, with addenda d/- 21/7/17 and 8/8/..

1. (a). The 58th Division will relieve the 48th Division in the line on the night 28/29th August 1917.
   (b) The 51st Division will relieve the 11th Division in the line on the night 29/30th August, 1917.
2. (a) The 48th Division will be concentrated in the ST.JAN.TER BIEZEN area with divisional headquarters at WORMHOUDT.
   (b) The 11th Division will be concentrated in the OOSTHOEK area with divisional headquarters at "X" Camp.
   (c) 51st Divisional Headquarters will be at BORDER CAMP A.30.b.2.5.
3. The Main Dressing Station will remain commanded by Lieutenant-Colonel D.RORIE, D.S.O..R.A.M.C.T.F. and the tent sub division of his ambulance will be supplemented by two more tent sub divisions of the 51st Division who will take over their portion of the Main Dressing Station in relief of the personnel of the 11th Division.
   The 58th Division will detail a complete tent division to work their portion of the Main Dressing Station in relief of the personnel of the 48th Division.
5. The Walking Wounded Collecting Post will remain commanded by Major G.F.WHUTE, R.A.M.C.T.F. and his personnel of the 51st Division working there will be made up to one tent sub division in relief of that of the First Division. (11th)
   The 58th Division will arrange for one tent sub division to be sent to the Walking Wounded Collecting Post in relief of that of the 48th Div.
6. The Corps Sick Collecting Station and Skin Depot will remain as heretofore.
7. The personnel of the Corps Rest Station will remain as at present constituted.
8. Field Ambulances of the 11th and 48th Divisions will take over sites vacated by the 51st and 58th Division.
9. The 58th Division will detail a field ambulance to be parked at the Main Dressing Station to assist in working there when called upon to do so by the O.C.
10. The A.Ds.M.S. 11th and 48th Divisions will arrange to provide, on temporary loan, sufficient R.A.M.C. personnel to maintain the 51st & 58th Divisions at war establishment until reinforcements arrive. Details to be arranged between the divisions concerned.
11. Field Ambulances of the 11th and 48th Divisions on being relieved will only take away with them their approved mobilization equipment.
    All sector stores, reserve of blankets and stretchers will be handed over and receipts taken.
12. The motor ambulances of the 11th and 48th Divisions will move with their division and all cars requiring to be overhauled will be sent to the O.C. 24 M.A.C.Workshops at L'EBBE FARM. It must be understood however that this transport is to be held at Corps disposal.
    Divisions being relieved will place their Ford ambulances at the disposal of the divisions taking over the line from them for use when considered necessary. Arrangements to be made between A.Ds.M.S. direct.
13. The wheeled stretchers of the 11th and 48th Divisions will be placed at the disposal of the A.Ds.M.S. 51st and 58th Divisions respectively.
14. All details of relief in connection with advanced aid posts and relay posts etc will be arranged between A.Ds.M.S. direct.
15. Divisions taking over the line will arrange for refreshment posts to be instituted east of the canal for use of walking wounded.
16. Completion of the above reliefs to be reported to this office accompanied by copies of receipts for stores etc taken over.
17. ACKNOELEDGE.

XVIII Corps.
25th August, 1917.

Colonel,
Deputy Director of Medical Services.

Issued to Sign.l

DISTRIBUTION.

```
Copy No 1 to D.M.S. Fifth Army.
Copy No 2 to "G" XVIII Corps.
Copy No 3 to "A" XVIII Corps.
Copy No 4 to A.P.M.          ..
Copy No 5 to G.O.C.,R.A.,    ..
Copy No 6 to G.O.C. H.A.     ..
Copy No 7 to S.M.T.O.        ..
Copy No 8 to 51st Division.
Copy No 9 to 58th Division.
Copy No 10 to 48th Division.
Copy No 11 to 11th Division.
Copy No 12 to A.D.M.S. 11th Division.
Copy No 13 to       ..          ..
Copy No 14 to       ..          ..
Copy No 15 to       ..          ..
Copy No 16 to       ..    48th Division.
Copy No 17 to       ..          ..
Copy No 18 to       ..          ..
Copy No 19 to       ..          ..
Copy No 20 to       ..    51st Division.
Copy No 21 to       ..          ..
Copy No 22 to       ..          ..
Copy No 23 to       ..          ..
Copy No 24 to       ..    58th Division.
Copy No 25 to       ..          ..
Copy No 26 to       ..          ..
Copy No 27 to       ..          ..
Copy No 28 to O.C. No 24 M.A.C.
Copy No 29 to O.C. No 24 M.A.C. A.S.C.
Copy No 30 to O.C. C.M.D.S.
Copy No 31 to O.C. C.R.S.
Copy No 32 to O.C. W.W.C.P.
Copy No 33 to O.C. C.S.C.S.
Copy No 34 to D.D.M.S. XIV Corps.
Copy No 35 to D.D.M.S. XIX Corps.
Copy No 36 to D.D.M.S. XIII Corps.
Copy No 37 to D.A.C.G. XVIII Corps.
Copy No 38 to D.A.P.C. XVIII Corps.
Copy No 39 War Diary.
Copy No 40    ..
Copy No 41 File.
Copy No 42 File.
```

August 1917 – Chart shewing <u>Wounded</u> Adms by Units – ①

Unit	Approx. value
1/1 Bucks	270
1/1 Ox & Bucks	180
1/4 R. Berks	175
1/5 Glosters	240
1/5 R. Wwk. R.	185
1/6 "	190
1/7 "	175
1/8 "	185
1/4 Gloster	145
1/6 "	170
1/7 Worcester	165
1/8 "	100
1/5 R. Sussex	100
RHA 240 Bde	34
" 241 "	65
II/2 A.C.	10
RE 1/1H Fld Coy	34
" 1/1S "	30
" 1/1T "	28
R.A.M.C.	76
1/3 M.G. Coy	54
1/4 "	34
1/5 "	52

War Diary of
A.D.M.S. 48th Division.

Period September 1st – 30th 1917

Summary of Medical War Diaries
of 48th Div. 18th Corps. 5th Army

Western Front Ops. Sept. 1917.

A.D.M.S. Col. Pickard.
D.A.D.M.S. Capt. J.J.H. Beston.

Phase "D" 1. Passchendaele Ops. July–Nov 1917
(a) Ops. commencing 1/7/17

21(e) FOOD.

Hygiene 4.

Rations - Withdrawal of - Economy in, etc.

Sept. 16th.	Moves.	F.A. 1/2nd S.M.F.A. to Licques.
17th.	Moves.	To Zoutkerque.
28th.		To Brake Camp A.30d.1.5. (28).
30th.	Casualties.	Total wounded admitted during Sept. 139.

Appendices.

1. R.A.M.C. Operations Order No.5. dated 14/9/17.
2.   do.   do.   No.189. dated 18/9/17.
3. Table General distribution sick in back area.
4. Admin. Inst.Order No.76. dated 24/9/17.
5. R.A.M.C.Order No.191 dated 25/9/17.
6. Mov. Order No. S/303 dated 25/9/17. (48th Div.)
7. Table total adms. by units for Sept.
8. Chart of admissions and evacuation by units for September.

Sept. 16th.		Moves. F.A. 1/2nd S.M.F.A. to Licques.
17th.		Moves. To Zoutkerque.
28th.		To Brake Camp A.30d.1.5. (28).
30th.		Casualties. Total wounded admitted during Sept. 139.

Appendices.

NOTE:- All appendices attached to 1st copy.

1. R.A.M.C. Operations Order No.5. dated 14/9/17.
2. do. do. No.189. dated 18/9/17.
3. Table General distribution sick in back area.
4. Admin. Inst. Order No.76. dated 24/9/17.
5. R.A.M.C. Order No.191 dated 25/9/17.
6. Mov. Order No. S/303 dated 25/9/17. (48th Div.)
7. Table total adms. by units for Sept.
8. Chart of admissions and evacuation by units for September.

WAR DIARY
or
INTELLIGENCE SUMMARY.

(Erase heading not required.)

Army Form C. 2118.

Place	Date	Hour	Summary of Events and Information	Remarks and references to Appendices
WORMHOUDT	1.9.17	—	Division at Rest as for 3rd August. A.D.M.S. visited all three Field Ambulances. A.D.M.S. visited 2/1 Wx. B. XVIII Corps	
WORMHOUDT	2.9.17 3.9.17		Routine work	
WORMHOUDT	4.9.17		A.D.M.S. visited all Field Ambulances & 2/2 Canadian Casualty Clearing Station. Capt HUGHES. F. R.A.M.C. T.F. attached to 2/5th Fd Amb. B Cn was created.	
WORMHOUDT	5.9.17		A.D.M.S. attended D.D.M.S. Conference with all Quartermasters of the Units of the Division & R.C. Ch. D. held by A.D.M.S. A.D.V.S. attended. Capt W. MACDERMOT & CHARRIS R.A.M.C. T.C. joined Division for duty	
WORMHOUDT	6.9.17		Routine work Lieut-Col A.A. HINGSTON, OC 1/2nd Wx. Field Amb'ce essa on leave. Capt. K. O. P. R. Finney R.A.M.C. T.F. detached for temporary duty with Wel H.Q. Group. A.D.M.S. inspected Sanitarium of Tunnellers Camp (ST JAN TER BIEZEN) Capt H. READ R.A.M.C. T.F. reported for duty.	Sheet Belgium 27/40000

WAR DIARY
or
INTELLIGENCE SUMMARY.

(Erase heading not required.)

Army Form C. 2118.

Instructions regarding War Diaries and Intelligence Summaries are contained in F. S. Regs., Part II. and the Staff Manual respectively. Title pages will be prepared in manuscript.

Place	Date	Hour	Summary of Events and Information	Remarks and references to Appendices
WORMHOUDT	7.9.17 8.9.17		} Routine work	
WORMHOUDT	9.9.17		Routine work	
WORMHOUDT	10.9.17	-	1st Lieuts L.B. MOORE & W.S. PIPER USA Medical Service reported for duty. O.B.M.S. inspected Sanitation of ROAD Camp (2T JANTERBIEZEN)	
WORMHOUDT	11.9.17 12.9.17	-	Situation unaltered Routine work.	
WORMHOUDT	13.9.17	-	O.B.M.S. visited all three Field Ambulances.	
WORMHOUDT	14.9.17	-	Orders received for the move of the Field Ambulances on the Division moving into Back Training Area	App I
WORMHOUDT	15.9.17	-	O.B.M.S. proceeded on Base leave (B.1.4.O) from O.C. 1/3rd Lky Field Amb. preparing to follow. Capt Robert Smith, & Challans proceeded to England to R.Army Medical College, Millbank, London for duty in India. Trusts being made authority D.G.M.S. 1/2 and 1/3rd Ky Field Ambulances moved to ZECQUES	Ref Map Calais 13.
WORMHOUDT	16.9.17			
WORMHOUDT	17.9.17	10a.m	Division moving to ZOUTKERQUE AREA 1/1 Ky Field Ambulance arrived ZOUTKERQUE 1/3rd Lky Field Ambulance arrived BLANC PIGNON	Ref Map HAZEBROUCK 5A " "

WAR DIARY
or
INTELLIGENCE SUMMARY.
(Erase heading not required.)

Army Form C. 2118.

War Diary ADMS, 40th Div.

Place	Date	Hour	Summary of Events and Information	Remarks and references to Appendices
ZOUTKERQUE	18.9.17	-	All Field Ambulances visited. Arranged for 1/2nd Rly Field Ambulance to take on all the sick of the Division.	
ZOUTKERQUE	19.9.17 20.9.17 21.9.17		Routine work.	
ZUTKERQUE	22.9.17 23.9.17 24.9.17		Routine work. Division in training. Capt. Kennel reported for duty. Capt. Kennel relief of duty with 32nd Division. Capt's J MCCLANS reported for duty.	
ZUTKERQUE	25.9.17	-	BADMS visited ADMS 58th Division. ODMS X VIII Corps with reference to relieving the field Ambulances of 58th Division at ADS DUHALLON & the XVIII Corps Main Dressing Station.	Sheet 28 A 23 C 1·4
			Arrangements for move of 1/2nd & 1/3rd Rly Field Ambulances A Duns arrived back from leave.	App 2.
ZUTKERQUE	26.9.17		Transport of "B" & 1/2nd Rly Field Ambulances proceeding to ESQUELBECQ in route for forward area. 1/2nd Rly Field Ambulance moved up to GRASSE-PAYELLE in route for entraining at ARDRUICQ.	
ZUTKERQUE	27.9.17		F.Q. Transport of 1/2 marches to XVIII Corps Main Dressing Stn. (Sheet 28.A.23.A.1.1) C.M.D.S. " " " entrained at ARDRUICQ, detrained at BRIELEN, marched to GWENT Personnel " " " entrained at ARDRUICQ, detrained at BRIELEN, marched to GWENT FARM.	
			Transport of 1/3 RA marched to GWENT FARM (Sheet 28.A. 28.D. 5.5) Personnel " " " entrained at ARDRUICQ, detrained at BRIELEN, marched to BRAKE CAMP.	
BRAKE CAMP	28.9.17 28.C.8.1.5 20.d.1.5		GWENT FARM. 1/4th Bearers moved to BRAKE CAMP. 1/3 RA took over ADS DUHALLOW collection from Rl. Bnl area of XVIII Corps 1/2 FA took over dressing Stn of C.M.D.S.	

Army Form C. 2118.

WAR DIARY
or
INTELLIGENCE SUMMARY.   A.D.M.S. 40 Div
(Erase heading not required.)

Place	Date	Hour	Summary of Events and Information	Remarks and references to Appendices
BRAKE CAMP Sheet 28. A.30.d.15	30.9.17		The 1/1st F.A., who had remained behind in the back area near ZUTKERQUE, until 2 Inf. Bgdes of the Div., today moved into the forward area by train, encamping at L'EBBE FARM (Sheet 24.F.23.c.6.3) R. Michener Col	appendices 1) Route Order 189 " 191 3) XVIII Corps administration Instructions no. 76 of 24.9.17 2) Nos. of sick & wounded by units 2) Chart of sick admns & evacuation

app (3)

Diary

With reference to D.M.S. Instructions under his No 11/76 d/d 13-7-17, this office No M.16/58 d/d 14-7-17, all sick West of BERQUES - NOORPEENE Railway to ST OMER except self-inflicted wounds.

The following table shows the distribution of cases from Divisions in the back areas.

Class of Case,	Unit to which sent,	Location,
General Sick including Officers,	10 Stationary Hospital, 58 General Hospital, 59 do.	ST OMER whichever is receiving,
Infectious & Venereal,	7 General Hospital,	MALASSISE
Shell-Shock Officers & Neurasthenia,	7 General Hospital	MALASSISE
Ophthalmic,	4 Stationary Hospital,	ARQUES,
Dental,	10 Stationary Hospital,	ST OMER
Dental for units East of WATTEN - ST MOMELIN Line,	Dental Surgeon, 5 days per week, 8 cases from each Field Ambulance. Wednesdays & Fridays, reserved for fillings, Dental Surgeon to arrange his programme for these 2 days.	RUBROUCK

All cases of ordinary sick and N.Y.D.N. are to be retained in Field Ambulances for fourteen days.

ADMINISTRATIVE INSTRUCTIONS ISSUED WITH XVIII Corps
order No. 76 of 24th September 1917.

Reference 1/100000 map Sheet 6A (Hazebrouck).

1. The 48th Division is relieving the 58th Division in the right sector of the Corps Front on the night of the 27th/28th September, 1917.

2. On completion of relief the 58th Division (less Artillery, R.E. and Pioneers) is moving to the RECQUES area.

3. All details in connection with the handing over of advanced aid posts etc. will be arranged direct between the two Divisions concerned.

4. The A.D.M.S. 48th Division will detail one complete tent division of a field ambulance to proceed to the Corps Main Dressing Station to work their portion, in relief of a similar party of the 58th Division.

5. The A.D.M.S. 48th Division will detail one complete tent sub-Division to proceed to the Corps Walking Wounded Collecting Post in relief of a similar party of the 58th Division.

6. The following sites are placed at the disposal of the A.D.M.S. 48th Division for accommodation of field ambulances.

   Corps Main Dressing Station.
   Gwent Farm.
   L'Ebbe Farm.

7. The motor transport of the 58th Division will move with its division but will be held at Corps disposal for use when required at short notice.

8. 15 large cars of the 48th Division will be sent to the O.C. 24 M.A.C. at the Corps Main Dressing Station by 12 noon 27th September.

9. The A.D.M.S. 58th Division will set aside sufficient personnel to maintain the 48th Division at war establishment, on temporary loan until reinforcements arrive. Details to be arranged between divisions direct.

10. A.Ds.M.S. 18th and 58th Divisions will arrange to lend 2 Ford cars to the 11th and 48th Divisions respectively to assist in carrying out evacuation from the front line. Similarly the wheeled stretchers of the 18th and 58th Divisions will be placed at the disposal of the A.Ds.M.S. 11th and 48th Divisions for use if required.

11. The Field Ambulances of the 58th Division on relief will only take with them their approved mobilisation equipment. All sector stores, oxygen cylinders etc. reserve of blankets and stretchers will be handed over to the incoming units, receipts taken and copies forwarded to this office.

12. Completion of the above moves to be reported to this office
13. Acknowledge.

P.M. Davies

C.H.Q.
25/9/17.

Issued to Signals at 11 A.M.

Brigadier General,
D.A. & Q.M.G. XVIII Corps.

P.T.O.

DISTRIBUTION.

```
Copy Nos. 1-5    11th Division.
          6-10   18th Division.
          11-15  48th Division.
          16-21  51st Division.
          22-26  58th Division.
          27     "G".
          28     G.O.C.R.A.
          29     G.O.C.H.A.
          30     C.E.
          31-32  D.D.M.S.
          33     S.M.T.O.
          34     A.P.M.
          35     D.A.C.G.
          36     D.A.P.C.
          37     D.M.S. 5th Army
          38     O.C.M.D.S.
          39     O.C.W.E.C.P.
          40     O.C.C.R.S.
          41     O.C.C.S.C.S.
          42     O.C. 24 M.A.C.
          43     O.C. 2 M.A.C.A.S.C.
          44     D.D.M.S. 14th Corps.
          45     D.D.M.S. V Corps.
       46-47-48  File
          49-50  War Diary.
```

SECRET. No 191,

48th Division,

R.A.M.C. ORDER by Lt-Colonel T.A.GREEN, RAMC.T,

A/A.D.M.S. 48th Division,

25th Sept. 1917,

1. The Transport of the 1/2nd & 1/3rd S.Mid. Field Ambulances will march together tomorrow (26th inst.) to ESQUELBECQ under the command of Captain SOUTTER.   They will rendezvous at the Bridge, NORDAUSQUES at 8 a.m.   Route via EPERLECQUES, WATTEN, CLITRES, MEROKEGHEM.

2. On the 27th inst. the transport will proceed to their respective destinations as follows,-
    1/2nd S.Mid.Field Ambulance to XVIII Corps Main Dressing Station.
    The transport of the 1/3rd S.Mid. Field Ambulance to GWENT FARM.

3. The Personnel of 1/2nd S.Mid. Field Ambulance & 1/3rd S.Mid. Field Ambulance will entrain at ARDRUICQ on the 27th inst. at a time to be notified later, and will detrain at BRIELEN.

4. Thence the 1/2nd S.Mid. Field Ambulance will proceed to XVIII Corps Main Dressing Station and relieve the 2/1st Home Counties Field Ambulance at that Station on 27th/28th inst. O.C. 1/2nd S.Mid. Field Ambulance will detail 1 Officer with 1 Tent Sub-division to relieve the Tent Sub-division of the 2/1st Home Counties Field Ambulance at XVIII Corps Walking Wounded Collecting Post on the 28th inst.

5. The 1/3rd S.Mid. Field Ambulance will relieve the 2/2nd & 2/3rd Home Counties Field Ambulances at the Advanced Dressing Station, Divisional Collecting Post, and Relay Posts on the 28th inst.

6. O.C. 1/2nd S.Mid. Field Ambulance will, on arriving in the new area, arrange with the O.C. No 24 M.A.C. for the collection of the Sick of 48th Division.in the forward area.

7. The 1/1st S.Mid. Field Ambulance will collect the Sick of the Division from the whole area of the back area, and evacuate cases which will not be well in 48 hours, and will continue to render the usual returns to this office.

8. Completion of moves to be reported to this office.

9. ACKNOWLEDGE.

TAGreen

Lt-Colonel,
A/A.D.M.S. 48th Division

Secret   RIP   Diary

48th Division.
No. S/303.

Orders for Move of 1/2nd and 1/3rd S.M. Field Ambulances.
----

1. Personnel of 1/2nd and 1/3rd S.M. Field Ambulances will move by rail on 27th instant from AUDRUICQ.
   Detraining Station BRIE LEN.
   Time of train will be wired to A.D.M.S. as soon as known.
   Captain YOUNG, Headquarters, 145th Inf. Bde., will allot accommodation for 10 Officers and 400 O.R. on the train.

2. The transport of these 2 Ambulances under command of Captain SUTER, R.A.M.C. will move on 26th instant to ESQUELBECQUES.
   Route - NORDAUSQUES - EPERLECQUES - WATTEN - MERCKEGHEM.
   Advance Party to report to Town Commandant, ESQUELBECQUES for billets 2 hours before arrival of column.

3. The march will be continued on the 27th instant to XVIII Corps Area. Route - HOUTKERQUE - ST JAN TER BIEZEN.

4. The destination on 27th instant will be -

   1/2nd S.M. Field Ambulance.   A.23.c.2.8.
   1/3rd   -do-   GWENT FARM.

5. ACKNOWLEDGE.

                                    H. Crawshay Major
                                    DAQMG
                                         for Lieut-Colonel.
                                    A.A.& Q.M.G. 48th Division.

25-9-17.

                George Smith

Distribution.

   Copy 1. XIX Corps.
     " 2. XVIII Corps.
     " 3. "G".
     " 4. A.D.M.S.
     " 5. 58th Division.
     " 6. 145th Inf. Bde.,
     " 7. O.C. 48th Div. Train.
     " 8. Retained.
     " 9.   "

48th Division

Total admissions by Units, for month of September 1917.

Unit	Sick Admissions Totals	Diarrhoea	Scabies	Venereal	Wounded Totals
1/1 Bucks Batt.	49	7	3		6
1/4 Ox & Bucks	47	1	1		4
1/4 Roy. Berks	29	1	3		4
1/5 Glosters	33	3			47
1/5 R. War. R	38	4		1	47
1/6 "	51	16			1
1/7 "	43	2	2		-
1/8 "	65	22			1
1/4 Glosters	48	1	10		1
1/6 "	74	18	4		-
1/7 Worcesters	60	5	2		1
1/8 "	49	6	4		-
1/5 Roy. Sussex	44				10
R.F.A. 240 Bde	9				10
" 241 "	33				24
" 48 D.A.C	14				11
R.E. 474 Field Coy	15				15
" 475 " "	5				4
" 477 " "	8				-
143 M.G. Coy	12	5			1
144 "	10				-
145 "	12	1	1	1	2
143 T.M.B	3				-
144 "	2			1	1
145 "	3				-
48 Div. Supply Col	1				1
1/1 S.M. Field Amb	6				-
" 2 "	6				-
" 3 "	3				-
145 Inf. Bde H.Q	1				-
48 Div Salvage Coy	4				-
" " H.Q	3				5
" " Signals	11				1
" " Train	6	2			-
" " Mob. Vet. Sect	1				-
242 Employment Coy	2				-
Grand Totals	**800**	**94**	**27**	**3**	**139**

—Adms —Evacs.   CHART SHEWING SICK ADMs AND WASTAGE — BY UNITS — off (8)

SEPTEMBER 1917

Vol 31

CONFIDENTIAL

War Diary
of
A.D.M.S. 48th Division
from 1-10-17 to 31-10-17.

Vol. XXXI.

COMMITTEE FOR THE
MEDICAL HISTORY OF THE WAR
Date -5 JAN 1918

WAR DIARY
or
INTELLIGENCE SUMMARY.

ADMS 46 Div

Army Form C. 2118.

Place	Date	Hour	Summary of Events and Information	Remarks and references to Appendices
BRAKE CAMP (S.Sheet 28 A.30.d.15)	2.10.17		Conference of C.Os., Fd. Ambs. Here, afterwards one of M.O.s of 143 Inf. Bgde. Discussed war position of RAPs, which are very far back, Fuse of Reserve Inf. Stretcher Bearers attached to RAPs.	

	3.10.17		Saw O.C., 143 Inf. Bgde. He agreed to following :—
			 a) Regt. S.Bs. to remain with Coy. to collect wounded into proper in shell holes.
			 b) Reserve Inf. Bearers to take over from there & carry to RAPs, in two relays, one from line ½ way back, the other to RAP.
			
			          o ⎫ front line
			     HUBNER o ⎬
			     (D.1.c.4.6) o ⎭
			       VICTORIA (O.P) Company Groups
			          ⎰⎱ Regt. S.B.
			      Reserve Inf. Bearers
			 RAP
			 (MONT du
			 C.6.c.H.Bou)
			 RAP
			 (JANET- C.12.d.34
			     Reserve Inf. Bearers
				attached

	4.10.17- 6 am		Opern. Order (RAMC No.9) issued. Div. advanced on a one Brigade front by two stages, from V. 25.c.8.5 - D.19.a.3.4 to V. 26.a.8.6 — D.3.c.5.5.	

WAR DIARY
or
INTELLIGENCE SUMMARY.   A.D.M.S. 40th Div

Army Form C. 2118.

Place	Date	Hour	Summary of Events and Information	Remarks and references to Appendices
BRAKE CAMP	4.10.16		First lying cases arrived at ADS at 8.30am by car. Light railway was broken in 5 places badly by shell fire, so that it could not be used till 10.0am. After that it went well, it was used for walkers, sitters, & less serious lying cases. The journey down took 1 hr, ambulance car took 20 minutes. Evacuation went on smoothly, the great difficulty being the actual collection in the front line. On the whole the cases were not so serious as in the engagements of August, there being very few severe wounds of the lower extremities. There were a considerable no. of cases coming to the ADS from adjoining divisions & of men trav. their own to them.	6.10.16–2.30pm Total through ADS Officers 25 OR 365 — 390 Regimental OR 2 3 34 — 36 Total 426 Remnde OR No 2 Ambulance
"	5.10.16		Wounded still coming in at ADS. Action has been successful. RAP's being formed at HUBNER.	
"	6.10.16		Weather very bad, much rain. Headquarters warned of likelihood of trench feet. By 6.0 pm this evening those wounded in the attack had passed through ADS.	
"	7.10.16		I inspected Reune relay posts, also RAPs at HUBNER & JANET. Arranged with Sun. Hoghs to have Regt RAP at HUBNER. R. cannot be moved because of want of accn. at VICTORIA. Arranged also for burrows sheets to be provided at RAPs for shelter of wounded here	

Army Form C. 2118.

WAR DIARY or INTELLIGENCE SUMMARY.

(Erase heading not required.)

Place	Date	Hour	Summary of Events and Information	Remarks and references to Appendices
BRAKE CAMP	7.10.17		The following is a summary of casualties passing through 2 ADS from 6.0 a.m. on 4.10.17:—	

46th Division

	Lying	Sitting	Walking	Officers	Totals
6 am 4th – 6.0 pm 4th	74	13	158	15	260
6 pm 4th – 6.0 am 5th	35	30	42	7	114
6 am 5th – 6 pm 5th	37	6	22	1	66
totals 5th	146	49	222	23	440
6 pm 5th – 6 am 6th	12	7	—	1	20
6 am 6th – 6 pm 6th	19	11	10	2	42
6 pm 6th – 6 am 7th	4	4	—	1	8
6 am 7th – 6 pm 7th	2	—	2	—	4
	183	71	234	27	514

11th Division

6 am 4th – 6 am 5th	17	8	35	—	60
5th – "	14	4	8	—	26
6th – "	2	—	—	—	2
7th – 6 pm	1	—	3	—	4

New Zealand Division

6 am 4th – 6 am 5th	32	10	77	1	120
5th – "	8	1	2	1	14
6th – "	1	—	1	—	2
7th – 6 pm	—	—	1	—	1
	80	23	126	—	229

46th Divn. casualties passing through 2 other ADS's

	11th Divn	New Zealand		Totals
	41	34		75
	66	45		111
	3	2		5
	110	81		191

Summary of 46th Divn casualties

Through ADS Duhallow 514
11th Divn ADS 110
New Zealand ADS 81
                 ———
                 705

Army Form C. 2118.

WAR DIARY
or
INTELLIGENCE SUMMARY.

(Erase heading not required.)

ADMS 48th Div.

Place	Date	Hour	Summary of Events and Information	Remarks and references to Appendices
BRAKE CAMP	7.10.16 8.10.16		Issued Routine Orders. Received 48th Divn. Administrative instructions for forthcoming operations.	Attack Operations attack
	9.10.16		144 Inf. Bgde. attacked on a 3 Battn. front at 5.20 am 4 R Gloster 6 R Gloster 1 R Worcester (In reserve 8th Worcesters)	
			Very little found was gained. A further attack at 5.0pm by 7 R Worcesters also failed to gain a pack.	
		9 am	First wounded from attack reached ADS — walkers.	
		11 am	First train arrived, but it had in error collected many casualties from WIELTJE, in the 49th Divn area on our right. (Note — apart from this we evacuated the 49 Divn — see table attached)	
		11.35am	Received wire from 144 Bgde that 2/Lt S.E. MILLIGAN, RAMC (T.C.) M.O. to 1/4 Worcesters had been killed. He was struck by a small piece of shell case below the orbit, presumably the bone of the brain was injured, he died in a few minutes. Captain SOUTTER 1/3rd S.M.FA was sent to replace him.	
		1pm	Received note to say that the Marine Inf. Scorers for left side only reported at Bn am.	

WAR DIARY
or
INTELLIGENCE SUMMARY.

Army Form C. 2118.

ADMS 48th Division

Place	Date	Hour	Summary of Events and Information	Remarks and references to Appendices
BRAKE CAMP	9.10.17 — Cont'd	noon	Traffic on road delaying evacuation bye ars but not seriously	
		12.30pm	Some congestion at VANHEULE, mainly because many wounded from 49th Divn. are reporting here	
		1.0 pm	VANHEULE clear	
		5.0 pm	50 Infty sent up to replace some of those working in front of R.A.P. who are tired out	
		9.0 pm	Evacuation going smoothly. Report that it is hung up on the night because of sniping	
"	10.10.17	10.0 am	Fair number of wounded during night. 8 9th Divn arrived at ADS to take over staff & collection of wounded:— 2 Lt. FO Amb. for E. of CALIFORNIA 1st South African F.A. for ADS	
		2.0 pm	Parties of 1st 2nd	
		6.0 pm	Relief complete. Recd parties of 9 K Divn left as follows:— 2 Offrs & 42 O.R. to work EG DCP (ST JULIEN) " " " " " at A.D.S., DUHALLOW } to clear field of 45th Divn on relief by 9 K Divn. Rest Headquarters moved to X Camp	

WAR DIARY
INTELLIGENCE SUMMARY. 40th Divn ADMS

Army Form C. 2118.

Place	Date	Hour	Summary of Events and Information	Remarks and references to Appendices
X Camp E⁹ (Sheet 57 A.16.c.3 y)	11.10.18	10 am	Field reports clear by Regtl. M.O.s. Ranic bearers + reserve Inf.y withdrawn (see table of casualties attached) (raine evacuation in October 10th by DASC attached).	12th by DASC attached
		30 pm	Received 4th Divn. instructions for move from 5th Army to 1st Army area. For move Fld. Ambs. are attached to Inf. Bgdes. (See Rouic Order No. 192 – attached).	
TERNES (Hens toroure) E.1	12.10.18		Preparations for move. Div¹. Headquarters moved here this morning. 11/4 F.A. left HOUDOUTRE at 5.45 p.m. to detrain to LIGNY ST FLOCHEL. I visited Headquarters (ADMS) of 2nd Canadian Divn at VILLERS au BOIS + went with him to ADS 4 VIMY RIDGE.	
"	14.10.18		Visited DDMS. V Corps, ADMS 2nd Canadian Divn, Fd. Ambce sites at VILLERS au BOIS, ESTREE CAUCHIE, + FRESNICOURT. Issued RAMC open order no. 11 + medical arrangements (no.193) – attached.	
VILLERS CHATEL (Hens toroure) H.2	17.10.18		Headquarters moved here today by road. Moves of Fd. Ambs. to new area completed today (see open order 11).	

Army Form C. 2118.

WAR DIARY
or
INTELLIGENCE SUMMARY.
(Erase heading not required.)

A D M S 4th Div.

Place	Date	Hour	Summary of Events and Information	Remarks and references to Appendices
CHATEAU D'ACQ Sheet 36B W.30.b.2.5	18.10.17		Div. Headquarters moved here by road today. Visited ADS, NEUVILLE St VAAST.	
	19.10.17		Routine office work.	
	20.10.17		Visited LA CHAUDIÈRE, DARTMOUTH Post.	
W30.b.2.5	21.10.17	—	Routine office work. D.A.D.M.S. returned from leave.	
W30.b.2.5	22.10.17	—	A.D.M.S. visited trenches inspecting site for aid-posts, stretcher relay posts in preventing trench foot. Also for water & drying arrangements to 4th Fld. Field Ambulance took over V Corps Rest Station from 2nd Canadian Division. A.D.M.S. attended Conference A.D.M.S. V Corps.	
W30.b.2.5	23.10.17	—	A.D.M.S. visited Field Ambulance at ESTRÉE-CAUCHIE being taken over by 13rd Fld. Fld. Ambulance. Interviewed with a V Corps Skin & Scabies Station. Then visited 4th Fld. Field Ambulance at V Corps Rest Station and 13rd Fld. Field Ambulance. Capt. McDERMOTT RAMC T.C. proceeded to England Convalescence.	
W30.b.2.5	24.10.17	—	A.D.M.S. held a Conference with OCs. Field Ambulances. A.D.M.S. visited Divisional Baths at NEUVILLE-ST.VAAST, BERTHONVAL - Mt ST. ELOY. Also 13rd and 14th Field Ambulances.	

Army Form C. 2118.

WAR DIARY
or
INTELLIGENCE SUMMARY.
(Erase heading not required.)

Instructions regarding War Diaries and Intelligence Summaries are contained in F. S. Regs., Part II. and the Staff Manual respectively. Title pages will be prepared in manuscript.

Place	Date	Hour	Summary of Events and Information	Remarks and references to Appendices
W30b.2.5.	25.10.17	-	Situation unchanged. Weather unsatisfy. A D.M.S. visited R.A.P.s & R.A.M.C. Posts of Right Secta. 1/2nd Lin Field Ambulance & Baths at MONT ST ELOY	
W30b.2.5.	26.10.17	-	Situation unchanged. Weather stormy, cold & wet. Routine Office work.	
W30b.2.5.	27.10.17	-	A.D.M.S. visited 1/2nd Lin Field Ambulance and with O.C. proceeded to AUX RIETZ to which place the Head Quarters of that Ambulance are moving	
W30b.2.5	28.10.17	-	A.D.M.S. visited A.D.M.S.59th Division. He with O.C. 1/3rd Lin Field Ambulance proceeded to FOSSE No.10 A.12.b. (Sheet 36B moon) to inspect & has Rec (corr 8/12)	
W30b.2.5.	29.10.17	-	Situation unchanged. Wet & cold. A.D.M.S. visited Sn chSe & Quarry in T.16 d 9.3. where preventive measures against trench P. & anti-spraying room are being carried out. H.Q. 1/2nd Lin Field Ambulance arrived to AUX RITZ. A.D.C.I.S. (2 Lieut MAROEUIL 1/2000)	
W30b.2.5.	30.10.17	-	Situation unchanged. Weather improving. A.D.M.S. attended Conference D.D.M.S. & Corps. A.D.M.S. visited 1/3rd Lin Field Ambulance	
W30b.2.5.	31.10.17	-	Weather fine & warm. A.D.M.S. visited Divl. Baths MONT ST ELOY. 1/3rd Lin Field Ambulance & I Corps Rest Station. 1/11 Lin Field Amby. Capt J.D.SMYTHE. 1/3rd Lin Field Ambulance reported for duty from sick leave in England.	

Divisions on Right & Left:-
31st Division on Right
59th Division on Left

Total sick admissions for month = 1053   Last month 811
Average sick admissions per day = 33.96   "   "   27.03
Total average strength for month = 15210   "   "   10992
Sick percentage = .69   "   "   .43

Total wounded for month = 1475

R Hulme Col

App 1   War Diary

SECRET.

48th Division R.A.M.C. OPERATION ORDER No 7,
by COLONEL R. PICKARD, C.M.G., A.M.S.
A.D.M.S. 48th Division.

3rd October 1917.

Ref. Map Sheet BELGIUM 28 N.W. 2,
1/10,000

1. The Division will attack on its present front on a day and hour to be given later.

2. The following Medical Posts will be established -

			RAMC Officers	RAMC Bearers
REGTL. AID POSTS.	Left, MON DU HIBOU,	C.6.c.2.3.	-	40
	Right, JANET FARM,	C.12.d.5.5.	-	40
RELAY POSTS.	ST JULIEN,	C.12.c.4.6.	-	20
		C.18.a.1.7.	1	20
	VANHEULE FARM	C.17.d.2.6.	1	20
	TIN HUT	C.23.a.4.2.	-	20
DIVISIONAL COLLECTING POST.	CALIFORNIA TRENCH,	C.22.b.7.1.	2	Half Tent Subdivn. 20 Bearers
BEARER POSTS, (local casualties)	CANOPUS TRENCH,	C.17.a.4.6.	-	8 "
	ADMIRALS CROSS ROADS,	C.22.c.5.5.	-	8 "
	LA BELLE ALLIANCE,	C.20.d.4.3.	-	Reserve Bearers.
ADVANCED DRESSING STATION.	DUHALLOW,	C.25.d.3.0.		2 Tent Subdivns.

3. EVACUATION OF WOUNDED.
   (a) Lying & Sitting: By car from Relay Post (C.18.a.1.7) ST JULIEN, to Divisional Collecting Post, and thence by rail or car to Advanced Dressing Station DUHALLOW, thence to Casualty Clearing Station or Corps Main Dressing Station by No 24 Motor Ambulance Convoy cars.
   10 Motor Ambulance Convoy cars will be allotted for working between the Divisional Collecting Post and Advanced Dressing Station.
   (b) Walking; On foot to Divisional Collecting Post, CALIFORNIA TRENCH, then by rail or on foot to Advanced Dressing Station. From Advanced Dressing Station by Lorries to Corps Walking Wounded Collecting Post
   (c) Cases other than those East of STEENBEEK; will go to nearest Relay Post.
   (d) Light Railway; 2 trains of 3 waggons each will be provided. A spur line terminating near Divisional Collecting Post will be used for loading.
   Line is controlled by O.C. No 29 Light Railway Coy. TROIS TOURS.
   Orderlies will be provided by O.C. 1/3rd S.Mid. Field Ambulance.

4. **DUTIES OF O.Cs.**
   FIELD AMBULANCES.

   (a) O.C. 1/3rd S.Mid. Field Ambulance will be in charge of the evacuation from Regimental Aid Posts to Advanced Dressing Station.
   Personnel, (1) Bearer Divisions of 3 Field Ambulances;
   (2) 2 Tent Subdivisions of 1/3rd S.Mid. Field Ambulance.

   (b) O.C. 1/1st S.Mid. Field Ambulance will be in charge of Advanced Dressing Station, DUHALLOW, and passing over of cases to Motor Ambulance Convoy.
   Personnel, 2 Tent Subdivisions 1/1st S.Mid. Field Ambulance;
   1 Medical Officer 58th Division.

   (c) O.C. 1/2nd S.Mid. Field Ambulance will be in charge of a Section at Corps Main Dressing Station.
   Personnel, 2 Tent Subdivisions, and 7 Nursing Orderlies from 1/3rd S.Mid. Field Ambulance;
   2 Medical Officers 58th Division.

5. **RESERVE INFANTRY BEARERS.**
   1½ Companies will be detailed.
   3 Platoons will report at Advanced Dressing Station on "Y" day; at 5 p.m.;
   (2 Platoons will be sent to Regimental Aid Post MON DU HIBOU, 1 to Regimental Aid Post JANET FARM.)

   3 Platoons will report at Advanced Dressing Station on Z day at 9 a.m.
   The latter will be at the disposal of the A.D.M.S.

6. Attention is drawn to -
   (a) 48th Division R.A.M.C. Operation Order No.3, paras. 6, 8, 9, & 10;
   (b) 48th Division R.A.M.C. Circular Memo.No 2 of 31-7-17;
   (c) D.M.S. Fifth Army Circular Memo. No 41 d/d 1st Sept.1917.

7. All German wounded prisoners will have their documents taken away from them at the Advanced Dressing Station; these will be made up into packets and handed to 48th Divisional Headquarters.

8. ACKNOWLEDGE.

R. Pickard
Colonel,
A.D.M.S. 48th Division,

TP D.M.S.Fifth Army,
D.D.M.S.XVIII Corps,
H.Q."A" 48th Divn,
O.Cs. 1/1,1/2,1/3,S.M.Fd Ambs.

SECRET,

48th Division R.A.M.C. OPERATION ORDER No 8,

1. The Division will make a further advance today.

2. R.A.M.C. Relay Posts will be established at,
    (a) HUBNER FARM,
    (b) P (VICTORIA FARM, C.7.b.3.2.)
   where wounded will be taken over from Regimental Bearers or Infantry Bearers.

3. The 3 Infantry Platoons working between Regimental Bearers of 143 Inf.Bde. will be relieved by 3 Platoons 145 Inf. Bde. On relief the former will report to A.D.M.S. at A.D.S.
   The 3 Platoons will be distributed 1 to R. side 2 to Left side and will work between Regtl Bearers and Relay Posts (para.2)

4. The 3 Reserve Platoons are returned to units.

                                          Colonel,
                                    A.D.M.S. 48th Divn.

4-10-17,
3.45 p.m.

SECRET.

48th Division R.A.M.C. OPERATION ORDER No 9,
by COLONEL R. PICKARD, C.M.G., A.M.S.

7th October 1917,

Ref. Map Sheet BELGIUM 28 N.W.2,
1/10,000

1. The Division will attack on its present front on a day and hour to be given later.

2. The following will be the Medical Posts for the operations,

			Off.Bearers
REGIMENTAL AID POSTS,	Right, JANET,	C.12.d.5.5.	40
	Left, HUBNER,	D.1.c.4.6.	40
R.A.M.C. RELAY POSTS,	MON DU HIBOU,	C.6.c.2.3.	
	TRIANGLE,	C.6.c.7.2.	20
	ST JULIEN	C.12.c.4.6.	40
DIVL. COLLECTING POST.	ST JULIEN	C.19.a.1.7.	½ Tent Subdvn 40 Bearers
RESERVE BEARER POSTS,	VANHEULE	C.17.d.2.6.	½ Tent Subdvn
	CALIFORNIA	C.22.b.7.1.	10 Bearers
	LA BELLE ALLIANCE,	C.20.d.3.0.	Reserve tent
ADVANCED DRESSING STATION,	DUHALLOW,	C.25.d.3.0.	2/subdvns

3. EVACUATION will be by hand and wheeled stretcher to Divl. Collecting Post, thence by cars or rail from C.17.b.3.9. to Advanced Dressing Station.

4. RESERVE INFANTRY BEARERS, Three Platoons will be available on Y day, 1 will be used in front of JANET, 2 in front of HUBNER.

5. DUTIES of O.Cs. Field Ambulances;
    As in R.A.M.C. Operation Order No 7 d/d 3.10.17.

6. ACKNOWLEDGE.

R. Pickard

Colonel,
A.D.M.S. 48th Division

SECRET. ADMINISTRATIVE INSTRUCTIONS
in connection with 48th Div. Order No. 223.

8.10.17.

MEDICAL 1.

A. The following posts will be established:-

Regtl. Aid Posts:	JANET FARM	Right.
	HUBNER	Left.
RELAY POSTS:	TRIANGLE	C.6.c.72.
	ST. JULIEN	C.12.c.46.
DIV. COLLECTING POST	ST. JULIEN	C.18.a.17.
BEARER POSTS.	VANHEULE FARM.	
	CALIFORNIA	C.22.b.71.

ADV. DRESSING STN. DUHALLOW.

B. EVACUATION by hand and wheeled stretchers to D.C.P. Thence by rail and Car to A.D.S.

C. PERSONNEL.
145 Inf. Bde. will detail from 1/5 Glouc. R. 3 complete platoons for work under the A.D.M.S, to report at A.D.S. DUHALLOW at 5 p.m. 'Y' day.
This party will report with rations for Z and Z + 1 days.

PROVOST 2.

PRISONERS.
The Adv. Div. Collecting Post will be at CHEDDER VILLA. Prisoners will be taken to this point by Brigade Escorts and will be taken over by the A.P.M. who will give a receipt for all taken over. Thence they will be taken to the Divisional Cage, CANAL BANK.

STRAGGLERS POSTS.
The arrangements will be the same as on Oct. 4th vide APPENDIX IX to 48th Div. Order No. 219.

PERSONNEL.
145 Inf. Bde. will detail from 1/5 Glouc.R. the following parties to report to A.P.M. CANAL BANK at 6 p.m. 'Y' Day.

	Off.	N.C.Os	Men.
For escort duties and guard at CHEDDER VILLA.	1	2	24
For guard at CANAL BANK Cage.		1	6
For Stragglers Posts.	1	4	15

These parties will bring rations for 'Z' and 'Z'+ 1 days.

DUMPS 3.

Ammunition and Grenade Dumps are established as follows:

Main Div. Dump		C.22.c.57.
Adv. " "	CORNER COT.	C.17.b.96.
Bde. Dump.	Trench Board track S. of HUBNER.	D.1.c.74.

The amounts at these dumps have been communicated to Staff Captains.

WATER 4........

- 2 -

WATER. 4.

A Divisional Water Dump of 400 petrol tins is established at C.17.b.96.
The guard in charge will issue full tins in exchange for empty ones.

RATIONS 5.

1000 complete Rations are dumped at JANET FARM and approximately 5000 at C.17.b.96. These may be issued on demand of an officer 48th Division.

SOUP KITCHENS. 6.

Divisional Soup Kitchens are established at HILL TOP and VANHEULE.

7. ACKNOWLEDGE.

G H Barnett
Lieut.-Colonel,
A.A. & Q.M.G., 48th Div.

```
Copy No. 1 - 'G'
  "   "  2 - C.R.A.           Copy No. 7 - XVIII Corps.
  "   "  3 - C.R.E.             "    "  8 - A.P.M.
  "   "  4 - 143 Inf.B de.      "    "  9 - A.D.M.S.
  "   "  5 - 144  "    "        "    " 10)
  "   "  6 - 145  "    "        "    " 11) Retained.
                                "    " 12)
```

SECRET.   Copy No. 9

AMENDMENTS TO ADMINISTRATIVE INSTRUCTIONS
in connection with 48th Div. Order No. 223.

8.10.1917.

The following amendments will be made to Administrative Instructions issued with 48th Div. Order No. 223.

Para. 2, line 1. For CHEDDAR VILLA substitute ST. JULIEN.

Sub-heading '**Personnel**', line 4.

"For escort duties and guard at CHEDDAR VILLA

Off.	N.C.Os.	men.
1	2	24

substitute

"For escort duties and guard at St. JULIEN,

Off.	N.C.Os.	men.
1	4	40

Lieut.Colonel,
A.A. & Q.M.G., 48th Division.

Distribution:-

To all recipients of Administrative
Instructions in connection with
48th Division Order No. 223.

SECRET

App 7 Drawy

48th Divn. R.A.M.C. OPERATION ORDER No 10,

9th Oct 1917.

Ref. Map Sheets 28 & 27.

1. The 48th Division will be relieved in the line by the 9th Division on the night 10/11th October.
2. (a) The 1/1st S.Mid. Field Ambulance will pass over the Advanced Dressing Station, DUHALLOW, to the incoming Field Ambulance of the 9th Division on the 10th inst. It will move to SCHOOL CAMP.
   (b) ~~O.C.~~ 1/3rd S.Mid. Field Ambulance will hand over R.A.M.C. Posts in the area East of the Canal to the incoming Field Ambulance of the 9th Division It will move to L'EBBE FARM.
   (c) The 2 Tent Subdivisions of the 1/2nd S.Mid. Field Ambulance will be relieved at Corps Main Dressing Station by a Tent Division of the 9th Division. Their Tent Subdivision at the Corps Walking Wounded Collecting Post will be similarly relieved by a Tent Subdivision of the 9th Division. They will move to TUNNELLERS CAMP.

   All these moves to be complete by 6 p.m. on the 10th inst.
   In the case of (a) and (b) sufficient personnel will be left behind to deal with the casualties of the 48th Division still to be collected. Further orders will be given on this point. The Officers and personnel of the 58th Division will be passed over to the 9th Division.
   In handing over material strict accuracy must be exercised and great care taken that no material is left in the field.
3. SICK. The Field Ambulances will collect the sick in their new camps.
4. A.D.M.S. Office is situate at X Camp A.16.c.2.4.
5. ACKNOWLEDGE.

R. Pickard
Colonel,
A.D.M.S. 48th Division.

To D.M.S. Fifth Army
D.D.M.S. XVIII Corps,
H.Q. "A" 48th Divn,
O.Cs 1/1, 1/2, 1/3 S.M.F.Ambs.
A.D.M.S. 9th Divn.

Secret

Diary

CASUALTIES dealt with at Advanced Dressing Stn. DUH ELO", from 6 a.m. 9th to 6 a.m. 11th Oct 1917.

	48th Division.				Officers.	Other Formations.			Officers.
	Lying.	Sitting.	Walking.	TOTAL.		Lying.	Sitting.	Walking.	TOTAL.
9th, 6 a.m. – 6 p.m.	24	50	158	232	–	67	63	201	371	8
6 p.m. – 6 a.m.	31	22	31	84	2	17	36	84	137	7
10th 6 a.m. – 6 p.m.	28	9	19	47	4	1	–	–	–	–
3 p.m. – 6 a.m.	11	1	9	21	–	–	–	–	–	–
11th 6 a.m.										
	94	82	217	434 *	6	44	99	395	538 *	15

48th Divn Casualties collected) At A.D.S. 11th Div. 57
at adjoining A.D.Ss. Noon 9th –)   "   " 49th " 24
Noon 9th.)   ───
                                               515 *

* Officers included in the Totals.

R Violen
Colonel,
A.D.M.S. 48th Division.

App 9 Diary
Secret

48th Division, R.A.M.C. ORDER No 192,

by COLONEL R. PICKARD, C.M.G., A.M.S.

11th Oct. 1917,

1. For the purposes of the forthcoming move the Field Ambulances of the Division will be affiliated as follows,-
   1/1 S.M.Fd Ambce to 144th Inf. Bde;
   1/2 S.M.Fd Ambce to 145th Inf. Bde;
   1/3 S.M.Fd Ambce to 143rd Inf. Bde.
   Orders will be issued to the Field Ambulances by the Brigades concerned.

2. Each Field Ambulance will be responsible for the collection of Sick of its Brigade during the move and on arrival in the new area.

3. A.D.M.S. Office in "X" Camp will close on the 13th inst. at Noon, and reopen at the same day and hour at a place to be notified later.

4. ACKNOWLEDGE.

R. Pickard
Colonel,
A.D.M.S. 48th Divn.

TO H.Q. "A",
O.Cs 1/1, 1/2, 1/3 S.M.F.Ambs.
H.Q 143, 144, 145 Inf. Bdes.

SECRET.

R.A.M.C 48th Division OPERATION ORDER No 11,

14th Oct. 1917.

1. The 48th Division will relieve the 2nd Canadian Division in the line.

2. MOVES & DUTIES
   OF FIELD AMBULANCES;

   (a) 1/1st S.Mid. Field Ambulance will move to FRESNICOURT on the 15th inst. It will take over the duties of the Corps Rest Station when the Field Ambulances of the Canadian Division move out.

   (b) The 1/2nd S.Mid. Field Ambulance will send an Advance Party on the 15th inst. to the 5th Canadian Field Ambulance at MONT ST ELOI to learn the method of clearing from the line, and to take over the posts and material. The main party will move to MONT ST ELOI and will take over the collection of sick and wounded from the line, to be completed by Noon on the 17th inst.

   (c) The 1/3rd S.Mid. Field Ambulance will send an Advance Party on the 15th inst. to take over,-
   (1) Field Ambulance encampment at CHATEAU DE LA HAIE;
   (2) Medical Detention Room and encampment at VILLERS AU BOIS;
   (3) Field Ambulance encampment at QUATRE VENTS;
   (4) Corps Infectious Hospital at ESTREE CAUCHIE.
   On the 16th inst. the main party will move to,-
   (1) CHATEAU DE LA HAIE,-   Headquarters.
   (2) VILLERS AU BOIS,-   1 Tent Subdivision.
   (3) QUATRE VENTS,-   1 N.C.O. & 4 men.
   (4) ESTREE CAUCHIE,-   1 Tent Subdivision.

3. ACKNOWLEDGE.

R. Pickard
Colonel,
A.D.M.S. 48th Division.

H.Q. "A",
O.Cs. 1/1, 1/2, 1/3 Fd Ambce,
D.D.M.S. Vth Corps,
A.D.M.S. 2nd Canadian Divn.
D.M.S. 1st Army,

SECRET *app "* *Diary*

NO 193,

48th Division MEDICAL ARRANGEMENTS.

1. POSTS as follows,- Ref. Map Sheet LENS 1/100,000
   " 36C S.W.1/20,000

   Regimental Aid Posts, Right, T.16.c.5.9. Junction of TEDDY GERARD & TORONTO Rd.
                   Left, T.15.a.6.6. PEGGIE Trench,
                        T.8.c.9.6. HAYTER Trench.
   Relay Post, T.8.a.5.7. Head of Light Railway.
   Divisional Collecting Post, T.22.c.6.4.
                        T.25.a.9.4. VIMY,
                        S.18.c.9.3. BOIS DE CHAUDIERE,
   Advanced Dressing Stations, NEUVILLE ST VAAST
                        AUX RIETZ.

   Medical Detention Rooms, CHATEAU DE LA HAIE, VILLERS AU BOIS.
   Corps Rest Station, FRESNICOURT.
   (including Scabies)
   Corps Infectious Diseases Hospital, ESTREE CAUCHIE.
   Casualty Clearing Stations, BRUAY, BARLIN.

2. 1/2nd S.M.Fd Ambulance will collect Sick and Wounded from the front line.
   1/3rd S.M.Fd Ambulance will collect Sick from the remaining portion of the Divisional Area, establishing Detention Huts at VILLERS AU BOIS and CHATEAU DE LA HAIE, in addition to staffing Corps Infectious Hospital at ESTREE CAUCHIE.

3. (1) Cases likely to recover in 48 hours will be detained at the 1/3rd S.M.Fd Ambulance;
   (2) Cases likely to be well in over 2 days and under 14 days will be sent to Corps Rest Station.
   (3) Cases likely to exceed 14 days will be sent to Casualty Clearing Station at BRUAY or BARLIN.

4. Instructions regarding Infectious cases and other special cases will be issued later.

R. Pickard
Colonel,
A.D.M.S. 48th Division.

14-10-17,

48th Division, MEDICAL ARRANGEMENTS, No 194.

18th Oct. 1917,

1. Field Ambulances admitting patients will keep the A. & D. Book and render A 36.

2. All cases sent to Corps Rest Station will be shewn in the books of the Field Ambulances sending them, as Transfers to the Field Ambulance running the Corps Rest Station (at present the 1/1st S.Mid. Field Ambulance), and in the books of the latter as Transfers from the Field Ambulance sending them to the Corps Rest Station.

3. (i) Cases may be detained in the Field Ambulances for 48 hours if circumstances permit, and if they are likely to recover in that time. At the end of that time they must be either discharged to duty, if fit, or admitted to the Field Ambulance and transferred to Corps Rest Station.
   (ii) Cases likely to take from 2 to 14 days to recover will be admitted and transferred to the Corps Rest Station.
   (iii) Cases likely to take more than 14 days will be admitted and sent to Casualty Clearing Station.

4. Each Field Ambulance admitting cases will send a Daily State from 8 a.m. to 8.0 a.m. In order to adjust this to the Noon state which has been previously sent, the state for 8 a.m. on the 19th inst will be for the period Noon 18th to 9.0 a.m. 19th.
   In the state "Divl. Rest Station" will be altered to "C.R.S".

6. Nominal rolls of all Officers & Other Ranks of the Division evacuated to Casualty Clearing Station must ~~be~~ accompany the daily state.

Colonel,
A.D.M.S. 48th Division.

SECRET.

EVACUATION from the line held by the 48th Division
- T.17.d. - T.2.a. -

1. **RIGHT SECTOR.**

   R.A.P., T.18.c.5.9.5. Support Line R.A.Ps. T.27.d.2.5.(out of
                                                                                               Divl.area
                                      T.20.b.0.7.KURTON.

   Cleared by (a) TOAST TRENCH to Junction with CANADA,
                          thence to D.C.P. -
             VANCOUVER, there they are loaded into
                        cars and go to -
             NEUVILLE ST VAAST via WILLERVAL;
   or   (b) In the dusk or misty weather, overland
                  by track to VANCOUVER;
   There is a third alternative,- the MONT FORET Railway
                     from S.18.c.9.5. to VIMY, but this is
                     exposed to view, and is not used, for
                     that reason. TOAST TRENCH end has been
                     much shelled.
   D.C.P., 22.c.7.4. VANCOUVER.
        Personnel, 1 Officer 30 Other ranks (including those
                working from R.A.P to this post).
        Accommodation, 30 lying and about 40 sitting cases.
        Evacuation by car to NEUVILLE ST VAAST.

2. **LEFT SECTOR.**

   R.A.P., T.15.a.5.7½ PEGGIE.
        Evacuation by PEGGIE TRENCH to KURTON TRENCH, thence
                  by Railway to D.C.P., LA CHAUDIERE.

   R.A.P., T.8.c.9.6. HAYTER.
        Evacuation by HAYTER TRENCH to RAILWAY EMBANKMENT,
                 thence by Light Railway to D.C.P.
                 at LA CHAUDIERE.
   R.A.M.C.Posts, VIMY (T.25.a.9.4),
              Personnel 5 Other ranks, for local casualties.
             DARTMOUTH (T.8.a.6.8), at present there is a
                holding party at this post, which is
                unfinished.
   D.C.P., LA CHAUDIERE (S.18.c.85.4).
        Personnel, 1 Officer 30 Other ranks (including
              those working between this and the R.A.Ps.)
        Accommodation, 30 lying cases, about 30 sitting.
        Evacuation by car to NEUVILLE ST VAAST.

3. **ADVANCED DRESSING STN.** NEUVILLE ST VAAST, A.3.c.1.1.

        Personnel, 2 Officers 1 Tent Subdivision.
        Accommodation, 12 lying cases.

                                                    Colonel,
                                          A.D.M.S. 48th Division

23-10-17

— Adms — Evacs   Chart shewing Sick
October 1917   Admissions & Wastage by units

app 114

www.ingramcontent.com/pod-product-compliance
Lightning Source LLC
Chambersburg PA
CBHW081425300426
44108CB00016BA/2307